Between Markets and Governments

Konstantinos Loizos

Between Markets and Governments

An Institutional Analysis of Development Banking and Economics in Greece

palgrave
macmillan

Konstantinos Loizos
National and Kapodistrian University of Athens
Centre of Planning and Economic Research (KEPE)
Athens, Greece

ISBN 978-3-031-88526-6 ISBN 978-3-031-88527-3 (eBook)
https://doi.org/10.1007/978-3-031-88527-3

This Palgrave Macmillan imprint is published by the registered company Springer Nature Switzerland AG.
The registered company address is: Gewerbestrasse 11, 6330 Cham, Switzerland

Dedicated to my beloved companion in life, Maria

Acknowledgements

This book is the result of research the majority of which was conducted in the intellectual environment of the Economics Department at the National and Kapodistrian University of Athens. I would like to thank George Krimpas, Stavros Thomadakis, and Michalis Psalidopoulos for their friendship and for being an inspiration in my work, always being full of ideas that guided me in fascinating paths of thought. I owe special thanks to Professor Michel Zouboulakis who had the patience to read the entire manuscript and provide me with valuable suggestions. I would also like to thank Kostas Kostis, George Dotsis, Chrysafis Iordanoglou, Matthias Thiemann, and two anonymous referees for being kind enough to read parts of the book and provide their comments, and the Chairman of the Centre of Planning and Economic Research (KEPE) Panagiotis Liargovas and the library staff of this organization for their continuous support. All remaining errors are my responsibility. I am also indebted to the editorial team of Springer Nature for their support and assistance. This book is dedicated to my beloved wife Maria for her life-long love and support.

December 2024 Kostas Loizos

Competing Interests The author declares the following as potential competing interests: The author was a non-executive member of the Board of Directors of the Hellenic Development Bank (HDB) and the Hellenic Development Bank of Investments (HDBI) from June to October 2019

Contents

About the Author

Konstantinos Loizos is a senior research fellow at the Centre of Planning and Economic Research (KEPE) and a visiting lecturer at the Department of Economics, National and Kapodistrian University of Athens, Greece. As a researcher, he has also worked with the Bank of Greece and the National Confederation of Commerce and Entrepreneurship. His research has been published in academic journals including the *Journal of Economic Issues*, *Journal of Post Keynesian Economics*, *Journal of Economic Surveys*, *International Review of Financial Analysis*, and *Economics and Business Letters* as well as in peer-reviewed edited volumes. He has also been the author or co-author of three books and editor of three volumes about economic theory, banking, and the history of institutions in Greece. His research interests include development finance and financial regulation-deregulation, with emphasis on development banking and bank regulation, and the theory and history of economic institutions.

Abbreviations

AFD:	Agence Française de Développement
BNDE/BNDES:	Banco Nacional do Desenvolvimento Economico e Social (Brazilian National Bank of Economic and Social Development)
BSTDB:	Black Sea Trade and Development Bank
CCCE:	Caisse Centrale de Coopération Économique
CCFL:	Caisse Centrale de la France Libre
CCFOM:	Caisse Centrale de la France d'Outre-mer
CDP:	Cassa Depositi e Prestiti
DEKO:	Public Enterprises and Organizations
DFCs:	Development Finance Companies
DFIs:	Development Finance Institutions
EAPs:	Economic Adjustment Programs
ECU:	European Currency Unit
EEC:	European Economic Community
EFSI:	European Fund for Strategic Investments
EIB:	European Investment Bank
EIF:	European Investment Fund
ELTI:	European Long-Term Investors
EMS:	European Monetary System
EMU:	European Monetary Union
ERM:	Exchange Rate Mechanism
ESG:	Environmental, Social, and Governance
ETBA:	Hellenic Industrial Development Bank
ETEAN:	Hellenic Fund for Entrepreneurship and Development
ETEBA:	National Investment Bank for Industrial Development
EU:	European Union

GDP:	Gross Domestic Product
GSIs:	Global Standard Institutions
HDB:	Hellenic Development Bank
HDBI:	Hellenic Development Bank of Investments
IBRD:	International Bank for Reconstruction and Development
IFC:	International Finance Corporation
IfG:	Institution for Growth
IMF:	International Monetary Fund
IOBE:	Foundation for Economic and Industrial Research
IR:	Industrial Revolution
KfW:	Kreditanstalt für Wiederaufbau
LDCs:	Less Developed Countries
MFP:	Multi Factor Productivity
MSMEs:	Micro, Small and Medium Enterprises
NEFI:	Network of European Financial Institutions for SMEs
NPL:	Non-Performing Loans
NSFR:	Net Stable Funding Ratio
OAE:	Organization for Business Restructuring
OBA:	Industrial Development Corporation
OXOA:	Economic Development Financing Organization
PPP:	Public-Private Partnerships
R&D:	Research and Development
ROA:	Return on Assets
ROE:	Return on Equity
SEV:	Hellenic Federation of Enterprises
SMEs:	Small and Medium Enterprises
TANEO:	New Economy Development Fund
TCE:	Transaction Cost Economics
TE:	Investment Bank
TEMPME:	Guarantee Fund for Small and Very Small Businesses
TFP:	Total Factor Productivity

List of Figures

List of Tables

CHAPTER 1

Introduction

The crisis of 2007–2008 and its consequences for the global economy were followed by a revived interest in development banking both in theory and in policy. The World Bank and the European Union have sponsored conferences and published policy papers assessing the role of national development banks in countering the adverse effects of economic recession and reconsidering their place in the future financial landscape. This contrasted an intellectual and policy environment of distrust to the idea of development banking during the financial liberalization era of the 1980s and 1990s. However, development banking was closely related to efforts for industrialization and economic development both in the nineteenth and twentieth centuries. Hence, questions arise about why and how such institutions were considered obsolete in the late twentieth century before they attracted again the interest of policy makers just after the outbreak of the Global Financial Crisis in the early twenty-first century.

This book is inspired by the above questions to provide a novel approach to development banking based on the Original Institutional Economics which is considered as a more encompassing and comprehensive theoretical approach for our purposes when compared to the New Institutional Economics. The aim is to form a theoretical model of development banking that would identify its distinctive features and, at the same time, highlight its possible risks. Such a point of view aspires to provide a more comprehensive theory and a modern approach to development banking as

K. Loizos, *Between Markets and Governments*,
https://doi.org/10.1007/978-3-031-88527-3_1

a useful mechanism for financing economic development and promoting institutional development in a globalized economic environment.

The argument of this book is that an answer to the previous questions should be looked for in the prevailing financial regimes and their relationship to development banks in the context of the implemented government policies. Hence, simple ahistorical arguments, for or against development banking, miss the point that every economic organization should be assessed within the context of the particular institutional conditions that characterize the specific historical period in which it operates. This is more so the case for development banks that were essentially dependent on the prevailing financial regime and the related government policy. The financial regime of financial repression/regulation during the post-war period, when the Bretton Woods international monetary arrangements were in their heyday, was a fundamentally different institutional environment than the financial regime of financial liberalization after the collapse of the Bretton Woods system.

In addition, our argument rejects the simplistic view of development banks as mere instruments of cheap finance that disregards their contribution to institutional development. However, this means that development banks as instruments of economic and institutional development are special organizations that cannot be adequately described in the context of financial risks' categorization in conventional banking theory. After all, modern development economics places a great emphasis on institutional issues that were rather disregarded in the past. Hence, an institutional approach to development banking seems both promising and topical.

Institutional economics is a vibrant and expanding field of study that attempts to provide a comprehensive understanding of economic behavior. The discipline counts in its ranks two Nobel laureates, Oliver Williamson and Douglass North, and two major figures in the history of economic thought, John R. Commons and Thorstein Veblen. Despite the differences between Original and New Institutional Economics, there is a growing debate about their compound impact on economic thought. The argument of this book is that, in the study of development banking, the New Institutional Economics can be thought of as a particular case of the more general and encompassing theoretical framework of the Original Institutional Economics, especially concerning the relationship between development banks and the prevailing financial regime and the role of development banks in institutional change. In this sense, concepts such as the types of economic transactions, "reasonable" pricing and the prevailing public purpose, problem-solving institutional reform along with changing habits of thought, and instrumental versus ceremonial values in institutional change, form the basis for a comprehensive institutional theory of development banking.

The proposed model is then employed to illuminate the case study of the Greek economy in the post-war period, with a focus on the role of development banking in its socioeconomic transformation, having passed through alternative financial regimes. Greece has been chosen as the object of our case study for many reasons. First of all, because it is an economy that experienced a fundamental economic and social change that brought it from the ranks of developing economies to those of developed ones and the family of Eurozone economies. The second reason is that Greece, despite the above, went through several severe and protracted crises in the wake of the Global Financial Crisis which still torments its people and has left its scar on the economic and social conditions in the country. Finally, Greece is an interesting case because its development banking organizations, which had been present in the financial sector since the early 1960s, stopped operating in the early 2000s, only to reappear in 2019 within the new European context for promotional banks.

Having in mind these specificities of the Greek case and with the help of the institutional methodological tools of storytelling and pattern modeling, we identify the major turning points in the economic history of post-war Greece, and we recount its institutional development. In this context, the story about the role of Greek development banking in supporting this economic and institutional transformation and in being transformed by it, is being told. The analysis reaches the conclusion that the major risk that Greek development banks have encountered was an institutional-political rather than an economic or financial risk. This institutional-political risk was derived from the dependence of Greek development banks on government policy with respect to the prevailing financial regime and the ability or inability of the government to formulate a long-term institutional and economic development policy in the midst of conflicting interests that were represented by different social groups in the Greek society. Hence, the success and sustainability of the most recent efforts to revive the idea of development banking for the benefit of Greek economic development depend on whether the government is able to follow a long-term development and financial policy plan. This plan should consider development banks as critical instruments of institutional change in favor of sustainability and innovation rather than as short-sighted cheap-finance vehicles.

The book contributes to the current literature on development banking in many respects. First of all, it provides a comprehensive institutional theory of development banking that goes beyond the conventional theories that focus on financial risks or the juxtaposition of market failures with government failures. Our dynamic theory provides an institutional justification for the heterodox approach that emphasizes the active role of the state in shaping markets. It also advances beyond that by looking at the internal relationship between development banks and the state and by locating their major risk, the institutional-political risk, in government policies about the prevailing financial regime. Moreover, the institutional foundations of our theory about the role of development banks in institutional change clarify further their dynamic "mission-oriented" role which is proposed by the heterodox literature, and emphasize their internal transformation. Then, the empirical part of this book provides an analysis of Greek development banking which, to our knowledge, is unique in terms of the time span that it covers and the methodological approach of Original Institutional Economics that it employs. Development banking in Greece is a rather understudied area of research. Therefore, this analysis contributes to the debate about the impact of development banking on economic and institutional development in post-war Southern Europe.

To achieve the above objectives the book is divided into two parts. The first part attempts a review of the ideas of development banking and development finance both on historical and theoretical grounds. These ideas are then related to the issue of financial development as a particular aspect of institutional development, thus highlighting the importance of institutions for development finance. The latter naturally guides us to a discussion of Original and New Institutional Economics as we are looking for theoretical foundations of a novel approach to development banking. Contrasting the ideas of Oliver E. Williamson to those of John R. Commons and those of Douglass C. North to those of Thorstein Veblen an argument is formed on how the Original Institutionalists provide us with a more comprehensive and open-ended theory of institutions and institutional change. On these grounds, a theory of development banking is formulated in this book which aspires to be representative of the historical experience of development banking so far, realistic and policy useful in the context of evolving economies.

The second part of this book is a case study of the Greek economy and the Greek experience of development banking during the post-World War II period until today. The Greek economy is a small peripheral European economy which, however, did transform during this period from a developing to a developed economy. In addition, the Greek economy was harshly hit by the Global Crisis of 2008 and became the object of interest in international economic circles both academic and policy ones in the last decades. Finally, the Greek economy experienced five different phases of economic development and two financial regimes which make it a good illustration of how development banking evolved in the European periphery. Hence, the second part uses a storytelling approach to narrate the history of Greek development banking in the context of macroeconomic and institutional developments in Greece during these six decades. The analysis shows the contribution of the main era of development banking in 1963–2002 to economic and institutional development and narrates the internal transformation and changing role of Greek development banks having in mind the theoretical framework of the first part of the book. The analysis also explores the evolution of development banking after the accession of the country to the Eurozone and the establishment of the Hellenic Development Bank in 2019. Then, the final chapter of the book summarizes this discussion by providing preliminary answers to three open questions about the future of development banking with a focus on the Greek case.

PART I

An Institutional Reconsideration of Development Banking

CHAPTER 2

Development Banking in the History of Economic Development

2.1 Introduction: Development Banking and Industrial Financing: The Birth of an Idea

Capitalism had been synonymous with capital accumulation and economic growth long before the idea of economic development was established in the economists' jargon. The connection between economic (material) progress and the well-being of the people has been at the root of classical political economy such as Adam Smith and Ricardo (Arndt 1984: 7). "Economic development" is a term which has been in use mostly after World War II and has been related to a wide spectrum of goals in addition to economic growth such as higher living standards, increasing income per capita, rising control of man over the environment, reduction of poverty and inequality (Arndt 1989: 1). However, the common ground between the original idea of material progress as this has guided economic policies in the nineteenth and early twentieth centuries and that of economic development from 1945 onward seems to be the idea of modernization coupled with industrialization (Arndt 1989: 2, 13). Modernization entails a mental and cultural revolution in peoples' everyday lives which made possible a new set of motives conducive to rising income and prosperity. At the bottom-line is what Tawney indicates as the differing characteristic between the traditional and modern man: For the latter, continuous economic progress is an ideal that guides its actions and culminates in economic change being the rule rather than the exception (Arndt 1989: 11).

K. Loizos, *Between Markets and Governments*,
https://doi.org/10.1007/978-3-031-88527-3_2

This is an important observation because, as we will argue in this book, development banking should be understood as a dynamic organization which is formed and evolves at the intersection of changing agents' beliefs that drive their economic behavior. On the other hand, industrialization has been the material basis of this modernization since the First Industrial Revolution initiated in the British islands. Hence, the, historically, twin concepts of industrialization and modernization have also characterized the birth and evolution of development banking during the last two centuries.

Development banking is an idea that dates back to nineteenth-century policies to finance industrialization in the so-called backward countries. The focus was on continental Europe as opposed to England whose industrialization was not characterized by any significant involvement of banks in long-term financing. The capital accumulation required for the Industrial Revolution in Great Britain came from profits generated in agriculture along with those derived from external trade and small industrial units while banks provided the necessary working capital. Moreover, entrepreneurial, managerial, and technical skills were developed gradually while the social status and economic role of entrepreneurs have been well-established in British society. This was not the case for backward economies in continental Europe because of scarce capital, less confidence in the prospects of industry, and projects that needed high capital-output ratios. In this context, a particular type of banking was needed, distinct from commercial banking, since the latter banks were reluctant to embark on long-term lending. Long-term financing of industry entailed risks they were less willing to assume while they didn't have the expertise and experience to assess the related risks. Eventually, the crucial difference between commercial banking in industrialized England and development/industrial banking was the practice of the former to provide short-term capital and that of the latter to extend long-term finance (De Aghion 1999; Gerschenkron 1962: 13–14; Diamond 1957: 19–20).

Indeed, the long-term provision of borrowed capital was related to the specific needs for rapid industrialization of backward countries in nineteenth-century continental Europe such as the Netherlands, France in the era of Napoleon III or Germany. The idea was to catch up with the industrialization process already commenced in the British islands in the spirit of the material progress ideology described above. This venture entailed significant government involvement therefore, the first government-sponsored bank of this type was the Société Générale pour

Favoriser l'Industrie Nationale established in Brussels in 1822. In the early nineteenth century the typical French entrepreneur ran a small family business and was unwilling to take great risks or to get involved in new uncertain ventures. In such a background, three institutions for industrial financing were created in France between 1848 and 1852: the Crédit Foncier, the Comptoir d'Escompte, and the Crédit Mobilier of the Pereire brothers. Finally, in Germany the idea of universal banking was born where long-term industrial banking was combined with short-term commercial banking (De Aghion 1999; Gerschenkron 1962: 12–14; Diamond 1957: 23). As we shall explain below, banks with a purpose to promote economic development such as the Crédit Mobilier in France or the German Universal Banks were the prototypes on which development banks' proliferation after the World War II was based. Yet, it seems that the model institution for industrial/development banking which became the object of imitation in other European countries, despite its eventual failure in 1867, has been the Crédit Mobilier (Gerschenkron 1962: 13).

2.2 The Crédit Mobilier and the German "Great Banks": The Prototypes of Industrial Banking

Industrialization in Continental Europe has been in many respects a French affair as France was the source of both skills and capital exported to other countries in the process of economic development between 1850 and 1870. The emblematic institution of this process, the Société Générale du Crédit Mobilier was established in November 1852. Émile and Isaac Pereire built on Saint-Simonian notions of "mobilization of credit" and the combination of banking and industry to promote the idea of industrial development with a particular focus on railway network building. Saint-Simonian influences indicated also a sort of ideological difference between development and commercial banking as far as industrial banks were treated as instruments of (planned) economic development and the Pereire brothers considered themselves as bearers of a mission rather than as simple bankers. Indeed, the Sain-Simonian movement considered industrialization as a means to raise the welfare of the great majority of people, and hence, industrial banking had a role to play in this regard. Although Crédit Mobilier, as a private company, sought to make a profit, it did so by following the government's industrial development policy (Gerschenkron 1962: 23; Diamond 1957: 23; Cameron 1953). The Crédit Mobilier affected economic development in Europe and elsewhere in many ways. It participated in the establishment of banks which promoted industrial development such as the Bank für Handel und Industrie in Darmstadt which was the model for the German "great banks". Besides negotiations with the Austrian government concerning the building of the Austrian State Railway and other projects, it prompted the competitors of the Pereira brothers, the Rothschilds to establish their industrial bank in Austria, the Kreditanstalt für Handel und Gewerbe. The influence of the model of the Crédit Mobilier spread also in the nineteenth century in Spain, Switzerland, Russia, Italy, the Netherlands, and the Ottoman Empire. Eventually, the impact of the Crédit Mobilier on the economic development of continental Europe was directly or indirectly very significant despite its rather short period of operation (Cameron 1953).

It is important to note that the Crédit Mobilier had been a factor in both industrial and financial development around Europe through the implementation of its railway financing (De Aghion 1999). The Crédit Mobilier initiated a type of banking where industrialization and credit mobilization met each other in an organization that was meant to achieve both private financial and social economic gains. However, this prototype institution of the nineteenth century paradoxically presented the whole set of problems that development banks still face: Should profitability be a criterion of the contribution of development banks in economic development, and how to reconcile private profitability with social gains? How to measure their contribution to income growth as a justification for their involvement in industrialization? More notably, the contribution of the Crédit Mobilier and this sort of banks to the economic development of France, Europe, and other countries all over the world cannot be assessed only on the grounds of the financial success of the enterprises they supported. One should also focus on the intangible benefits of their operation concerning the diffusion of technical and organizational skills and banking techniques along with the spread of the "idea of development and the spirit of enterprise". This is probably the most important legacy of the Crédit Mobilier as a model bank for the future of development policies (Cameron 1953). Hence, the Crédit Mobilier was the prototype for the double role of development finance institutions as promoting both economic and institutional development. Furthermore, the bank of the Pereire brothers also highlighted a major contradiction of such institutions between private profitability and bureaucracy. The Crédit Mobilier was a private, profit-seeking bank without red tape procedures but its need for immediate profit had been its major shortcoming, given that it financed long-term projects. Hence, government sponsorship might alleviate this constraint yet, at the possible expense of bureaucratic inefficiency and government corruption (Cameron 1953).

As we have already mentioned above, the Crédit Mobilier served also as a model for the German "great banks". The latter, according to Gerschenkron (1962: 13–14) initiated universal banking[1] that combined the idea of Crédit Mobilier with ordinary commercial banking activities. German universal banks were more financially sound rather than the Crédit Mobilier and they managed to develop a close relationship with the enterprises they financed both through mechanisms of effectively long-term credit extension and with participation in corporate boards to exert control not only on financial but also on crucial managerial decisions about the operation of the firms. However, for both, the Crédit Mobilier and the German "great banks" the justification for their establishment in the specific environment of nineteenth-century continental Europe was to meet the need for long-term industrial loan capital in backward countries characterized by both material and institutional "deficits": scarcity of capital, especially when the required capital/output ratios related to the size of plants and the scale of the industrialization attempts were very high, and an unfavorable entrepreneurial climate toward industrial activities (Gerschenkron 1962: 14).

However, there was a crucial difference between the Crédit Mobilier and the German universal banks: although both were engaged in "active banking" for industry only the latter proved financially viable. As Piero Sraffa points out in his lectures on continental banking, the Crédit Mobilier started its operation with a policy of matching the maturities of assets and liabilities but later on it changed its business model by backing long-term financing with short-term deposits. When the Crédit Mobilier faced liquidity problems, the Banque de France neither supported it nor let it issue long-term bonds. This was not the case with German universal banks. The German state through the Reichsbank was ready to provide the necessary liquidity to these banks as a lender of last resort. The universal banks

[1] According to the World Bank (1989), "universal banking" is used as a term to define the combination of commercial banking (accepting deposits and extending loans) and investment banking (issuance, underwriting, placement, and trading of firms securities) along with close banking and industry links which are manifested in seats reserved for the banks on supervisory boards and proxy voting rights of these banks on behalf of shareholders that have deposited their shares with them (World Bank 1989: 50).

were private institutions but were also instruments of the German state receiving its support in case of need. This was certainly a case of "planned institution building" (Chandrasekhar 2016: 22–23; De Cecco 2005).

The prototype of the Crédit Mobilier was disseminated beyond the European continent and notably in Asia where the Industrial Bank of Japan was founded in 1902. The latter became the model for development finance institutions in other countries such as India (Diamond 1957: 36). Furthermore, in the early twentieth century, especially after World War I, a new wave of industrial financing institutions appeared in Europe because of the need for reconstruction after the war and the Great Depression that hit the world after the Wall Street Crash of 1929. These institutions included the Société Nationale de Crédit à l'Industrie founded in Belgium in 1919, the Crédit National pour Faciliter la Réparation des Dommages causés par la Guerre in France, the National Economic Bank founded in Poland and the "Industrial Mortgage Bank" in Finland in 1924, the Industrial Mortgage Institute in Hungary in 1928, the Bankers' Industrial Development Company established in Great Britain in 1930 and the Credit for Industry Ltd in 1934, the Instituto Mobiliare Italiano in 1931 and the Instituto per la Reconstruzione Industriale established in Italy in 1933. An important difference with the nineteenth-century institutions was that in the twentieth century, the ownership structure of development banks was characterized by a high degree of dispersion among other financial institutions while projects were co-financed with other banks. Indeed, the above cases refer to joint ventures with the participation or support of private banks, large firms, and the government (Thorne and du Toit 2009; De Aghion 1999; Diamond 1957: 30–31).

2.3 The Post-WWII Experience in Europe and Around the World

Development banking after World War II was justified on the same grounds as industrial financing in the nineteenth and early twentieth centuries, though its rise and demise were closely related to the rise and fall of alternative views of development finance for Least Developed Countries as these will be discussed in the next chapter. However, it is possible to identify the major features of modern development banks by browsing through the relevant literature in the post-WWII period.

The first modern development finance institution was the International Bank for Reconstruction and Development (IBRD) which was an offspring of the Bretton Woods agreement in 1944 and the Marshall Plan for the reconstruction of Europe after World War II. The first loan of the IBRD was extended to France in 1947. The establishment of this international institution was followed by the creation of various national development finance institutions. The Industrial Development Bank of Canada was founded in 1944 to support industrial enterprises with a special focus on small ventures. The German Kreditanstalt für Wiederaufbau was established in 1948 to finance infrastructure and industrial projects using mainly the Marshall Plan funds. Moreover, in 1949 the Industriekreditbank A.G. succeeded the Bank für Deutsche Industrieobligationen which had been established in 1924. In 1945, the Industrial and Commercial Finance Corporation and the Finance Corporation for Industry were founded in Great Britain and the Herstelbank in the Netherlands. Outside Europe, the Export Bank of Japan was founded in 1950, and the Japan Development Bank in 1951 both with developmental mandates. In 1953, the Brazilian National Bank of Economic Development (BNDE)—subsequently BNDES—was founded to finance energy and transportation infrastructure projects and in 1954 the Korean Reconstruction Bank—later renamed Korea Development Bank—to help the economy in the wake of the Korean war (Mazzucato and Penna 2016; Lazzarini et al. 2015; Diamond 1957: 31). In India, among the many institutions established were the Industrial Finance Corporation of India in 1948 and the Industrial Development Bank of India in 1964. Finally, one of the most important development finance institutions because of the size of its assets and its international reach is the China Development Bank which was established in 1994 to finance the reshaping of the productive base of the Chinese economy. The bank emphasized medium and long-term loans for the provision of basic goods and the completion of public infrastructure projects (Musacchio et al. 2017; Chandrasekhar 2016: 26–29). However, there were some differences between the development banks established in the post-WWII era and their counterparts in the nineteenth century: The post-war banks were usually more specialized in their activity and enjoyed in greater degree of government sponsorship and support. The latter took the form of increasing government participation in their share capital, concessional loan financing, and government guarantees to their bond issues. In addition, post-war governments, more often than not, participated in their boards of directors and influenced their banking policies.

Finally, at least until the late 1950s, it appears that post-war development banks were primarily engaged in providing loans to established firms rather than participating in the equity capital of nascent enterprises (Diamond 1957: 29–30).

The number of development banks has proliferated during the post-World War II era all over the world. At the end of the 1990s, there were more than 550 development banks of whom 520 were national development banks in 185 countries (Bruck 1998). In 2017 the World Federation of Development Financing Institutions numbered 230 members. Finally, concerning the year of establishment of development banks still in operation according to the responses in a World Bank survey in 2017, 16% were founded before 1945, 37% between 1945 and 1979, 22% between 1980 and 1999 in the era of financial liberalization and, 25% after 2000 (De Luna-Martínez et al. 2018). However, the participation of the government in post-World War II development finance institutions was predominant, and co-financing with other banks was limited in most cases, as opposed to the case in the early twentieth-century institutions. Furthermore, according to the 2017 survey, only 10% of the development banks surveyed followed a wholesale lending model (lending to other financial institutions), 40% a retail model (lending directly to customers), and 50% a mixed lending model. Finally, the countercyclical role of development banks during the global financial crisis of 2008–2010, when private commercial banks and capital markets were off limits for many private firms, has sparked new support and interest by policymakers for these institutions. Furthermore, despite reservations concerning the quantitative effect of development banking on economic development, its qualitative impact was not questioned (Griffith-Jones et al. 2018: 1; De Luna-Martínez et al. 2018; De Luna-Martínez and Vicente 2012; De Aghion 1999). This qualitative feature of development banking is closely related to its modernization mission which in turn dovetails with its role in institutional development.

Moreover, recent events in the European Union have provided additional support for the "making of the European field of development banking" within the new international interest in this kind of finance. The communication published by the European Commission in July 2015 considers national development banks as significant vehicles to promote investment projects in cooperation with European Union institutions and urged member states lacking a national development bank to establish one. The European Commission has hoped for a network of national development banks to emerge as a complement to the European Investment Bank (Mertens et al. 2021: 1).

However, a defining characteristic of the historical evolution of development banks in the post-World War II period was the financial environment or the financial regime under which they were operating. Normally, a development bank established in the 1950s or the 1960s would have been part of a financial system characterized by strict administrative regulations within the international context of the Bretton Woods monetary system. This era was characterized as the period of financial repression as opposed to financial liberalization that ensued from the collapse of the Bretton Woods regime in the 1970s and became a policy recommendation included in the IMF's structural adjustment programs during the late 1980s and thereafter. In this context, development banks were less favored and their activity declined (Griffith-Jones 2022; Loizos 2018). During the post-WWII period, the ideas of central planning and import substitution served the purpose of both economic reconstruction and economic development. For some development banks supporting employment and entrepreneurship supplemented the goal of shoring up specific sectors of the economy. However, by the late 1980s-early 1990s the economic development model changed to the one of export-led growth amid liberalized markets and rising competition worldwide. Development banks had to adapt by facilitating privatizations and shifting their focus toward the financing of small and medium enterprises (SMEs) and the support for innovation and sustainability projects (Musacchio et al. 2017). The views toward development banks evolved from the traditional model of the 1950s to reservations about their efficiency to eventually, an eclectic view that recognizes their distinctive role as developmental agencies operating in a market-friendly financial environment (Gutierrez et al. 2011). However, the international financial regime affected the prevailing financial regime within each country and hence, government policies toward financial institutions such as development banks (Hermann 2010; Bruck 1998). Eventually, the Global financial crisis of 2008 and subsequently the fallout of the COVID-19 pandemic led to a renewed interest in development banking worldwide, both for countercyclical finance and for funding the necessary transformation of the economies toward sustainable growth (Griffith-Jones 2022).

The history of development banks after 1945 is closely related both to the financing of economic development and to financial development in the face of institutional underdevelopment. As was the case for their nineteenth-century predecessors in continental Europe, it seems that the presence of both economic backwardness and inadequate institutional infrastructure called for the establishment of special financial institutions with the name "development banks" or "development finance companies" (DFCs) (Gordon 1983). Besides, the term "economic development" has come to replace the term economic "material progress" to characterize the changing economic and social conditions in societies after 1945 (Arndt 1989: 1).

Both economic and institutional underdevelopment as a double handicap for economies to overcome is reflected in the need for the provision of long-term financing. Normally, funding of investment projects should emerge from the capital market, that is, from a market mechanism without government involvement. An efficient capital market should theoretically ensure increased liquidity to investors and continued public assessment of the firm's performance. However, amid economic and institutional underdevelopment only a few large established firms will be able to access the capital market for long-term financing. For the same reasons, the risk aversion of savers for such risky investments is high in these markets. On the other hand, the presence of economic underdevelopment might also imply the existence of unexploited investment opportunities and therefore, the possibility for profitable projects if initial financing were possible. In terms of prices, the presence of high interest rates reflects the riskiness of the general economic environment in a less developed economy which in turn becomes an impediment to the implementation of such projects. Nonetheless, a great deal of this aggregate risk is correlated with institutional underdevelopment and the inadequate protection of individual investors.

To put our earlier discussion of industrialization and modernization in context, development banks have come to fill this "underinvestment" gap with their expertise (Krahnen and Schmidt 1994: 12), insofar as their dual role has been to respond to both economic and financial underdevelopment. Development banks were entitled to provide long-term finance to leading sectors of the economy that had acquired increased importance for the development of the backward country. From this point of view, they answered the problem of economic underdevelopment. On the other hand, they were also designed as institutions to fill the institutional "gap" in areas such as entrepreneurship and promotional activity, modern corporate management (including financial management), and capital market development. Yet, one must not forget the specific or relative character of these institutions both in time and in space. Indeed, as Diamond (1957: 38) observed early on, development banks as financial institutions are the offspring of the specific conditions that gave birth to them and evolve as these conditions change and the economy develops. These country-specificity and historical-specificity features will prove to be defining characteristics of development banks' nature as organizations as will be explained in subsequent chapters.

2.4 Financing Priority Projects: Lending and Promotional Activity of Development Banks

Development banks, called also policy banks or development finance institutions (DFIs) or development finance companies (DFCs), or national promotional banks are so diverse among different countries in their form, size, performance, mandates, funding sources, governance arrangements, and activities that we can argue that there is no generally accepted definition of them in the development finance literature. In addition, development banking is a rather understudied field in financial economics with relatively few theoretical and empirical studies (De Luna-Martínez et al. 2018; Lazzarini et al. 2015; Thorne and du Toit 2009; Levy-Yeyati et al. 2004). Indeed, in their long history, development banks have been owned by a variety of stakeholders, both private and public, though government sponsorship in various forms has been a common feature. Some development banks have directed their financing and promotional activity to public enterprises, others to private firms while some of them have served both the private and public sectors. They engage in a variegation of activities which might concern the economy as a whole or specific sectors and regions thus, being characterized as national or regional organizations.[2] All of the above, together with differences in their sources of funding or their specific relationship with the government, contribute to the great variety of forms that development banking has taken in different countries with different social, economic, and political environments and over different periods (Smallridge and de Olloqui 2011; Diamond 1957: 1). A development bank can be defined as a state-owned financial institution or

[2] A significant category of development banks is, of course, the multinational development banks. In this study, however, we will deal only with the national development banks and only marginally with the multinational ones, such as the World Bank or the European Investment Bank, to the extent that they affect the operation of the former.

a bank "...with at least 30% state-owned equity..." that promotes, by its legal mandate which has been provided by the state, socioeconomic goals and "promotional activities" that are related to a specific region or sector and are associated with high social returns. Because of their expertise and accumulated knowledge both of local conditions and national government policies, can stimulate long-term financing in critical areas such as environmental sustainability, innovation, and social and human capital development (Colombo and Cuda 2023; Fernández Arias et al. 2019; De Luna-Martínez and Vicente 2012: 4). In the context of this definition, these organizations do much more than conventional financial institutions usually do, not only providing capital to finance investment projects, especially in the private sector, but also disseminating entrepreneurial, technical, and management skills to the private sector (Diamond 1957: 4–5). Alternatively, development banks play four key roles: (a) countercyclical role against speculation-ridden markets, (b) capital development role related to the provision of public goods, (c) venture-capitalist role in risky and innovative endeavors, and (d) mission-oriented role concerning crucial societal issues and problems. Through these functions they attempt to mitigate the impact of shocks as diverse as financial and economic ones, environmental and social challenges, or even extraordinary crises like the Covid-19 pandemic, the moment they help to create and shape markets and promote innovation (Colombo and Cuda 2023; Bilal 2021; Mazzucato and Penna 2018: 260–269; Mazzucato and Penna 2016)

Development banks provide loans or equity financing, including venture capital, for investment projects. Their clients include micro, small, and medium enterprises (MSMEs) and start-ups, large private firms, state-owned enterprises and local governments, other financial institutions, and households. "Plain vanilla loans" or equity financing are considered to have the more pronounced policy impact in terms of structural transformation. Furthermore, equity participation entails a share in profits when a project is successful thereby rewarding the bank for assuming higher risk. These are usually industrial projects or projects related to SMEs, start-ups, and innovative firms, or infrastructure undertakings with high economic priority which yield an appropriate financial and economic return. It is usually the case that private financial institutions have been unable or unwilling to finance these projects. Development banks also provide quasi-equity financing, such as mixed equity and debt instruments or preferred stock along with risk-sharing financial instruments and guarantees against financial losses. As lenders, they can offer either first-tier (retail) or second-tier (wholesale) lending which takes the form of partial or full rediscounting of loans extended from other financial institutions. It is noteworthy that development banks played a significant role in countering the procyclical activity of private sector lending in the global financial crisis. This countercyclical role is important, both for shoring up investment in the downturn of the economic cycle and for sustaining the structural transformation of the economy during crises. However, the size of the development banks with respect to the financial system in a country is crucial for the success of its countercyclical activity. Besides, development banks might act countercyclically either by lending directly to the economy or by on-lending through private banks. In addition, development banks sometimes take a seat on the board of the companies they finance to monitor their activities and advise them on how to deal with shortcomings. Their funding sources have included international institutions such as the World Bank and the International Monetary Fund, local governments, and own bond issues held by private investors in national and international markets. Deposits from the general public are less common but deposits from government institutions are permitted in many cases. The leverage of public funds with private ones is necessary when fiscal resources are limited (Griffith-Jones 2022; Mertens et al. 2021: 6, 24; Brei and Schclarek 2018: 298; De Luna-Martínez et al. 2018; Griffith-Jones et al. 2018: 1, 3–4, 15; Musacchio et al. 2017; Chandrasekhar 2016: 23; De Luna-Martínez and Vicente 2012; Gordon 1983).

The development banks or development finance companies (DFCs) that have been established from 1948 onward usually have the mandate to provide loans or equity financing chiefly to industrial projects. Those should be investment projects with a high economic priority which are also expected to yield a reasonable financial and economic return. Credit provided at preferential terms is preferred when the receiving firm suffers from credit constraints that prohibit its access to finance but at the same time, its project may bring about positive spillover effects in the economy. Loans subsidized by the government have been provided to these institutions at low or zero interest rates, to fulfill their purpose. However, such arrangements are meant to be just a temporary solution to their financing problem. Subsidized lending can provide a false picture of investment opportunities for both the financial institution and its customers while increasing the bank's dependence on government support and distorting competition with other financial institutions. Hence, the idea is that in due course, development banks should rely more on market sources and raise funds by floating their own securities. However, in many cases, for these bond issues to be marketable, government guarantees are provided. Fundraising is an operation on the liabilities side of their balance sheet. On the other hand, the placing on the market of a portfolio of corporate securities held by DFCs as part of their financing activity is an operation on their asset side. However, both can contribute to capital market development, as will be shown below (Fernández Arias et al. 2019; Gordon 1983; Diamond 1957: 68, 82–83).

As noted above, commercial banks, besides governments, have been significant shareholders of development banks. On the other hand, providing loans to finance long-term investment projects demands both the capacity to ward off liquidity risks and the special skills required to assess the variety of risks attached to claims with long maturities. The sources of funds available to development banks deal with the first issue while their expertise in handling long-term projects provides them with an advantage over commercial banks (Diamond 1957: 46).

The complementary role of development banks concerning private commercial banks is stressed in the literature since development banks are supposed to crowd in instead of competing with other financial institutions (De Luna-Martínez et al. 2018; Moslener et al. 2018; Rudolph 2009). It is argued that if development banks' activity addresses specific market failures, which imply that private financial institutions were unable or unwilling to fill the specific market niche, then they do not engage in unfair competition with commercial banks and they do not distort market equilibrium outcomes. Even in the case of countercyclical lending by development banks, the latter should roll their activity back when private financial institutions have regained their financial health and vigor and are able to serve the economy. Yet, successful countercyclical intervention implies that development banks should have a continuous minimum presence in the market to gain familiarity with specific sectors and be able to scale up their lending asap when it is needed. This is the "Sleeping Beauty" approach, or "Sleeping Beauty Syndrome" as the Conference Board of Canada has called it. On the other hand, a financial system with a variety of financial institutions, including development banks, is more diversified thereby enhancing competition, reducing systemic risk, and promoting more realistic policy responses. Second-tier lending means that development banks lend to commercial banks which in turn on-lend to borrowers. This practice removes any concern about the lack of diligent lending practices on behalf of the development bank due to political interference or insufficient risk management, reduces operating costs, and diffuses risk-sharing with the private sector. The downside of this practice is that it may be less effective in achieving the bank's developmental goal measured in terms of social returns and structural transformation results. This is because commercial banks that select the projects to be financed are less keen on choosing projects with high social returns that also carry higher risk. In addition, interest rates charged to borrowers are usually higher than when a development bank lends directly to private firms. However, in the latter case operating costs rise substantially, especially when a development bank operates many branches throughout the country to reach its target financing group. Nevertheless, the choice between direct lending or second-tier lending is also a country-specific issue that depends on historical and cultural factors that characterize each economy (Griffith-Jones 2022; Fernández Arias et al. 2019; De Luna-Martínez et al. 2018; Gutierrez et al. 2011: 11; Smallridge and de Olloqui 2011).

Direct lending is not the only way to promote investment projects in specific sectors. Another way is the one related to the promotional role of a DFC namely, its "direct entrepreneurial activity" when it takes the initiative to set up businesses in targeted sectors. Promotional activity is considered the ultimate and perhaps the more risky contribution of development banks to institutional and economic development. In the relevant literature, it ranks third in the hierarchy of DFC activity after long-term financing and equity participation. The DFC initially sets up a business in a sector of interest, but the ultimate objective is to transfer the control of the firm in due course to prospective entrepreneurs at a profit. The development bank attempts to fill an entrepreneurial gap in that country given that its entrepreneurial class is small and is characterized by poor industrial experience. In this sense, the development bank is assuming an entrepreneurial role concerning the identification, formulation, initiation, and execution of a project. However, there is a high risk and a related cost to this, otherwise beneficial operation for a backward economy. If such an enterprise proves to be unsuccessful or less successful than expected, then the bank might not be able to find buyers for the firm's equity stock and the subsequent losses will impact its profitability. It follows from this kind of risk that the development bank should maintain a relationship of close monitoring and control with the enterprise it promotes or sponsors. Besides, an important difference between a development bank and a commercial bank is that the former conditions its financing to a firm less on tangible collateral and more on an intangible asset such as its close relationship with the firm's management. In this context, it is not always possible for a development bank to avoid the perplexity of risks associated with its financing activity. The lack of managerial skills in many developing economies requires in many cases the bank's representation in the board of directors and/or its direct participation in everyday management activity. The risk taken by the bank in the latter case is the confusion of the roles of entrepreneur (risk-taker) and financier (risk-averter) in the same person representing the bank (Kuiper 1968a: 7, 10–11, 17–18, 22–23; 1968b: 52, 54–55, 57).

However, the choice between secured loan financing and equity financing hinges also on the kind of collateral that a bank might demand to secure its repayment. At least, this is the normal banking practice. The ability of the borrower to post collateral is related to the efficiency of the legal system in securing property rights. If such protection is in short supply, then the bank should base its financing decisions on assessing the quality of management of the borrower and the capacity of the proposed project to generate adequate cash inflows (Diamond 1957: 51). However, equity financing might encounter a different kind of obstacle: the entrepreneur's unwillingness to accept bank's participation to the firm as co-owner with a share in profits and a say on management issues. In any case, the reluctance of borrowers to disclose information about their business might be overcome by the entrenchment of a relationship between the bank and the borrower which is based on trust and is founded on common interests. The latter indicates the crucial role of development banks in changing ingrained habits of thought within the business community. In addition, when the bank's participation in the board is accompanied by technical assistance to the firm's management this provides an additional incentive for the entrepreneur to enter this deal. This is particularly the case when the bank's board membership increases investors' confidence in the good quality of the project and facilitates the sale of the firm's securities on the market (Fernández Arias et al. 2019; Diamond 1957: 52–53, 78). In addition, equity participation may be the preferred choice of the bank when the distribution of returns is so skewed that its risk/return characteristics make it a better choice than lending or providing guarantees (Fernández Arias et al. 2019). The provision of guarantees, on the other hand, is preferred when a borrower with a project that promises high returns has limited access to finance because of low creditworthiness and extreme risk aversion on behalf of commercial banks while, at the same time, the development bank that provides the guarantee possesses higher quality information about the value of the posted collateral or it is in a better position to enforce the contract implementation (Fernández Arias et al. 2019).

Specialization in a particular field or a more general mandate that embraces more sectors and activities is a distinct dilemma for development banks. Specific mandates might include the provision of financing to segments of the economy such as agriculture, small and medium enterprises (SMEs), external trade, industrial firms, infrastructure projects, and even local governments. A general mandate is usually related to a multipurpose goal such as boosting social and economic development (Fernández Arias et al. 2019; De Luna-Martínez et al. 2018). Focusing on the problems of a particular area (country or region) might be the advantage of a regional or national development bank that has a better understanding of local problems, circumstances, and inhabitants thus reducing asymmetric information between lenders and borrowers. Besides, a narrow mandate is more amenable to monitoring and measurement of performance. In this sense, a narrow mandate related to a particular market failure may be preferable even if it lacks flexibility. Moreover, a national development bank with a very broad range of activities could gain from portfolio diversification but it might also provide insufficient financing to each activity while specific fields of financing are intertwined with risks particular to them such as agriculture or small manufacturing firms. In addition, a broad mandate makes the bank's activity less transparent to stakeholders and more amenable to political pressures while it increases the probability of competition with other financial institutions. On the other hand, specialization increases the need for additional personnel employed in different specialized organizations, fails to exploit economies of scale, and, at the same time, may increase the concentration risk and raise the costs of policy coordination among different institutions (Fernández Arias et al. 2019; De Luna-Martínez et al. 2018; Griffith-Jones et al. 2018: 5; Minsky et al. 1993; Diamond 1957: 48–50). In short, even though a restrictive mandate may be a safer solution for a bank looking for financial security, it may make a mediocre contribution to financing economic development which is the main reason for setting up a development bank in the first place (Fernández Arias et al. 2019).

2.5 Development Banks as Agents of Institutional and Capital Market Development

As depicted in the previous sections, development banks have been the offspring of government response to both economic and institutional backwardness. Therefore, both institutional development and change are inscribed in the core of their mandate (Gordon 1983). The non-financial services that development banks provide and which contribute to institutional reform and change include: (a) Providing technical assistance, business advice, mentoring, and merchant banking services to its corporate clients; (b) Contributing to developing human capital, networking, and strategic planning; (c) Promotion of innovation, structural change and financial inclusion (d) Promoting the provision of public goods, including environmental sustainability and the transition to a green economy (Mertens et al. 2021: 6; Griffith-Jones et al. 2018: 3; Chandrasekhar 2016: 23; Mazzucato and Penna 2016; Minsky et al. 1993). The role of development banks in the structural transformation of the economy is particularly important to the degree that this transformation relates to novel and innovative sectors surrounded by deep fundamental uncertainty. In this respect, development banks possess both the long-term perspective of growth and the necessary skills to cope with hurdles related to insufficient funds and knowledge (Griffith-Jones 2022).

Countries where capital is relatively scarce and a great degree of uncertainty governs long-term expectations, are usually characterized by underdeveloped and shallow capital markets. Savings might be inadequate, but they are always there, even in small amounts. Well-functioning financial markets are essential in transferring savings from surplus units to those who are willing to undertake the risk of an investment project and possess the skills to carry it out. However, stimulating and channeling local savings to productive uses might need to cope with multiple hurdles besides poverty including incumbent social values and the general political, economic, social, and psychological environment. The project of economic development eventually culminates in the willingness of economic agents and the ability of government policies to change prevailing habits that go beyond traditional ways of economic activity (Diamond 1957: 9–12). Therefore, financing economic development takes more than supplying the necessary capital. It seems to be an institutional exercise from the very beginning wherein an interaction between individual initiative and the general economic, social, and legal environment takes place. Indeed, as early as the late 1950s Diamond (1957: 13–16) notes that the mobilization and transfer of savings to fund investment requires a legal apparatus and well-established practices that would provide savers with the required safeguards against deep uncertainty about prospects. Such safeguards might include sound banking practices, regulations that protect the consumers of financial services, limited liability laws and corporate organization of firms, and a legal system that protects property rights and facilitates their transfer thus, increasing the marketability of capital goods. The above should contribute to building up capital markets conducive to growth if they establish investors' confidence in them. However, such capital markets demand the willingness of market participants and entrepreneurs to overcome traditional ways of thinking in doing business and take advantage of the new legal infrastructure. Moreover, they entail the ability of entrepreneurs to acquire new technical and managerial skills and of employees to acquire new labor skills related to the new industrial activity. Hence, the multitude of factors that contribute to underinvestment in particular economic sectors relates to the inadequate mobilization of savings because of the inability of economic agents to detect and their unwillingness to exploit new investment opportunities, the shortage of institutions, legal infrastructure, and financial techniques which are conducive to economic growth and the lack of necessary entrepreneurial and technical skills and managerial expertise. If the above are the "ingredients of effective investment" then development banks have been set up to provide at least some of them (Diamond 1957: 16–17).

Hence, in addition to their financing role, DFCs should contribute to institutional development in an economy by promoting more efficient and accurate methods for assessing investment projects, improving the practices of accounting and financial reporting for their clients, and training them in modern management techniques. The institutional role of development banks is not a byproduct of their financing role. Therefore, development banks need to have adequate qualified staff with advisory and technical skills on a permanent basis while conducting research to spot profitable outlets for investment and provide training to private firms (Diamond 1957: 58). In the above context, besides their financial services, development banks offer non-financial services as well. The latter include consulting and management services to firms along with technical assistance, all of them having the aim to promote entrepreneurship. The very function of consulting by development banks has evolved as economies in the world move forward from the import-substitution model to the export-led growth model. Initially, banks' employees involved in this service focused either on specific industries and sectors or on general economic planning. Later, the focus shifted to companies' growth strategies, the efficiency of day-to-day operations, and advising on human resources (Musacchio et al. 2017). As Diamond and Gulhati (1973) point out, the institutional development brought about by the operation of DFCs is one of the main reasons why the World Bank has been interested in supporting these institutions. Institutional development and change have been brought to the fore through DFCs' help in building entrepreneurial and technical skills, training professional staff, and fostering leadership, which should normally provide the necessary impetus for institutional change. As Diamond and Gulhati (1973) put it, DFCs are considered by the World Bank as permanent agents capable of transforming the economic and social environment of Less Developed Countries (LDCs) by providing locally devised solutions to locally emerging problems. On the same basis, Diamond (1982: 118–119, 121) points out that the developmental role of DFCs is not limited to the provision of finance because it extends to the transformation of existing conditions in an economy through active rather than passive intermediation, involving the development of skills and the acquisition of habits and attitudes on behalf of the trainees that would change the mindset of the local business community.

A particular institutional implication of development banks' activity is their impact on capital market development. Development banks contribute to capital market development by floating their own securities, stocks, or bonds, by underwriting their clients' issues of stocks and bonds, and by selling on the market their holdings of securities. However, hesitant entrepreneurs and potential investors with little experience in the related financial instruments might impede capital market development. In this case, development banks are well placed to propose changes in law and motivate behavior that is more conducive to growth (Diamond 1957: 55). Gustafson (1968a: 25–26, 29, 31–32, 34–35) stresses the importance of capital market development as a goal for DFC policies. Development banks often design new financial instruments with attractive risk-return characteristics for capital market participants. At the same time, DFCs are actively involved in a long-term process of changing investor attitudes and practices. The latter contributes to capital market development as far as the operation of an orderly market with increased liquidity and limited fraud is concerned. The development of the capital market presupposes, and the activity of the DFCs provides, a series of institutional changes that should promote business ethics, together with the public disclosure of financial accounts and the standardization of accounting practices, intending to protect the interests of minority shareholders and thus contribute to the dispersal of shareholdings. To achieve these goals, DFCs are expected to educate their clients in modern business practices and suggest to the government changes in the law that will help the development of the capital market, especially concerning the policy on taxation of securities income.

Long-term funding is normally a function performed by the capital markets. In this sense, development banks become capital market substitutes when they provide long-term loans to businesses. DFCs also substitute for capital markets in a more fundamentally institutional but at the same time provisional way. When investors are uncertain about the liquidity of their holdings in new companies' securities, development banks can enhance the marketability of these shares through their screening and monitoring of companies' projects as experts in the field. Then, one post-investment service that a development bank could provide is to place on the market the securities of a successful company that was originally financed by the bank. In this sense, Gustafson (1968a: 33, 38–39, 42) emphasizes the importance of the "roll-over" of a DFC's stock portfolio to the market, together with the bank's participation in certain companies, as a factor that increases public confidence and improves the conditions for future public offerings of these companies' stock. Furthermore, for Diamond (1957: 56–57) the question is whether a development bank should engage in quick revolving of its funds invested in other firms' securities. Swift selling its placements might entail that it is obliged to keep the worst securities and hence deteriorate its portfolio and probably its profitability and reputation. On the other hand, fast revolving provides fresh funds to be invested in new ventures and contributes to the deepening of the capital market. However, this post-investment service of the bank is based on its during-the-investment capital market substitute role. A development bank also acted as a capital market substitute when it decided where to invest the funds it borrowed from domestic or foreign sources and when it expected its future repayment to take the form not only of interest or dividends but also of possible capital gains after selling these securities on the market. The latter provides a direct link between the bank's operation and the development of the capital market to the degree that the initial operation of the bank as a capital market substitute becomes a channel that promotes rather than impedes the eventual development of the market itself both in terms of the volume of transactions and in terms of a rising market value. However, the latter requires DFCs to sell corporate securities from their portfolio at market prices as Gustafson (1968a: 42, 44) points out. Hopefully, these prices would reflect lower required rates of return as the bank's close monitoring of these firms becomes an additional safeguard for the individual investor. Reducing the initially high required rate of return on the market means that the capital market becomes more accessible to prospective firms. In this respect, the role of development banks in reducing the institutional barriers to financial development in a less developed country is crucial.

2.6 Constraints in Development Banks' Operation and Financial Management

When development banks act as financiers of investment projects and agents of institutional change they face important constraints. These constraints relate to the dual role of a development bank as both a financial institution and a promoter of economic development and depend on government policy and how this affects the bank's financial viability. Development banks need to evaluate project proposals in both economic and financial terms. However, the government and its developmental priorities are crucial in this respect as this has long been recognized in the literature (Bhatt 1982; Mathew 1968, 1982). Bhatt (1982: 70–71) identifies three criteria that a project should meet to be accepted for funding. These include the financial rate of return which relates to a project's financial soundness, the economic rate of return in terms of income generation and savings, and finally the yield of the project in terms of competitive efficiency (the domestic cost per unit of foreign exchange saved). Then these measured rates of return should also act as a communication tool between the bank and the government in the bank's efforts to influence public policy and make economically sound projects financially viable. De Luna-Martínez et al. (2018) and Mathew (1968: 91, 97–99, 101–104), on the other hand, indicate the paradox of private DFCs having to reconcile their financial performance as private enterprises with the fulfillment of the government's developmental goals. In this respect, DFCs are vulnerable to the whims of the government, as they are directly dependent on its support for their survival, given the high risk of financing small and innovative companies at below-market rates. The main concern is that lending money to support financially dubious projects that are important to the government's development objectives threatens the very existence of development banks as banking institutions. Furthermore, government interference when accompanied by corruption phenomena renders the relationship with DFCs even more problematic. Things get worse when there is unfair competition between private and state-owned DFCs at the expense of the former. Besides, during the 1980s and 1990s, state ownership had been related to poor performance for development banks (Gutierrez et al. 2011).

Dependence on government funds and support is dictated by the ability or the inability of the development bank to provide financing to its clients on reasonable or preferential terms. The government's participation in the development bank's equity and government subsidies are needed in most cases. On the other hand, an appropriate mix between equity and debt should be the one that would provide enough capital to absorb risks and at the same time, so much debt as to increase the profitability of its equity. However, the share of the government in the bank's equity relates to its involvement in management. In this respect, the composition of the board of directors of the bank and its dependence on government is crucial. The board of directors can operate as a shield for the management against public and private pressures. In any case, a major safeguard against pressures on the management emanating either from the government or from private interests might be the dispersion of ownership of the bank. Furthermore, competent management is necessary for establishing a "working relationship" with the government which secures both the necessary flexibility in financial decisions and management's accountability toward the elected government (Gutierrez et al. 2011; Diamond 1957: 68–72, 78).

Mathew (1982: 281–282, 287–288) indicates that financially viable development banks together with limited government interference in their management are the only guarantees in favor of the public interest. This is important as far as the access and credibility of DFCs to financial markets are at stake. Moreover, the goal of development banks to reverse the path-dependence of economic and institutional underdevelopment can only be successfully achieved if, in addition to reducing their dependence on government financial support, they maintain a market orientation in their activities. However, as the World Bank (1976) points out, persistent dependence of DFCs on official funds emerges because of government-administered low lending rate policies, underdeveloped capital markets that prohibit DFCs from mobilizing domestic funds, and government regulations that impede foreign borrowing by DFCs or favor government securities at the expense of banks' securities. However, we should note that besides governments, commercial banks have been the major source of equity capital for development banks in the post-WWII era. In addition, diffused ownership shields management from undue involvement either of the government or of private shareholders (Diamond 1957: 45, 61).

The government-imposed constraints on development banks' operation also extend to the appropriate financial management policies followed by these banks as, Gill (1982), Raghavan (1982), and Gustafson (1968b) point out. This is because depressed profitability implies diminishing returns for the bank's shareholders and at the same time reduces the opportunities of the DFC to tap funds from alternative sources other than the government. Specifically, Gustafson (1968b: 63, 73–74) emphasizes the need for DFCs' management to act as if they maximize shareholders' wealth to raise additional equity and debt capital from the markets thereby limiting future concessional funding by state agencies. To this end, debt-equity ratios should be set at levels that do not jeopardize the solvency of banks in difficult times. In addition, ratios representing the delay in recovery of loan proceeds (defaulted interest plus principal over total interest plus principal) and the soundness of the portfolio (defaulted loans over total loans) should be considered as indicators of the risk assumed. In the same sense, Raghavan (1982: 200, 202–204) shows the need for a readjustment of DFCs' financial policies toward market sources as far as the expansion of their operation and the related demand for funds renders official sources inadequate. In this sense, policies should be considered that would enhance profitability by increasing interest rate spreads. Thus, Gill (1982: 213–214) argues that as the sophistication of the economy increases and development banks face increased competition from other financial institutions and the capital market, a change in attitude within the financial management of DFCs toward the acceptance of market discipline is in order. According to Diamond (1957: 81–84) if the question is whether a development bank should make a profit, the answer is that it should for various reasons. If the development bank is privately owned and needs to attract private capital, the expectation of profits is needed to motivate investors. Even if the bank is state-owned, prudent management dictates that it still needs to make profits to accumulate capital that can be used to absorb losses and finance future ventures. It is a matter of financial viability and efficiency which implies that a financial organization should at least cover its operating and financing costs. Profitable undertakings in a bank's portfolio are more readily sold on the market and at the same time, the bank has a greater capacity to borrow from the market, being a lucrative business. Finally, a profitable development bank, either public or private, depends less on government assistance and becomes a paradigm for the economic community of its country, that serving the purpose of economic development on sound financial grounds is possible.

Even though the above literature registered concerns about development banking some decades ago, this discussion remains topical. In agreement with these authors, we think that although a development bank has to assess both the socioeconomic return of a project to be financed and its financial return, the latter might be more important for its mandate to promote financial development. This is because no investor would ever trust the bank's monitoring of a project as a safeguard against the assumed risks attached to it if the related financial return is not an important—at least in the long run—factor in the project's evaluation. However, this cannot be an absolute criterion when considering the multiplicity of development banks' goals and not just the ones related to financial development. Fernández Arias et al. (2019) even talk about the "impossible trinity" referring to the ability of a successful development bank to satisfy simultaneously three conditions: to address a specified market failure, to act in a way that does not crowd out the private sector and to be profitable. They conclude that financial viability should not be an absolute criterion for the success of a development bank that has to meet the other two conditions as well. More lenient conditions such as capital preservation may be more plausible. Furthermore, since financial performance is more easily measured than the fulfillment of the developmental objectives of a bank, its management may prefer to emphasize the former rather than the latter. It seems that many development banks emphasize criteria of financial performance such as profitability, operating efficiency, and disbursement indicators because they have not developed the skills to assess their developmental performance. However, performance evaluation is important since development banks operate in niches where markets are in infancy or non-existent. Therefore, internal evaluation systems should take the place of lacking market signals. Proper performance assessment which will include the developmental impact of the bank is necessary for accountability to the public (De Luna-Martínez et al. 2018). The idea is to move beyond traditional measures of bank profitability such as return on equity (ROE), return on assets (ROA), Net Interest Margin, or non-performing loan ratios and use indices that take into account the costs and benefits that are intrinsic to development banking such as subsidies and social benefits (Francisco et al. 2008). Gutierrez et al. (2011) argue that the objective of a development bank should not be profit maximization but financial sustainability, in the sense of generating sufficient income to fulfill its mandate without imposing a financial burden on the state. When financial sustainability is combined with successful fulfillment of developmental goals then this is an example of a healthy public development bank. However, it is difficult to describe the benchmark case of a healthy development bank because of the variety of mandates and the specific socioeconomic circumstances that characterize the operation of these financial institutions. Yet, common minimum dimensions for a comprehensive evaluation of development banks' performance should include (a) public policy objective and corporate governance, (b) developmental effect, and (c) financial and operational criteria (Smallridge and de Olloqui 2011). On the other hand, private ownership of development banks is not a solution to performance issues because it comes with strings attached. While private ownership may be beneficial in terms of market funding, streamlined governance, and up-to-date risk management, it carries the risk that the bank's development objective will be sacrificed in favor of higher profitability in competition with other private banks. In any case, according to the World Bank 2017 survey, more than 90% of development banks reported positive ROE and ROA ratios though these have been below the national averages during the period 2011–2015 while 61% of responders reported non-performing loan ratios less than 5% (De Luna-Martínez et al. 2018; Griffith-Jones et al. 2018: 19).

Eventually, a development bank will be in a better position to realize its developmental goals, including environmental and social sustainability, if it has a clear mandate, competent management, and follows good governance practices probably accompanied by the use of innovative practices to address specific market failures under appropriate regulation and supervision (Colombo and Cuda 2023; Griffith-Jones et al. 2018; De Luna-Martínez and Vicente 2012; Gutierrez et al. 2011). Development banks' underperformance has been often associated with vague and confusing mandates and poor governance since inadequate board of directors along with a lack of management skills invite political interference. Ideally, mandates should be enshrined in laws and clearly define a target sector related to a market failure, rules of cooperation with the private banking institutions, and a minimum level of efficiency related to the financial sustainability of the development bank. Mandates should also be under regular review to ascertain that they are still relevant for the changing economic and institutional environment (De Luna-Martínez et al. 2018; Gutierrez et al. 2011; Rudolph 2009). Last but not least, development banks' performance depends also on the external environment that they face and especially on macroeconomic policies and financial conditions. Government policies that contribute to lower inflation, dampened cyclicality, external balance, and financial development for the benefit of the real economy are instrumental in improving both the financial and developmental performance of development banks (Griffith-Jones et al. 2018: 6).

References

Arndt, H.W. (1989) *Economic Development. The History of an Idea*, Chicago and London: The University of Chicago Press.

Arndt, H.W. (1984) *The Rise and Fall of Economic Growth. A Study in Contemporary Thought*, Chicago and London: The University of Chicago Press.

Bhatt, V. V. (1982) "On a Development Bank's Selection Criteria for Industrial Projects", in Diamond W. and Raghavan V. S. (eds.) *Aspects of Development Bank Management*, EDI Series in Economic Development, Baltimore and London: The Johns Hopkins University Press, pp. 60–79.

Bilal, S. (2021) "The Rise of Public Development Banks in the European Financial Architecture for Development", Elcano Royal Institute Working Paper 12/2021, Madrid: ETTG/Elcano Royal Institute. Available at https://media.realinstitutoelcano.org/wp-content/uploads/2021/12/wp12-2021-bilal-rise-of-public-development-banks-in-european-financial-architecture-for-development.pdf accessed 23 May 2024.

Brei, M. and Schclarek, A. (2018) "The Countercyclical Behaviour of National Development Banks in Latin America and the Caribbean" in Griffith-Jones S. and Ocampo J. A. (eds.) *The Future of National Development Banks*, New York: Oxford University Press, pp. 278–301.

Bruck, N. (1998) "The Role of Development Banks in the Twenty-First Century", *Journal of Emerging Markets*, 3: 39–67.

Cameron, R. E. (1953) "The Crédit Mobilier and the Economic Development of Europe", *The Journal of Political Economy*, 61(6): 461–488.

Chandrasekhar, C.P. (2016) "National Development Banks in a Comparative Perspective" in Calcagno, A., Dullien, S., Márquez-Velázquez, A., Maystre, N., and Priewe J. (eds.) *Rethinking Development Strategies after the Financial Crisis Vol. II: Country Studies and International Comparisons*, New York and Geneva:

United Nations, pp. 21–30, available at https://unctad.org/system/files/official-document/gdsmdp20152_en.pdf Accessed 21 Oct. 2023

Colombo, M. and Cuda, M. (2023) "The Role of Public Development Banks & Institutions in the Implementation of the United Nations' Agenda 2030: A survey in Europe", Discussion Paper No. 179. Directorate General Economic and Financial Affairs (DG ECFIN), European Commission, available at https://economy-finance.ec.europa.eu/document/download/2e0e5ab7-c684-40d7-9d03-e21432e99b62_en?filename=dp179_en.pdf Accessed 21 Oct. 2023

De Aghion, B. A. (1999) "Development Banking." *Journal of Development Economics* 58: 83–100.

De Cecco, M. (2005) "Sraffa's Lectures on Continental Banking. A Preliminary Appraisal", *Review of Political Economy*, 17(3): 349–358.

De Luna-Martínez, J., Vicente, C. L., bin Arshad, A., Tatucu, R., and Song, J. (2018) "2017 Survey of National Development Banks", World Bank Group Global Report, (May) available at https://documents1.worldbank.org/curated/en/977821525438071799/pdf/2017-Survey-of-National-development-banks.pdf Accessed 13 Oct. 2023

De Luna-Martínez, J. and Vicente, C. L. (2012) "Global Survey of Development Banks", World Bank Policy Research Working Paper No 5969, Washington, DC. available at https://documents1.worldbank.org/curated/en/313731468154461012/pdf/WPS5969.pdf Accessed 20 Dec. 2016

Diamond, W. (1982) "The Impact of Development Banks on their Environment" in Diamond W. and Raghavan, V. S. (eds.) *Aspects of Development Bank Management*, EDI Series in Economic Development, Baltimore & London: The Johns Hopkins University Press, pp. 116–135.

Diamond, W. (1957) *Development Banks*, Baltimore & London: The Johns Hopkins University Press

Diamond, W. and Gulhati, R. (1973) "Some Reflections on the World Bank's Experience with Development Finance Companies", IBRD Economic Staff Working Paper, No 145, (Feb.), available at https://documents1.worldbank.org/curated/en/884731468740126062/text/multi0page.txt Accessed on 30 Oct. 2023.

Fernández Arias, E., Hausmann, R., and Panizza, U. (2019) "Smart Development Banks", Inter-American Development Bank (IDB) Working Paper Series No IDP-WP-1047, Washington, DC., available at https://publications.iadb.org/en/publications/english/viewer/Smart_Development_Banks_.pdf Accessed 30 Oct. 2023

Francisco, M., Mascaró, Y., Mendoza, J. C., and Yaron, J. (2008) "Measuring the Performance and Achievement of Social Objectives of Development Finance Institutions", World Bank Policy Research Working Paper WPS4506, available at https://documents1.worldbank.org/curated/en/949841468036879814/pdf/wps4506.pdf Accessed 21 Oct. 2023

Gerschenkron, A. (1962) "Economic Backwardness in Historical Perspective" in A. Gerschenkron, *Economic Backwardness in Historical Perspective*, Cambridge, Mass, pp. 5–30.

Gill, D. B. (1982) "Development Banks and the Mobilization of Financial Resources", in Diamond, W. and Raghavan, V. S. (eds.) *Aspects of Development Bank Management*, EDI Series in Economic Development, Baltimore and London: The Johns Hopkins University Press, pp. 213–232.

Gordon, D. L. (1983) "Development Finance Companies. State and Privately Owned. A Review", World Bank Staff Working Papers, No 578, available at https://documents1.worldbank.org/curated/en/928181468741004629/text/multi-page.txt Accessed 25 Oct. 2023

Griffith-Jones, S. (2022) "The Role Public National Development Banks Play in the Structural Transformation of Developing Countries", United Nations Conference on Trade and Development, April, available at https://unctad.org/system/files/information-document/BRI-Project_policy-brief-01_en.pdf Accessed 30 Oct 2023

Griffith-Jones, S., Ocampo, J. A., Rezende, F., Schclarek, A. and Brei, M. (2018) "The Future of National Development Banks" in Griffith-Jones S. and Ocampo, J. A. (eds.) *The Future of National Development Banks*, New York: Oxford University Press, pp. 1–36.

Gustafson, D. (1968a) "Promoting Broader Ownership of Private Securities in the Low Income Countries" in Diamond, W. (ed.) *Development Finance Companies: Aspects of Policy and Orientation*, Baltimore: The Johns Hopkins Press, pp. 25–48.

Gustafson, D. (1968b) "Financial Policy Problems of Development Finance Companies" in Diamond, W. (ed.) *Development Finance Companies: Aspects of Policy and Orientation*, Baltimore: The Johns Hopkins Press, pp. 59–90.

Gutierrez, E., Rudolph, H. P., Homa, T. and Blanco Beneit, E. (2011) "Development Banks. Role and Mechanisms to Increase their Efficiency", World Bank Policy Research Working Paper WPS5729, available at https://documents1.worldbank.org/curated/en/912941468045550498/pdf/WPS5729.pdf Accessed 28 Oct 2023

Hermann, J. (2010) "Development Banks in the Financial-Liberalization Era: The Case of BNDES in Brazil", *CEPAL Review*, 100: 189–203.

Kuiper, E. T. (1968a) "The Promotional Role of a Development Finance Company", in Diamond, W. (ed.) *Development Finance Companies: Aspects of Policy and Orientation*, Baltimore: The Johns Hopkins Press, pp. 5–24.

Kuiper, E. T. (1968b) "Relationship Between a Development Finance Company and the Management of Enterprises it Promotes, Sponsors, or Finances", in Diamond, W. (ed.) *Development Finance Companies: Aspects of Policy and Orientation*, Baltimore: The Johns Hopkins Press, pp 49–58.

Krahnen, J. P. and Schmidt, R. H. (1994) *Development Finance as Institution Building. A New Approach to Poverty-Oriented Banking*, London & New York: Routledge.

Lazzarini, S. G., Musacchio, A., Bandeira-de-Mello, R., and Marcon, R. (2015) "What Do State-Owned Development Banks Do? Evidence from BNDES, 2002–09", *World Development*, 66: 237–253.

Levy-Yeyati, E. L., Micco, A. and Panizza, U. (2004) "Should the Government Be in the Banking Business? The Role of State-Owned and Development Banks", Inter-American Development Bank Working Paper No 517, available at https://publications.iadb.org/en/publications/english/viewer/Should-the-Government-Be-in-the-Banking-Business-The-Role-of-State-Owned-and-Development-Banks.pdf Accessed 2 Nov. 2023

Loizos, K. (2018) "The Financial Repression-Liberalization Debate: Taking Stock, Looking for a Synthesis", *Journal of Economic Surveys*, 32(2): 440–468.

Mathew, P. M. (1982) "Government and Development Bank Relations", in Diamond, W. and Raghavan, V. S. (eds.) *Aspects of Development Bank Management*, EDI Series in Economic Development, Baltimore and London: The Johns Hopkins University Press, pp. 277–294.

Mathew, P. M. (1968) "Relations Between Governments and Development Finance Companies", in Diamond, W. (ed.) *Development Finance Companies: Aspects of Policy and Orientation*, Baltimore: The Johns Hopkins Press, pp. 91–108.

Mazzucato, M. and Penna, C. R. C. (2018) "National Development Banks and Mission-Oriented Finance for Innovation" in Griffith-Jones, S. and Ocampo, J. A. (eds.) *The Future of National Development Banks*, New York: Oxford University Press, pp. 255–277.

Mazzucato, M. and Penna, C. R. C. (2016) "Beyond Market Failures: The Market Creating and Shaping Roles of State Investment Banks", *Journal of Economic Policy Reform*, 19(4): 305–326.

Mertens, D., Thiemann, M. and Volberding, P. (2021) "Introduction: The Making of the European Field of Development Banking" in Mertens, D., Thiemann, M. and Volberding, P. (eds.) *The Reinvention of Development Banking in the European Union. Industrial Policy in the Single Market and the Emergence of a Field*, New York: Oxford University Press, pp. 1–32.

Minsky, H. P., Papadimitriou, D. B., Phillips, R. J., and Randall Wray, L. (1993) "Community Development Banking. A Proposal to Establish a Nationwide System of Community Development Banks", The Jerome Levy Economics Institute of Bard College, Public Policy Brief No 3 available at https://www.researchgate.net/publication/5163193_Community_Development_Banking_A_Proposal_to_Establish_a_Nationwide_System_of_Community_Development_Banks Accessed 5 Nov. 2023

Moslener, U., Thiemann, M. and Volberding, P. (2018) "National Development Banks as Active Financiers. The Case of KfW", in Griffith-Jones, S. and Ocampo, J. A. (eds.) *The Future of National Development Banks*, New York: Oxford University Press pp. 63–85.

Musacchio, A., Lazzarini, S. Makhoul, P. and Simmons, E. (2017) "The Role and Impact of Development Banks. A Review of their Founding, Focus, and Influence", (Report to the World Bank). Washington, D.C.: World Bank. Available at https://people.brandeis.edu/~aldom/papers/The%20Role%20and%20Impact%20of%20Development%20Banks%20-%203-9-2017.pdf Accessed 5 Nov. 2023

Raghavan, V. S. (1982) "Some Issues Relating to Financial Policies of Development Banks", in Diamond W. and Raghavan V. S. (eds.) *Aspects of Development Bank Management*, EDI Series in Economic Development. Baltimore and London: The Johns Hopkins University Press, pp. 196–212.

Rudolph, H. P. (2009) "State Financial Institutions. Mandates, Governance, and Beyond", World Bank Policy Research Working Paper WPS5141 available at https://documents1.worldbank.org/curated/en/114531468159602791/pdf/WPS5141.pdf Accessed 13 Nov. 2023

Smallridge, D. and de Olloqui, F. (2011) "A Health Diagnostic Tool for Public Development Banks", Inter-American Development Bank (IDB) Technical Notes No. IDB-TN-225, available at https://publications.iadb.org/en/publications/english/viewer/A-Health-Diagnostic-Tool-for-Public-Development-Banks.pdf Accessed 3 Nov. 2023

Thorne, J. and du Toit, C. (2009) "A Macro-Framework for Successful Development Banks", *Development Southern Africa*, 26(5): 677–694.

World Bank (1989) *World Development Report 1989*, Washington D.C., available at https://openknowledge.worldbank.org/server/api/core/bitstreams/97d36d98-ce0c-516d-bfa6-d57cbd4da318/content Accessed 20 Oct. 2023

World Bank (1976) *Development Finance Companies*, Sector Policy Paper 11020, Washington D.C., (April), available at https://documents1.worldbank.org/curated/en/317061468763754287/text/multi0page.txt Accessed 3 Oct. 2023

CHAPTER 3

Development Finance and Financial Development in Economic Theory and Policy: The Importance of Institutions

3.1 Development Finance and Post-WWII Theories of Economic Development

Browsing the literature on economic development and its financing it is possible to distinguish two different periods, each one referring to different policy recommendations and theories of development finance. These periods are closely related to the economic conditions prevailing in less developed countries (LDCs) in the context of the international financial and monetary architecture. The first period spans the decades of the 1950s and 1960s. During this period, there was a widespread conviction among governments and economic theorists for the necessity of development planning as a policy recommendation, especially for the "backward" countries. Economic backwardness is a complex condition with many aspects including industrial structures, institution building, and "intellectual climate" or "ideology". Nevertheless, Marx's claim in the preface of *Das Kapital* that "The industrially more developed country presents to the less developed country a picture of the latter's future" (Gerschenkron 1962: 6–7) characterized that period of hope and optimism for economic

This Chapter draws partly on ideas presented in the article Loizos (2018) published in the *Journal of Economic Surveys*, 2018, copyright John Wiley & Sons Ltd., available online https://onlinelibrary.wiley.com/doi/10.1111/joes.12195

K. Loizos, *Between Markets and Governments*,
https://doi.org/10.1007/978-3-031-88527-3_3

development worldwide. After all, the world economy in 1945 had recently experienced the consequences of two major disasters: the Great Depression of the 1930s and the Second World War. However, the economic development of LDCs as a policy agenda of developed economies in the West was an offspring of the War itself for many reasons. The New Order and Co-Prosperity Sphere propagated by the Axis countries of Germany and Japan respectively, demanded an alternative authoritarian proposal for the post-war world. Franklin Delano Roosevelt's "Four Freedoms Speech" on January 6 1941 included the freedom from want "…which, translated into world terms, means economic understandings which will secure to every nation a healthy peacetime life for its inhabitants-everywhere in the world" (Roosevelt 1941). The latter was an example of a different democratic alternative. Moreover, if the Great Depression challenged laissez-faire policies and highlighted the decisive role of the state in shoring up fickle inter-war economies, the war economy that followed showed to the people how effective the government was in coordinating a nations' productive forces to achieve an ultimate goal (Carvalho 2009; Arndt 1989: 43–44). If that goal in wartime had been to defeat the Axis, it could change into a post-war priority for reconstruction and economic development in both developed and developing countries alike. Additional reasons for this post-World War II interest in economic development were the collapse of the colonial system and the rise of national independence movements in the former colonies which sparked hopes for the future in these countries along with the new international order which was marked by the increased influence of the Soviet Union. It is worth mentioning that for the Marxist economists of the era economic development was almost identical to the degree of industrialization in a country. Moreover, economists in the Marxist tradition such as Charles Bettelheim, who studied soviet planning in the inter-war years, became advocates and experts of economic planning in the post-war period and participated in "planning doctor" missions in developing countries. The Third World that emerged in this way compounded with a post-war public opinion in Western countries with rising humanitarian concerns, shaped an intellectual climate in favor of economic development objectives. The theoretical framework of development planning to improve living standards for the population was eventually articulated in three major themes: the formation of real capital, the contribution of human capital, and the role of international trade as factors of growth. The development policies agenda of the era included financing for priority sectors, import-substitution policies compound with support for infant industries, state ownership of financial institutions, central planning, and administrative controls on prices (Allisson 2024; de la Torre et al. 2017: 78; Carvalho 2009; Arndt 1989: 49–50, 54). The above constituted the main elements of "classical developmentalism" which was founded on a "developmental class coalition" that comprised industrialists, workers, and bureaucrats in the service of the national goal for industrialization and economic development (Bresser-Pereira 2015).

As FitzGerald and Vos (1989: 18) indicate there was a strong theoretical underpinning of this strand of thinking emerging from the ideas of J. M. Keynes (1936 [1973]) that cast doubt on the ability of the market mechanism to achieve optimal allocation of resources from the point of view of long-term economic growth. Especially, the contradiction between short-term speculative horizons and long-term investment (Keynes (1936 [1973]: 150–161) indicates the inevitable role of state intervention in favor of social objectives for long-term growth planning (Keynes 1936 [1973]: 375–378). Such ideas had left their mark on the New Deal policies though Keynes himself seems to have been even more radical by calling for the "socialisation of investments" to bring about full employment (Mazzucato and Penna 2016: 314; Keynes 1936 [1973]: 378). Nonetheless, economic development is a much richer notion than mere economic growth. Economic development entails changes in the economic and social structure of a country, it is accompanied by a rise in the living standards of the majority of the population, and it has an impact on multiple dimensions of everyday life including social and cultural features and it implies changes in the way people think about their ability to progress (Arndt 1989: 52–53).

Industrialization or economic development called for both fixed capital formation and the growth of technical knowledge. The ideological framework had been provided by the Soviet example of five-year plans. After all, Soviet planning had proved more effective than free markets during the depression and war years. In this context, government intervention was not challenged in either the academic or political debates. Major theoretical contributions in this tradition include the ideas of Rosenstein-Rodan for "planned industrialization", "big push" and "balanced growth", which were developed further by H. Singer, R. Nurkse and G. Myrdal. H. Singer expounded the idea of a big push that would make possible the escape from the "vicious circle" of underdevelopment through a substantial initial boost of investment on a broad range of industries under a specific development plan. The long gestation periods before investment in real capital yielded beneficial results on economic growth, had made state intervention necessary for the accomplishment of the developmental goal. In this sense, G. Myrdal explained how the vicious circle can transform itself into a virtuous one according to his hypothesis of "circular cumulative causation". Myrdal understands economic development as a "cumulative process" based on Rostow's (1956) necessary take-off for economic growth which would be self-sustained. Notably, Rostow examines dimensions of the take-off which include the required supply of loanable funds, the sources of entrepreneurship, and the leading sectors of the economy, and emphasizes the need for institutions and a political and social environment that would be conducive to growth. Finally, R. Nurkse developed further the idea of Rosenstein-Rodan for "balanced growth" (Levy-Yeyati et al. 2004; Arndt 1989: 57–59). On the other hand, F. Perroux argued in the 1950s in favor of "growth poles" namely, that there are specific points or poles in an economy where growth takes place. If this is the case, then planning and coordination of policies are needed that would target these poles in favor of regional economic growth (Caloffi and Serra 2022)

This debate was further enriched in the 1960s as the focus moved from physical to human capital formation. The discussion revolved around "brain drain", the role of technical progress and growth of knowledge, the importance of education as an investment in human capital, and the role of culture and tradition in adapting new methods provided by technical assistance along with institutions building (Arndt 1989: 60–66). In the context of a debate about protectionism and planning as opposed to free trade and market economy, import substitution was proposed as a solution for quick industrialization of less developed countries in the context of R. Nurkse's advocacy of balanced growth and P. Prebisch and G. Myrdal's thesis that free international trade could not promote growth in LDCs. It was considered that inelastic world demand for primary products and the combination of monopolistic conditions in the market for industrial products of developed economies versus the competitive conditions in the market for LDCs' primary products, resulted in the deterioration of the terms of trade for the less developed "peripheral" economies and contained the diffusion of the benefits of technical progress to them. Prebisch argued that as agricultural productivity increased in LDCs, the prices of their exports would fall because international markets for their products were more competitive than those for industrial goods from developed countries. Agricultural specialization by LDCs was therefore not a viable long-term option. Industrialization was inevitable as a policy choice. Myrdal suggested that international trade is contributing to rising inequality between nations, while Nurkse highlighted the asymmetry in relations between the center and periphery, given that most industrial production is concentrated in developed Western economies. Hence, Myrdal proposed that LDCs should impose restrictions on imports, which in many cases were already in place during the war and afterward, as a means to protect their industries. In this context, W. A. Lewis and A. O. Hirschman suggested that LDCs should protect their "infant industries" until they reach a certain "threshold" of development (Carvalho 2009; Arndt 1989: 73–75).

From a different perspective, the above discussion also highlights the problems associated with financing economic development. Four dimensions in development financing describe the complexity of this issue and its interdependence with other economic policies: the relationship between consumption and investment, public investment and fiscal conditions, the balance of payments and foreign currency shortages, and the development of local financial markets and institutions. In terms of "real" resources, developing economies are facing a dilemma since higher investment expenditure implies lower consumption expenditure. Very poor countries with meager income levels may not be able to squeeze consumption further and therefore, foreign aid is inevitable. On the other hand, public investment to build up infrastructure with high social returns is necessary. Public development banks can play a central role in financing these projects. However, in fiscal terms, the necessary funds can only come from rising taxes, increasing public debt, or newly printed money with the corresponding impact on taxpayers' disposable income, on the government's borrowing costs, or possibly on monetary stability. Moreover, since capital accumulation in LDCs is dependent on imports of capital goods and other materials the availability of foreign currency is crucial to meet the relevant payments. If the proceeds from exports are not enough, then capital inflows should make up for the shortfall. Finally, the degree of development that has been achieved by domestic financial institutions and markets is critical for development finance. Investments in real assets correspond to financial claims which make up portfolios of investors in financial markets. Financing economic development becomes even more complicated as monetization of the economy progresses and money appears as a monetary asset side by side with financial assets and liquidity premium emerges as the return for safety amid uncertainty. The institutional structure of financial markets is also important along with their regulation concerning financial inclusion and financial fragility. Economic development brings about financial development, the growing diversification of financial services along with rising complexity of financial processes which may increase financial fragility (Carvalho 2009).

The above theories of economic development and issues in development finance were conditioned by the historical experience of the 1920s and 1930s where "latecomers", such as the Soviet Union, achieved a remarkable step forward in economic development and industrialization, implementing development planning as opposed to the woes of the Western market economies under the Great Depression (Arndt 1989: 57–58; FitzGerald and Vos 1989: 18). A combination of these two factors, advances in economic theory and historical experience, called for further government intervention to guide the process of economic development and industrialization. The financial aspects of this policy recommendation included administratively low interest rates and government-ridden credit allocation to provide funds to what Rostow (1965: 1–21) would call industries in "leading sectors". These priority sectors would benefit from below-market preferential interest rates and credit quotas imposed on private banks. Administrative interest rates implied ceilings on deposit and loan rates as a way to reduce the financing cost of both borrowers and banks (de la Torre et al. 2017: 79–80). Thinkers such as Arthur Lewis, Alexander Gerschenkron, and Gunnar Myrdal were in favor of an increased presence of the government in the financial system to promote its economic growth policies (Levy-Yeyati et al. 2004). As FitzGerald and Vos (1989: 3) point out, development finance was considered to be a passive supporter of long-term development policies including policies of structural transformation without paying attention to short-term problems of debt imbalances and possible economic instability.

The previous ideas of interventionism/protectionism were criticized by an alternative strand of thought which was built around the theme of liberalization and especially the beneficial effects of free international trade.[1] The international dimensions of development finance and the "two-gap" model which has been associated with the work of H. B. Chenery paved

[1]A different kind of critique against classical developmentalism came from dependency theorists who focused on the center-periphery antithesis and development-underdevelopment polarization (Bresser-Pereira 2015; Carvalho 2009; Arndt 1989). Since our focus is on development finance rather than on economic development theories we will not elaborate further on these ideas.

the way for this critique. It was argued that the key constraints to LDCs' growth were twofold: the insufficiency of domestic savings to support the financing of investment (the "savings gap") and the inadequacy of LDCs' exports—mainly of primary goods—and of foreign aid to finance the required imports in capital equipment (the "foreign exchange gap"). The two gaps between domestic saving and investment on the one hand, and exports and imports on the other, could be filled by the inflow of foreign savings and foreign exchange in a liberalized external sector of the economy. These ideas doubted the benefits of import-substitution strategies as well since they seemed to be unsuccessful in economizing on foreign exchange reserves and reducing the dependence of LDCs on world markets. On the contrary, international trade was now considered to be a major factor of economic development toward outward-looking strategies of industrialization (Arndt 1989: 77–79, 82–84; FitzGerald and Vos 1989: 33–34; Thirlwall 1976: 13). Hence, during the 1980s and 1990s a new theoretical and policy consensus emerged under the banner of financial and economic liberalization which were expressed in privatizations and neo-liberal economic policies and took their comprehensive form in the so-called Washington Consensus. As is explained in the next section, administratively low interest rates were considered to be the cause rather than the result of underdeveloped capital markets and financial underdevelopment (Mazzucato and Penna 2015; Levy-Yeyati et al. 2004).

3.2 Alternative Financial Regimes: The Financial Repression—Financial Liberalization Debate and the "Washington Consensus"

The above conflicting ideas about development finance in the post-WWII world assumed the institutional form of alternative financial regimes that split this period into two major subperiods: The period of financial repression/regulation that extends from 1945 to mid-1970s, or even to mid-1980s in some cases. The financial arrangements that mark this period are related to the Bretton Woods regime, the dominance of Keynesianism, and the interventionist role of the state in the economy. The second period is characterized by financial liberalization and deregulation, is an offspring of the collapse of the Bretton Woods regime and is associated with laissez-faire neo-liberal ideas that favor the dominance of markets over political arrangements (Loizos 2017; Wade 2008; Mallick and Agarwal 2007;

Chakraborty 2002). We will employ in this book the term "financial regime" in the way it is used in the above literature because we think it is both comprehensive and illuminating of the post-WWII situation in development finance. The advantage of this term is that it goes beyond the realm of ideas and expresses the institutional and policy dimensions of alternative views of development finance that were considered in the previous section. In this sense, the transition from financial repression/regulation to financial liberalization/deregulation was a "regime change" (Wade 2008) that needs to be discussed further in this section.

The McKinnon-Shaw financial repression/liberalization model constitutes the financial aspect of the new liberalization doctrine and reflects the theoretical debates concerning economic conditions during the 1970s and 1980s. The historical setting was now one of rising inflation and unemployment in the background of the two oil crises of 1973 and 1978–1979. This phenomenon of stagflation led to a radical re-examination of the, till then, followed policies and their theoretical underpinnings. Fry (1995: 3–19) describes this "revolution" in two dimensions: (a) by questioning the instruments used during the 1950s and 1960s for promoting economic development. These included the imposition of interest rate ceilings, the obligation of commercial banks to maintain high required reserves with the state-controlled Central Bank, and the administrative funnel of funds to selected investment programs; (b) by questioning the theoretical foundations of such policies and especially the validity of the Keynesian liquidity trap and hence of the need for government deficit spending. Focusing on the economic problem of the day, inflation was set at the center of academic and policy interest, and all the previous policies were assessed from this perspective.

In this context, state ownership of banks in LDCs was put into question since the empirical evidence has not been encouraging. It seemed that government ownership of financial institutions did not contribute to financial development and economic growth while fiscal conditions in these economies deteriorated. Moreover, government participation in commercial banks was associated with poor financial performance and asset quality. These criticisms are open to challenge as the direction of causality between the activity of state banks and the degree of economic and financial development is not straightforward. For example, financial underdevelopment may be the cause rather than the result of government intervention in financial markets. Furthermore, state banks may show low profitability because they are engaged in socially desirable projects that yield low financial returns rather than because of bad management. Nevertheless, these criticisms do have a point when we are considering the political environment and the historical experience. Directed lending may indeed lead to misallocation of resources when it is influenced by political cronyism and electoral cycles rather than by social welfare considerations. On the other hand, historical experience is mixed since it shows the success of directed lending in East Asian countries such as Japan, Korea, Taiwan, and China but failure in many developing economies around the world. Moreover, development banks were successful in promoting industrialization in Europe and Japan and there were successful examples of state-owned banking in Indonesia and Thailand. However, the majority of cases in developing countries were not supportive of government ownership of financial institutions (de la Torre et al. 2017: 80–82).

Hence, a new perspective was adopted concerning the relation between economic development and financial development whereby the causal relationship was reversed, with financial development preceding economic development. In this context, Shaw's (1973) "debt-intermediation view", followed Goldsmith's (1969) observation concerning the correlation between financial development and output growth (Fry 1995: 28), and emphasized the role of financial institutions and financial deepening to improve the allocation of credit. This would be achieved in less developed economies by unifying a fragmented capital market and diminishing uncertainty concerning the future rates of return on both real and financial assets (Shaw 1973: 48–49, 72–73). In this sense, inside money[2] becomes important in a model where a positive relationship is established between financial intermediation and incentives to save on the one hand and the quality of investment on the other hand (Shaw 1973: 72,75). Besides, financial intermediaries are characterized by risk diversification, economies of scale in lending activities, and lower transaction costs, which are themselves growth-promoting (Shaw 1973: 76–77). Hence, the whole discussion focuses on the effects of financial repression versus financial

[2] According to Gurley and Shaw (1960: 73, 363–364) inside money is to be distinguished from outside money in the sense that the first refers to government debt (money) issued in exchange for private domestic debt (private securities) while the second pertains to the case of money issue that is backed by foreign or government securities or gold. The distinction is important for financial development issues as far as an increased weight of inside money indicates increased intermediation of the domestic financial system and the development of financial markets for private and public debt.

liberalization concerning the intermediation of the financial system between savers and borrowers.

The original thesis raised several questions concerning the role of finance in economic development especially in the specific institutional context of LDCs' economies. The critique was initiated first by the Neostructuralist tradition as this was developed by Lim (1987), Buffie (1984), Kohsaka (1984), Taylor (1983: 91–103), and Van Wijnbergen (1982, 1983, 1985). Neostructuralists do not address the relation between financial liberalization and financial development directly. However, their remark about the persisting presence of unofficial curb markets in the financial structure of LDCs challenges the assumed causality between financial liberalization and financial development. Moreover, they acknowledge that these segmented curb markets are characterized by inefficient financial intermediation regarding risk diversification, collection of information, and project appraisal (Kohsaka 1984). Nevertheless, rising interest rates in organized markets do not necessarily lead to financial deepening if unorganized money markets are present and they absorb the excess demand for loans. The fact that the official banking system is burdened with reserve requirements, as opposed to curb markets, indicates that the latter may offer more efficient intermediation than the former. This means that the curb market rate will remain high as demand for curb market loans rises. Since this is the rate that equilibrates the credit market (Lim 1987), it is also the rate that enters the aggregate supply function. As the curb market rate rises, it contributes to cost-push inflation which might counteract the deflationary impact of rising real interest rates on aggregate demand (Van Wijnbergen 1983). The crucial assumption made by Neostructuralists is that curb market assets and bank deposits are closer substitutes than unproductive assets and deposits. Hence, rising official rates after financial liberalization generate a flow of funds out of curb markets and into time deposits which reduces the total amount of lending to the private sector due to official reserve requirements (Loizos 2018). If this is the case, then financial deepening is undermined by official reserve requirements that reduce loan supply contrary to what is happening in the curb market. At least this is the short-run effect while in the long run, a rise in savings might increase loan supply from the official sector (increase financial intermediation) and lower the curb market interest rate (Buffie 1984).

From the point of view of the role of the government in development finance, the criticism mounted by the McKinnon-Shaw school belonged to a laissez-faire approach. This perspective gained support from evidence concerning the developing economies of the 1970s and 1980s, which demonstrated increasing government failures surpassing market failures. Eventually, the proposed program of reforms against protectionist policies, subsidized financing, and government participation in financial institutions became known as the "Washington Consensus" (de la Torre et al. 2017: 84). The "Washington Consensus" was an agenda of policies proposed in 1990 that summarized the critique to development policies of the 1950s and 1960s and at the same time constituted a recipe to be followed by developing economies in Latin America (Babb 2012; McCleery and De Paolis 2008; Williamson 2008: 14). Policy recommendations included fiscal consolidation aiming at stabilizing developing economies but first and foremost a wave of market liberalization which included financial liberalization, privatizations, and deregulation (Williamson 2008: 16–18; Gore 2000). More importantly, the "Washington Consensus" was effectively a comprehensive declaration of a "paradigm shift". It signaled an abandonment of the historical analysis of the 1950s, 1960s, and 1970s which was followed by a focus on economic and social transformation of developing economies The new fad was an ahistorical assessment of economies' performance which stressed functionality in a laissez-faire context (Gore 2000). The term "consensus" referred to the policies endorsed by the International Monetary Fund, the World Bank, the Inter-American Development Bank, the US government, and think tanks in Washington with an interest in development policies (Babb 2012; Williamson 2008: 21). That "consensus" reserved a limited role for the state which should have "got out of the way" and should have left private markets to operate unhindered. What if an efficient operation of markets presupposes at least effective regulation and competition policies, especially in the financial sector? Is it enough to get the prices right? (Marangos 2009; Stiglitz 1998).

The Post-Keynesian school, building on previous critical observations in the literature, offered its own critique of the laissez-faire approach described in financial liberalization theories and Washington Consensus policies. At first, the assertion that a liberalized banking sector can lead to a stable financial system is doubted on the grounds of Stiglitz and Weiss's (1981) asymmetric information between borrowers and lenders and the related notions of adverse selection and moral hazard. Hence, Arestis and Demetriades (1999) indicate that rising interest rates may ration out "sensible" borrowers in favor of risky borrowers to increase the probability of default because of adverse selection. A related notion is that of moral hazard where borrowers engage in projects different from those approved by the lender. This might increase further the cost of borrowing and make the adverse selection problem worse. However, the same problems can arise in the relationship between depositors and banks in the face of inadequate supervision. Arestis and Demetriades (1999) and Mishkin (1996) observe that banks may take on excessive risks having in mind that if these projects prove to be profitable they will reap the benefits of their investment policy, and if they prove to be bad loans, deposit insurance provides a net of protection and the Central Bank a backstop ultimately paid by the tax-payer. Hence, both Arestis and Demetriades (1999) and Mishkin (1996) stress the need for developing countries to build an adequate institutional infrastructure that would regulate and supervise the financial system along with measures to enhance the legal framework concerning financial markets operation and transparency. We agree with Arestis and Demetriades (1999) that the above observations call for a post-Keynesian view of uncertainty as fundamental ignorance about the future that is not reducible to probabilistic calculations of risk. A way to handle this kind of uncertainty is the establishment of conventions such as contractual arrangements, along with institutional setups that are related to banking supervision and regulation. Nevertheless, the true meaning of "conventions" in the Post-Keynesian terminology is that they are vulnerable to the mass psychology of the public (Keynes 1936 [1973]: 154). Hence, there is nothing inherently stable in these institutional formulations.

A further fault of the financial liberalization thesis according to Arestis (2005) is the neglect of the role of the stock markets both by McKinnon (1973) and Shaw (1973) and by Fry (1997) who consider the role of stock markets in financial intermediation as being less important than that of commercial banks in developing countries. According to Arestis and Demetriades (1999), stock markets are crucial in the process of financial liberalization for three reasons: (a) higher interest rates make borrowing more costly and encourage firms to issue equity; (b) stock markets are a major channel through which international funds enter the economy; and (c) stock market development is very often a condition of financial liberalization policies encouraged by the International Monetary Fund (IMF) and the World Bank. However, according to Singh (1997) stock markets in LDCs exhibit problems such as excess volatility, lack of transparency, and insider trading. This is because, the instant liquidity feature of stock markets when combined with the poor regulation and inadequate information dissemination in emerging markets, contributes more to the arbitrary pricing of securities and unjustified volatility rather than to the efficient allocation of resources. In this context, Arestis and Demetriades (1999) emphasize the distinction between short-run and long-run capital inflows in an emerging stock market after financial liberalization. Short-run capital flows relate to speculation activity that is facilitated by stock market deregulation. The main consequences of these flows are destabilizing for the following reasons: (a) They often lead to a sharp appreciation of the exchange rate and loss of competitiveness or an accommodating monetary policy to fix the exchange rate which may generate inflation. (b) Because of capital inflows, asset prices rise which results in rising wealth of their holders that may end up in an increase in import demand for consumption on the one hand, and increased optimism of financial institutions and rise in speculation on the other. (c) The short-term nature of these capital inflows indicates how easily they can be transformed into outflows after an even minor adverse shock in the economy to provoke a sharp decline in asset prices and the exchange rate with the related consequences for the stability of the financial system and the real economy. On the contrary, long-term capital inflows in the form of direct productive investment are not speculative and can contribute to increased growth through both their direct impact on real investment and their indirect effect on the whole economy concerning technology transfer and skill diffusion effects.

In the above context, Arestis and Glickman (2002) explain the crisis in Southeast Asia in 1997–1998 by referring to an open-economy Minskyan framework. Specifically, domestic financial liberalization along with free capital flows increased the indebtedness of firms in these economies and the ratio of foreign debt over foreign currency reserves of each country in the region. This transformed sovereign states into speculative and Ponzi units lacking both the regulatory instruments and the institutional infrastructure that would prevent euphoria in capital markets from becoming a full-blown crisis or at least mitigate the latter. Indeed, financial crises in Latin America, East Asia, and Russia disproved the validity of the Washington Consensus policies among some critical economists, including Joseph Stiglitz who accused the IMF of "market fundamentalist ideology". On the other hand, it is worth noting that capital account liberalization encouraged by the IMF was not included in the original list of the "Washington Consensus" policies drawn up by John Williamson (Babb 2012; Williamson 2008: 21).

3.3 Bridging Development Finance and Financial Development: The Case for Institutions

John Williamson in his historical account of the "Washington Consensus" is very careful in emphasizing the historical and country specificity of the agenda as he explains that the proposed policies were targeting the problems of Latin American economies in the particular conjuncture. This was the case for both the original and the new agenda which stressed the importance of legal, political, and economic institutions depending on the specific needs of each country. The government was now vested with a new role as being responsible for building an institutional environment that would enable private economic initiative (Marangos 2009; Williamson 2008: 14–15). Country specificity, a preference for discretion versus rules, and a focus on institutions were at the forefront by the mid-2000s as the World Bank and the IMF assessed the policies followed during the 1990s. The Bretton Woods institutions acknowledged the need to improve regulation and supervision in financial and commodity markets along with streamlining legal systems and combating corruption. Governance issues, financial, and labor market institutions were also on the list that made up the so-called "Augmented Washington Consensus" of "second-generation" reforms which, in a sense, shifted the focus from "getting the prices right" to "getting the institutions right" (Rodrik 2006). The same logic is followed by the "Amended Washington Consensus" which further establishes the "responsibility of the government" in building the necessary institutional infrastructure of the economy (Marangos and Whalen 2011: 162).

In this intellectual climate, Arestis and Stein (2005) introduce their "institutional perspective" as an alternative to the mainstream financial liberalization model. A system of legal rules, norms, and incentives that would prevent corruption and enhance transparency is necessary. Also, the existence of adequate bankruptcy laws along with prudential supervision and regulation of the banking system is inevitable to prevent financial crises that might emerge because of the financial liberalization process. In short, an institutional perspective of finance that would enhance the capacity of financial organizations to adapt to the needs of economic development is the general motif of the authors' view. However, what is crucial in this argument, as is apparent in Arestis and Demetriades (1999), is the recognition of the underlying Keynesian fundamental uncertainty that surrounds the financial liberalization process. Such uncertainty can only be coped with an active regulative role of the state to form the appropriate legal framework of institutional arrangements and conventions, thereby acknowledging both the need to smoothen the process of financial reform and its limitations. These arguments reflect Minsky's (1995) observations that relate fundamental uncertainty to the institutional features of capitalist economies. According to Minsky, Keynes's notion of "beliefs" as mental models that guide behavior with varied degrees of rationality, emphasizes the role of institutions amid uncertainty and the need for government intervention to establish those institutions that mitigate this uncertainty.

Moreover, as Studart (1995: 48) puts it, the post-Keynesian view is the one where finance precedes saving in the context of a finance-investment-saving circuit. On the other hand, the "liberal" view pertains to a loanable funds framework where the causality runs from saving to investment. Arestis (2005) indicates the direction of this causality as a shortcoming of the orthodox financial liberalization approach. According to the post-Keynesian tradition the causality runs from investment, as spending that generates income, to saving as a function of income and not the other way around. Hence, in this sense, we can argue that the inadequacy of saving in LDCs is not due to below-market interest rates but due to inadequate growth of output and income of which saving is a function. More importantly, this argument stresses the role of banks as lending institutions independently of the accumulated savings (deposits) so that, within the banks themselves, the causality also runs from lending to deposits (as loans generate more deposits) rather than the other way around. Hence, investment is more dependent on profit expectations and aggregate demand than on savings. But expectations highlight the role of institutions to mitigate uncertainty as already explained above.

Furthermore, the above observation about the role of banks in financing investment is of major importance in LDCs because of the predominance of banking institutions as intermediaries between surplus and deficit units in the supply and demand for funds. However, this role is better understood in Studart's (1995: 63–65) framework of "functionality of the financial structure". The concept of "functionality" connects directly the existing financial structure to the financing needs of the economy in the process of economic development. A financial system is functional, according to Studart (1995: 64), if it provides adequate finance for investment, maintaining, at the same time, its stability—or avoiding financial fragility. In this sense, the "functionality" of the financial sector and its institutions, including different types of banks, is an issue that concerns both developing and developed economies. However, what distinguishes this view from the "liberal" one is the reversal of the causality between financial development and economic development. Financial liberalization was supposed to promote financial development as a prerequisite for economic growth in a unilateral relationship among them. On the contrary, according to the post-Keynesian view, the needs of a growing economy bring about the necessity for financial development as finance becomes more "functional" in promoting economic development. Both the experience of British industrialization which showed a "spontaneous" process of development of financial markets and the examples of German universal banks or the Japanese "zaibatsu" that indicated a close relationship between banks and industry, can be explained as emerging by the needs of economic development for securing efficient financing and funding mechanisms (Studart 1995: 71–73). In this context, Joan Robinson (1952: 86) points out that "where enterprise leads finance follows" as high prospects of profit that give rise to "a strong impulse to invest" find their way to realization through the development of institutions that accommodate financing needs. Robinson (1952: 86–87) refers to examples of institutional developments such as the invention of the corporate form of the joint-stock company or the new lending practices introduced by the German banks' participation in industrial firms. In this sense, financial liberalization cannot be considered to promote economic development independently of what is "functional" for an economy with specific institutional characteristics (Studart (1995: 74–75). Besides, we should add, that financial development cannot be assessed independently of what is "functional" for economic development for different economies, with different institutional endowments in different historical times.

Furthermore, what the "liberal" view emphasizes concerning financial development are the benefits of enhanced financial intermediation per se. Indeed, Levine (1997) identifies the functionality of the financial system with its ability to decrease risk by enhancing liquidity and diversifying idiosyncratic risk, allocate capital efficiently to investment uses by lowering the costs of acquiring information and coping with principal-agent problems among firms' stakeholders, pooling and channeling savings between surplus and deficit units, and facilitate the exchange through contracts that reduce transaction costs. However, the underlying guiding principle of this definition of financial development is what Fry (1995: 293–316) describes as the minimization of transaction and information costs. Contrary to this rather static view, the post-Keynesian approach to financial development takes the form of "active" intermediation as far as banks assume an active role in lending activity. In the finance-investment-savings circuit, banks funnel newly created money to finance investment and promote economic development, while financial markets promote the stability of the system (Studart 1995: 64–65) through funding mechanisms that enhance liquidity and diminish financial fragility. In this sense, financial liberalization might harm financial development and investment expenditure if, as Arestis (2005) indicates, it leads to increased financial fragility. This would be the case if banks engage in more risky lending and if financial liberalization promotes speculative activity in the stock markets by the facilitation of short-run capital flows at the expense of long-term direct investment projects (Arestis and Demetriades 1999). In short, rising liberalization of intermediation irrespective of the institutional structure and the functional needs of the real economy might impact the volume and stability of economic growth. Furthermore, the existence of banking oligopolies in LDCs—in contrast with the McKinnon-Shaw perfect competition assumption—might lead to high interest rate margins and reduce any assumed financial deepening, especially in the context of inadequate bank regulation. In addition, the need for domestic banks to cope with increased competition might strengthen the oligopolistic structure of the industry through mergers and acquisitions.

In the context of the preceding discussion, the concept of development banking is treated in a manner that is open to interpretation, contingent upon the predisposition of each school of thought concerning government intervention in the promotion of economic development. Consequently, development banks are perceived either as remnants of financial repression regimes that impede economic and financial development or as a means to promote economic development in situations of thin financial markets. Indeed, Fry (1995: 362–365) points out that development banks were not as effective at mobilizing domestic savings—although he recognizes that they managed to attract foreign capital—and highlights their ineffective allocation of capital to productive investments. Furthermore, he indicates that the emergence of several specialized institutions with the responsibility to finance specific priority sectors led to a segmentation of the market for credit resulting in reduced competition among financial institutions and high intermediation costs. Conversely, Studart (1995: 75) posits that development banks serve as "compensating mechanisms" that circumvent the issue of thin capital (funding) markets. In a similar vein, Chang and Grabel (2005) consider development banks as one of the means for providing long-term finance in underdeveloped financial systems according to the idea that a financial system is "functional" if it meets the financing needs of economic development. Clearly, behind these conflicting views lies the controversy mentioned above concerning the causality between financial liberalization and economic development. If the causality runs from financial system liberalization to economic development then development banks are just part and parcel of a distorting regime. If, on the other hand, the "functionality" of a specific financial structure depends on whether it serves the needs of economic development for given institutional characteristics of an economy, then development banks are justified in underdeveloped institutional environments for both financial and economic development.

Taking stock of our discussion so far, we can identify financial development with increased "active" intermediation between deficit and surplus units in the service of the following ultimate goals: (a) increase in the volume and the efficiency of allocation of resources for investment purposes according to the "functional" needs of the economy and (b) maintenance of the stability of the financial system. However, as the above discussion reveals, disentangling the puzzle of the relationship between economic and financial development is a difficult task. We believe that certain features of the debate in development finance contributed to this difficulty: (a) the conducting of the discussion mainly at a macroeconomic level without paying adequate attention to the microeconomic effects and foundations, and hence, (b) the examination of institutions as a static constraint of economic activity—at a macro level—rather than as a factor of transformation of economic relations and hence as contributors to financial development. Indeed, identifying financial development with enhanced intermediation implies identifying the former with the appropriate nexus of institutions through which intermediation is implemented more or less successfully. Although economic and financial development is made visible at the macroeconomic level, the policies for them—to be effective—must take account of the agents that would set them in motion. Hence, paying attention to the microstructure of the economy is necessary. On the other hand, an abstract set of axiomatic ahistorical hypotheses might not yield the desired result as long as the object of financial development is both dynamic and institutional. Hence, we need an approach that would take into account both of these factors: the need for microfoundations and the central role of institutions.

3.4 Further Issues About Institutions and Economic Development

The discussion presented in the previous sections of this chapter concluded that the crucial understudied link in the development finance—financial development relationship is the role of institutions and the specific institutional environment in which the relevant policies are implemented. However, the kind and type of institutions that are needed to boost growth are yet to be determined. Hence, Arestis and Demetriades (1999) stress the importance of the legal infrastructure of LDCs concerning contract enforcement, bankruptcy procedures, and banking regulation and supervision. Institutional underdevelopment and financial liberalization in an environment characterized by a general retreat of financial regulation may precipitate the manifestation of severe financial crises (Arestis and Glickman 2002). What these approaches stress is the inefficiency of financial liberalization policies in economies institutionally unprotected to absorb the consequences of international short-term capital flows and globalized markets. Arestis and Stein (2005) take a step forward by proposing a theoretical framework for institutional transformation that would take into account the existing institutional matrix of each country concerning norms, rules, incentives, and existing capacities of financial organizations to assume the burden of transformation toward a more liberalized regime. Hence, the type of institutions seems to be dependent on country-specific characteristics. Is there a historical dimension as well?

The institutional perspective is also followed by another strand of literature expressed by Rajan and Zingales (1998a, 1998b, 2003a, 2003b) who identify the "great reversal" from developed capital markets to financially repressed regimes during the period of the Great Depression. Financial repression regimes are characterized at the institutional level by a relationship-based system among incumbent large firms, banking oligopolies, and the government. An important ingredient of this system is the regulation of capital flows that insulates the financial system from external competition and market discipline. More importantly, investor protection assumes non-price forms such as a specific monopoly power of the bank over the firm it finances—for example, the bank in question is the main lender of the firm while it uses its connections with managers, politicians, etc. as a means of contract enforcement. In a sense, hierarchical control is substituted for market control and makes the efficiency of the legal system and contract enforcement less important. Furthermore, dissemination of information is rather discouraged than encouraged, since this would endanger the whole system of relationship finance. In this sense, financial repression is an impediment to financial development. However, we should point out that this remains a historically specific assessment in the sense that what made financial repression/regulation successful in the wake of the Great Depression and World War II was no longer present in the 1990s or the 2000s.

The historically specific dimension is better grasped in the literature about legal systems and institutions that purport to establish a system of investor protection from management and/or shareholder opportunism. This is the theme of La Porta et al. (1997, 1998) and Modigliani and Perotti (1997). Modigliani and Perotti (1997) indicate that financial liberalization, not followed by the appropriate institutional development concerning legal rules for investor protection and their enforcement, might lead to banking crises and instability. This is because poor enforcement of legal rules renders market transactions unreliable. The result is a shift of institutionally underdeveloped economies to systems characterized by long-term relations. On the other hand, La Porta et al. (1997, 1998) focus on the specific *kind* of the prevailing legal system—common or civil law—and its effect on investor protection and financial development. It is assumed that law enforcement and investor protection are poorer in civil law compared to common law countries. Then, swings in financial development are meant to be explained by differences in the historically determined institutional environments between countries.

Finally, a new political economy perspective on financial regulation and development is followed by Pagano and Volpin (2001). In a "corporatist" sense, the state, and hence, its interventionist policy, reflects the balance of power between conflicting interests that affect the formation of the legal framework which determines the dispersion of control rights between different stakeholders within the firm. Coalition governments, which are associated with corporatism, permit an institutional environment with low investor protection as opposed to high employee protection. This is the case in Continental Europe, while countries with Anglo-Saxon traditions are characterized by high investor and low employee protection. Hence, investor protection is determined by the degree of diffusion of shares (concerning the issue of controlling shareholders) and the power of management. Eventually, the cost of "corporatism" which is now the basis for explaining a specific form of financial regulation, is the low degree of financial development because of a low degree of investor protection.

The above discussion concludes that whatever the country, financial system, or historical period, institutions in their variety are important for economic development. Acemoglou and Robinson (2013: 42–43) argue that institutions are the reason why different nations exhibit so diverging paths of development. It is the interaction between political and economic institutions as the former determine the type of the latter while both form the set of incentives that condition the behavior of economic agents and political actors. Eventually, underdevelopment and poverty are not the consequence of unfavorable geography, cultural differences, or even ignorance (Acemoglou and Robinson 2013: 48–68). The first two explanations carry with them a fatalistic point of view while the latter might be considered rather naïve. Fatalism entails that even if institutions have a role to play, they are subjected to geographical or cultural factors that are considered more or less enduring and unchanged (Chang 2011; Evans 2007: 36). A more balanced argument would not overemphasize the bearing of these factors and at the same time would focus on a determinant which is present in all historical examples of economic development and which conditions the relationship between human and nature (geography) and between human beings themselves (culture) along with the perception of these phenomena by economic and political agents (ignorance or knowledge). This is what Acemoglou and Robinson (2013: 79–81, 429–430) propose when they distinguish between inclusive and extractive institutions. The idea is that inclusive economic institutions which are supported by inclusive political institutions protect and enforce property rights thereby boosting investment, innovation, and growth. This is not the case with extractive institutions which benefit small elites at the cost of the prosperity of the great majority of the population. Again, property rights are at the center of this argument and political institutions that underlie each type of economic institution and the rivalry between different social groups to control them play a crucial role. In the end, political and economic institutions interact to generate the level of economic development for a country quite often in a path-dependent manner.

Following the above argument institutional imitation might be a sensible policy if political elites are ready to import inclusive institutions into their country. However, institutional transplantation is only half the answer, as the successful operation of formal institutions requires the successful supporting functioning of informal institutions such as habits and values, which may be lacking in this country. Hence, when a country imports foreign "good practices" adaptation to local circumstances is in order. Institutional change, innovation, and development in every economic sector including the financial sector is not possible if the relevant process does not enjoy the legitimacy derived from the local culture (Chang 2007b: 29–30). This argument is in direct contrast to the orthodox GSI argument according to which governments in developing countries are called for to adopt Global Standard Institutions (GSIs), the ones that emanate from Anglo-American development traditions and have been the centerpiece of IMF and World Bank proposals to developing economies. However, what is beneficial and rational for a given country is not necessarily benevolent for a different country in a different epoch as it is explained below. More importantly, neither culture nor traditions and modes of thought are rigid and fixed in the long run. On the contrary, there are elements in the institutional matrix that characterize a country in every specific historical period that contradict each other and may pull that country in different paths of economic development (Chang 2011).

Yet, a critical question to be answered is whether institutional development is the result or the cause of economic development. The orthodox view seems to maintain a causality that runs from financial development, as a deliberate policy of Western-style institution building to economic development as an outcome. Chang (2007a: 13) claims that the causality runs the other way around in many historical examples of developing countries. Furthermore, institutional development, cultural changes, and economic development interact with each other since economic agents are not characterized by immutable preferences. If institutions can play a "constitutive" function then economic development—for example, the process of industrialization—can bring about the development of necessary institutions to support this process and, at the same time, change agents' preferences. Moreover, human agency is important to understand institutional change since members of a society make choices dependent not only on their "objective" social position but also on ideologies and on how they perceive their interests (Chang 2007a: 10; 2007b: 27–28).

In the same vein, Rodrik (2006) focuses on a fundamental issue in institutional policy. The same institutional goal may be achieved by different means in different contexts. In other words, policies are operational and successful only within societies with specific cultural features. This is another way to say that both country and historical specificity matter and incentives provided to economic agents are critical. Institutions are "context-specific tools" and different historical periods and countries demand different institutions as the legitimacy and efficiency of these institutions may change with time and space. In this sense, the effectiveness of the government's role is also dependent on social and cultural differences between countries (McCleery and De Paolis 2008; Reinert 2007: 67). In this context, Arestis and Stein (2005) and Arestis et al. (2003) call for a process of "institutionalization" of reforms and new practices in the sense of their internalization in agents' behavior. This approach sets the role of institutions at a higher level of complexity since setting up institutions is not enough. These institutions should motivate economic agents to act in such a way so that development goals are endorsed by them and advanced by their behavior. More than that, the government should be able to inspire agents to act in a way that is conducive to changing behavior and enable them to restructure their value system. The above observations open a whole new perspective to the issues of development finance, economic development, and financial development which stresses the importance of social goals along with economic ones, the dimension of historical time and conditions, and the role of the balance of power between different social strata. Social goals include social justice, falling inequality, and enhanced personal liberty which is not confined to economic liberty. Historical time and context bring to the forefront institutional development and change in historically specific contexts. Finally, power issues remind us that the process of economic development is not free of conflicts among social groups with different access to means that enable them to meet their interests (Marangos and Whalen 2011: 166–169; Evans 2007: 47).

It seems as though the question about economic development and development finance reveals its dynamic and multilevel nature when it is treated as a "process". In this setting, development is construed as both economic growth and social structural change which means that institutional transformation under specific historical conditions for different countries is the desired outcome. Hence, development cannot be measured only in terms of GDP growth but also in terms of falling social inequality and rising environmental concerns. It is in this sense that Amartya Sen (1999) talked about "development as freedom" (Carvalho 2009). Development finance is bound to respond to this multidimensional economic and social development and development banks have been established historically as a key financial organization to promote such developmental approaches as will be shown below. Moreover, financial development is a path-dependent process that hinges on the specific institutional environment of a given country. Such an institutional context is the product of historical developments in a particular country that have shaped it. Hence, implementing reforms that are conducive to financial development is again an issue of historical and country specificity (de la Torre et al. 2017: 92). However, according to Polanyi (1944 [2001]) the state assumes a role in creating and shaping markets (Mazzucato and Penna 2016) including financial markets. The "social capabilities" that are necessary for development include an array of institutions such as political, commercial, or financial institutions. Furthermore, the government and especially development banks have a crucial part to play in forming and enhancing social capabilities. Eventually, following Polanyi, the antithesis between markets and the government seems unfounded (Mazzucato and Penna 2016). Therefore, straying away from "pure" explanations that emphasize either the role of the government in an interventionist mood or the role of unfettered markets in a neo-liberal crescendo we will agree with Boyer (2006: 66) that unadulterated approaches are not the way to go forward. At least, this is where an institutional perspective of economic development and development finance drives the discussion in this book. In the next chapters, we will try to explore the specific conditions of this interaction and synergy between markets and the government walking away from dogmatic explanations.

References

Acemoglou, D. and Robinson, J. A. (2013) *Why Nations Fail. The Origins of Power, Prosperity and Poverty*, London: Profile Books

Allisson, F. (2024) "Charles Bettelheim and World War II, or the Making of a Planning Doctor", *History of Political Economy*, 56: 283–304.

Arndt, H. W. (1989) *Economic Development. The History of an Idea*, Chicago and London: The University of Chicago Press.

Arestis, P. (2005) "Washington Consensus and Financial Liberalization", *Journal of Post Keynesian Economics*, 27 (2): 251–269.

Arestis, P. and Demetriades, P. (1999) "Financial Liberalization: The Experience of Developing Countries", *Eastern Economic Journal*, 25(4): 441–457.

Arestis, P. and Glickman, M. (2002) "Financial Crisis in Southeast Asia: Dispelling Illusion the Minskyan Way", *Cambridge Journal of Economics*, 26 (2): 237–260.

Arestis, P. and Stein, H. (2005) "An Institutional Perspective to Finance and Development as an Alternative to Financial Liberalization", *International Review of Applied Economics*, 19 (4): 381–398.

Arestis, P., Nissanke, M. and Stein, H. (2003) "Finance and Development: Institutional and Policy Alternatives to Financial Liberalization", The Levy Economics Institute of Bard College Working Paper No 377 available at https://www.levyinstitute.org/pubs/wp377.pdf Accessed 18 Nov. 2023

Babb, S. (2012) "The Washington Consensus as Transnational Policy Paradigm: Its Origins, Trajectory and Likely Successor", *Review of International Political Economy*, 20(2): 268–297.

Boyer, R. (2006) "Half a Century of Development Theories. An Institutionalist Survey", in Stathakis, G. and Vaggi, G. (eds.) *Economic Development and Social Change. Historical Roots and Modern Perspectives*, London and N.Y.: Routledge, pp. 29–73.

Bresser-Pereira, L. C. (2015) "Reflecting on New Developmentalism and Classical Developmentalism", FGV Sao Paulo School of Economics Working Paper No 395 available at http://www.bresserpereira.org.br/Texto-Discuss%C3%A3o/379-Reflecting-TD395.pdf Accessed 3 Nov. 2023

Buffie, E. F. (1984) "Financial Repression, the Neostructuralists, and Stabilization in Semi-Industrialized Economies", *Journal of Development Economics*, 14(3): 451–482.

Caloffi, A. and Serra, M. (2022) "Revisiting Perroux's Development Poles: the Cases of Italy and Brazil", Instituto de Economia, No 425, available at https://www.eco.unicamp.br/images/arquivos/artigos/TD/TD425.pdf Accessed 5 Sep. 2024

Carvalho, F. J. C. (2009) "Financing Development", *International Journal of Political Economy*, 38(4): 5–24

Chakraborty, L. S. (2002) "Fiscal Deficit and Rate of Interest: An Econometric Analysis of the Deregulated Financial Regime", *Economic and Political Weekly*, 37(19): 1831–1838.

Chang, H.-J. (2011) "Institutions and Economic Development: Theory, Policy and History", *Journal of Institutional Economics*, 7(4): 473–498.

Chang, H.-J. (2007a) "Institutional Change and Economic Development: An Introduction", in Chang, H.-J. (ed.) *Institutional Change and Economic Development*, N.Y.: United Nations University Press, pp. 1–14

Chang, H.-J. (2007b) "Understanding the Relationship between Institutions and Economic Development – Some Key Theoretical Issues", in Chang, H.-J. (ed.) *Institutional Change and Economic Development*, N.Y.: United Nations University Press, pp. 17–33.

Chang, H.-J. and Grabel, I. (2005) "Reclaiming Development from the Washington Consensus", *Journal of Post Keynesian Economics*, 27(2): 273–291.

De la Torre, A., Gozzi, J. C. and Schmukler, S. L. (2017) *Innovative Experiences in Access to Finance. Market-Friendly Roles for the Visible Hand?*, Washington D.C.: World Bank Group.

Evans, P. B. (2007) "Extending the 'Institutional' Turn: Property, Politics, and Development Trajectories" in Chang, H.-J. (ed.) *Institutional Change and Economic Development*, N.Y.: United Nations University Press, pp. 35–52.

FitzGerald E.V. K. and Vos, R. (1989) "The Foundations of Development Finance: Economic Structure, Accumulation Balances and Income Distribution", in FitzGerald, E.V. K. and Vos, R. (eds.) *Financing Economic Development. A Structural Approach to Monetary Policy*, Aldershot: Gower, pp. 17–54.

Fry, M. J. (1997) "In Favour of Financial Liberalization", *Economic Journal*, 107(442): 754–770.

Fry, M. J. (1995) *Money, Interest and Banking in Economic Development*, 2nd Ed., Baltimore: Johns Hopkins University Press.

Gerschenkron, A. (1962) "Economic Backwardness in Historical Perspective" in Gerschenkron, A. *Economic Backwardness in Historical Perspective*, Cambridge, Mass, pp. 5–30.

Goldsmith, R. W. (1969) *Financial Structure and Development*, New Haven: Yale University Press.

Gore, C. (2000) "The Rise and Fall of the Washington Consensus as a Paradigm for Developing Economies", *World Development*, 28(5): 789–804.

Gurley, J. G. and Shaw, E. S. (1960) *Money in a Theory of Finance*, Washington D.C.: The Brookings Institution.

Keynes, J. M. (1936 [1973]) *The General Theory of Employment, Interest, and Money*, reprinted in *The Collected Writings of J. M. Keynes*, Vol. VII, MacMillan.

Kohsaka, A. (1984) "The High Interest Rate Policy under Financial Repression", *Developing Economies*, 22(4): 419–452.

La Porta, R., Lopez-de-Silanes, F., Shleifer, A., and Vishny, R. W. (1998) "Law and Finance", *Journal of Political Economy*, 106(6): 1113–1155.

La Porta, R., Lopez-de-Silanes, F., Shleifer, A., and Vishny, R. W. (1997) "Legal Determinants of External Finance", *The Journal of Finance*, 52(3): 1131–1150.

Levine, R. (1997) "Financial Development and Economic Growth: Views and Agenda", *Journal of Economic Literature*, 35(2): 688–726.

Levy-Yeyati, E. L., Micco, A. and Panizza, U. (2004) "Should the Government Be in the Banking Business? The Role of State-Owned and Development Banks", Inter-American Development Bank Working Paper No 517, available at https://publications.iadb.org/en/publications/english/viewer/Should-the-Government-Be-in-the-Banking-Business-The-Role-of-State-Owned-and-Development-Banks.pdf Accessed 2 Nov. 2023

Lim, J. (1987) "The Neostructuralist Critique of the Monetary Theory of Inflation: The Case of the Philippines", *Journal of Development Economics*, 25(1): 45–61.

Loizos, K. (2017) "Alternative Financial Regimes and Development Banks in Greece 1963–2002: What Have We Learned?", *Economic Alternatives*, 1: 34–50.

Loizos, K. (2018) "The Financial Repression-Liberalization Debate: Taking Stock, Looking for a Synthesis", *Journal of Economic Surveys*, 32(2): 440–468.

Mallick, H. and Agarwal, S. (2007) "Impact of Real Interest Rates on Real Output Growth in India: A Long-Run Analysis in a Liberalized Financial Regime", *Singapore Economic Review*, 52(2): 215–231.

Marangos, J. (2009) "What Happened to the Washington Consensus? The Evolution of International Development Policy", *The Journal of Socio-Economics* 38(1): 197–208.

Marangos, J. and Whalen, C. J. (2011) "Evolution without Fundamental Change: The Washington Consensus on Economic Development and its Significance for Post-Keynesian Institutionalism", in Whalen C. J. (ed.) *Financial Instability and Economic Security after the Great Recession*, Cheltenham, UK and Northampton, MA, USA: Edward Elgar, pp. 153–173.

Mazzucato, M. and Penna, C. R. C. (2016) "Beyond Market Failures: The Market Creating and Shaping Roles of State Investment Banks", *Journal of Economic Policy Reform*, 19(4): 305–326.

Mazzucato, M. and Penna, C.C.R. (2015) "Beyond Market Failures: The Market Creating and Shaping Roles of State Investment Banks." Working Paper No. 831, The Levy Economics Institute of Bard College, available at https://www.levyinstitute.org/pubs/wp_831.pdf Accessed 18 Oct 2023

McCleery, R. K. and De Paolis, F. (2008) "The Washington Consensus: A Post-Mortem", *Journal of Asian Economics*, 19(5–6): 438–446.

McKinnon, R. I. (1973) *Money and Capital in Economic Development*, Washington D.C.: Brookings Institution.

Minsky, H. P. (1996) "Uncertainty and the Institutional Structure of Capitalist Economies", *Journal of Economic Issues*, 30(2): 357–368.

Mishkin, F. S. (1996) "Understanding Financial Crises A Developing Country Perspective" NBER Working Paper, No 5600, available at https://www.nber.org/system/files/working_papers/w5600/w5600.pdf Accessed 3 Nov. 2023

Modigliani, F. and Perotti E. (1997) "Protection of Minority Interest and the Development of Security Markets", *Managerial and Decision Economics*, 18(7–8): 519–528.

Pagano, M. and Volpin, P. (2001) "The Political Economy of Finance", *Oxford Review of Economic Policy*, 17(4): 502–519.

Polanyi, K. (1944 [2001]) *The Great Transformation: The Political and Economic Origins of Our Time*, Boston, MA: Beacon Press.

Rajan, R. G. and Zingales, L. (1998a) "Financial Dependence and Growth", *American Economic Review*, 88(3): 559–586.

Rajan, R. G. and Zingales, L. (1998b) "Which Capitalism? Lessons from the East Asian Crisis", *Journal of Applied Corporate Finance*, 11(3): 40–48.

Rajan, R. G. and Zingales, L. (2003a) "The Great Reversals: The Politics of Financial Development in the Twentieth Century", *Journal of Financial Economics*, 69(1): 5–50.

Rajan, R. G. and Zingales, L. (2003b) *Saving Capitalism from the Capitalists: Unleashing the Power of Financial Markets to Create Wealth and Spread Opportunity*, Princeton University Press.

Reinert, E. S. (2007) "Institutionalism Ancient, Old, and New: A Historical Perspective on Institutions and Uneven Development" in Chang, H.-J. (ed.) *Institutional Change and Economic Development*, N.Y.: United Nations University Press, pp. 53–72.

Robinson, J. (1952) "The Generalization of the General Theory" in Robinson J. *The Rate of Interest and Other Essays*, London: Macmillan, pp. 67–142.

Rodrik, D. (2006) "Goodbye Washington Consensus, Hello Washington Confusion? A Review of the World Bank's 'Economic Growth in the 1990s: Learning from a Decade of Reform'", *Journal of Economic Literature* 44(4): 973–987.

Roosevelt, F. D. (1941) "Annual Message to the Congress", January 6, US National Archives, available at https://www.archives.gov/milestone-documents/president-franklin-roosevelts-annual-message-to-congress Accessed 23 Nov. 2023

Rostow, W. W. (1965) "Leading Sectors and the Take-off" in Rostow, W. W. (ed.) *The Economics of Take-off into Sustained Growth*, New York, pp. 1–21.

Rostow, W. W. (1956) "The Take-off into Self-Sustained Growth", *Economic Journal*, 66(261): 25–48.

Sen, A. (1999) *Development as Freedom*, New York: Alfred Knopf.

Shaw, E. S. (1973) *Financial Deepening in Economic Development*, New York: Oxford University Press.

Singh, A. (1997) "Stock Markets, Financial Liberalization, and Economic Development", *Economic Journal*, 107(442): 771–782.

Stiglitz, J. E. (1998) "More Instruments and Broader Goals: Moving toward the Post-Washington Consensus", Keynote Address, The WIDER Annual Lecture, Helsinki, Finland, January 7, available at https://core.ac.uk/download/pdf/161443692.pdf Accessed 3 Nov. 2023

Stiglitz, J. E. and Weiss, A. (1981) "Credit Rationing in Markets with Imperfect Information", *American Economic Review*, 71(3): 393–410.

Studart, R. (1995) *Investment Finance in Economic Development*, London and New York: Routledge.

Taylor, L. (1983) *Structuralist Macroeconomics: Applicable Models for the Third World*, New York: Basic Books.

Thirlwall, A. P. (1976) *Financing Economic Development*, London & Basingstoke: Macmillan.

Van Wijnbergen, S. (1982) "Stagflationary Effects of Monetary Stabilization Policies: A Quantitative Analysis of South Korea", *Journal of Development Economics*, 10(2): 133–169.

Van Wijnbergen, S. (1983) "Interest Rate Management in LDCs", *Journal of Monetary Economics*, 12(3): 433–452.

Van Wijnbergen, S. (1985) "Macroeconomic Effects of Changes in Bank Interest Rates: Simulation Results for South Korea", *Journal of Development Economics*, 18(2–3): 541–554.

Wade, R. (2008) "Financial Regime Change?", *New Left Review*, 53: 5–21.

Williamson, J. (2008) "A Short History of the Washington Consensus" in Serra, N. and Stiglitz, J. E. (eds.) *The Washington Consensus Reconsidered. Towards a New Global Governance*, Oxford: Oxford University Press, pp. 14–30.

CHAPTER 4

Transactions and Governance: An Institutional Explanation of Financial Regimes

4.1 New and Original Institutional Economics: From the Particular to the General

In order to reconsider financial regimes as institutional frameworks that impact development finance we need to look beyond the macroeconomic treatment of both the liberal school of the McKinnon-Shaw tradition on the one hand and the Neostructuralist school on the other hand. This is because their analysis, which we have outlined in Chap. 3, disregards an implicit assumption they make concerning the operation of markets at the micro-level. Their argument in favor of or against financial liberalization as opposed to financial repression/regulation hinges on the efficiency of macroeconomic policies and variables, such as the liberalization of interest rates or capital flows, on the availability of funds for saving and investment and their allocation. Hence, the discussion implies the effectiveness of official and organized markets as opposed to curb markets without questioning the issue of market organization as an institutional mechanism within the broader institutional environment in which the economy operates. On the other hand, the Post-Keynesian tradition takes a closer look at the issue of the liberalized markets and their proper functioning, but again the discussion takes on a macroeconomic perspective with an emphasis on international financial flows. Eventually, the debate about institutions from all strands of literature, especially in the context of the Washington Consensus, needs to be further elaborated on the basis of institutional

K. Loizos, *Between Markets and Governments*,
https://doi.org/10.1007/978-3-031-88527-3_4

theory in order to improve our understanding of the role of institutions and financial regimes in modern development finance.

This chapter and the following one focus on institutions as the most promising theoretical base for the study of the relationship between financial structures and economic development and therefore, for setting out a theory of development banking. However, this is done in an orderly way in the sense of looking for a reconstruction of the above-expounded theoretical and historical debate using the tools of Institutional Economics in its two main forms: Original Institutional Economics and New Institutional Economics. In this chapter, we examine the approaches of John R. Commons and Oliver Williamson, a Nobel 2009 prize winner, about the notion of "transaction" as construed by the two authors and how this relates to financial regimes and reform. In the next chapter, we explore more thoroughly the thorny issue of institutional change in economic development through an examination of the work of Thorstein Veblen and Douglass North.

The reader might wonder why we have chosen to look for theoretical underpinnings for our approach to development banking in *both* institutionalist traditions. The differences between the Original and the New Institutional Economics are well documented in the literature. So, why not just choose one of them and get on with it? The New Institutionalists, for example, make use of a modified rational choice model which is based on methodological individualism while they also embrace formalism. Eventually, their approach to institutions is dictated by concerns about efficiency and economizing on transaction costs. The Original Institutionalists, on the other hand, give much more emphasis on cultural issues and their methodology is holistic rather than individualistic and formalistic. In this sense, social and political forces, and especially issues such as power and conflict or ideology are more central to their thought rather than efficiency (Rutherford 1995). Of course, there are differences among thinkers who ascribe to the same theoretical tradition. A strand of literature concerning the Original Institutional Economics characterizes Veblen's thought as a kind of cultural Darwinism that imposes its requirements on individual perception and action while Commons seems to emphasize the possibility of regulation through collective action which means that people can form their social order through a democratic process. On the other hand, within the New Institutional Economics, Williamson's approach acknowledges the limitations of individual rationality without questioning further the endogeneity of individual preferences since his focus is on governance structures and economizing within a given institutional environment. On the contrary, North's preoccupation with institutional change led him to examine more thoroughly the role of ideology and culture in shaping individual choices along with power and path-dependence without completely abandoning methodological individualism, rational choice, and efficiency/inefficiency concerns (Groenewegen et al. 1995; Rutherford 1995).

The above indicates that interesting and useful ideas to cope with the issues of institutional and economic development and the role of development banks may probably be found in both theoretical traditions. This is at least the initial credo of any student of financial and institutional economics who values pluralism and open-minded approaches. However, as will be apparent below, we think that the Original Institutional Economics point of view is more encompassing and comprehensive, but this is not to disregard the merits of New Institutionalist ideas in specific circumstances. Hence, according to our view, New Institutionalist ideas could be considered a special case of Original Institutional Economics and interesting ideas such as Williamson's "asset specificity" and "safeguards" and their relationship to a range of governance structures from markets to hierarchies should be assessed in this context. On the other hand, North himself had gone through different stages in his thought from his early neoclassical approaches to late developments that focus on ideology and culture (Vandenberg 2002) thus approaching the Original Institutional theses, however without taking this journey to its conclusion. A second reason to examine both the Original and the New Institutionalist theoretical conceptions is that the institutionalist turn in mainstream thought about economic development, as this is expressed in the Washington Consensus institutions such as the World Bank, has been inspired to a large extend by the New Institutional Economics. At least from the mid-1990s, the ideas of New Institutional Economics appear in the Bank's documents concerning the role of the state, governance structures, and institution building (Stein 2008: 94–107). Therefore, a comprehensive institutional approach to development banking would not be possible unless both the Original and the New Institutional Economics were briefly surveyed and assessed.

4.2 O. Williamson's Transaction Cost Economics and Governance Structures

The term "transaction" might sound vague, non-specific, and hence, ultimately non-useful in economic modeling. After all, every economic activity can be seen as a transaction between two parties. However, as Furubotn and Richter (2008: 49–50) indicate, the concept of "transaction" obtains particular importance for economic analysis if it is conceived in the double sense given by Williamson (1985: 1) and Commons (1931). In its first meaning, transaction relates to the act of technologically determined transfer, within a broad sense of division of labor. In the second meaning, the transaction relates to property rights transfer and hence it is legally vested. Combining technological necessities arising from the division of labor with explicit or implicit property and contract rights on goods and services disengages transaction from its unique relation to markets and permits its use to describe any form of economic conduct. In this sense, Furubotn and Richter (2008: 50) assert that transactions are the social activities that underpin economic institutions.

However, the question arises. Even if this is the case, what difference does it make if we include the term "transaction" in our economic models? In what respects do these models change? To answer this question, we have to remember that transaction is an economic activity and every economic action has its costs. Coase (1937, 1960) emphasized transaction costs and property rights and how the existence of positive transaction costs may lead to market inefficiency (Stein 2008: 88, 91). In this sense, what makes "transaction" important is not itself as a new economic category among others, but the related costs that come with it when it enters economic model building. Arrow (1969), as reported also by Williamson (1991a), gives a general definition of transaction costs as the "costs of running the economic system". This definition implies that an economic structure is a system of institutions within which economic activity takes place at a cost. Furubotn and Richter (2008: 51–55, 568) analyze and categorize the various forms of costs entailed in creating, maintaining, or changing economic institutions. The double sense of transaction explained above is maintained in the definition of transaction costs. Hence, transaction costs relate to the costs of defining property and contract rights (Williamson 2000) and measuring the related claims and the underpinning resources. Another kind of transaction cost relates to the enforcement of these rights with the establishment of an appropriate legal environment and legal mechanisms either formal or informal corresponding to explicit or implicit rights. Furthermore, the need for the transfer of these rights entails information and bargaining costs that fall also into the category of transaction costs. Finally, a general division of transaction costs between "fixed" and "variable" helps us distinguish the initial stage of forming a new institution—where fixed costs come in—from the subsequent stage of developing this institution where transaction costs depend on the volume of transactions. These variable costs can take the form of search and information costs, bargaining and decision costs, and finally, supervision and enforcement costs. Transaction costs are the analogy of frictions in mechanical systems in the sense that their existence provokes failures in market operation (Williamson 1985: 19; 1996: 58). Then, according to Williamson (1996: 46) economic institutions in capitalism purport to reduce transaction costs or in his terminology "economize on transactions costs".

The basic hypotheses of Transaction Costs Economics (TCE), according to Williamson (1979) include: (a) bounded rationality that describes the limited ability of economic agents to calculate all possible future contingencies in the course of the implementation of a transaction either because of the extremely high costs of such an operation or because of fundamental ignorance about the future (Furubotn and Richter 2008: 4). Hence, even the more complex contracts are "unavoidably incomplete" (Williamson 2000). Moreover, one of the major goals of economic organizations is to "economize on bounded rationality" (Williamson 1996: 43) (b) Opportunism is a major characteristic of human behavior which effectively means that agents are "self-interested with guile" (Kreps 1990: 744; Williamson 1985: 47). This claim entails that market participants may deliberately misguide contracting parties as the information they provide may not be accurate or it may be partial and misleading. Not all people but some of them behave opportunistically sometimes. However, it costs to verify whether a contracting party is worth your trust or not (Williamson 1996: 48, 56). In other words, the one party of the contract might effectively breach it in the course of its implementation if he had the opportunity. Bounded rationality and opportunism combined imply that transactions should be structured in such a way as to economize on our limited ability to calculate all possible outcomes and contingencies and at the same time provide for protection against opportunistic behavior (Furubotn and Richter 2008: 5; Williamson 1996: 44, 48). But, for this threat to be meaningful another hypothesis is necessary. (c) That the above-mentioned transactions refer to investments with a high degree of "asset specificity". "Asset specificity" is synonymous with non-marketability of the incurred costs of investment so that the two parties are tied up in a relationship that is necessary either for both or at least for one party to maintain it. These kinds of "idiosyncratic" investments refer to cases such as specialized physical capital investments and human capital investments which are, however, of a recurring kind (Williamson 1979). Hence, the various types of asset specificity include: (1) Site specificity such as in the case of proximity in the location of premises which implies lower costs of transportation and of maintaining inventories. (2) Physical asset specificity when there is a need for investment in specialized assets tied to the production of specific goods. (3) Human asset specificity which relates to learning-by-doing or team cooperation cases and the related costs. (4) Dedicated assets where particular investments, such as the expansion of a plant, are made at the request of a particular customer (Williamson 1996: 59–60; Williamson 1985: 95–96). However, since the rate at which these transactions occur is of importance, (d) the fourth hypothesis relates to the frequency of the transaction. Eventually, the above indicate the three dimensions in which we can describe all transactions and these are the degree of asset specificity, the degree of uncertainty, and the frequency of the transaction. However, among those three, asset specificity is the most important in Transaction Cost Economics in the sense that the cost of removing a transaction-specific investment from its current use or user and transferring it to another is almost prohibitive and implies a significant loss in value (Williamson 1996: 45).

The above observations suggest that the crucial point made by the Transaction Costs Economics analysis is that relatively frequent "asset-specific" transactions between opportunistic bounded rational agents entail "maladaptation costs" (Klein 2000: 467) after the signing of the contract given that contracts are incomplete in the context of fundamental uncertainty. The solution to this problem is the design of specific "governance structures", that is guidelines of appropriate adaptations to changing conditions during the implementation of the contract. Governance structures are a way to mitigate the conflict between the parties of a contract for the mutual benefit of both parties by giving the appropriate incentives for the contract implementation (Williamson 2000). The problem is to match specific governance structures to specific kinds of transactions under the above criterion of efficiency. Indeed, Williamson (1996: 39, 45–46) juxtaposes efficiency with power to the degree that resource dependency issues that emerge in an incomplete contract are known ex-ante to the contracting parties. Therefore, they can tackle them in the context of efficiency as asset specificity, price, and governance structures are determined simultaneously (Williamson 1996: 39, 45–46). Furthermore, power is akin to a strategizing point of view while efficiency pertains to an economizing consideration (Williamson 1991c). In other words, power pertains to an ex-post consideration of contracts while Transaction Cost Economics examines contracts in their "entirety". Furthermore, if both parties are in a position to benefit from a specific contractual arrangement that is more efficient than some other alternative, they both have an incentive to select it (Williamson 1985: 258). One might point out that in this case, Williamson disregards the possibility of unequal bargaining power between the contracting parties which means that power and efficiency cannot be compared and contrasted. Moreover, Williamson's assertion that firms emerge due to efficiency rather than power considerations is challenged on various grounds in the literature which indicates that efficiency and power may co-exist. Furthermore, big corporations may appear not because of rising asset specificity and transaction costs but because of technological progress and a rising tendency toward monopoly power (Pitelis 1998; Dugger 1987). Nevertheless, Williamson (1991c) is right to point out that at the bottom-line efficiency or cost economizing is important.

Hence, Williamson (2000) indicates a hierarchy of governance structures from simple to complex as follows: spot markets, incomplete long-term contracts, firms, regulation, and public bureaus. According to Williamson (1979), markets relate mainly to non-specific transactions of whatever frequency and of standardized products. Furthermore, the non-specificity of assets means that contracts are mainly of short-term nature (Kreps 1990: 751–752) and hence "classical contracting", where all contingencies are described by the contract, is the appropriate governance structure here. However, as the level of asset specificity—idiosyncrasy—of the transaction increases and as far as occasional transactions are concerned, "neoclassical or trilateral contacting" is the relevant governance structure. Here, a third party—an arbitrator—substitutes the complete description of contingencies in the contract as a means to alleviate future maladaptation of the contract. However, the more interesting case is the one where frequent, long-term highly specific investments are concerned. In this case, the establishment of specialized governance structures is efficient because of the recurring nature of the transaction since the cost of such a structure can be recovered (Williamson 1979). These specialized governance structures are referred to as "relational contracting" and range from bilateral governance to unified governance as the idiosyncrasy of the relevant investment increases. An example of a unified governance structure is the internalization of the transaction with the establishment of a firm although now further costs emerge in the form of bureaucratic costs and the reduced role of market incentives. However, an interesting observation of Williamson (1979) is that the maturing of an industry that implies a lower degree of uncertainty might lead to a reversal from unified to bilateral governance and consequently to more market-based solutions.

4.3 Transaction Cost Economics and Financial Markets

Financial markets and financial institutions in general are a special kind of economic institutions where claims on future streams of money are traded. As far as financial instruments are contracts concluded between debtors and creditors for the allocation of these income streams under uncertain future economic conditions, institutional considerations in finance seem indispensable from the standpoint of economic analysis proper. Given the previous analysis, the most important insight of Transaction Cost Economics (TCE) that is of interest to us is the extension of the notion of transaction to cover any form of economic organization, not just that of the market. Williamson (1996: 6) indicates that the notion of "transaction" becomes the unit of economic analysis to the degree that the latter focuses on how transactions are organized or "governed". Then it is easy to conceive economic organization of any form as a means to economize on transaction costs and hence compare different forms of economic organization from this point of view. In this sense, transaction costs relate to the formation and functioning of specific financial institutions—of which markets are only one form—as compared to their efficiency in allocating funds between surplus and deficit units. Indeed, Williamson (1991a) favors an "analysis of discrete structural alternatives" in the sense that hierarchies employ different means to carry out transactions that otherwise would have taken place in the market. The crucial point here is the search for organizational efficiency which is the object of "first-order economizing" as opposed to second-order marginal analysis of mainstream economics. Different governance structures such as markets, hybrids, or hierarchies, have different capabilities of adapting to changing circumstances. Williamson (1993b) insists that first-order economizing should precede second-order marginal considerations more so when issues of economic development are at stake. A market and a command economy may be equally efficient in marginal terms but what about, for example, bureaucratic costs or other structural divergence between two different institutional setups?

Nevertheless, it could be argued that TCE is not the appropriate framework to use when analyzing financial transactions. After all, the origin and development of TCE literature are associated with the industrial organization of product markets by describing the conditions under which moving from the market to a hierarchical organization such as the firm might be efficient in transaction costs economizing respects. Williamson (1975) is preoccupied with exactly this issue in the context of an "organizational failures framework" where vertical integration, firm size, market structure, and issues of monopoly and oligopoly are examined. However, Williamson (1979) gives a preliminary answer to this critique. He considers his model of matching governance structures with transactions pertinent to the case of capital markets as well. He bases his assertion on the observation that the critical element in financial transactions is the "ease of verification" of future income streams. Indeed, one can argue that thin capital markets which are characterized by rising uncertainty, limited calculability of future contingencies, varied degrees of frequency of transactions, and highly asset-specific transactions call for relational governance structures. On the other hand, as the financial system develops, asset specificity decreases—although opportunism is always present—and market-based solutions may become more justifiable. Hence, a developed capital market with an adequate institutional infrastructure where information dissemination is continuous and reliable may not need a special governance structure other than the market itself. On the contrary, a less developed legal infrastructure and investment culture among market participants and weak enforcement of contract rights render the market an inefficient governance mechanism. Additional governance mechanisms may be necessary to ensure that profitable projects obtain the finance they need.

The rest of this section is an attempt to check Williamson's (1979) claim for the usefulness of TCEs' framework in explaining financial phenomena. The case in point is financial repression/regulation by introducing a new microeconomic perspective in the old-fashioned financial repression/liberalization or regulation/deregulation debate. Hence, a more comprehensive approach would be to start from the basic elements of financial transactions and attempt to reformulate them in the light of Williamson's (1985: 32–35) "simple contracting schema". The main idea is that asset specificity (k), safeguards (governance) of contracts (s), and price (p), are determined simultaneously because of the inevitability of their interaction when a financial contract is signed. As far as we introduce asset specificity and governance considerations, along with price, in the determination of the financial contract, we take a decisive step away from the traditional liberal view. Remember that the level of interest rates is considered by the McKinnon-Shaw school as a major obstacle to financial and economic development. Hence, the importance that is given to price determination is disproportionately greater than that given to institutional issues, the latter being limited to the appropriate "sequencing" of the fiscal, monetary, and exchange rate policies in the process of liberalization to preserve macroeconomic stability. This "sequencing" is the optimal order of economic liberalization. In this sense, fiscal consolidation should precede the liberalization of the financial system while international capital flows should be liberalized after domestic liberalization has been completed along with the achievement of domestic price stability (McKinnon 1993: 4–10). Of course, the "Washington Consensus" in its various forms introduces further institutional considerations relating to property rights assignments and institution building in general (Marangos and Whalen 2011: 154–162). However, this shift of the focus from "getting the prices right" to "getting the institutions right" (Rodrik 2006) is not able to provide a comprehensive view of alternative financial regimes but rather juxtaposes regulation to deregulation and liberalization without further elaboration.

Returning to Williamson's terminology, as explained above, asset specificity refers to transaction-specific investments in the sense that "non-marketable" transaction expenses are incurred (Williamson 1979). A financial contract between a lender and a borrower becomes transaction-specific to the degree that the transaction costs for its conclusion are asset-specific, namely specific to the particular asset and hence, not possible to be retrieved through the market. The more difficult it is to verify the future income streams from an asset, the higher these costs will be. In other words, the degree of "ease of verification" of financial returns has the same meaning as "the degree of transaction-specific investment" (Williamson 1979). However, the degree of asset specificity depends on the existence and efficiency of an institutional framework for the operation of the capital market that includes issues such as investor protection against managerial or shareholder opportunism, reliable information dissemination, safeguards against default of the borrower, etc. Furthermore, these governance characteristics of the market have an effect on the prices of the financial instruments by determining their ability to reflect the genuine profitability of the project.

Note that the degree of asset specificity is not the same as the degree of liquidity/marketability of a financial asset but these two are related. Therefore, in a capital market with a developed institutional framework, verification costs of asset returns are low and hence, non-marketable (specific to the related asset) transaction costs are also low, which contributes to increased liquidity/marketability for the asset. Hence, asset specificity (k), when translated in financial terms, is predominantly an institutional—rather than a technical—issue closely related to the other two characteristics of contractual safeguards (s) and price (p). Considering asset specificity as an indicator of non-marketability of the incurred transaction costs points to the core of the institutional infrastructure of an economy and hence to the microeconomic underpinnings of financial repression/regulation or liberalization as a financial structure/regime. For Williamson (1996: 41–42) the crucial or "canonical" governance choice is between buying something in the market or producing it internally at the level of the firm. This entails that his theory implies microeconomic decisions at the level of the individual firm where the issue of vertical integration and the optimal size of this firm is examined. However, the same choice in the case of finance takes on a macroeconomic perspective as far as the alternatives are between capital markets on the one hand and hierarchical or hybrid modes of governance at an economy-wide level on the other hand. In this sense, financial repression/regulation is the institutional framework that governs contractual relations between firms-borrowers and investors-suppliers of financial capital, when a high degree of asset specificity (low degree of ease of verification) and institutional underdevelopment pose safeguard hazards and raise the price of capital to a level prohibitive for investment.

Williamson (1991a, 1991b) distinguishes the three main types of governance structures—market, hierarchy, and hybrid mode—in terms of their major distinctive characteristics. The latter include differences in the ability to adapt to changing circumstances and in the relative weight between incentive intensity and administrative controls.

Changes in asset specificity determine the type of adaptation needed and hence the related mode of governance. Markets are characterized by type A (autonomous) adaptation where prices are sufficient to reflect changes in demand and supply. As asset specificity increases and we move away from markets toward hybrids or hierarchies, type C (coordination) adaptation predominates where conscious attempts to overcome coordination failures substitute for market autonomy. Setting the above logical argument in a historical perspective may describe—in terms of shifts between markets and hierarchies—differences between alternative financial systems depending on their development. The level of economic development is a decisive factor concerning institutional development. Hence, a less developed economy may be characterized by rather primitive financial structures because of its low level of economic development. In such an economy, the rudimentary or limited level of monetary transactions justifies a situation of institutional underdevelopment. On the other hand, there is no unique relation between the level of economic development and the development of capital markets as Rajan and Zingales (2003: 212) indicate. Indeed, financial markets lost their previous significance as a source of finance after 1929 and throughout the whole period up to the deregulation wave of the 1980s. The point to be made here is that financial repression/regulation might be interpreted as emerging from the need for type C adaptation as transaction-specific investments increase (ease of verification decreases) and liquidity risk increases in a system. Hence, disrupting events in economic history such as the Great Depression in the 1930s led many developed countries with large capital markets in the political decision for the "great reversal" toward financial repression/regulation. Such interpretations of financial development make Williamson's (1991a, 1991b) analysis of adaptation needs pertinent to the understanding of financial repression/regulation.

Nevertheless, there is a price to pay when we move from markets to hierarchies, and when conscious attempts replace the autonomous adaptability of the system. This price is the cost of degrading incentives versus the benefits of administrative control. In type A adaptations, prices are adequate guides of decision, providing agents with the necessary incentives to adapt efficiently. Full-information prices in developed markets are supposed to be less vulnerable to opportunistic distortions. Yet, in cases of bilateral dependency where type C adaptations are needed, and where prices are not fully informative, the need for decisions based on fiat leads to the joint effect of degrading high-powered incentives—that is incentives guided by prices—and rising bureaucratic costs (Williamson 1991a). The costs of bureaucracy, as explained in Williamson (1985: 148–152), relate to three major issues: (a) the propensity of decision-makers in a hierarchy to overstate their ability to solve complex problems or their strategic inclination to use the means provided by the organization to meet their preferred subgoals; (b) the fact that internal organizations forgive errors more often than markets; (c) the logrolling effect, namely the propensity of hierarchies to renew reciprocal relations among agents within it even if this is not justified on the grounds of efficiency calculations. On the other hand, incentives within hierarchies are rather "flat" (Williamson 1991a) in the sense that greater effort is not reflected in larger pecuniary or non-pecuniary compensation. However, the developmental role of the state also highlights a different dimension in bureaucratic and other public costs related to economic development. According to Williamson (1994) administrative costs and compensation for investors who are committed to maintaining a longer-term perspective when investing in a country may be socially desirable and efficient. On the other hand, investors' commitment presupposes the government's credible commitment toward those investors that will boost investment in durable assets which are highly asset-specific but also have great importance for economic development.

Nevertheless, the implication for financial repression/regulation regimes is that the decisive role of the state in forming or affecting prices of capital and guiding its supply in a rather hierarchical form may lead to the additional burden of bureaucratic costs and diminished private incentives for efficient allocation of resources. Bureaucratic costs in a financially regulated regime may take the form of preferential relationships between government officials and specific agents with distorting effects on investment financing. It may also be the case that these officials meet their short-term political goals at the expense of the long-term declared goals of government policy. Then flat non-market incentives may simply worsen this result. Although such costs are indispensable in hierarchical organizations, it is a question whether are offset by the gains of this form of governance. The competence of the political and administrative personnel of a government and its agencies is pertinent to this net calculation. Nevertheless, the prevailing financial regime is a matter to be determined by the particular historical conditions given the type of adaptation needed by the real economy.

4.4 A More Encompassing Approach to Transactions: J. R. Commons's Legacy

Using Williamson's notion of transaction and its simple contracting schema we were able to build a conceptual bridge between the two alternative financial regimes: financial repression/regulation and financial liberalization/deregulation. At least we could have been able to do so if we had imagined a financial repression regime as a hierarchical order on the one hand, and a financial liberalization regime, where unfettered markets flourish, as the representative of the market type of governance structure. However, the analogy is not yet well-established for at least a couple of reasons. It is true that in Williamson's terms, we can speak about a range of governance mechanisms that span from the market to the firm as the unified governance of hierarchy (Furubotn and Richter 2008: 183–184; Williamson 1991a). However, the question arises whether Williamson's argument can describe more complex and encompassing institutional arrangements such as a financial regime which is the outcome of combined economic and political decisions. Williamson himself provides us with a hint on at least two occasions. When he discusses the relationship between public sector (or political) contracting and private sector contracting or the possible similarities between alternative forms of redistribution and governance. According to this analysis, a direct redistribution program, which is the least costly but most easily undone by a new government corresponds to the market as a governance mechanism. On the contrary, an indirect redistribution program with strong ties between the interest group and the political elite is the most costly because of large deadweight losses and corresponds to the hierarchy mode of governance. Then, an indirect redistribution program with weak ties between interest groups and politicians may correspond to a hybrid governance mechanism in private sector contracting (Williamson 1996: 200, 212). However, this mere analogy does not take us far enough into the intricacies of the interaction between political decisions and financial arrangements or how the former frames the latter.

A more pertinent example is provided by Williamson (1993a) in his discussion of trust for economic organization. This is an example of a regulation that "…can serve to infuse trading confidence into otherwise problematic trading relations" (Williamson 1993a: 477). The argument goes that if regulation of a market can instill trust between contracting parties then market participants may be more willing to engage in transaction-specific investments. He even stresses the intentional character of establishing a regulatory mechanism that implies a special role that is attributed to the government. In Williamson (1979: 259) he becomes more specific about the relationship between capital markets and governance structures where in this case the analogy is between "degree of transaction-specific investment" and "degree of verification" as already mentioned above. However, for a theory that characterizes transaction as simply the act that occurs when "...a good or service is transferred across a technologically separable interface..." (Williamson 1996: 58) and which reduces the "...scope of the concept of transactions to a microeconomic dimension more adequate to ... methodological individualism..." (Guedes and Jeronimo 2023: 75) this is the farthest you can go.

Transaction in J. R. Commons is more than a physical transfer. It even transcends the act of exchange. Transaction is an economic and social configuration that is particular to capitalism as a form of organizing social and economic life. In this sense, the concept of transaction describes both an underlying material and a social relationship. The material relationship refers to the interaction between the human being and nature and the social relationship describes the interaction between human actors (Guedes and Jeronimo 2023). Indeed, economics as a science implies this double interaction which is partly physical and partly social. Humans transcend their biological limitations by developing their social traits, but physical constraints are present when they interact with nature in the production process. On the other hand, production takes place only in the form of particular social relationships. Hence, transaction in Commons is a much richer concept than in Williamson, and if transaction is understood in the above double sense then Commons is right to consider it the unit of his analysis (Furubotn and Richter 2008: 41). As Commons segregates the proprietary from the engineering aspect of the economy, the social part predominates over the physical one and hence, the social form of transaction has in Commons the meaning of transfer of legal rights of ownership rather than of physical items. This is apparent when the object of exchange is financial assets or intangible assets. The contract which describes this transfer of property rights, as "rights to scarcity" (Kaufman 2003), is a legal and social construct itself but this kind of exchange does not necessarily imply a harmony of interests between the contracting parties. On the contrary, Commons's approach to transaction involves both a conflict of interest between the two parties and the existence of mutually dependent interests. Human beings attempt to cope with scarcity by settling conflict, taking account of interdependence among them, and looking for order. The first derives from the fact that ownership by someone is equivalent to the exclusion of someone else from access to this good or asset. In other words, ownership generates a kind of "contrived scarcity" which relates to "scarcity value" as the owner of the good excludes others from their access to it. On the other hand, the interests of the contracting parties are mutually dependent since they both have an incentive to conclude the relevant transaction. Eventually, what comes out of this interaction is the expectation of order from both parties as this is expressed in the working rules of the particular society. However, these rules that resolve conflicts and retain order are the outcome of collective action in the context of fundamental uncertainty about an unknowable and unforeseeable future (Kemp 2009: 61–62; Kaufman 2003). Furthermore, the characterization of rules as "working" rules indicates their functionality within a given society which is governed by specific objectives, and therefore, their ability to be modified via collective action if conditions change (Atkinson 1983).

For Commons, there are three types of transactions: The bargaining transaction, the managerial transaction, and the rationing transaction. The bargaining transaction is concluded between legal equals after a voluntary accord between them and it is governed by scarcity as explained above. The outcome of a bargaining transaction is the process of exchange on the market. Moreover, the managerial transaction pertains to the relationship of individuals who are legally unequal in the sense that one of them is superior to the other and the other is inferior to the first. The managerial transaction relates to production and efficiency in the context of a firm that uses labor as a factor of its production. Finally, there is the concept of rationing transaction which is also a relationship of command between legally superior and legally inferior. However, in this case, the legal superior is a group of people and the legal inferior is an individual. This concept is identified with sovereignty and distribution as it involves the distribution of burdens and benefits. In a rationing transaction at least the quantity or the price is determined by the legal superior. Moreover, all of these kinds of transactions taken together are necessary for the student of institutions to be able to describe a particular organization or a particular "going concern" as Commons puts it. Bargaining, managerial, and rationing transactions include the two means of coordination of economic activity: prices and command (Kemp 2009: 64–65; Kaufman 2003; Ramstad 1996). This characteristic of Commons's theory of transaction is probably what makes it such a powerful tool in describing economic activity in different financial regimes and historical circumstances.

For the sake of exposition and being fully aware of the methodological differences between Commons's and Williamson's approach and the divergent conceptual underpinnings of their theories (Kemp 2006; Ramstad 1996), one may observe that Commons's bargaining and managerial transactions may be (imperfectly) reflected in Williamson's treatment of transaction when the latter examines the different forms of governance from the market to the firm. Even if this is a rather superficial observation, nevertheless it has the merit of revealing with sufficient clarity the significant shortcoming of Williamson's exposition as opposed to Commons's. Williamson's theory, as it is preoccupied with and confined to private ordering, is not able to incorporate a notion of transaction that is appropriate to sovereign or public activity. On the contrary, Commons with his more encompassing theory is capable of providing a comprehensive approach to transaction that includes all three manifestations of economic activity: production, with the notion of managerial transaction, exchange with the notion of bargaining transaction, and distribution with the notion of rationing transaction. The latter implies, not a voluntary, but a commanding distribution of benefits and liabilities to the members of a collective entity (Ramstad 1996). The meaning of rationing transactions cannot fit in Williamson's categorization of markets, hybrids, and hierarchies (Valentinov 2009). Although the bargaining and managerial transactions are useful in describing a pendulum between markets and hierarchies in the terminology of Williamson, the rationing transaction is indispensable in incorporating the state sovereignty as an entity of collective action which is closely related to decisions relating to the prevailing financial regime and the process of economic development. Furthermore, as indicated by Dugger (1996), Commons's theoretical concern was to expand state sovereignty in favor of the less powerful while Williamson aimed at restricting this type of sovereignty. Moreover, Commons's treatment of the notion of sovereignty as the relative power to resolve conflicts of interest is much more comprehensive since it includes the authorities of the state, the business concern, and the cultural concern which is related to the power of opinion. Therefore, a theory that aims to explain the role of public authority and is capable of doing this without disregarding the authority of other important organizations in an economy is more useful in approaching the relationship between financial regimes, the government, and economic development.

The rationing transaction refers to the collective actions taken by a group of individuals that allocates certain "rights and duties" to particular individuals and it is subject to collective bargaining. Commons relates the rationing transaction with the extant power structures that may lead affected individuals to organize so that they can collectively claim a different distribution or rationing of output. Hence, for Commons, the rationing transaction is directly related to the political process in which democratic representation and arbitration among social groups is essential (Kemp 2009: 70–71).

However, the question may arise: in what respect is the notion of rationing transactions useful in describing a financial regime or a financial institutional environment? First of all, a financial regime is described by and is composed of a body of rules and expected patterns of behavior that are established by a sovereign state as was the case both in the case of financial repression and in the subsequent case of financial liberalization and its evolution in the context of the Washington Consensus. Even if the latter was more a set of policy "recipes" and proposals by international institutions, they eventually became incorporated into the legal system of each nation that sought to abide by them. A financial regime takes, in fact, the form of a political transaction between an organized group of individuals, which in this case may be the sovereign state and particular individuals affected by the rationing transaction, the financial market participants in our case. However, if the proper form of allocation arranged by the rationing transaction concerns benefits and income, how it is reconciled with a representation of the financial regime as the output of such a transaction? First of all, rationing for Commons includes both quantity and price rationing or even price fixing (Chavance 2012; Commons 1934[2017]: 680). Moreover, Commons's rationing transaction, as mentioned by Guedes and Jeronimo (2023), is not confined to the distribution of real goods and services or monetary values but also to the allocation of power among constituents. Indeed, power and its distribution are at the core of Commons's theory as will be also explained below. Commons (1931) refers to examples of rationing transactions that involve legislative action or even state decrees that call for "negotiation" but also "command and obedience". Hence, the rationing transaction is central in Commons's approach along with his idea that all costs are "instituted" rather than being the outcome of some kind of friction. Therefore, the procedures and conventions established by rationing transactions and the related distribution of power become the basis for carrying out bargaining and managerial transactions (Pessali and Fernández 1999; Ramstad 1996). Moreover, if we follow Kaufman (2003) that property rights are a strategic determinant of the form of economic organization then, different distribution of property rights through rationing transactions can better explain the range of alternatives between perfect decentralization (market economy) and perfect centralization (command economy) rather than varieties of asset specificity. In this sense, a particular financial regime can be thought of as a specific arrangement resulting from a political decision that allocates and redistributes both income and power among individuals or individual organizations that participate in financial markets.

Moreover, there is a further categorization of transactions in Commons's texts concerning the type of choice one can make in economic activity. In this case, there are two kinds of transactions: Routine transactions comprise the majority of decisions and represent patterns of behavior that do not diverge from the usual, normal, or regular ones. On the other hand, strategic transactions refer to choices that become critical in creating value by correcting a limiting factor namely, a particular problem that calls for a solution. If a difficulty, as a limiting factor to action is overcome, then complementary factors related to traditional modes of operation are set in motion. In this sense, a managerial decision that improves the efficiency of production and creates use value and profits may be considered a strategic transaction. The same holds for a bargaining transaction which generates income for a firm by excluding others from access to a product and thus causes prices to rise in its favor (Kemp 2009: 55–58, 62). Extending the above examples to the case of rationing transactions we may conceive the decision of a polity on the financial regime as a strategic transaction that overcomes the difficulties or problems caused by the previous regime and improves the allocation of resources both economic and power ones.

4.5 Reasonable Value, Negotiation and Reform

This section takes up the second reason why analogies between Williamson's theory and financial regimes are incomplete and this reason concerns the role of prices. Prices are examined in Williamson's contracting schema where they interact with asset specificity and safeguards. The idea is that rising asset specificity should drive upward either prices or safeguards. If the latter happens then prices might stay low to the benefit of economic development (Williamson 1985: 33). As Furubotn and Richter (2008: 307) point out, Williamson takes the constitutional and legal framework in an economy as given when it examines the various governance mechanisms. Hence, the social formation or the social determinants of the elements that affect governance structures are left to the background. However, this is exactly what we need to address when talking about financial regimes that frame private financial contracts. In other words, the way that prices are formed is not independent of the way safeguards are provided for given asset specificity. However, since in financial markets asset specificity is directly related to the verification of asset returns as explained above, neither asset specificity is independent of the social determinants of prices and safeguards.

The mainstream approach considers markets and competition as natural phenomena that exist beyond cultural or historical differences among different nations or regions. Eventually, institutions or customs are irrelevant since markets are driven by a natural logic that leads to self-regulation. Institutions may only act on top of this naturalistic structure for better or for worse, but they are not integrally necessary to the functioning of the market. Therefore, the social framework in which markets are embedded is also irrelevant according to the mainstream view. The above indicates that prices determined in the market under competitive conditions have also a "natural", rather than social, quality that leads to a corresponding equilibrium that is characterized by efficiency or cost minimization (Ramstad 2001). If the market mechanism and the prices which are formed therein have the quality of a natural process and outcome, the latter being an equilibrium outcome, then "naturally" we end up to the conclusion that public regulation is "unnatural". In this case, there is no way to explain in a meaningful way why financial repression was the mainstream approach in the post-WWII period and how changing social and economic conditions led to institutional change in the deregulation era. In the above naturalistic mentality, it is even more difficult to form a theory about development banks that are so intimately linked to the prevailing financial regime.

Commons, on the other hand, provides us with a theory of price formation which is a social process centered on the notion of reasonableness or reasonable value. A reasonable value is a value defined in social terms and which is conditioned by history and the state of technology in each historical era. According to Commons (1936: 237), the theory of reasonable value includes "ethics, public welfare, or national public interest" in economic theory. Therefore, the reasonable value in Commons is not abstract but pragmatic, empirically derived from the best practices of historically functioning organizations (Kemp 2009: 26; Dugger 1996). In Commons, an exchange is not characterized by harmony of interests but on the contrary, by conflict. Conflict is derived from scarcity and scarcity values are correlated with prices which are signals provided in a social context. In the end, order is not produced spontaneously but it is the outcome of "...collective control of individual behavior through working rules" (Kemp 2009: 50, 62; Ramstad 2001: 256). Hence, a reasonable value is a manifestation of the "...rationality of systems that imposes a form of rationality upon individuals" (Kemp 2009: 75). In other words, it is not a rational value as this is perceived by an abstract rational individual but rather a rational value which expresses what is rational for a society in particular historical time. So, if order is not automatic but comes about through the adoption of working rules how are the latter characterized? Working rules include laws enacted by the legislature, decisions of the courts, rules established within business associations and trade unions, and social norms and customs. These formal and informal working rules could be described as "(property) rights" since they determine the distribution of scarce resources among individual agents. Commons asserts that working rules are a way to allocate incentives for action and fix expectations of market participants about future action. If certain patterns of behavior implied by the instituted working rules are being repeated in social exchanges, they become habitual and customary and in this sense, they are considered by economic actors as "natural". In this process of formation of working rules, the sovereign ultimately determines the prevalent working rules according to its perception of public purpose. The state chooses to consider as a public purpose a specific set of private purposes according to the economic class that determines the ethical beliefs of the political elite (Kaufman 2003; Ramstad 2001). Then, "Every transaction is weighed ... according to what is deemed to be a public purpose" (Commons 1924: 326).

Indeed, as Kemp (2009: 76–77) remarks, reasonable value is a concept directly related to sovereign power as an allocator of rights and duties to individuals having in mind the public purpose and the will of society. Despite Commons's emphasis on the role of the courts, and especially the Supreme Court to determine the public purpose of the era and hence, affect the meaning of reasonable value, it is the public opinion and the custom that finally determines the content of reasonableness. However, the latter, as we have shown above, is also related to the balance of power between different social groups or economic classes. Hence, it is important to note that, contrary to the mainstream view, the market system is not the derivative of a spontaneous order but an artificial conscious construction where the state structures incentives and transforms with its working rules the private into public purposes. In the context of circular causation between individual volitions and action on the one hand and working rules on the other hand, equilibrium is the outcome of some kind of "institutional balance" as working rules adapt to circumstances while prices are also institutionally determined through socially endorsed rules such as property rights (Ramstad 2001).

By defining reasonableness in a way that serves the public purpose of the era, reasonable value becomes inseparable from the social context, and prices, in turn, are perceived as being a social construct that is subject to modification and readjustment if that is approved by society. In short, prices for Commons are publicly administered prices (Kemp 2009: 136) under the criterion of reasonableness as defined above. Public purpose relates to the democratic process as a factor that determines economic development and especially the possible alternatives to achieving it (Kemp 2009: 132). Therefore, introducing the public purpose in reasonable value determination introduces explicitly a social parameter in the definition of an economic variable which, in the face of democratic negotiations, spells out the importance of the balance of power in the economy.

According to Commons, a value can be considered "reasonable" if it is the outcome of a bargaining process between two contracting parties in conditions of persuasion rather than coercion. However, coercion is not just the use of force or the threat of such use. It is also a form of economic coercion on behalf of the party with the larger ownership of resources. This difference in terms of property gives the ability and power to the party that possesses the greater amount of resources to wait until the weaker party concedes in an agreement that is favorable to the first. Commons had in mind the difference in power between corporations and workers and favored government involvement in the form of regulation and a regulatory commission as a "fourth branch of government" to generate reasonable rules through negotiation between the interested parties (Ramstad 2001). Hence, for Commons, some form of economic regulation is necessary to obtain reasonable values, and reasonable values are reflected in the so-called "negotiated economy" which has been the historical paradigm in Scandinavian economies. At the bottom-line reasonable values are regulated values in the sense of being the outcome of compromise between interested parties however imperfect this might be (Ramstad 1991).

In addition, the theory of reasonable value is also a theory of reform. The term "reasonable" is related to the practices that are considered the best possible ones at a given stage of technological development. Furthermore, reform and institutional change are meant to be the offspring of a process of democratic participation of interested parties where the economist assumes the role of informed counselor. For Commons, reform means a change in regulations based on what is considered socially reasonable in a particular historical period (Kemp 2009: 79, 119–120). The role of government in general, in Commons's setup, is multiple. Commissions are considered by him to be the "fourth branch" of government. However, commissions are negotiation hubs between representatives of social classes or interest groups and the government. This way to solve a class conflict, a process of "joint bargaining.. between representatives of opposing organized interests" (Commons 1934 [2003]: 858 reported by Kitagawa 2020: 318) assumes its full meaning in the term coined by Commons (1935): "collective democracy" as opposed to "individualistic democracy" in Adam Smith. In collective democracy, working rules are decided by an investigation process of best practices and a related negotiation process among interest groups with the support of the state and the counseling role of professional economists. Hence, progressive change is closely related to collective democracy because collective democracy, as described above, is a way to identify what is reasonable and it is the best means to persuade, rather than coerce, individual agents to accept this kind of reasonableness (Kitagawa 2020). In other words, no top-down imposition of working rules is possible in the long run. On the contrary, the foundation for the progressive evolution of working rules should be looked up in the way individuals internalize these working rules and under which conditions they do so. In this respect, Commons's collectivism differs from Williamson's individualism to the degree that reasonableness cannot be defined otherwise (Dugger 1996). Against an individualistic psychology implied by Williamson, Commons argues in favor of a decision-making individual which is embedded in a social environment that conditions its behavior through customs and formed habits. This kind of "institutionalized man" way of action depends on individuals' participation in community life and the habits they have acquired because of this membership (Ramstad 1996). Therefore, Commons's assumption of interdependent utility functions and his emphasis on forbearance contradicts Williamson's opportunism in the pursuit of self-interest. Commons does not disregard the possibility that in some cases cooperation may pay off more than self-interest and individuals have an incentive to value collective good more highly than their independent and isolated preferences. In this respect, trust among individuals and a priority of other-regarding over self-regarding behavior may also reduce transaction costs. Furthermore, markets may guide behavior through the "high-powered" incentives derived from prices and self-interest, but organizations and hierarchies are also governed by high-powered incentives of a different quality such as the promotion of team spirit which may also be responsible for high levels of performance within an organization (Kaufman 2003). Eventually, individuals may willingly accept collectively imposed restrictions in their actions if they value collective fairness. On the other hand, "reasonable" rules for Commons are meant to promote both efficiency and fairness. This is not in contrast with individual liberty or with self-interest per se if we recall Commons's (1951: 21) definition of institutions as "collective action in control, liberation, and expansion of individual action" (Ramstad 1996; Atkinson 1983: 1060). All these observations are important justifications for an institutional framework that is formed and reformed as the deliberate outcome of negotiation and conscious collective action.

Besides, the notion of reform is at the core of Commons's analysis of capitalism in two respects. First, economics, as Commons understands it, is better described as political economy to the degree that the working rules of economic organizations are formed or endorsed by collective action. Furthermore, economics is an evolutionary social science because these working rules are in a process of inescapable change and development as circumstances and conditions change (Kaufman 2003). However, institutional change is not comprehensibly explained unless it is the outcome of some kind of cooperation guided by an amalgamation of self-interest, omnipresence of power, and some sense of fairness. In fact, for Commons, economic reform emerges as a negotiation between social groups where interest, power, and fairness codetermine the outcome (Atkinson 1983). To be more specific, institutional reform comes about through a process of artificial selection where human volition interacts with working rules, and the new formal rules are shaped by the modification of customs within going concerns. In this process of artificial selection the notions of power and legitimation are crucial (Chavance 2012). Hence, it is important at this point to embed the above ideas of Commons about reasonableness and reform in his understanding of the economy as being in fact "a managed economy" in the sense that economic and institutional development come about by collective action and his insistence for democratic participation. After all, for Commons, the state is construed as a "creative entity" in forming the economic process in historically and culturally specific conditions (Whalen 2022). We believe that the above constitutes a set of hypotheses or a framework of analysis that is able to guide us further in understanding economic and financial development in a dynamic and comprehensive way.

4.6 Summing up: Transactions, Governance, and Financial Markets

The conclusion to be derived from the above discussion is that the Institutional Economics of Williamson and Commons can provide us with powerful theoretical tools that can be used in explaining alternative financial regimes. These regimes are conceived as institutional structures of incentives for market participants given the peculiarities of financial markets. Commons's theory of transactions is more encompassing than the one developed by Williamson and it has the ability to approach more closely the features of financial regimes as structures endorsed by public authorities which have material consequences for market participants. On the other hand, Williamson's contracting schema and especially his emphasis on asset specificity and safeguards are useful to the student of financial regulation as they provide a practical model to approach the relationship between financial regulation and the level of financial development. However, from a macroscopic point of view, asset specificity in financial markets is a rather relativistic concept that depends on the ease of verification of asset returns and hence on the level of financial development. At the same time, safeguards and asset prices are also dependent, among other factors, on the level of financial development, which, after all, reflects institutional development and reform. Hence, encompassing Williamson's governance analysis into Commons's institutional analysis is necessary for our purposes.

Moreover, Commons's treatment of the market mechanism and prices' determination provides a comprehensive framework for understanding the alternation of financial regimes. Reasonableness is the central concept in this case since it implies an artificial way of market operation and price determination where bargaining and negotiation within a regulatory framework are the norm. In addition, public purpose and the way it expresses and promotes private purposes, whomever these may be, justifies the involvement of government and public authorities in this process. However, note that this framework might become an explanation for both the strict financial repression/regulation regime and the subsequent deregulation or financial liberalization regime, probably enhanced by a different form of regulation such as prudential regulation (Walter 2003). The important point here is that the type of financial regime reflects what is considered to be "reasonable" for a society in a given historical period and the latter reflects the balance of power between different social groups. Hence, the prevailing financial regime is indeed the outcome of social negotiation whether this is instituted as Commons would have wanted it or not. In this respect too is Commons's theory more comprehensive than Williamson's. Williamson was right to point out that institutional and economic development may decrease the level of asset specificity and reverse the trend at the micro-level from hierarchies to markets. Nevertheless, Williamson is not able to identify the social developments in which governance mechanisms are embedded because he takes them for granted. Moreover, if financial regimes are the object of analysis, the social context is not given, and such reversals reflect the changing balance of power and ideologies in a society. In the next chapter, we will be more specific on such issues but for now, the above suffice to determine the relative importance of Williamson's and Commons's analyses as we move from mere analogies to more fundamental issues.

References

Atkinson, G. W. (1983) "Political Economy: Public Choice or Collective Action?", *Journal of Economic Issues*, 17(4): 1057–1065.

Arrow, K. J. (1969) "The Organization of Economic Activity: Issues Pertinent to the Choice of Market versus Non-Market Allocation" in *The Analysis and Evaluation of Public Expenditures: The PBB-System*, Joint Economic Committee, 91st Cong., 1st sess., Vol. 1, Washington, D. C.: Government Printing Office, pp. 59–73.

Chavance, B. (2012) "John Commons's Organizational Theory of Institutions: A Discussion", *Journal of Institutional Economics*, 8(1): 27–47.

Coase, R. H. (1960) "The Problem of Social Cost", *The Journal of Law and Economics*, 3: 1–44.

Coase, R. H. (1937) "The Nature of the Firm", *Economica*, New Series, 4(16): 386–405.

Commons, J. R. (1951) *The Economics of Collective Action*, New York: The Macmillan Company.

Commons, J. R. (1936) "Institutional Economics", *American Economic Review*, 26(1): 237–249.

Commons, J. R. (1935) "Communism and Collective Democracy", *American Economic Review*, 25(2): 212–223.

Commons, J. R. (1934[2017]) *Institutional Economics: Its Place in Political Economy Vol. 1*, London & New York: Routledge.

Commons, J. R. (1934 [2003]) *Institutional Economics: Its Place in Political Economy Vol. 2*, New Brunswick, USA & London, UK: Transaction Publishers.

Commons, J. R. (1931) "Institutional Economics", *American Economic Review*, 21(4): 648–657.

Commons, J. R. (1924) *Legal Foundations of Capitalism*, New York: The Macmillan Company.

Dugger, W. M. (1987) "The Economic Institutions of Capitalism", *Journal of Economic Issues*, 21(1): 528–530.

Dugger, W. M. (1996) "Sovereignty in Transaction Cost Economics: John R. Commons and Oliver E. Williamson", *Journal of Economic Issues*, 30(2): 427–432.

Furubotn, E. G. and Richter, R. (2008) *Institutions and Economic Theory. The Contribution of the New Institutional Economics*, 2nd Ed., Ann Arbor: The University of Michigan Press.

Groenewegen, J. Kerstholt, F. and Nagelkerke, A. (1995) "On Integrating New and Old Institutionalism: Douglass North Building Bridges", *Journal of Economic Issues*, 29(2): 467–475.

Guedes, S. N. R. and Jeronimo, R. C. (2023) "A Concept of Two Authors: Commons and Williamson on Transactions", *Journal of Interdisciplinary Economics*, 35(1): 61–82.

Kaufman, B. E. (2003) "The Organization of Economic Activity: Insights from the Institutional Theory of John R. Commons", *Journal of Economic Behavior and Organization*, 52: 71–96.

Kemp, T. (2009) *Progress and Reform. The Economic Thought of John R. Commons*, Saarbrücken, Deutschland: VDM Verlag Dr. Müller.

Kemp, T. (2006) "Of Transactions and Transaction Costs: Uncertainty, Policy, and the Process of Law in the Thought of Commons and Williamson", *Journal of Economic Issues*, 40(1): 45–58.

Kitagawa, K. (2020) "From Judicial Sovereignty to Collective Democracy: The Development of J. R. Commons' Perspective on Progressive Institutional Change", *Journal of Economic Issues*, 54(2): 316–321.

Klein, P. G. (2000) "New Institutional Economics" in Bouckaert, B. and De Geest, G. (eds.), *Encyclopedia of Law and Economics*, Vol. I. The History and Methodology of Law and Economics, Cheltenham, Edward Elgar, pp. 456–489 available at https://reference.findlaw.com/lawandeconomics/0530-new-institutional-economics.pdf Accessed 19 Nov. 2024.

Kreps, D. M. (1990) *A Course in Microeconomic Theory*, New Jersey: Princeton University Press.

Marangos, J. and Whalen, C. J. (2011) "Evolution without Fundamental Change: The Washington Consensus on Economic Development and its Significance for Post-Keynesian Institutionalism", in Whalen C. J. (ed.) *Financial Instability and Economic Security after the Great Recession*, Cheltenham, UK and Northampton, MA, USA: Edward Elgar, pp. 153–178.

McKinnon, R. I. (1993) *The Order of Economic Liberalization: Financial Control in the Transition to a Market Economy*, 2nd Ed. Baltimore: John Hopkins University Press.

Pessali H. F. and Fernández, R. G. (1999) "Institutional Economics at the Micro Level? What Transaction Costs Theory Could Learn from Original Institutionalism (In the Spirit of Building Bridges)", *Journal of Economic Issues*, 33(2): 265–275.

Pitelis, C. N. (1998) "Transaction Costs and the Historical Evolution of the Capitalist Firm", *Journal of Economic Issues*, 32(4): 999–1017.

Rajan, R. G. and Zingales L. (2003) *Saving Capitalism from the Capitalists: Unleashing the Power of Financial Markets to Create Wealth and Spread Opportunity*, Princeton University Press.

Ramstad, Y. (2001) "John R. Commons's Reasonable Value and the Problem of Just Price", *Journal of Economic Issues*, 35(2): 253–277.

Ramstad, Y. (1996) "Is a Transaction a Transaction?", *Journal of Economic Issues*, 30(2): 413–425.

Ramstad, Y. (1991) "From Desideratum to Historical Achievement: John R. Commons's Reasonable Value and the 'Negotiated Economy' of Denmark", *Journal of Economic Issues*, 25(2): 431–439.

Rodrik, D. (2006) "Goodbye Washington Consensus, Hello Washington Confusion? A Review of the World Bank's 'Economic Growth in the 1990s: Learning from a Decade of Reform'", *Journal of Economic Literature*, 44(4): 973–987.

Rutherford, M. (1995) "The Old and New Institutionalism: Can Bridges be Built?", *Journal of Economic Issues*, 29(2): 443–451.

Stein, M. (2008) *Beyond the World Bank Agenda. An Institutional Approach to Development*, Chicago & London: The University of Chicago Press.

Vandenberg, P. (2002) "North's Institutionalism and the Prospect of Combining Theoretical Approaches", *Cambridge Journal of Economics*, 26(2): 217–235.

Valentinov, V. (2009) "Mapping the Third Sector in John R. Commons' Typology of Transactions", *Journal of Economic Issues*, 43(4): 917–930.

Walter, A. (2003) "Implementation in East Asia. Financial Liberalization and Prudential Regulation in East Asia: Still Perverse", London: LSE Research Online available at https://eprints.lse.ac.uk/797/1/Financial_liberalization_and_Prudential_Regulation_%2D%2D_Benu_Schneider_book.pdf Accessed 7 Nov. 2024.

Whalen, C. J. (2022) "The Institutionalist Method and Vision of John R. Commons", *Journal of Economic Issues*, 56(4): 1006–1018.

Williamson, O. E. (2000) "The New Institutional Economics: Taking Stock, Looking Ahead", *Journal of Economic Literature*, 38(3): 595–613.

Williamson, O. E. (1996) *The Mechanisms of Governance*, New York, Oxford: Oxford University Press.

Williamson, O. E. (1994) "The Institutions and Governance of Economic Development and Reform", *The World Bank Economic Review*, 8(suppl_1): 171–197.

Williamson, O. E. (1993a) "Calculativeness, Trust, and Economic Organization", *Journal of Law and Economics*, 36(1): 453–486.

Williamson, O. E. (1993b) "Transaction Cost Economics and Organization Theory", *Industrial and Corporate Change*, 2(2): 107–156.

Williamson, O. E. (1991a) "Comparative Economic Organization: The Analysis of Discrete Structural Alternatives", *Administrative Science Quarterly*, 36(2): 269–296.

Williamson, O. E. (1991b) "Economic Institutions: Spontaneous and Intentional Governance", *Journal of Law, Economics, and Organization*, 7(Special Issue): 159–187.

Williamson, O. E. (1991c) "Strategizing, Economizing, and Economic Organization", *Strategic Management Journal*, 12(S2): 75–94.

Williamson, O. E. (1985) *The Economic Institutions of Capitalism*, New York: Free Press.

Williamson, O. E. (1979) "Transaction-Cost Economics: The Governance of Contractual Relations", *Journal of Law and Economics*, 22(2): 233–261.

Williamson, O. E. (1975) *Markets and Hierarchies. Analysis and Antitrust Implications*, N.Y. and London: The Free Press.

CHAPTER 5

Habits and Cognition: Exploring the Process of Institutional Reform

5.1 From Transactions and Governance to Institutional Formation and Change

This chapter is about institutional change and reform. The reason for this interest is the historical fact that the operation of development banks has always been dependent on the prevailing financial regimes and because these banks played a role in institutional development and change. These remarks should have been clear by now, given the historical evidence and the theoretical debate about development banks, development finance, and financial development expounded in the previous chapters. On the other hand, whatever is true about institutional change in general is also true for institutional change in the financial sector in particular, despite the intricacies and specificities of financial markets. New Institutionalist economists' references, such as those of Oliver Williamson and Douglass North, to issues relating to the governance and development of capital markets, are proof of this assertion. For this reason, looking more closely at how individuals make decisions and contribute to institutional change does not detract from the main research question of this book, which is the role of development banking between markets and governments. After all, North (2005: 170) himself defines economics as "a theory of choice" by intentional individuals, a science whose study helps us understand the process of decision-making in human societies.

K. Loizos, *Between Markets and Governments*,
https://doi.org/10.1007/978-3-031-88527-3_5

In Chap. 4 we reviewed the ideas of John R. Commons and Oliver Williamson on transactions, governance, reasonableness, and negotiation in an attempt to build a framework for explaining alternative financial regimes. We demonstrated how Commons's rationing transactions and a framework of negotiation and reasonableness may become the basis for understanding alternative forms of "regulating" markets. We also noted that Commons's theory of reform is based on the above ideas, but we didn't delve further into this issue. What are the social, cultural, and economic forces behind the process of institutional formation? How is institutional change possible and why did it come about in the first place? Is it a top-down or a bottom-up process? What is the role of different social groups and elites? Which is the distinct role of individual perception and action, and of group ideology and collective action?

The literature on the above perennial questions concerning institutional change is vast and ever-expanding. It would be naïve and a distraction from the purpose of this book to cover, even superficially, this rich and diverse literature. However, what we can do in this chapter is to use the above questions as guiding strings in our short review of the ideas of two groundbreaking thinkers in this area: Thorstein Veblen and Douglass North, a Nobel 1993 prize winner. The reason for focusing on these two authors is twofold: At first, Thorstein Veblen has been a leading figure in Original Institutional Economics and a major inspiration for all subsequent work in the institutional formation and change within this strand of literature. Secondly, Douglass North provides, in our opinion, the most developed and comprehensive approach to institutional change within the New Institutional Economics tradition. After all, his contribution to understanding "economic and institutional change" by using combined tools from economic theory and economic history (Nobel Prize Organization 1993) gave him the Nobel prize. In addition. North's work and ideas have influenced the attitudes and policies of international organizations such as the World Bank (Stein 2008: 98–107; World Bank 1997, 2002).

The sections of this chapter do not have the intention to discuss in detail the vast and growing interdisciplinary literature on institutional change. Our goal is much more modest. We attempt to review some salient institutional tools for understanding financial and economic development along with institutional reform reflected in the change in financial regimes, by using the ideas and notions developed by Thorstein Veblen and Douglass North. Due to limited space, we will not embark on strict periodization of North's ideas which can be found in the relevant literature concerning the development of his thought (Von Staden and Bruce 2015; Vandenberg 2002; Dugger 1995; Groenewegen et al. 1995; Rutherford 1995). However, a separate section is devoted to his emphasis on cognitive issues which is the main breakthrough of his last works. Likewise, our account of Veblen's ideas is necessarily focused on an elementary exposition of the relationship between instincts, habits, and beliefs and the interaction between technology and institutions in the process of institutional change.

5.2 Institutional Matrices, Economic Agents' Behavior and Change in D. North

"Institutions are the humanly devised constraints that structure political, economic, and social interaction" (North 1991). In this well-known definition, North shows that his interest extends beyond micro-contractual relationships and governance mechanisms which has been the case for Williamson. His analysis concerns institutions as social constructs on a macro scale which encompasses the economic, political, and social spheres in their interrelation. Therefore, as Furubotn and Richter (2008: 307) point out, although both North and Williamson emphasize the role of transaction costs, North examines the evolutionary aspect of the institutional structure while Williamson takes the "constitutional and legal framework", the macro-context as given. In this sense, and from the perspective that it is of interest to this book, North can escape from the "analogies trap" we pointed out when we talked about Williamson's attempt to extend the explanatory ability of his model to public sector contracting or public regulation. North's approach, even from his definition of institutions, is a direct attempt to elaborate on institutional formation and change in a comprehensive and dynamic social context. Contemplating the functionality of institutions, it seems that for North institutions are effectively constraints on individual perception and action. Such constraints may be both informal and formal. Informal constraints include routines, customs, conventions, tradition, and codes of conduct while formal rules comprise constitutions, laws, and property rights. Therefore, formal rules pertain to both political and judicial rules and economic rules and contracts. Furthermore, the ability of informal constraints to perpetuate in time reflects their embodiment in agents' habits that affect their behavior. These institutional constraints are imposed so that effective cooperation is possible, given the existence of uncertainty, complexity, transaction costs, and increased specialization in the economy (North 1990: 25, 47, 83; 1991).

North's theoretical ideas are closely related to his historical perspective. According to North (1991), institutions determine transaction and production costs, and, in this sense, economic history is the narrative of institutional evolution and transformation. This is because institutions build the incentive structure faced by the agents of an economy and in this sense, they determine the direction of change in economic life. Will there be a pro-growth social and economic transformation or a bout of decay will follow? At the end of the day, North's macro-dynamic perspective, as opposed to Williamson's micro-static one, can be seen in that he is interested in explaining the economic performance of different nations throughout their history and in their current comparison. Economic performance depends on the combination of established formal rules, informal norms, and their enforcement. The key here is to probe further into the formation and enforcement of property rights which appear as formal constraints and the role of political institutions in this process, rather than take this institutional environment for granted. Political institutions affect economic performance through their function to define and enforce property rights. In addition, one needs to take into account that formal rules can change in a very short time but informal norms need more time to change and this happens in a gradual fashion (North 1991, 1994). Hence, once again history matters.

North provides a historical narrative about the relationship between the division of labor, trade, transaction costs, and institutions. Local trade in small villages is supported by a network of social and personal relationships which act as informal constraints on individual behavior thus, reducing transaction costs. However, as specialization and division of labor increases, trade opportunities beyond the local level appear and markets expand further. However, this happens at the expense of the established personal network between traders. Impersonal exchange is now the norm and transaction costs, both pre-contractual and post-contractual, rise. Long-distance trade is a case in point where agency and enforcement costs increase sharply. Finally, in modern capitalism where services, including finance, banking, and insurance, predominate over other forms of economic activity, the importance of transaction costs and property rights protection rises. This is how North's reading of history establishes the importance of political institutions and their evolution, as guarantors of impersonal contract enforcement. At the same time, he points out that the evolution path described above is not a necessity but a possibility that has been realized in some parts of the world but not in others (North 1991).

The crucial point in this argument is the existence of an "institutional matrix" that defines the opportunity set or the "pay-offs" of agents as incentives for acquiring knowledge and selecting particular actions (North 1995: 15, 17). The institutional matrix includes both political and economic organizations and generates increasing returns for its members. North (1990: 5) defines organizations as "groups of individuals bound by some common purpose to achieve objectives". Hence, in the above framework, the viability of organizations depends on the structure of the incentives given by the existing institutions and the response of agents to these incentives. Furthermore, the above-mentioned increasing returns culminate in path-dependence in economic history (North 1991)[1] which raises the question of how is institutional change possible.

According to North (1994, 1995: 15), institutional change is a continuous and incremental process that comes about in the context of an interaction between institutions and organizations in an environment defined by widespread scarcity "If institutions are the rules of the game, organizations, and their entrepreneurs are the players". However, note that this is a two-sided relation. On the one hand, the institutional framework determines the kind of maximizing behavior for the organization. On the other hand, this maximizing behavior is a source of institutional change (North 1990: 78) as far as changes in relative prices—i.e. changes in the ratio of prices of factors of production, changes in the cost of information, changes in technology—alter the incentive structures (North 1990: 83–84). Hence, "organizations and their entrepreneurs", with their purposeful action affect the direction of institutional change in an incremental fashion (North 1990: 73). The decisions that people make in their everyday activities are usually ordinary routine decisions. However, some of them call for some kind of "recontracting" in their relationship with organizations which may require changing the existing rules and norms (North 1994). Nevertheless, institutional change can only be

[1] Path-dependence is a concept which originated in the works of Arthur (1989) and David (1985) in the form of technological path-dependence. The idea was then extended to explain institutional path-dependence as economies find themselves locked in, in inefficient institutional structures. See Zouboulakis (2015).

incremental and subject to the bargaining power of different groups of agents. Organizations prevailing in this bargaining game are able to affect the polity toward changing the political rules (North 1990: 79) which also entails a change in economic rules concerning the specification and enforcement of property rights (North 1990: 47–48). A change in relative prices that enhances the bargaining power of a specific social group may engender a change in the rules in favor of this group (North 1981: 29–30). In short, the way institutions are formed does not guarantee their efficiency in terms of social welfare but rather it is an indicator of the bargaining power of specific groups that are in a position to shape new formal rules that serve their interests (North 1990: 16; 1994). Indeed, the process of institutional change implies that entrepreneurs of organizations recognize new opportunities and they attempt to modify the rules by influencing political decisions, if they are economic organizations, or by changing the rules they set themselves, if they are political organizations. Especially, the change in informal constraints occurs through everyday interaction among organizations. As new forms of informal conventions or norms emerge through this process, the old ones fall into disuse (North 1995: 16).

As indicated above, North is interested in the differing performance of economies through time and, in comparison among them. Why do some economies perform better than others? Economies are populated by organizations that struggle for survival and hence, they seek to possess knowledge and acquire skills that will help them survive in a competitive environment by raising the efficiency of their organization in that particular environment. However, the specific type of knowledge they are looking for prescribes their perception of possible opportunities that they identify and their subsequent action. But this kind of action is part of an incremental process of institutional change (North 1995: 15–16). In this context, North (1991) remarks that there is no necessary reason for all societies to cultivate those skills and knowledge that favor pro-growth institutional development. This is not to say that people are willingly engaged in wasteful activity. Rather it is the case that the maximizing behavior that pays off in a given society is not necessarily friendly to economic development. It depends on the institutional framework in each society and epoch which defines the opportunities that direct maximizing economic activity. If in a particular society, piracy is associated with high returns, then it pays off to invest in piracy skills. A completely different situation will emerge if the higher returns in a different society come from pursuing a productive occupation (North 1995: 17). Therefore, there are increasing returns to existing institutions in lowering transaction costs as initial setup costs for new institutions are high and the kinds of knowledge and skills that pay-off are specific to the incentive structure of the existent institutional framework (North 1990: 78). Furthermore, coordination between contracting parties on the expectations built into the formal rules and into the informal constraints that evolve within the existing institutional structure will decrease uncertainty (North 1990: 95). For example, in early modern Europe, rising economies of scale, as trade rose, gave the incentive and resources for more sophisticated and innovated means of contract enforcement. At the same time, the improved ways of contract enforcement reduced transaction costs and increased the returns on trade and thereby its volume (North 1991). In this context, "path dependence means that history matters" (North 1990: 100) and it is inevitable in determining the future course of the economies as being the "yesterday's choices" which "are the initial starting point for today's" choices (North 1995: 20).

The relationship between formal and informal constraints and the crucial role of the latter indicates North's focus on everyday activity and interaction as the source and support of long-lasting institutions. North (1991) stresses the importance of enforcement mechanisms that were created by merchants organized in guilds such as the codes of conduct that preceded more formal rules such as mercantile law. Eventually, the mixing and interaction between those rules that were enforced by mechanisms internal to merchant organizations and those enforced by the polity enhanced the efficiency of these modes of contract enforcement. Furthermore, North (1990: 37, 44; 1995: 22) argues that informal constraints in the form of norms, conventions, and codes of conduct are significant generators of continuity and path-dependence because of their strong cultural affiliation and their part in incremental institutional evolution. This is an important point that we will pursue in the next section.

Then North (1990: 137–138) asks "How does one reverse the increasing returns characteristics of a particular institutional matrix?". The answer justifies the crucial role of the polity in implementing such policies that would change the incentives of action by changing the relative prices and hence, the perceptions, norms, and ideologies of groups that are willing to accept radical changes. In short, North's (1990: 112) model attempts to understand both institutional persistence and institutional change in a framework characterized by an established incentive context that determines action in the face of incomplete information, subjective apprehension of reality, and positive transaction costs. Then, the key to the future course of an economy is the ability or inability of incremental change which is derived from the maximizing behavior of organizations in their attempt to overcome the increasing returns characteristics of existing institutions in decreasing transaction costs. Since the viability of existing organizations in a given society hinges on the institutional matrix that prescribes the incentives of action then, institutional change is necessarily incremental and path-dependent. Revolutionary change is the exception rather than the rule since only incremental change is compatible with the survival of incumbent institutions. On top of that, formal rules derive their legitimacy from informal norms which alter only gradually through time. In addition, informal constraints, being cultural constraints that take the form of customs and traditions, are, to some degree, immune to top-down policies. Therefore, a revolutionary change which possesses the property of abrupt rupture with the previous institutional structure will find its pace retarded by the slow change of informal norms. On the other hand, institutional change cannot diverge from the type of knowledge favored by the existing institutional matrix. Having said that, it is essential to underline that the crucial variable in the development of economies is the expanding stock of knowledge that they accumulate along with the ability of individuals and organizations to learn from their experience (North 1990: 6; 1994; 1995: 18–20). Nevertheless, a reversal of path-dependence is possible and can occur from unintended consequences of chosen actions, external factors but mainly by purposeful action of the polity for radical change as this is supported by the groups of constituents that favor such change (North 1990: 138). On the other hand, the nature of the polity as an agent that promotes long-run developmental goals and not short-run electoral purposes is important. This is translated in North's (1990: 48,138) conception of the state as an agent supported by and supporting these social groups that are prone to change as this is reflected in the altering of the pay-off matrix they face.

North and Shirley (2008: 288–291) and North (1991) indicate the crucial effect that political institutions have on financial institutions and their stability since the former guarantee the property rights of private agents. Their concern is financial development in the sense of capital market development. Hence, they emphasize both the accountability of different political agents to different social groups and the importance of securing property rights against the government's ability to abuse its power in order to encroach private property rights on assets. Financial development requires both a government that has the ability to enforce contracts and at the same time imposes limits on its discretion. Impersonal exchange requires impersonal rules that would restrain both the government, which resorts to the capital market to issue its debt, and private organizations. Historically, the solution to this problem has been given by the development of parliamentary democracy, the separation of powers in the state, and the government's credible commitment to protect property rights which ultimately should reduce transaction costs. This implies that government action in shaping and respecting an appropriate institutional framework is necessary. On the other hand, financial development, as a form of institutional development, is the offspring of incremental change. North and Shirley (2008: 293–295) argue that an indication of imminent institutional change is the lack of congruence between political and economic institutions, but the direction of change is not predetermined. According to North (1990: 101, 112) reversals of established paths start from above, from an initiative of the political actors but change is incremental and depends on the bargaining power of different social groups and the historical past that sways current perceptions and decisions. Moreover, North (1991) stresses the particular importance of political organizations in countering the increasing returns generated by path-dependent institutions. Therefore, breaking the path-dependence in an underdeveloped economy or just altering its growth path requires both political initiatives at the high level and institutional incremental change in everyday economic transactions. The argument expounded in this book is that such incremental institutional change should be supported by the operation of development banks, along with other factors, and this should not be disregarded when assessing the contribution of these institutions to economic development and reform. In a sense, this is an argument about the relationship of political and economic institutions in institutional and economic development that belongs to the research agenda of North and Shirley (2008: 295) however, without necessarily agreeing with their conclusions.

A quite different but pertinent problem is how well the political process responds to the demand for institutional change. A Transaction Costs approach that stresses the importance of such costs in political markets also underscores their inefficiency. Indeed, how one can measure the object of political transactions which is in fact "promises for votes"? Furthermore, the rational choice model of the new political economy is not capable of explaining the choices that dictate the long-run path of economies and societies and their impact on growth. Instead of emphasizing rational choice models, it is worth the effort to examine the predominant ideologies in specific societies and their conditioning of decisions (North 1995: 23). Furthermore, the initiative for change should come from governments or rival small elite groups rather than from a polity's constituents due to the free-rider problem namely, the costs that agents have to incur to dispute a status quo or their inability to act as conscious purposeful large groups (North 1981: 31–32). On the other hand, the stability of political institutions is important for successful economic change, and this depends on the support provided to them by social organizations, on the norms that can legitimize the new rules put forward by political institutions, and on how responsive institutions and systems of beliefs are on political calls for change (North 1994). Therefore, for North the top-down political initiative for change is important but the bottom-up support of this initiative is crucial. This is the reason why he stresses "adaptive efficiency" (North 1990: 80–81; 1994) to changing conditions which appears to be a property formed by some societies in a long-lasted process as historical time unfolds. Adaptive efficiency relates to problem-solving and the ability of a society to learn from its experience, innovate, and assume risk as it develops through time.

Summing up the above analysis, we can think of incremental institutional change as the offspring of interaction between the institutional framework of a society on the one hand, and the purposeful action of agents given their perceptions and beliefs, or of "organizations as behavioral entities in their own right" on the other hand (North 1990: 73; 2005: viii, 26, 59). In this theoretical framework, development banks can be conceived as purposeful entities/organizations whose dynamic nature and transformation defines them as reflections of the financial system's development between two financial regimes: repression and liberalization. However, government policies are crucial in this context, as they are the ones that have an impact on the long-term viability of financial institutions (North and Shirley 2008: 288) by setting out the matrix of motives and constraints within which development banks operate.

5.3 Ideology, Cognition, and Beliefs: D. North's Emphasis on Individual Perceptions

Institutional change is important for the study of economic and financial development since it implies the study of economic and social dynamics which are intimately related to history. This is the point of view of this book which is congruent with North's approach to economic change. North (1994) conceives economic change from two perspectives: (1) In terms of the pace of change which depends on how quickly organizations and their members learn. (2) In terms of the direction of economic change which hinges on how people perceive the pay-offs they expect to gain if they possess different types of knowledge. The second point is crucial because it is not just that the specific institutional structure recompenses a specific behavior attached to the acquired knowledge but it is that agents perceive that it does so according to their mental models. In other words, it is not just that institutions matter, but "ideas matter" (Denzau and North 1994) as well. Most importantly, for North (2005: viii, 38) the evolutionary change in human history differs substantially from Darwinian evolution in the sense that humans are purposeful conscious creatures and they are guided in their actions by intentions that are conditioned by their perceptions and beliefs. Their ultimate intention is to reduce the uncertainty that surrounds their action. Therefore, the selection mechanism that governs their evolution includes their choices.

North (1994) defines his approach to economic history and the problem of economic change as an "institutional/cognitive approach". In this sense, a crucial variable in North's schema of institutional change is the way individuals, as members of organizations, perceive their environment and direct their actions. Individual perceptions are the major determinant of the choices made and a source of path-dependence. Therefore, along with incumbent organizations that block institutional change so that they can survive, the beliefs that support a particular institutional structure also resist fundamental changes and contribute to path-dependence (North 2005: 77). In turn, perceptions are related to ways of interpretation of the acquired information namely, of "mental constructs". After all, North (1995: 20, 24–25) himself distinguishes his approach from the game theoretic one exactly because of his focus on cognition issues as an alternative to the standard rational choice theory and calls for a research agenda that will explore the interrelationship between culture, beliefs, mental models and institutions.

Furthermore, North (1994) criticizes the neoclassical rationality assumptions and their disregard for institutions. He considers his approach as a "modification of neoclassical theory" in which he combines the neoclassical precepts of scarcity and competition with a modified rationality assumption and the inclusion of time as support of a learning process. Since the information that individuals receive is necessarily incomplete and since they process this information using their subjective models, the latter cannot self-adjust away from fallacious conceptions by the information feedback (North 1990: 16). However, North (2005: 24) seems more determined to distinguish himself from neoclassical precepts to the degree that he considers rational choice as necessarily socially and institutionally embedded. On top of these remarks, one should be aware of the fact that humans have to deal with a world characterized by extreme complexity and Knightian fundamental uncertainty which is not open to probabilistic calculations. Throughout its history, the human being has managed to reduce the uncertainty emanating from its natural environment but at the expense of increasing the complexity of the human environment. The result is a non-ergodic world whose underlying structure is constantly modified, making its comprehension more difficult and open to non-rational interpretations (North 2005: 16; Denzau and North 1994). This observation extends the argument about the importance of institutions to the significance of individuals' mental models and perceptions for shaping these institutions.

Understanding the formation and functioning of mental models, which are "...the internal representations that individual cognitive systems create to interpret the environment..." (Denzau and North 1994: 4) is central to comprehending how decisions are made in conditions of profound uncertainty. North (1994) cites an enlightening paragraph by Simon (1986: S211) who claims that if human knowledge and human ability to make complex calculations and processing is limited then reality and its perception are two separate things. Therefore, a theory of how people make decisions should not confine itself only to the appropriate mode of reasoning but should also heed the way a decision maker subjectively perceives the relevant problem, "his or her frame". Based on these insights North (1994) attempts to unfold the process of learning as the formulation of a structure of interpretation of our world based on our experience of it. The world we have in front of us has both natural and cultural characteristics that inform our categorization of phenomena to achieve their perception or, in other words, to form our mental models which attach our interpretation to specific objectives and goals of action. However, continuous experience feeds back to this learning process and contributes to the evolution of our mental models. Learning, in this context, implies both confirmation of existing classifications in our mind and/or their revision.

North (1994) points out that the human process of learning is accomplished through a "representational redescription" where the human mind continuously reorders its mental models in such levels of abstraction so as to be able to use them in different situations. The important point here that distinguishes North's approach from the neoclassical rational model is that this process of "representational redescription" is, according to North, the origin of both human creativity and the ideological beliefs that condition human decisions. Denzau and North (1994) seem to approach the Original Institutional Economics preference for inductive reasoning as opposed to the deductive one. Indeed, Denzau and North (1994) argue that in situations where information is limited and complexity abounds, deductive rational reasoning is not the appropriate procedure to follow. Instead, an inductive method is more fruitful according to which agents form internal mental models to interpret the environment and learn from it in order to shape their decisions even if they are not able to know the entire sets of alternative actions and their consequences. To use a philosophical term, North (2005: 2) seems to agree with some kind of agnosticism when he admits that we may never be able to know the "reality" we deal with but nevertheless we can form beliefs, no matter how imperfect they might be, about it and derive from these beliefs both positive and normative theories. Moreover, the similarities with the methodology of Original Institutional Economists continue as North (2005: 27, 31) defends "pattern matching" as a mental process in which we try to find similarities between our experiences and make use of analogy to derive generalizations that are culturally embedded. Eventually, patterns are identified through a trial-and-error inductive process.

Of course, each person has their own perceptions about the external environment which may not concur with the perceptions and interpretations of a different individual. This is the canonical case. However, the common cultural conditioning of a group of individuals provides the basis for their similar—not identical—mental models. This is the effect of cultural learning on individual perception and action (Denzau and North 1994). Eventually, learning does not have only a synchronous cross-sectional dimension concerning the sharing of beliefs among the members of the same group or society. Learning also has an intertemporal dimension as cultural learning or the transfer of acquired knowledge and interpretations between generations which often take the form of myths and dogmas of various kinds. The latter constitute belief structures that underpin formal and informal constraints of behavior. In this way, Denzau and North (1994) establish a crucial link between the mental models as perceptions of the world and institutions as the realization in the action of these perceptions that shape the external environment.

Learning is necessary for organizations to survive in a competitive environment characterized by ubiquitous scarcity (North 1994). It seems that there is a virtuous or vicious circle here which requires further exploration. Indeed, North (1995: 17) insists that different cultural heritages lead to different interpretations of the same information and hence, to different reactions. In addition, the information they get from the impact of their choices is again interpreted imperfectly, and hence, it cannot lead by itself to a self-correction of choices and actions to an optimum outcome which is the same for all economies. North is right to underscore that there is also a kind of mental or cultural path-dependence which is probably the ultimate source of economic path-dependence. Then the key to reversing the course of an economy trapped in underdevelopment is to resolve this fundamental issue of mental and cultural path-dependence.

"Culture provides a language-based conceptual framework for encoding and interpreting the information that the senses are presenting to the brain" (North 1990: 37). In other words, culture provides the framework of learning in the sense of "categories and priors" while the shared mental models equip individuals with a language and a group of concepts that facilitate communication among them and provides the basis for the convergence of their individual mental models (Denzau and North 1994). Hence, culture is important in North's argument as a conditioning factor that interacts with problem-solving as a daily activity of economic agents along with their ability to learn in a continuous interplay with their environment (North 1995: 17–18, 24). However, the specific common culture and learning experience of a group of individuals implies that they share common or congruent mental models which also reflect common ideologies and institutions that may differ from those of other groups of individuals with completely different cultural inheritances and experiences. Moreover, the imperfect information feedback from these experiences, as explained above, is not able to bring these differing learning processes and cultural effects together toward some equilibrium that would reflect a common representation of reality (Denzau and North 1994). This is an important point that highlights North's emphasis on the importance of cultural learning for institution building, and especially for the success of the operation of institutions or the effects of transplanting institutions in different cultural environments. Besides, North (2005: 159) puts it quite bluntly: "…the institutions that have emerged in the Western world, …, do not have to be faithfully copied in developing countries. The key is the incentive structure that is created, not the slavish imitation of western institutions". This is an implication of his theory to which the international organizations of the Washington Consensus should have paid more attention.

In addition, culture is related to historical time to the degree that the latter does not refer only to contemporaneous experiences that inform agents' mental models but also the "cumulative experience" that has been acquired by previous generations and transmitted to present-day decision-makers through culture. Hence, culture refers to an accumulated stock of knowledge that includes the crystallization of centuries of experience in language, technology, and practices and expresses itself in inherited rules, norms, and beliefs. The cultural context of human action consists of a grid of physical and human capital. The first pertains to the accumulated techniques and material instruments while the latter refers to stored knowledge and institutions. Culture is a central concept for North because it supplies the natural vehicle for path-dependence. This is because learning is not unconditional. On the contrary, our past "collective learning" or culture conditions our present learning (North 1994, 2005: 6, 48–49). The problem for North (1994) is that such conditioning means that a society may not be able or well-prepared to cope with new challenges beyond the scope of the established belief systems. In this context, the question is to provide the incentives for acquiring the suitable type of knowledge that hinges not only on perceived monetary rates of return but also on the degree of social forbearance to human creativity and innovation.

How do ideologies relate to the learning process and the mental models of individuals? In the face of uncertainty and complexity and under the urge of action human beings need to form explanations about the world around them. Hence, even when a scientific explanation is not available because of information limitations, action may be guided by myths, dogmas, religions, or other belief systems. This is not necessarily a bad thing to the degree that it helps the human species to survive in the long process of evolution (Denzau and North 1994). Furthermore, if mental models have a subjective element that can be identified with individuals as the locus of such models, ideologies have necessarily a collective connotation. Therefore, North (1990: 111) argues that ideologies form the subjective ways by which we perceive and understand the world around us and North (1994) defines ideologies as the "shared frameworks of mental models" which refer to groups of individuals. As shared mental models, ideologies represent a shared, by the members of the particular group, interpretation of real phenomena. However, ideologies also include an element of vision on how to reshape the social environment around us. In other words, ideologies represent both interpretations of the real world and suggestions on how to handle or change it (Denzau and North 1994). However, ideas need to transform themselves into action in order to make a difference by changing the surrounding environment. In this respect, ideologies with their visionary normative element aim at furnishing positive mental models that guide action (Denzau and North 1994). Yet, to the degree that ideologies shape agents' actions, these agents have to pay the price defined by the relevant institutional framework if they want to act according to their own ideas (North 1990: 111). In this respect, the degree to which ideology, as a motive for action, will succeed in transcending the free-rider problem, as North (1981: 32) hoped would do, is an open issue. On the other hand, North (2005: 56, 100) is more optimistic about the efficiency of political processes than he was in his past writings as far as behavior in political markets reflects "moral and ethical norms". Such norms might seem to be "non-rational" but they express ideological beliefs that make political markets more effective in a non-ergodic world surrounded by uncertainty. The necessary condition for such effectiveness is the existence of democratic procedures that introduce a process of trial and error with no predetermined end. The successful metamorphosis of the Western world, as opposed to less developed countries, concerning the institutions and beliefs that can deal with human environment uncertainties instead of physical environment uncertainties is a case in point.

Furthermore, ideologies and perceptions are subject to change to the degree that agents' activity enriches their experience, though the latter is conditioned by the mental models that are culturally endorsed. But "fundamental changes in relative prices" will change ideas and informal norms in an incremental and slow process (North 1990: 138). Denzau and North (1994) provide a more detailed exposition of this process of change. Changes in mental models include both a slow process of incremental change that is long-lasting along with radical changes in a short period of time. In the process of gradual change mental models are enhanced with new meanings and the evolution of old ones which generate new concepts, and modify the "climate of opinion" in a society and inform its ideas. Then an ideology crisis occurs either because of the conflict between the evolving climate of opinion and the guardians of the old ideological interpretations or because of inconsistencies and disharmonies in the old ideological paradigm. Finally, in a more structural spirit, North (2005: 126) summarizes an outline of a dynamic theory where institutional change depends on revisions of beliefs held by the entrepreneurs of organizations that act in order to change their environment. However, the impact of this initial perturbation will be a modified set of opportunity costs for organizations that act as substitutes or complements of the abovementioned organizations. The latter adds to the complexity of the whole process and to the difficulty of deciphering the final results of the initial change in beliefs. Therefore, more information on how interconnected organizations behave in structural terms is needed in order to predict the effects of particular policies.

If less developed economies suffer from an institutional matrix that does not incentivize productive activities because of vested interests combined with underdeveloped democracies then successful institutional policies should transcend these hurdles through three courses of action: (1) Support the new formal rules with complementary informal norms. (2) Support consensual democratic regimes instead of authoritarian ones so as for institutional change to have a long-term impact. (3) Direct external aid to the gradual development of skills of the indigenous population while at the same time respecting the cultural heritage of this population. The difficulty is that all of these policies take time to generate their results (North 2005: 159–160). However, the most important conclusion derived from this list is that without aiming at the support of informal norms, which are closely related to the way people habitually think and behave, institutional change may end up a disaster rather than a miracle cure for the developing world.

5.4 Looking Deeper in the Individual: Instincts and Habit Formation in T. Veblen

In the previous sections of this chapter, we examined the way North approaches the conundrums of institutional building and change and how he ended up with an "institutional/cognitive" model (North 1994) which emphasizes the role of ideology, bargaining power of social groups and individual perception in the process of incremental change and path-dependence. It is undeniable that North took a major step forward from the neoclassical conception of rationality when he emphasized the institutional embeddedness of individual perception in the context of a non-ergodic world, as we have mentioned in the previous sections. However, our impression is that North sets out the critical issues without being able to give those comprehensive answers that a theory of economic and institutional development requires because he remains trapped in his "modification of neoclassical theory" (North 1994). In this observation, we follow a growing strand of literature that assesses North's work and its contribution to contemporary institutional thinking.

Zouboulakis (2005) provides an account of radical critics of North's view of rationality and his methodological assumptions such as those of Milonakis and Fine (2007),[2] Fine and Milonakis (2003), and Ankarloo (2002). This literature asserts that despite subsequent North's emphasis on power and ideology, his view of rationality remains neoclassical as far as agents optimize with respect to relative prices. Furthermore, North falls into a "universalistic" fallacy in which incentives that normally characterize modern industrialized economies are used to explain behavior in different historical periods. This mode of thinking generates a form of ahistoricism despite North's emphasis on culture and historical specificity in his later writings. Zouboulakis (2005) is skeptical about the above sharp criticism of North's work, especially the one relating to the role of culture, ideology, and the interaction between the individuals and their social environment. However, he admits that North is not always able to escape the trap of universalism in favor of historical specificity while the role of power and that of conflict between social groups has not been adequately developed in North's writings. Furthermore, Fine and Milonakis (2003) insist that North's approach is ultimately founded on an individual rational choice model since institutions and ideology act rather as constraints on a maximization problem processed by the individual. On the other hand, according to Milonakis and Fine (2007), North considers power and conflict in an individualistic bargaining form since collectives are conceived by North as sums of rational individuals and history is the product of individuals either as rulers or as entrepreneurs. Finally, Ankarloo (2002)

[2] Zouboulakis (2005) refers to a previous version of the paper later published as Milonakis and Fine (2007).

confirms our impression that North straddles neoclassical economics and a more realistic approach with social and cultural connotations, and the way he chooses to resolve this tension is by reversing the relationship between history and our current perception of the world. It is not history that informs our understanding of modern societies but rather our current ideas form our perception of the past. Rutherford (1995) agrees with the foregoing debate that North, despite the development of his ideas from the mid-1970s to the mid-1990s, fails to provide a comprehensive theory of ideology while his treatment of social norms contradicts his insistence on individual maximization guided by selfishness. On the other hand, Groenewegen et al. (1995) recognize in North's later contributions a kind of individualism that they call "institutional individualism" or "structural individualism". The individual remains a cost-benefits calculator constrained by the existing institutions but at the same time, it is able to change the institutional edifice. Ideology and culture play a role in this process but most importantly historical specificity takes the form of path-dependence. Another strand of literature points out that North engages in a deductive use of economic theory on particular historical issues rather than employing a historical inductive approach in which theory is the outcome of observation and classification of historical evolution. Furthermore, his departure from the orthodoxy implied by the focus on power, ideology, and cognition is left incomplete because of his ambivalent treatment of history and the neoclassical remnants in his thought such as the role of relative prices, self-interest, and the question of efficiency of organizations. Notably, North places the change in relative prices at the beginning as a cause, not at the end as the outcome of the causality process in institutional change. Eventually, North provides us with scattered components of a theory instead of a coherent integrated theory (Vandenberg 2002; Dugger 1995). Finally, Von Staden and Bruce (2015) emphasize the "sociocognitive turn" of the later works of North since behind culture, learning as a patterned way of reasoning, the process of interpretation, and the formation of beliefs, they recognize the importance of intentionality and the reduction of the interaction between social structure and individual agency to a mental process. Yet, North's theoretical construction leaves beliefs ultimately unfounded since it overlooks the role of human predispositions and proclivities.

Therefore, the question posed in the second half of this chapter is whether Veblen's ideas about instincts and habit formation provide a more comprehensive approach than that of North to the biological and social-cognitive foundations of human behavior and institutional transformation. McCormick (2006: 1–5) delineates the difference between Veblen on the one hand and neoclassical and Marxian economics on the other, concerning human nature and behavior. Marxian economics recognizes the effect of the social environment on the way people perceive the world as opposed to the timeless utility-maximizing framework of neoclassical economics. It is, in a sense, the antithesis between nurture which can modify human behavior, and a passive, timeless "natural" conceptualization of human nature in neoclassical economics. Veblen (1919 [2016]: 59–60) provides in effect a synthesis of the above views since for him human behavior is the outcome of both natural and social determinants. Nature supplies humans with a substratum called instincts which are in fact some form of tendencies that govern behavior. On the other hand, human beings, as of their birth, are embedded into social groups which are bearers of particular habits of thought and conventions. These habits of thought and conventions are institutions that determine individual behavior as far as individuals are engaged in a learning process which may be called nurture.

We consider Veblen's focus on both natural and social forces that shape individual behavior as an understanding of human nature both in its constraints and in its possibilities. It is certainly a rejection of static neoclassical views by Veblen since he acknowledges the dynamic character of institutions as social constructs and their interaction with individual characteristics. However, it is also an advancement with respect to the Marxian view which may overemphasize nurture over natural constraints. The important point here, according to McCormick (2006: 6–8) is that instincts do not represent a kind of "reflexive actions that involve no thought". "Instincts" are in fact "propensities of human nature" (Veblen 1914 [2020]: 2–3) that guide behavior and provide the basic goals to which we direct our activity. But we need to employ a conscious process of reasoning to attain these goals. Human behavior is subject to the propensities of human nature which range from group-regarding to self-regarding ones. Hence, there is an interaction and, at the same time, an internal conflict within every human being between social awareness and selfishness. However, instincts are not immune to change though their evolution is slow and cannot account for economic and social change.

Therefore, we understand Veblenian instincts as the natural substratum of choice in the sense of a predisposition that directs decisions as an innate tendency. Moreover, it seems that the categorization of instincts by Veblen in group-regarding and self-regarding characterizes the inherent contradiction in every human being which is an individual consciousness that is necessarily socially embedded and conditioned. Indeed, the kinds of instincts associated with each of the above categories, as described by McCormick (2006: 8–17) are characteristic of the internal conflict that determines individual behavior. The instinct of parental bent indicates an interest in the future of humanity and the well-being of the generations to come while the instinct of workmanship relates to the advancement of the common good as far as an urge for creative and effective work contributes to the survival of human societies. However, creativity and survival here co-exist in the same way that satisfaction derived from socially useful work is possible and desirable. Finally, the instinct of idle curiosity is deeply rooted in human nature as the inherent want for knowledge. This curiosity is the source of scientific thinking which when combined with the instinct of workmanship becomes the origin of technological change and eventually, of institutional development. The above instincts are considered to be group-regarding while on the opposite side, there are self-regarding instincts such as self-preservation, self-aggrandizement, and predatory instincts. The instinct of self-preservation is antagonistic to that of parental bent in that our inherent tendency for survival may contradict our altruism or the care for our children. Self-aggrandizement also relates to an antagonistic perspective of the world where survival may mean that I need to have a higher status than others and I may need to achieve this even at the expense of the well-being of other members of my social group. Finally, the predatory instinct is even more assertive than the previous ones in imposing a selfish point of view since it is related to an urge to dominate others and show our superior status compared to them. In between these two major categories lies the instinct of emulation which is both the source of learning from others by emulating their behavior and of ranking them. At the bottom-line, emulation could be either socially beneficial or socially detrimental, depending on what kind of behavior someone imitates and why.

However, the Veblenian notion of instincts as propensities of behavior supplies the necessary basis on which habits of thought and beliefs are founded (Hodgson 2010). North, in his later writings, was looking for such a foundation of his system of beliefs in cognitive science but his approach lacked an explanation of differing individual behaviors that would emanate from individual characteristics per se. Ideology may explain the altruistic behavior of some people as opposed to the selfish behavior of other people but where does this ideological effect find correspondence in the way human individuals are biologically constructed? North (2005) alludes to the individual genetic architecture (Von Staden and Bruce 2015) but he lacks the much richer Veblenian theoretical construct of instincts, habits of thought, and beliefs, and hence, his sociocognitive turn is left incomplete. After all, the importance of instincts is highlighted by Barnett (2017) who points out the indispensable role of different kinds of instincts in providing a link between the biological-cognitive and the social-institutional determinants of human behavior in its complexity.

In the Veblenian tradition reasoning and choice depend both on biological and cultural factors namely, on instincts and habits respectively. Both instincts and habits are dispositions of behavior but instincts are biologically inherited while habits are culturally relayed to the individual. When an instinct is activated it can manifest as a reflex, an impulse, or an emotion. On the other hand, habits are the product of socialization namely, of learned behavior within social contexts. However, instincts are the foundation of habits and the latter are the foundation of reasoning and decision-making. First of all, there is an interaction between instincts and socialization since instincts as biological dispositions are the necessary biological apparatus that a human being needs in order to be able to participate in the socialization process. For example, a human being is born with the capacity of language which is necessary for communication with other human beings. In turn, the process of socialization and the particular cultural environment are important in triggering the manifestation of instincts. Language, for example, becomes over the course of time a cultural phenomenon. In addition, beliefs are dependent upon habits of thought since habits of thought provide the basis for interpretation of the world by framing our experience of it. The upshot of this convoluted framework is a more complex and realistic model of cognition and action which opposes the simple "beliefs first" model. The causality in the latter runs from beliefs to deliberation and then to action which, through the effect of experience, informs beliefs. The evolutionary model starts from instincts which affect habits and the latter impacts beliefs. Beliefs become the basis for deliberation and action but there is also interaction among all the above levels while action feeds back both to instincts (as a natural selection process) and to habits (as a cultural selection process). In other words, there is a "reconstitutive interaction" between individuals and institutions that transcends methodological individualism or methodological collectivism. In the interaction between individuals and structures, neither is reducible to the other. The above model does not refuse agents' intentionality, but it embeds it in an evolutionary framework. This happens because the process of "reconstitutive downward causation" through which institutions affect habits implies that the institutional structure does not affect directly the decisions of individuals but only the habits which are the basis for a change in agents' intentions. Hence, there is no direct influence of institutions on beliefs which means that individual agency or the ability of individuals to influence institutions is preserved despite their conditioning by these institutions (Hodgson 2010; Wrenn 2006; Hodgson 2002: 171; 2004).

In Veblenian thought the institutional structure is made up of formal laws and rules and informal ones which include customs, traditions, and habits of thought. Habits are the representation of behavior that is "common sense" in a social context. It is the behavior that makes sense to a group of people because this is the way they are used to behave when they act to achieve their goals which are dictated by their instincts as their predispositions. As Veblen (1899[2009]: 126) states "The situation of to-day shapes the institutions of tomorrow through a selective, coercive process, by acting upon men's habitual view of things, and so altering or fortifying a point of view or a mental attitude handed down from the past". Hence, people are shaped by habits which are both personal individual habits of behavior and also habits of group behavior which appear as conventions. These habits define the benchmark against which individual behavior and thinking are gauged and assessed. Finally, habits of thought that condition behavior are subject to learning through a socialization process but such a learning process is not a rational one. This kind of learning defines what is right and what is wrong for the different social groups we belong to, but segregating right from wrong is not the outcome of reasoning or the consequence of rational calculations. This is why the above-acquired habits are hard to change (McCormick 2006: 18–20).

North is talking about informal constraints and norms that change only gradually and are part of the cultural edifice of society. Veblen proposes a more encompassing notion of informal institutions by including the habits of thought in them. Moreover, habits of thought are endowed with a crucial role in the institutional structure as, by definition, become the connecting link between the individual and its social environment. Hence, if habits of thought are not necessarily the result of rational ways of thinking then, they also provide the basis for understanding how non-rational judgments about wrong and right, such as the religious ones which are founded on faith, are possible. But then habits of thought become also the basis for ideologies to develop as shared perceptions of the world and prescriptions about how to change it. In this respect, North's mental models attempt to acquire a meaning similar to that of Veblen's habits of thought. However, for North, as we have seen above, mental models are subject to continuous gradual modification along with short periods of abrupt change. On the contrary, for Veblen habits of thought are more difficult to change because they constitute a more fundamental and long-lasting process. In fact, North confuses the differing characteristics of instincts, habits, and beliefs when he uses the encompassing term "mental models". According to Wrenn (2006), habits and instincts are both part of mental models that an individual uses to interpret the world. When institutions impact habits of thought, they eventually sway an individual's mental models and cognition. Following the above Veblenian segregation among instincts, habits, and beliefs we consider habits of thought to have the same status as the mentality that characterizes the behavior of a group of people and which is more difficult to change, at least in a short period of time. On the other hand, we consider beliefs to be less difficult to revise both at the individual and at the group level. Ideology should embrace both habits of thought and beliefs and be identified with a value system that may have both a positive-progressive and a negative-regressive aspect in the sense of Bush (1987).

5.5 An Encompassing Approach to Institutional Formation and Change: Technology, Instincts, and Institutions

North's explanation of institutional change has at its center the individual who makes the decisions and optimizes. Veblen's theory, on the other hand, has a rather holistic focus. It is not so much whether culture or ideology appears in someone's writings but where the emphasis is given, or which is the governing principle of their thought. Rutherford (1995), making a comparison between New Institutional Economics and Original Institutional Economics, identifies methodological individualism and modified rational choice along with efficiency and economizing as the guiding principles in New Institutional Economics. On the contrary, Original Institutional Economics follow a holistic approach in which individual behavior is culturally conditioned, and social and political factors such as ideology and power are at the forefront of explanation. We do not think that North (2005) evades this categorization despite the much greater weight he assigns to ideology and culture. In his work, the individual remains at the center of the analysis, but in this case, it is the mind of the individual out of which reasoning about institutions and institutional change unfolds as Von Staden and Bruce (2015) point out. Emphasizing individual cognition may be useful if it is placed in the right context. The right context is the interplay of forces at the evolving holistic level that frame individual perception and action. Veblen is much more clear in this respect.

Evolution in societies emerges through the interaction of different levels that pertain to instincts, habits, and institutions. The first level refers to instincts that are divided into favorable for social well-being (workmanship, parental bent, and idle curiosity) and those that are detrimental to community life (predatory instinct and self-regarding ones). The predatory instinct and the instinct of workmanship are in tension between them at this level since the first elevates ceremonial habits of thought which praise domination and segregation on the basis of status, wealth, and power while the latter encourages scientific thinking and productive use of economic resources for the benefit of social well-being. At the second level of the evolutionary process, there exist habits of thought and action that are culturally determined and interact with instincts. Finally, at the last level, there are institutions that are based on habits (Baranes and Bucher 2022; Chavance 2009: 12). Crucial in the above interrelationship is the role of technology and its impact on institutional change or the so-called "Veblenian dichotomy" as this is usually referred to. If technology is identified with a dynamic drive to change, then institutions in their ceremonial aspect represent the static or conservative part of the culture (Lawson 2003). Institutions are characterized by inertia as they withstand change given slowly adapted instincts and habits (Chavance 2009: 14). Institutions are in fact a combination of useful and useless functions. We wear clothes to keep our bodies warm in the cold but, at the same time, we wear clothes that are "trendy" according to the social conventions of the era. A function is useful when it provides the solution to a problem, but it is useless when it serves a ceremonial purpose (McCormick 2006: 24–25). On the other hand, technological change depends both on instincts and on institutions. The instinct of idle curiosity becomes the source of new scientific knowledge but the direction of technological change hinges also on other instincts and whether group-regarding or self-regarding instincts dominate (McCormick 2006: 37–38). However, Veblen's preference for a holistic rather than individualistic approach manifests itself in his insistence that individuals express their idle curiosity as part of a community in which knowledge is specialized and each one of them possesses only a small part of it. Hence, technological change is a community matter to the degree that the larger the technological community, the greater the specialization will be which will also affect the rate of technological change (McCormick 2006: 35–36). After all, "…each move so made is necessarily made by individuals immersed in the community…, since all life is necessarily group life" (Veblen 1914[2020]: 103–104, also reported in McCormick 2006: 35).

Technological change also depends on institutions in various ways. First, the dominant habits of thought that characterize the institutional structure and are related to the controlling interests in a society, impact the type of technology that will advance. "Good" or "bad" technologies are judged in this context and according to the prevailing habits of thought be it, for example, those of business and profitability or those of ethics and religion or some combination of them (McCormick 2006: 38–39). Veblen introduces at this point a value judgment into technological change to the degree that "good" or "bad" depends on the prevailing habits of thought that are part of the dominant ideology. This is important because it implies that the success of economic development policies, to the degree that economic change is related to technological change, hinges on dominant ideological perceptions and vested interests of social groups that promote such ideological interpretations. Second, and in relation to the previous observation, dominant habits of thought in the realm of science take the form of "systems of knowledge" and of particular "schools of thought" that prevail and provide the conventional framework within which every new knowledge is assessed (McCormick 2006: 39–40). Veblen recognizes the existence of an adaptive form of rationality since intentional individuals may adjust their habits if circumstances change, but the prevalent ideology is not challenged because it provides the framework within which modes of thought should be ascribed. A change in ideology can come about only if such change is dictated by a modification "in the 'discipline' of life" (Rutherford 1995).

A major difference between mainstream economics and Original Institutional Economics is their stance toward values. Mainstream economics looks for "objective" positive knowledge that will provide normative-free interpretations of the world. On the contrary, Original

Institutionalists believe that values imbue the institutional edifice of the economy and hence, institutional change cannot be examined independently of them. Values are indeed normative in essence, but it is also true that any interpretation involves some kind of judgment. Values are the "standards of judgment" and as such they "correlate behavior". Therefore, institutional change implies "a change in the value structure of the institution" (Bush 1987: 1077–1078). Since values are part of the ideological scaffold of a society and in this way, they affect individual perceptions, we are tempted to conclude that institutional change is reducible to a change in value structures. Such an assertion does not mean that a modification in the value structure of an economy and society is sufficient for institutional change, but that the former is necessary for the latter to happen. In this sense, distinguishing between ceremonial and instrumental values makes possible an outline of the possible directions of institutional change. If value judgments concern distinctions that reproduce the dominance of one social class or group over another which are endorsed by traditional modes of thinking and ideological conceptions, then these judgments are related to ceremonial values. If, on the other hand, judgments pertain to a process of problem-solving for the benefit of the community, they are associated with instrumental values. It is instrumental values that are correlated with a change in the habits of thought that emanates from technological change. As new technology comes forth, instrumental values change in order to underpin the new habits of thought that are necessary to support the adoption of technological innovation. However, some degree of ceremonial dominance may be necessary in order to embed instrumental behavior within a culture. Such ceremonial dominance is the other aspect of ideology that is needed in order to warrant instrumental behavior in a community and stimulate its adoption. Eventually, since different cultures, and their ceremonial values, have different degrees of tolerance toward technological change, the degree or "index of ceremonial dominance" in a society is important for deciphering the direction of institutional change because it reflects the tolerance or "permissiveness" of this society toward technological change. Hence, if a change in the value structure takes the form of a change in the index of ceremonial dominance, then, only cases where that index falls and instrumental values displace ceremonial ones, are cases of progressive change (Bush 1987: 1085–1086). There are two phases in this process of institutional change. The first pertains to "ceremonial encapsulation" when new instrumental patterns of behavior are captivated by the ceremonial framework. Then, in the second phase, the new instrumental methods and values as they become widely diffused corrode the ceremonial framework and bring about progressive change (Baranes and Bucher 2022; Bush 1987: 1093, 1102). Eventually, democracy is the most appropriate environment for progressive change because it makes experimentation possible and because a long-lasting change is only feasible if behavior is not subject to radical modification given its correlation with other aspects of life in a given culture (Bush 1987). The importance of democracy for institutional change and economic development emanates also from the interaction between the bargaining power of different social groups and the dominance of mental models and ideas in a particular historical period and society. The more powerful social group can impose their preferred mental models and ideas which implies a framing of perceptions to the degree that these models guide the approval or disapproval of a given society for specific ideas and policies. In this respect, only democratic deliberation can contribute to changing the balance of power relationship and support a change of the institutional regime because it reduces the various costs of embarking on such a change. In the end, institutional change hinges not only on mental models but also on power (Altman 2023).

Therefore, in the interaction between technology and institutions, technological change is the one that provides the underlying dynamic force for change through the interplay between the instincts of workmanship and idle curiosity (Chavance 2009: 12; McCormick 2006: 40–41). New technologies are usually in conflict with old institutional arrangements which need to change and/or bring about the creation of new institutional arrangements that fit their purpose. In this way, technological change becomes a catalyst for widespread social reform which crucially takes the form of altered habits of thought and action. However, this is a slow process of change (McCormick 2006: 42–45). More importantly, the interaction between technology and institutions determines the direction of change as new and traditional modes of thinking clash. Technology brings with it a deepening of cause-and-effect mode of thinking. The process of learning how to use the new technology trains the mind to think in terms of causal reasoning. In other words, people disregard ceremonial aspects of life in favor of efficiency to the degree that a cause-and-effect way of thinking challenges old habits and puts forward institutional change (McCormick 2006: 46). Veblen (1904[2016]: 207–208) stresses that "...the mechanically employed classes, trained to matter-of-fact habits of thought, show a notable lack of spontaneity in the construction of new myths or conventions as well as in the reconstruction of the old". After all, "The change is always in the last resort a change in habits of thought" (Veblen (1919[2016]: 60). Hence, for Veblen, economic development is not just a case of capital accumulation or even of human capital accumulation. It is not mainly a matter of "accumulation" but rather a matter of changing habits of thought which will support a widespread institutional change. In this sense, economic development is not a matter of institutional development as this is usually perceived in the form of transplanting institutions from developed to developing economies North (2005: 159) agreed with this observation but he focused his objection to copying institutions from the western world to developing countries on the inability to build an adequate incentive structure in these economies. The problem in Veblenian terms is deeper than that since it implies the change in habits of thought, or mentalities as we have commented above which is a long and difficult process. Furthermore, institutions survive because "vested interests" that benefit from them resist their change and because of the sanctions imposed on those that violate the accepted behavioral patterns. However, the most important means of preserving an institution in the long run is for the economic and social agents to internalize them as being the correct way to behave. Therefore, institutions are necessarily slow to change in order to maintain social stability and their change takes place in small portions. When Veblen talks about institutions, he has mainly in mind the habits of thought in a society which, even in an era of revolution do not change easily (McCormick 2006: 25–27).

Institutional change for Veblen is a complex and multifactor process that may or may not result in progress since social evolution is unpredictable and open to various possibilities. In this sense, institutional change is an emergent outcome of the interplay among instincts, technology, and institutions where "emergence" is a salient feature of open systems. The process of cumulative causation implies an evolution without teleology. Cumulative causation has both a sequential and a recursive element. It is sequential in the sense of the irreversibility of time and successive transmutations of a cumulative nature. It is recursive because it implies both a relationship from cause to effect and feedback from the latter to the former. In this sense, institutions are both the object and the subject of an evolutionary selection and adaptation conditioned by the interaction between these institutions and individual action (Chavance 2009: 11, 15; Brette 2003). The process of cumulative causation indicates that every level of institutional evolution carries with it the sway of the past. In this way past institutions shape current behavior and provide incentives that may lead to either productive or predatory activity. Eventually, habits of thought and incentives affect the process of learning and the acquisition of that knowledge which will eventually lead to technological and institutional change (Rutherford 1995). Institutions may change because an exogenous shock hit the economy such as a war or a significant change in the climate for example. However, the most important source of institutional change is the endogenous process of interaction among instincts, technology, and institutions described above. The prevailing institutional structure dictates which type of instincts will dominate in a particular society, either the self-regarding or the group-regarding ones. In addition, this institutional structure as a system of habits of thought which makes up the culture of society generates the "central conventions". These "central conventions" reflect the dominant institutions of the era and are the basis for the assessment of other institutions in order to modify those institutions that deviate from dominant habits of thought. In this context, the predominance of "imbecilic" institutions is possible to the degree that these institutions service the interests of some social groups at the expense of others. In any case, technological change, which urges the change of old habits of thought and provokes social change, is not necessarily a promise for progress because of the complex and unpredictable interaction between technology, instincts and institutions that drive institutional change and its direction (Poirot 2008; McCormick 2006: 47–52).

5.6 Institutional Change and Development Banks as Organizations

At the bottom-line institutional change is about the interaction between individuals and structures. Hodgson (2000) clarifies this relationship by distinguishing between Ayres's cultural determinism and Veblen-Commons view. The priority of structure over the individual disregards the role of individual perception and action. On the other hand, both Veblen and Commons acknowledged the interaction between the social structure and individual beliefs and experiences. Hence, a reconstitutive downward causation process implies that individuals evolve through learning which takes place in specific social contexts. But for an individual "...The institution in which he finds himself is both the cause and effect of his beliefs..." (Commons 1899[1965]: 6–8, reported in Hodgson 2000:

326). In addition, "The growth and mutations of the institutional fabric are an outcome of the conduct of the individual members of the group, since it is out of the experience of the individuals, through the habituation of individuals, that institutions arise..." (Veblen 1919[2016]: 193, reported in Hodgson 2000: 326).

Therefore, the conclusion that can be derived from the previous discussion is that North's emphasis on individual intentionality, incentive structures, and eventually, individual perception in cultural contexts is right but incomplete. It lacks a comprehensive understanding of the complex interaction between technological innovation and institutional change and their foundation on an integrated approach to human nature that encompasses both its biological and social-cultural drivers. More importantly, the Veblenian notion of the habits of thought which is missing from North provides the centerpiece around which institutional change revolves since it can transcend the mainstream dogmatic descriptions of rational choice and represents the bridge between the biological property of instincts and the socially conditioned deliberation and reasoning process. The theory of institutional change in the Veblenian tradition that we examined in this chapter along with Commons's theory of reform that we described in the previous chapter provide a much more encompassing approach to reform and institutional change in financial markets than that provided by North, although particular remarks of the latter are useful in specific contexts, or they are able to take their full meaning only under the Original Institutionalist framework.

The interaction between the institutional structure and individuals that we examined in this chapter is mediated through the collectives, groups, and organizations in which individuals participate as members. Development banks are such kinds of organizations that participated and continue to take part in different degrees in institutional change both as instruments of finance for economic development and as protagonists of institutional development in the context of alternative financial regimes. Development banks, as our account of their evolution in the history and theory of economic development and development finance has shown, have been the reflection of financial reform and change in financial regimes through a process of financial development in which these banks themselves played a notable role as agents of government policy. Hence, a theory of development banking should draw from both the theory and history of development economics and development finance that we explored in Chaps. 2 and 3 of this volume and from the institutional approaches of alternative financial regimes and institutional change that we analyzed in Chaps. 4 and 5. A synthesis of these ideas in the context of the current theoretical literature about development banking is the object of the next chapter.

References

Altman, M. (2023) "Mental Models, Decision-Making, Bargaining Power, and Institutional Change", *Journal of Economic Issues*, 57(4): 1241–1259.

Ankarloo, D. (2002) "New Institutional Economics and Economic History", *Capital & Class*, 26(3): 9–36.

Arthur, B. (1989) "Competing Technologies, Increasing Returns, and Lock-In by Historical Events", *Economic Journal*, 99(1): 116–131.

Baranes, A. I. and Bucher, C. C. (2022) "Classification Systems and the Veblenian Dichotomy: An Interdisciplinary Approach to Social Stratification", *Journal of Economic Issues*, 56(2): 570–577.

Barnett, V. (2017) "Veblen's Two Types of Instinct and the Cognitive Foundations of Evolutionary-Institutional Economics", *Journal of Economic Issues*, 51(2): 541–562.

Brette, O. (2003) "Thorstein Veblen's Theory of Institutional Change: Beyond Technological Determinism", *European Journal of the History of Economic Thought*, 10(3): 455–477.

Bush, P. D. (1987) "The Theory of Institutional Change", *Journal of Economic Issues*, 21(3): 1075–1116.

Chavance, B. (2009) *Institutional Economics*, London & N.Y.: Routledge.

Commons, J. R. (1899 [1965]) *A Sociological View of Sovereignty*, N.Y.: Augustus Kelley.

David, P. (1985) "Clio and the Economics of QWERTY", *American Economic Review*, 75(2): 332–337.

Denzau, A. T. and North, D. C. (1994) "Shared Mental Models: Ideologies and Institutions", *Kyklos*, 47: 3–31.

Dugger, W. M. (1995) "Douglass C. North's New Institutionalism", *Journal of Economic Issues*, 29(2): 453–458.

Fine, B. and Milonakis, D. (2003) "From Principle of Pricing to Pricing of Principle: Rationality and Irrationality in the Economic History of Douglass North", *Comparative Studies in Society and History*, 45(3): 546–570.

Furubotn, E. G. and Richter, R. (2008) *Institutions and Economic Theory. The Contribution of the New Institutional Economics*, 2nd Ed., Ann Arbor: The University of Michigan Press.

Groenewegen, J. Kerstholt, F. and Nagelkerke, A. (1995) "On Integrating New and Old Institutionalism: Douglass North Building Bridges", *Journal of Economic Issues*, 29(2): 467–475.

Hodgson, G. M. (2010) "Choice, Habit and Evolution", *Journal of Evolutionary Economics*, 20(1): 1–18.

Hodgson, G. M. (2004) "Reclaiming Habit for Institutional Economics", *Journal of Economic Psychology*, 25(5): 651–660.

Hodgson, G. M. (2002) "Reconstitutive Downward Causation. Social Structure and the Development of Individual Agency" in Fullbrook, E. (ed.) *Intersubjectivity in Economics. Agents and Structures*, London & N.Y.: Routledge, pp. 159–178.

Hodgson, G. M. (2000) "What Is the Essence of Institutional Economics?", *Journal of Economic Issues*, 34(2): 317–329.

Lawson, T. (2003) "Institutionalism: On the Need to Firm up Notions of Social Structure and the Human Subject", *Journal of Economic Issues*, 37(1): 175–207.

McCormick, K. (2006) *Veblen in Plain English. A Complete Introduction to Thorstein Veblen's Economics*, New York: Cambria Press.

Milonakis, D. and Fine, B. (2007) "Douglass North's Remaking of Economic History: A Critical Appraisal", *Review of Radical Political Economics*, 39(1): 27–57.

Nobel Prize Organization (1993) Douglass C. North – Facts. NobelPrize.org. Nobel Prize Outreach AB 2024. Tue. 20 Feb 2024. https://www.nobelprize.org/prizes/economic-sciences/1993/north/facts/ Accessed 5 Dec. 2023

North, D. C. (2005) *Understanding the Process of Economic Change*, Princeton and Oxford: Princeton University Press.

North, D. C. (1995) "Five Propositions about Institutional Change", in Knight, J. and Sened I. (eds.) *Explaining Social Institutions*, Ann Arbor, Mich: University of Michigan Press, pp. 15–26.

North, D. C. (1994) "Economic Performance Through Time", *American Economic Review*, 84(3): 359–368.

North, D. C. (1991) "Institutions", *Journal of Economic Perspectives*, 5(1): 97–112.

North, D. C. (1990), *Institutions, Institutional Change and Economic Performance*, New York: Cambridge University Press.

North, D. C. (1981) *Structure and Change in Economic History*, N.Y. and London: W.W. Norton & Co.

North, D. C. and Shirley, M. M. (2008) "Conclusion: Economics, Political Institutions, and Financial Markets", in Haber, S., North, D. C., and Weingast, B. R. (eds.) *Political Institutions and Financial Development*, Stanford, California: Stanford University Press., pp. 287–296.

Poirot, Jr., C. S. (2008) "Eat Grubs and Live: The Habit-Instinct Problem in Institutional Evolutionary Economics", *Journal of Economic Issues*, 42(2): 407–413.

Rutherford, M. (1995) "The Old and the New Institutionalism: Can Bridges Be Built?", *Journal of Economic Issues*, 29(2): 443–451.

Simon, H. (1986) "Rationality in Psychology and Economics" *The Journal of Business*, 59(4), Part 2: The Behavioral Foundations of Economic Theory, S209-S224.

Stein, M. (2008) *Beyond the World Bank Agenda. An Institutional Approach to Development*, Chicago & London: The University of Chicago Press.

World Bank (1997) *World Development Report 1997: The State in a Changing World*, N.Y.: Oxford University Press.

World Bank (2002) *World Development Report 2002: Building Institutions for Markets*, N.Y.: Oxford University Press.

Vandenberg, P. (2002) "North's Institutionalism and the Prospect of Combining Theoretical Approaches", *Cambridge Journal of Economics*, 26(2): 217–235.

Veblen, T. (1919 [2016]) *The Place of Science in Modern Civilization and Other Essays*, Wroclaw: CreateSpace Independent Publishing Platform.

Veblen, T. (1914 [2020]) *The Instinct of Workmanship and the State of Industrial Arts*, Alpha Editions.

Veblen, T. (1904 [2016]) *The Theory of Business Enterprise*, Wroclaw: Independently Published.

Veblen, T. (1899 [2009]) *The Theory of the Leisure Class*, New York: Oxford University Press.

Von Staden, P. and Bruce, K. (2015) "Original and New Institutional Economics: Brethren Rather Than Foes? Lessons from the Sociocognitive Turn in "Late" Douglass North", *Journal of Economic Issues*, 49(1): 111–125.

Wrenn, M. V. (2006) "Agency and Mental Models in Heterodox Economics", *Journal of Economic Issues*, 40(2): 483–491.

Zouboulakis, M. (2015) "Customary Rule-Following Behaviour in the Work of John Stuart Mill and Alfred Marshall", *Journal of Institutional Economics*, 11(4): 783–801.

Zouboulakis, M. (2005) "On the Evolutionary Character of North's idea of Institutional Change", *Journal of Institutional Economics*, 1(2): 139–153.

CHAPTER 6

An Institutional Model of Development Banking

6.1 Introduction: Development Banks—The Peculiar Macro-micro Organizations

The theoretical and historical discussion in the previous chapters demonstrated the close relationship between development banks and the financial institutional environment or the financial regime, whether the one of strict regulation or the one of financial liberalization, that prevails in a particular era. Hence, we are not able to talk about a theory of development banking without taking into account this idiosyncratic feature of development banks. This observation will be more firmly established in this chapter which examines the various theories of development banks in the context of banking and financial theory and develops an institutional approach to these institutions.

A central conception of this chapter that characterizes its sections is the conception of development banks as peculiar macro-micro organizations. The idea is that development banks in their intimate relationship with the prevailing financial regime and government policy assume a macroeconomic dimension that distinguishes them from other types of financial institutions. Development banks, as agents of "macro-industrial policy plans" (Mazzucato and Penna 2016: 312) are fundamentally defined by the direction of government policy toward economic development in different historical periods and countries. This qualitative characteristic gives development banks a macro-dimension which contrasts with their

K. Loizos, *Between Markets and Governments*,
https://doi.org/10.1007/978-3-031-88527-3_6

microeconomic function as financial institutions with the goal to survive in a market economy. This second micro-dimension makes development banks comparable to other financial institutions in terms of financial performance and profitability. Therefore, the term "macro-micro organizations" attempts to summarize the internal contradiction that characterizes development banks as economic agents that should take care of their financial viability and at the same time serve social and economic development purposes (Krahnen and Schmidt 1994: 30). One may say that this characterization of macro-micro organizations probably fits the description of every public enterprise that is doing business in a market economy and is somehow controlled by the government whether it is fully owned by it or not.[1] However, the term "macro-micro" we have coined in this chapter intents to emphasize the contradiction between a public purpose *macroeconomic* function of these institutions in favor of economic development and their *microeconomic* "duty" to survive within a competitive environment. This second dimension is usually disregarded by governments under financially repressed/regulated regimes. However, this book argues that development banks are dynamic institutions that are able to survive in financially liberalized regimes as well, as the recent historical experience after the Global Financial Crisis has shown. Hence, the term "macro-micro" organizations intends to highlight the dynamic character of this contradiction for this kind of public enterprise that can be solved in favor of both socioeconomic development (the macro part) and financial viability of development banks (the micro part). As we will show in this chapter this peculiar character of development banks renders conventional banking theory inadequate to form a comprehensive theoretical model that would be able to explain their role in the economy. On the other hand, the inherent contradictions in development banking have generated a variety of theoretical approaches that emphasize particular aspects of their role.

In the following sections, after reviewing mainstream banking theory about issues concerning the conceptualization of development banking we present a survey of current theories of development banking. Our impression is that, even though these theories provide useful insights about the role of development banks for economic and institutional development and transformation, they lack a comprehensive theoretical

[1] For a widely accepted definition of public enterprises see Brittanica: https://www.britannica.com/money/public-enterprise, accessed on October 2024.

framework that will be able to underpin these considerations and conceive development banks in their entirety as macro-micro organizations. We assert that such a model can be found in the Original Institutionalist theory we presented in Chaps. 4 and 5. Hence, we conclude this chapter with our proposal for a theoretical dynamic institutional model of development banking and a methodological empirical framework on the same grounds.

6.2 Development Banks and Banking Theory

The following discussion outlines the difficulty of modeling development banks using the conventional tools of economic theory. In the literature on development finance, development banks are mainly treated as a subset of public banks rather than as a specific area of banking theory requiring its own particular modeling. We believe that the reason for this theoretical neglect and modeling misperception lies in the specific characteristics of these institutions, which make traditional banking theory only partially relevant to their case.

The previous historical and theoretical analysis showed that development banks are characterized by two major features: First, their direct dependence, concerning their form and means of operation, on government decisions and the general institutional infrastructure. Second, the property and goal of institutional transformation which is inherent in their nature and is related to their statutory goals. It could be argued that the first characteristic applies to every financial organization that operates within a regulatory framework formulated by the government. However, the degree of dependence of development banks on this institutional environment is much more profound and fundamental rather than in any other financial institution for three reasons: (1) Development banks raise the majority of their funds at concessionary interest rates, and this is only possible if there is a corresponding government policy that guarantees the low level of these interest rates, whether the bank operates within a financially repressed or liberalized regime. Such interest rates, in turn, make it possible for development banks to provide long-term finance to enterprises at below-market rates. (2) The spread between lending rates and borrowing rates is not always determined by the banks' management, although this is also true for commercial banks under financial repression. However, development banks may have less discretion than commercial banks in managing the synthesis of their assets and liabilities. Therefore, their dependence on government decisions is critical for their particular nature as banking institutions. On the other hand, their lending activity is closely related to the priorities set by the government concerning the financing of certain sectors of the economy. (3) The prevailing financial regime which informs government policies is of critical importance for the smooth operation of these banks as it is implied from point (1) above. The analysis in Chap. 2 which demonstrated the many forms and the internal institutional transformation of development banks over time provides historical proof for these remarks. Hence, the second distinctive characteristic of development banks is that they are both exposed to the general financial structure of the economy and are able to influence it through their routine operations. This point is related to the dual role of development banks outlined in the previous chapters: At first, they provide long-term loans to preferred sectors of the economy at low interest rates so as to accelerate economic development, especially in less developed economies. Secondly, they are supposed to act in a way that would contribute to financial development through their consulting services to the government and private enterprises and also by placing private, public, or their own securities on the stock exchange. Then, an interactive relationship between development banks and the institutional infrastructure implies their institutional transformation as an inherent characteristic of these banks since they need to remodel themselves from traditional development banks to merchant and investment banks to the degree that the capital market assumes an increasingly decisive role in industrial funding. So, the question arises how do these distinctive characteristics of development banks fit into traditional banking theory?

Swank (1996), Van Damme (1994), Bhattacharya and Thakor (1993), and Santomero (1984), indicate the following major issues in modern banking theory: (1) The question of the existence of financial intermediaries. (2) Asset allocation, credit rationing, and the composition of liabilities along with the choice of the capital structure. (3) Liquidity transformation function of banks when they fund illiquid assets with liquid liabilities and maturity transformation between short-term liabilities and long-term assets. (4) The borrowers' choice between banks and the capital market as a financing source and the bank-borrower relationship. (5) Profit maximization, operating efficiency, and risk management. (6) Banking regulation, its desirability and limits, and competition in the banking industry. (7) Special issues including the role of financial institutions in financial innovation and the differences between financial systems. The question is whether the above issues can shed light on the nature, functioning, and role of development banks and, in particular, their specificity compared to other banking institutions. Some of these issues are more relevant while others may be less relevant for the case of development banks given the close relationship between the activity of development banks and government policies. The question of liquidity and maturity transformation may not arise in the case of development banks as long as they fund their long-term loans with capital and subsidized long-term borrowing from the Central Bank or international development institutions such as the World Bank and the European Investment Bank. Furthermore, demand deposits were usually not offered in the traditional development banking model and only in some cases time deposits were accepted. Hence, the choice of liability and capital structure is not entirely at the discretion of development banks and the maturities of assets and liabilities are more closely matched than in the case of commercial banks. The problem of asset and credit allocation may also be less relevant as a choice problem since development banks are usually entitled to provide loans in sectors of the economy that are predetermined by the government. Hence, credit rationing becomes more of a government policy problem rather than a bank policy problem. Of course, there is an issue here concerning the financial viability of the projects chosen among those proposed within a priority sector and the tantalizing questions of operating efficiency and profitability. These issues relate to the ability of the bank's manager to select the right projects and the technical competence of the bank's personnel given the prevailing government policies and the respective regulatory framework. However, both public commercial and development banks are subject to these dilemmas. On the other hand, the reasons that justify the existence of financial institutions and relate to the reduction of transaction costs in the face of informational asymmetries apply to any financial institution. Therefore, such questions with broad relevance will not help us identify what is special about development banks.

Nevertheless, topics such as the choice between banks and capital markets, the structure of financial systems, and financial innovation are more relevant to our problem. One might observe that development banks are quite often established in situations where the capital market is very thin and underdeveloped so the choice between banks and the capital market for most firms is not realistic. However, focusing on the dilemma between banks and capital markets helps us understand the role of development banks initially as capital market substitutes, and later on as supporters of innovation and capital market development. Hence, issues that affect a borrower's decision between banks and capital markets, such as the creditworthiness and reputation of the borrower, the managerial skills and experience, or the informational rent extracted by commercial banks, are relevant to development banking. Development banks as capital market substitutes are expected to support borrowers who cannot have access to the capital market either because they do not have a previously established reputation or because they lack experienced management. On the other hand, as capital market promoters, development banks are supposed to disseminate management know-how to firms and help them build up a good reputation in the market so that they will be able to raise funds at low cost in the future and thus avoid possible extraction of information rents by commercial banks. Hence, the institutional activity of development banks which contributes to capital market development provides the opportunity for a wider range of companies to choose the source of their financing between commercial banks and the capital market. On the other hand, the issues of financial innovation and financial structure are pertinent to the institutional environment in which development banks operate and interact with other economic agents. Hence, the institutional role of development banks in shaping and promoting markets, their relationship with the structure of financial systems, and the impact of financial innovation should be part of a theory of development banking. Is this enough?

One issue that may require special attention when discussing the relevance of banking theory for understanding development banks is that of financial risks and risk management. Development banks are financial institutions and as such are subject to risks as every other financial intermediary. Swank (1996) describes two major and three derivative kinds of risks. According to his analysis, there is the credit risk, or the risk of borrower's default, and the funding risk, or the risk of withdrawal of funds by depositors. In addition, maturity mismatching gives rise to interest rate risk, while holding assets with variable values may entail price risk or exchange rate risk. Of the above, the credit or default risk is directly relevant to the case of development banks. On the other hand, for non-deposit institutions with limited maturity mismatching of assets and liabilities, liquidity or withdrawal risk may be small. Moreover, in the absence of significant maturity mismatches and given the preferential funding of loans by development banks, interest rate risk is less of a concern than in the case of commercial banks. Finally, price and exchange rate risk may be relevant to the degree that there is a significant portfolio of securities on the assets side of the balance sheet or foreign borrowing exposes the bank to risk from exchange rate fluctuation. Furthermore, given the above risk classification, Swank (1996) analyzes four types of banking theories: (1) Risk management theories that focus on a major risk aspect of banking operation among those we have described above. (2) Portfolio models that perceive the bank as a risk-averse manager of a portfolio where the liabilities of the bank are treated as negative assets. (3) Imperfect-market models that focus on the competitive structure of the banking industry. (4) Real resource models that model the bank not as an investor—as the portfolio models do—but as a producer of financial services with the related inputs and outputs. Bringing risks at the forefront of development banking theory is a fruitful approach, especially when this is combined with the role of the government, the state of competition, and operating and financial performance. However, the question is whether there is a major kind of risk that characterizes the particular nature of development banks as opposed to commercial banks and if this kind of risk is decisive for their performance.

Looking at the recent literature on development banking one may notice that there is indeed a particular focus on the risks that characterize the activity of these banks. Torres and Zeidan (2016) distinguish between general risks and those related to the specific mode of lending to the economy. General risks pertain to agency problems that are common to public banks but can also be mitigated if professional managers are in place. However, agency issues and crony capitalism increase the probability of misallocation of resources to failing companies. Excessive political influence on banks' decisions along with corruption becomes a major risk that compounds with reduced efficiency and crowding out of private banks. Specific risks, on the other hand, relate to the particular instruments used such as guarantees or preferential interest rates that may increase the cost of development banks' activity for the society as a whole or reduce the efficient allocation of resources. A particular kind of specific risk is the one that pertains to the life-cycle hypothesis for development banks as the latter need to change the nature and focus of their activity as the economy develops. From a different point of view, Griffith-Jones et al. (2022) and Griffith-Jones and Naqvi (2021: 91–92) identify two major kinds of risk: (1) "Real economy" risk which is associated with "natural" uncertainty, innovation, and technological change that generate a developmental impact with positive externalities to the economy. (2) Financial engineering risk which is connected to the type of financial instruments used by a development bank to attract private funds to a project. However, the risk, in this case, is the one of "subsidizing the profits of private investors, while socializing their risk of losses". Hence, there is a trade-off between rising leverage and falling policy steer. Therefore, development banks face the problem of how to maximize their developmental impact that entails high economic risk and at the same time minimize financial engineering risk associated with complex and non-transparent financial products and practices. In this context, an issue with importance is the kind of regulation that development banks should be subjected to. Whether development banks are deposit-taking institutions or not, is of some significance here although solvency, liquidity, governance, and accounting standards applicable to all seem to have gained the general agreement of policy makers. In this context, development banks are called up to streamline their risk management skills while a great proportion of national development banks worldwide are rated by international rating agencies (De Luna-Martínez et al. 2018). Yet, if non-deposit national development banks are the focus of interest then a specially tailored regulation may be needed. The reason is that Basel III-IV rules as they stand may inhibit the ability of development banks to finance risky innovative long-term projects with significant developmental impact or to act countercyclically. Basel's bias against long-term exposures, concentration risk, and the preference for shorter maturities implied by its Net Stable Funding Ratio (NSFR) liquidity indicator seems unsuitable for the role of development banks in supporting sustainable development and green transformation projects. Without disregarding the benefits from compliance with Basel rules concerning risk management and lower cost of funding from capital markets, it is noted that development banks do not take part in the payments system as commercial banks do and are less affected by market and liquidity risks because of the structure of their funding and the fact that they are less inclined to speculative practices. Hence, they are less likely to become a source of systemic risk (Gottschalk et al. 2022; Castro 2018: 244, 246, 252).

Summing up the above analysis, even if we acknowledge the presence of financial risks such as credit risk, price risk, exchange rate risk, or interest rate risk in development banking, for example when development banks engage in merchant and investment banking activities in a liberalized environment, even in this case we will not have found the "defining" kind of risk for this kind of banks. A point of difficulty here is the non-static nature of these institutions which relates to their deep dependence on the prevailing government policy and financial regime. In this sense, isolating only one of the above kinds of risks or focusing on specific aspects of their operation as financial services producers, portfolio managers, or risk managers will provide us with only partial answers concerning the nature of these banks, focusing only on one side of their operation. Hence, the previous discussion points to a specific direction concerning the defining risks for development banks as these are related to the political influence on them along with the distinction between financial and economic risks as they are reflected in their developmental role which should inform their regulation and supervision. Moreover, in the previous paragraphs of this section, we indicated the two distinctive characteristics of development banks: the critical dependence on government policy and the financial regime and the dynamic feature of institutional transformation. The first characteristic relates to various strands of the literature outlined above although the role of the government is not explicitly examined in a political economy framework. The second feature, which concerns the internal structure of development banks and their transformation, is only partially addressed in the literature.

Seeing things this way puts the emphasis on the dynamic nature of development banks and their normal transformation to investment banks after a sufficient level of financial development and proper functioning of the capital market in accordance with the life-cycle hypothesis (Torres and Zeidan 2016). The dynamic nature of these institutions is acknowledged by De Luna-Martínez et al. (2018), Gutierrez et al. (2011), Rudolph (2009), and Diamond (1982a: 15) and takes the form of the need for a continuous reevaluation and reorientation of banks' goals based on their growing experience and the evolution of national policy objectives. The sources of change identified in Diamond (1982b: 39) contain changes in government policy, in the structure of the real economy, and in the financial sector as the latter develops. In this sense, a dynamic institution means an institution inherently capable of transforming itself as the external environment changes. This transformation, according to our view, emerges almost naturally from the above-described dual role of these banks as both long-term financing institutions at depressed rates and capital market substitutes-promoters at market rates. The first kind of operation normally loses its central meaning after the development of the capital market and the proliferation of financial institutions. Indeed, as Diamond (1982b: 54) observes and Rezende (2018: 304) confirms, a development bank might need to adapt its operation to the changing environment as economic development proceeds by diversifying its activity toward "universal banking". In this sense, the second role increases in importance as financial institutions develop.

Given the above analysis, we propose to look for an encompassing dynamic theory that would examine development banks in their entirety as institutions that affect and are affected by the financial system and also that are characterized by an inherent feature of institutional transformation. If this is the case, then the major risk that characterizes the nature of development banks is not a pure financial risk but rather an institutional-political risk. It is the risk that the bank faces as the mode, scope, prospects, and financial soundness of its operation depends not on its own decisions but on government decisions concerning the prevailing financial regime and its development finance policies. Then pure economic and financial risks are rather derivatives of this major institutional-political risk. Even the contribution of development banks to capital market and financial development which is related to their holding and trading of securities, along with their internal transformation, depends on the government's willingness to improve the institutional infrastructure of the financial system. This means that even the realization of the dual role of development banks is subject to the decisions of the authorities.

6.3 Conventional Theories of Development Banks

Development banks are idiosyncratic organizations with both a microeconomic and a macroeconomic dimension inscribed in their nature and functionality as we have argued above. The previous section demonstrated the difficulty of conventional banking theories to grasp the defining characteristics of these organizations. This section will provide a short review of the recent literature on the main specific theories that have been proposed to explain the existence and evolution of development banks. In some respects, these theories overlap with the theories that have been proposed to justify the existence of state-owned financial institutions. Development banks are not restricted to the category of state-owned financial institutions. This is certainly not the case in many European countries including Greece, as will be shown in subsequent chapters. Nevertheless, even private development banks have mandates focusing on developmental goals and accepting the direction provided by governments in strategic issues. Furthermore, the dominance of public development banks is confirmed by the 2017 Survey of National Development Banks published by the World Bank Group in which the state owned the majority of shares in 95% of the banks surveyed (De Luna-Martínez et al. 2018). The above suggests that public national development banks are the characteristic example of development banking as it has evolved historically, and therefore a theory of development banking should draw its insights from such institutions where government influence plays a central role.

It is possible to identify four main theoretical views in contemporary mainstream economic thinking: the industrial policy or development view, the social view, the political view, and the agency or pro-market activism view. The first two carry a positive connotation since they refer to the assumed successful overcoming of market failures related to the goal of industrialization, economic development, and social welfare. The sources of market failures are identified with asymmetric information along with the implied costs to mitigate it, insufficient financing for socially desirable projects with low profitability, and the existence of poor institutions especially in LDCs. The third theoretical view has a negative meaning as it juxtaposes the above economic and social goals with politicians' personal perks and the goals of the businessmen who support them. The last takes an intermediate position between the positive and the negative approaches by emphasizing the trade-off between agency costs of government intervention and the derived social gains (De Luna-Martínez et al. 2018; Musacchio et al. 2017; Lazzarini et al. 2015; Gutierrez et al. 2011; Francisco et al. 2008; Levy-Yeyati et al. 2004).

The industrial policy or development approach to development banking rests on the classic economic development views that promoting industrialization and fostering entrepreneurship contributes to economic growth and increases economic and social welfare. This view is based on Gerschenkron's (1962), Myrdal's (1960), and Lewis's (1955) support for state-owned banks in the context of a general policy prescription of the era for government ownership of key economic institutions. Public intervention is justified on the grounds of scarce capital along with failures of the domestic financial system related to insufficient trust of the general public in the system and possibly widespread fraud and deceit. Constraints in the financing of activities in this context lead to underinvestment in infrastructure, key industrial sectors, and innovative projects. The state intervenes in the allocation of financial capital, thus becoming a substitute for market allocation. If the cost of financing, driven up by perceived riskiness and information asymmetries that surround such projects, is the major obstacle facing these firms, then subsidized lending by development banks that can offer lower interest rates with the support of governments, might be the solution. The same line of argument justifies the use of other kinds of support by development banks such as the participation of the latter in the equity capital of firms facing credit constraints, or the provision of services such as project identification and technical assistance. In many cases, development banks are also able to provide guarantees as an instrument that helps companies tap into the capital market for additional private funding. Eventually, development banks would secure the flow of loan and equity capital to priority sectors and industries in the context of pursued developmental policies to foster entrepreneurial activity in existing and new industries (de la Torre et al. 2017: 77; Musacchio et al. 2017; Lazzarini et al. 2015; Francisco et al. 2008; Levy-Yeyati et al. 2004).

According to this point of view, government involvement in development finance is necessary to unlock the "latent capabilities" of the private sector and contribute to economic development and rising income and employment. In addition, government intervention in the financing of infrastructure projects generates positive externalities that raise economic welfare and reduce costs while at the same time contributing to capital market development. Furthermore, innovation financing is related to learning externalities where acquired knowledge is diffused throughout entire economic sectors. On the other hand, development banks are well placed to act as coordinators of different agents and institutions taking part in the realization of major infrastructure projects (Musacchio et al. 2017). Finally, if the stakes are a dominant position in the world market in the context of export-led growth then development banks are able to identify and foster "national champions". If this is done with the use of subsidized credit with an eye to protectionism then government involvement may become detrimental to market competition (Musacchio et al. 2017).

According to the social approach to development banks, the latter are willing to finance projects that have a significant social impact even though their economic efficiency is debatable, i.e. they might have a negative net present value. For example, it may be socially desirable to support employment in a specific region of the country with less economic potential than others. This could be done either with subsidized credit or with participation in these firms' equity (Musacchio et al. 2017; Levy-Yeyati et al. 2004). The social view emphasizes a market failure related to the inability of private banks, being first and foremost profit maximizers, to cater to the needs of less privileged members of the population such as the poorer strata or those living in remote regions. The argument may be extended to the underfinancing of small enterprises with insufficient collateral because of their higher risk and rising transaction costs. The crux of this train of thought is that whatever activity that needs funding has a positive social value and broader beneficial effect on the community does not necessarily have a positive financial return (Francisco et al. 2008). In any case, the social view in some sense complements the industrial policy approach as a positive and affirmative stance concerning the role of development banks. Indeed, the social view justifies a more active role for state-owned banks in sectors where market failures take the form of information asymmetries with significant shortages of loan capital and sizable effects on the rest of the economy such as agriculture, sectors with a significant component of Research and Development (R&D) and those in need of large amounts of capital. The institutional environment is also important since the lack of or an underdeveloped institutional infrastructure which reduces confidence and trust in private financial institutions might justify the establishment of public institutions such as development banks which can foster financial development by transmitting their expertise to market participants. Moreover, development banks can play a stabilizing role in financial markets and the economy in general by acting countercyclically, especially when the economy finds itself at the trough of the credit cycle (Levy-Yeyati et al. 2004). The latter justifies both the development and the social approaches to the degree that financial and economic stability is necessary both for economic growth and for sustained social welfare. On another tone, the long-term developmental role of development banks is related to issues of asymmetric information and intervention to promote structural change while the short-term countercyclical role is associated with the difference between risk-averse private banks and a risk-neutral state which is able to mitigate procyclical behavior in credit markets. Put differently, the market gap that development banks aim to fill might be either of a demand-side cyclical nature or of a supply-side structural sort. Identifying the kind of gap is crucial for the success of the pursued government policies (Gutierrez et al. 2011; Smallridge and de Olloqui 2011). Indeed, since the state can spread the assumed risk both over time and over the population through its taxing and borrowing activities, it is also capable of decreasing significantly the social cost of risk as opposed to risk-averse private institutions (de la Torre et al. 2017: 76). This observation pertains both to developing and developed economies since extreme risk aversion may characterize mature capital markets as well and inhibit investment in risky but socially valuable projects such as infrastructure ones (Rezende 2018: 317).

If the industrial or development and the social views carry an interventionist flavor, the political view and partly the agency view follow a laissez-faire argument. Indeed, if the interventionist view emphasizes active government involvement in the financial sector, the laissez-faire view argues against it because of the market distortions that government intervention can cause (De Luna-Martínez et al. 2018). Governments have still a role to play in coping with market failures through direct subsidies to private banks and drafting regulations rather than directly controlling banks. This line of thinking is in favor of privatizations, second-tier lending, and institution building that would create an "enabling environment" such as securing creditor and shareholder rights, streamlining accounting systems and information dissemination, and enhancing prudential financial regulation (Francisco et al. 2008). In fact, these views led in many cases to the transformation rather than the liquidation of public development institutions as the history of development banks around the world has shown and, in this sense, a theory of development banking should be able to integrate into a comprehensive way both the interventionist approach and the laissez-faire approach as two moments in a dynamic financial organization. This is what the theory proposed in this book attempts to do in the last sections of this chapter.

More analytically, returning to the laissez-faire approach and the political view, the latter argues that financial markets are no different from other markets to require government intervention to improve their functioning and increase social welfare. Although cases of inefficiencies in market operation cannot be denied they are often overemphasized in the relevant literature and public ownership of financial institutions might not be the most effective way to address them. According to this view, what development banks are doing is to fund projects that are neither industrially nor socially important but rather the pet projects of politicians. Hence, it is not economic or social priorities that direct the decisions of development banks but rather political priorities that lead to capital misallocation and distorted market outcomes in both the financial and the real sectors of the economy (Musacchio et al. 2017; Levy-Yeyati et al. 2004).

This approach further categorizes the kinds and effects of government melding in financial markets with the help of two hypotheses: the soft-budget constraint hypothesis and the rent-seeking hypothesis. The soft-budget constraint focuses on how development banks are employed to shore up failing companies thus contributing to capital misallocation and decreased efficiency in the economy. If this is the case, this view argues, then government intervention is counter-productive, concerning the goal of economic and social development, for two interrelated reasons: Because it uses subsidized lending as a means to increase, rather than contain, inefficiency in the real sector of the economy. In addition, such misallocation of capital can only degrade incentives in the private sector to support developmental objectives. The rent-seeking approach takes this argument one step further by indicating that companies and projects that receive funding are not always those that are credit-constrained but rather the ones run by supporters of incumbent politicians. In the context of widespread "cronyism" even established entrepreneurs who would normally have been able to draw funding from the capital markets, prefer to exploit their political connections in order to gain access to lending on concessionary terms by development banks (Musacchio et al. 2017; Lazzarini et al. 2015). Therefore, the political view maintains that politicians are interested in maximizing their own welfare rather than the social one. They aim to secure the rents they extract by controlling development banks (Levy-Yeyati et al. 2004).

Summing up the above three mainstream approaches to development banking culminate in contrasting market failures to "government failures" (Griffith-Jones 2022; Musacchio et al. 2017) when describing the role and justifying the existence of development banks. Indeed, if the inability of the market to support a much-needed industrial policy or economic activity with significant positive social and environmental impacts justifies government intervention using development banks as financing instruments, the misuse of the latter leads to government failures that contradict the objectives set by the first two approaches. However, the last of the theories mentioned above which examines development banks as public institutions relies on this contradiction. The agency view focuses on the trade-off between two kinds of efficiency: (a) The allocative efficiency which allegedly improves under government intervention according to the industrial or development and the social view. (b) The bureaucratic efficiency or inefficiency of public institutions when they pursue their developmental goals (Levy-Yeyati et al. 2004). A similar to the agency view approach is the one described as the pro-market activism view (De Luna-Martínez et al. 2018; de la Torre et al. 2017: 77, 93–95; Smallridge and de Olloqui 2011). First of all, the form of government intervention is closely related to issues such as the incentives the government creates for financial institutions along with their monitoring and the level of institutional development. This approach accepts government interventions when they are cost-effective and they complement markets by assisting their development. Government intervention should be designed carefully to cope with specific market failures with the aim of ameliorating the enabling environment for financial markets. Although risk-sharing with the private sector is preferable, in the early stages of financial development the government might need to intervene directly in the financial markets. However, interventions should ultimately be market-friendly aiming at institutional reform and financial markets development. In addition, development banks need to be independent of political pressure and managed according to modern governance principles.

However, the market failure justification which appears to inform both the pro-interventionist and the laissez-faire approaches described above, is considered to be rather incomplete and, in some respects, restrictive by a strand of literature. A more comprehensive approach with a heterodox flavor is presented by Griffith-Jones et al. (2018), Mazzucato and Penna (2018), and Mazzucato and Penna (2016). The theory of market failures emphasizes the importance of information in financial markets and the inability of the latter to solve problems of information asymmetry between borrowers and lenders since financial contracts are fundamentally incomplete. If market failures exceed possible government failures, government intervention through financial regulation and the establishment of public national development banks may be justified. This allows for the "visible hand" of government to be considered as necessary and, in some cases, more effective than the "invisible hand" of markets. Besides, in the context of a learning society where knowledge and information are public goods, development banks might become an indispensable government instrument to overcome market failures in this area. Development banks can play a catalytic role as hubs for collecting and disseminating knowledge and fostering learning, as they are not focused on short-term profitability but on long-term development goals (Griffith-Jones 2022; Griffith-Jones et al. 2018: 7). However, whatever the sources of market failures such as negative externalities, public goods, information asymmetries or competition issues, they cannot take us too far. Development banks, in the context of market failure theory, are useful just to correct market "imperfections". Whether they do it successfully is of secondary importance to the essence of the argument. To put it differently, the market failure approach is only a partial justification for development banks since it does not take into account both the process of financialization of capitalist economies since the 1970s and the active, rather than passive, role of the state toward markets. Financialization and "money manager capitalism" (Minsky 1996) are closely related to speculation and short-termism in financial markets and provide a better explanation for the lack of finance for long-term investment and innovation than the one based on risk aversion and information costs. Moreover, the state has assumed historically an active role in "shaping and creating markets" rather than just passively correcting imperfections. When the "invisible hand" fails, the government can intervene and shape a market (Minsky et al. 1993). In this sense, Polanyi (1944 [2001]) has shown that the "state versus market" dichotomy is false since the "visible hand" in many respects has helped shaping the conditions for the "invisible hand". The above provides a "mission-oriented" justification for development banks in the context of government policies that purport to alter economic priorities toward new innovative industries, areas, and sectors Such missions and projects demand special knowledge and skills in the assessment of social and private returns where the former outweighs the latter (Griffith-Jones 2022; Mazzucato and Penna 2018: 257–258).

In the aforementioned heterodox context, development banks' countercyclical role during the 2008 Global Financial Crisis cannot be attributed to attempts to address coordination problems in the private sector. Such market failures usually result in procyclical behavior, with the risk appetite of market participants changing according to different stages of the economic and financial cycle. However, it is not the variability of risk aversion but the predominance of speculation that needs to be addressed. It is not a matter of "risk-neutral" development banks but of their countercyclical role with the eye in maintaining the pace of investment to a level that would promote capital development despite economic fluctuations. This is a view in the spirit of Keynes's (1936 [1973]) "socialisation of investments" rather than promoting public investment to instill confidence in the private sector. Furthermore, development banks are not simply instruments of public industrial policy that boost investment in public goods that are underproduced in the private sector or provide financing to facilitate entry into industries characterized by monopolistic structures in order to restore competitive equilibrium. Their role should be interpreted in dynamic Schumpeterian (1912 [1934]) terms where economic development is related to innovative processes that disrupt rather than rehabilitate static equilibrium. Development banks can contribute to developing technical capacities and the institutional infrastructure that renders industrialization and economic development an endogenous process of innovation in the context of a developmental state.[2] In this sense, development banks provide not just financial but also social capital in the sense of promoting trust and cooperation among different social groups that participate in economic development. In this context, the venture-capitalist role of development banks is better explained as supporting innovation in the face of fundamental uncertainty about future prospects rather than mitigating risk derived by information asymmetries in incomplete markets. Here we are dealing with development banking in the context of "entrepreneurial" rather than just "developmental" state within a modern perception of "industrial policy" when innovation-led growth is set at the forefront. Instead of the conventional practice of socializing risk and privatizing gains, public development banks' equity investments in such ventures may socialize gains too when they are successful. Finally, addressing societal challenges that generate negative externalities such as climate change is more than an issue of lacking equilibrium prices and markets. It is predominantly an issue of paradigm shift, a mission to challenge incumbent behaviors toward a new vision. It is an issue of cognition rather than of mere preferences. It is an attempt at institutional transformation with governments playing a crucial role in its success by using development banks as their instruments (Griffith-Jones et al. 2018: 24; Mazzucato and Penna 2016).

This approach sets a new perspective that is more dynamic and encompassing since both financial regulation and public development banks are seen as offspring of the development in capitalist economies and their structures. In this sense, the Global Financial Crisis of 2008 proved that financial development is not a guarantee for a rising and uninterrupted flow of investment expenditure in the real economy and hence, for economic development. It is neither a safeguard against financial instability. On the contrary, government presence in financial markets in the form of effective and comprehensive regulation and national development banks is necessary to smooth out economic cycles and foster financial stability. Governance issues are important and do make the difference between successful and unsuccessful government intervention but the justification of

[2] Although there is a diverse literature which distinguishes between old and new definitions, in general the term "developmental state" refers to government intervention in the economy with the intention to guide the developmental process (Ricz 2016).

the latter is indisputable. Moreover, development banks are dynamic institutions that are themselves subject to change as economic and financial development proceeds (Griffith-Jones et al. 2018: 8). Eventually, it seems that a consensus has been formed in the literature about development banks which acknowledges their significant role in mitigating procyclicality in credit markets, financing infrastructure projects, responding to market failures and contributing to structural transformation and change (Colombo and Cuda 2023). The question then is, which theoretical perspective better synthesizes these functions in a comprehensive theory of development banking?

6.4 Taking Stock: A Dynamic Theory of Development Banks as Hybrid Organizations Between Markets and Governments[3]

Our review of the theory and history of development finance and the idea of development banking should have now made clear that a theory of development banking should necessarily and foremost be founded on a theory of institutions and institutional development and change. Chapter 4 of this book set the theoretical framework for understanding the institutional structure that underpins financial regimes such as financial repression and financial liberalization which framed and conditioned the operation of development banks in the post-war period. Chapter 5 presented the salient elements of an analysis of institutional change and thus, it provided the tools of institutional theory that can be used in explaining development finance, economic development, and reform as an integrated social process of structural change. Development banks are those organizations that were shaped by government policies in the context of specific financial regimes and at the same time, they participated in economic and institutional development. In this respect, they can be characterized as peculiar macro-micro organizations with a close dependence on prevailing government policy and financial regime. In addition, they are organizations that can only be defined in dynamic terms both in the sense of their contribution to Schumpeterian processes where economic development breaks the vicious circle of path-dependence and underdevelopment and

[3] This section is derived in part from the article Loizos (2023) published in the *Journal of Economic Issues*, 2023, copyright Association for Evolutionary Economics, available on line http://www.tandfonline.com/10.1080/00213624.2023.2202561.

in terms of their dynamic adaption to changing economic and institutional conditions. Therefore, we argue that an institutional theory that can better grasp their relationship and interaction with the prevailing financial regime and at the same time can explain their role in financial development and change can provide a comprehensive understanding of these banks and their role in today's economies.

In Chap. 4 we showed how Commons's thorough theory of transactions and his approach to reasonable value, negotiation, and reform can explain the institutional framework that underpins financial regimes as the outcome of government policies. Development banks are embedded in financial regimes and, in this sense, they can be structurally described by the same conceptual framework of transactions and reasonableness. Development banks are hybrid institutions with features pertaining to both capital markets and typical banks. Development banks differ from the standard banking model since a commercial bank creates its own liabilities while a development bank reallocates liabilities created somewhere else in the financial system, just like the capital market. A typical capital market transaction has the features of Commons's "bargaining transaction" as described in Chap. 4: It is a legal transfer of wealth in the face of scarcity between legal equals (Kemp 2009: 64–66). On the other hand, development banks differ from capital markets because they are structured lending organizations, just like any other typical bank. However, a bank loan contract resembles Commons's description of the labor contract in the sense that it is a "bargaining transaction" before the contract is signed and a "managerial transaction" after the conclusion of the contract (Kemp 2009: 69). As explained above, the term "managerial" connotes some kind of hierarchy and control between a superior and an inferior for the sake of efficiency. The monitoring of loan contracts by banks implies some kind of command and control between a lender and a borrower that enhances the efficiency of financing. Finally, development banks differ from both capital markets and typical banks because they directly pursue socioeconomic goals. Socioeconomic welfare issues imply a process of distribution through collective bargaining and the involvement of the government and hence, it relates to Commons's "rationing transaction" (Kemp 2009: 64–65, 68, 70–71).

Therefore, development banks as substitutes for capital markets (Studart 1995: 75) can be defined by a dynamic combination of bargaining, managerial, and rationing transactions (Fig. 6.1) with two major features: (1) The first characteristic is the ability of development banks to switch

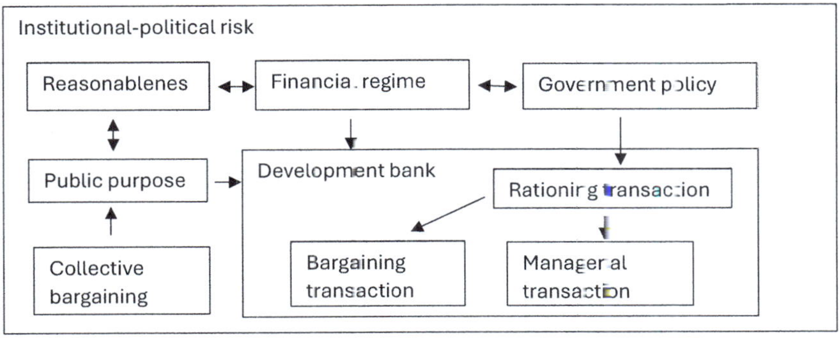

Fig. 6.1 Development banks and institutional-political risk (the arrows indicate the direction of effect). Source: Author's elaboration

between bargaining and managerial transactions depending on the circumstances. For example, on the assets' side, a development bank that finances a firm by participating in its capital and board of directors, effectively concludes a managerial transaction. The same transaction turns into a bargaining one when the development bank sells these securities on the market at a later stage. On the liabilities side, when a development bank extends long-term loans funded by official funds (loans provided by central banks, international organizations, etc.) but eventually at some point in time it floats its own bonds, the managerial transaction turns into a bargaining one. (2) The second feature is the priority of development banks' mandate to serve the public purpose over private profitability. In this sense, the combination of bargaining and managerial transactions is directly conditioned by a rationing transaction. Development banks are becoming instruments of resource allocation guided by the state after a process of collective bargaining. This idea is similar to Marois's (2022) dynamic view of public banks as fields of antagonism among social groups over the private interests that are to be served by their functions. It is, in a sense, a social struggle over the definition of public purpose in historically specific conditions.

According to our view, there is a guiding principle that binds together the above combination of transactions that constitute development banks as going concerns. This principle is Commons's idea of "reasonable value". "Reasonableness" is the notion that permeates the definition of financial regimes as socially constructed and politically supported, and of development banks as active organizations within these financial regimes. According to Commons bargaining transactions relate to scarcity plus the ability to withhold from others while reaching an agreement implies a continuum, from persuasion between legal equals to coercion between parties with different bargaining power (Kemp 2009: 65–66; Ramstad 1991, 2001). Managerial transactions relate to efficiency plus the ability to expand/grow and are characterized by degrees of coercion between superior and inferior. Finally, rationing transactions are associated with sovereignty and the ability of collective bargaining in the context of democracy and arbitration (Kemp 2009: 64–65, 68, 70–71). In an ideal world, a reasonable value would be the result of negotiation between the parties which is based on persuasion without the need to resort to any form of coercion (Ramstad 2001). More importantly, the term "reasonable" refers to a societal outcome that conforms to public purpose and reflects the public opinion and custom in a particular era and place (Kemp 2009: 75–77). In this sense, development banks are defined as the locus of a lender-borrower relationship that is organically embedded in the prevailing financial regime of a historical period. Such embeddedness entails that this lender-borrower relationship reflects "reasonable" pricing of finance and a reasonable composition of persuasion and coercion which is guided by public purpose and thus, it transcends the capital market or typical banking models. Since the term "reasonableness" is a historically specific characteristic of a society tied to the perception of public purpose in different periods and places, it can describe development banking in both financial repression and financial liberalization regimes. In addition, this definition incorporates our claim that the major risk that characterizes the nature of development banks is not a pure financial risk but rather an institutional-political risk to the degree that development banks as dynamic organizations are both subjects and objects of institutional change and they are dependent on government decisions concerning the prevailing financial regime (Fig. 6.1). Then pure economic risks are rather derivatives of this major institutional-political risk. Even the ability of development banks to change the synthesis of their assets and liabilities in support of capital market development may prove to be ineffective if the government is not prepared to amend the institutional infrastructure of the financial system.

However, development banks are themselves instruments of institutional change sponsored by the state as explained in the previous sections. Even the long-term financing activity of the banks can be considered an element of institutional change to the degree that it contributes to the changing structure of the economy toward industrialization and modernization. But also, the whole range of activities that we described above including promotional activities for new business, development of expertise, new methods of management and control, new accounting standards, new business ethics, and of course the development of the capital market contribute to the institutional transformation of the economy. As far as the financial sector is concerned, the role of development banks in overcoming the vicious circle of path-dependence is critical and it is the derivative of all these activities. Of course, path-dependence can emerge again to the degree that the state supports short-run political rather than long-term developmental goals. But even in this case, these effects should be reflected in the performance and operation of the banks.

The above remarks strengthen our assertion that it is not possible to examine a development bank with the same analytical tools as any other banking firm. More importantly, it is not possible to examine these institutions independently of the prevailing financial regime and the role of government policy. Furthermore, such a study is by its nature a dynamic and interactive one by focusing not on a static depiction of development banking at a particular point in time but on its evolution and transformation along with the evolution and development of the financial system itself. Furthermore, our short review of the economic history of development finance indicated that development banks emerged as a response to both economic and institutional backwardness. Hence, institutional development and change remained at the core of their mandate through the years (Gordon 1983).

As we have mentioned above, institutional change in Commons is profoundly related to problem-solving (Rutherford 1995) and emerges from collective action. Strategic transactions address limiting factors and involve critical choices that introduce new working rules (Kemp 2009: 58; Groenewegen et al. 1995). Institutional reform for Commons is both an individual and a collective issue: It involves the perception of limiting factors by individuals and their action to correct them and provoke change in institutions and in prevailing values. Moreover, it implies democratic participation and "reasonableness" as informed decision-making which is based on the current level of technology, instead of tradition and ceremonial values, or on the best practices given total social costs. This is Commons's progressive reform which takes into account both economic efficiency and social benefits and costs (Kemp 2009: 79, 83–89, 91–93). If development banks are defined by the notion of "reasonableness" as a societal conditioning feature that is inscribed in public purpose, then they are also privileged public agents of institutional change in the process of economic development.

However, in the recent critical literature about development finance and financial development, successful reform entails a process of "institutionalization" wherein economic actors internalize new practices in their behavior (Loizos 2018; Arestis and Stein 2005; Arestis et al. 2003). "Internalization" implies a change in agents' perceptions and behavior which Veblen's theory of institutional change can describe as part of an evolutionary theory of development banks. We have seen in Chap. 5 that in Veblen, institutional change is the outcome of the endogenous interaction among instincts, institutions, and technology. Given a natural substratum of instincts, technological change engenders institutional change which entails change in habits of thought and social conventions. On the other hand, it is important to note that the institutional structure determines whether group or self-regarding instincts dominate. Habits of thought are central since they evaluate institutions given established conventions and alter those that are not in accordance with them (McCormick 2006: 41, 49–51, 129). We argue that this Veblenian framework of institutional change is able to explain development banks as organizations with the potential to (a) contribute to a change in deeply seated habits of thought of firms' stakeholders concerning sustainable economic development and (b) promote a model of economic development and its institutional connotation which would emphasize group-regarding rather than self-regarding behavioral tendencies. It is an explanation that comprehends economic development as a profound structural social process rather than as a mere issue of efficiency and growth (Fig. 6.2).

An illustrative case is Veblen's Industrial Revolution (IR) example, where technological innovation causes a change in habits of thought as people learn to think in terms of cause and effect, and this generates further social change and innovations. The source of sensed awareness of the community concerning the need to alter its habits of thought is the change in material circumstances because of the new technology. The same result can come about by the contact of a society with other cultures (Bush 1987). However, development banks are historical creatures of the post-IR era when backward economies attempted to catch up with the pioneers of industrialization. In this case, the process of institutional change is less spontaneous than the British example and more deliberate and planned like the French or German examples (Gerschenkron 1962; Cameron 1953). This is exactly the historical case in which development banks as

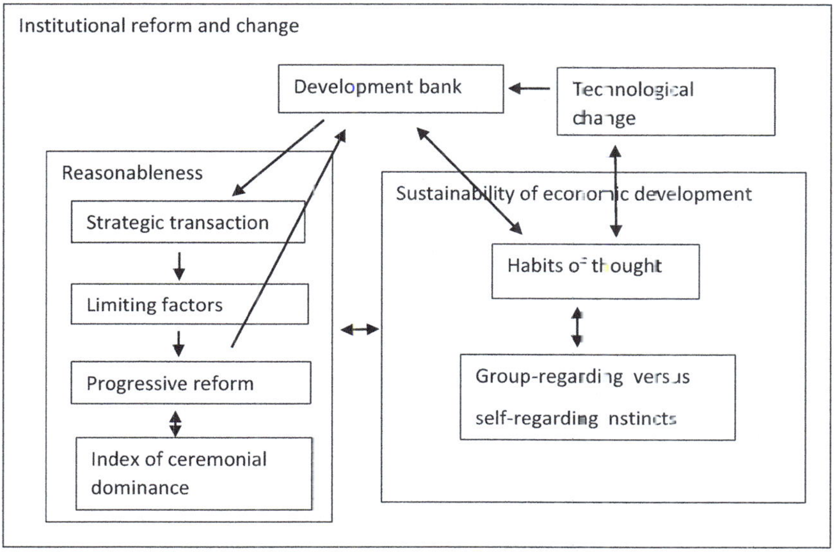

Fig. 6.2 Development banks and institutional change (the arrows indicate the direction of effect). Source: Author's elaboration

state-sponsored developmental agents introduce business practices and financing solutions that may bring about a change in the material circumstances and habits of thought of the community. Moreover, development banks in a progressive context could change the index of ceremonial dominance in society toward instrumental valuation in problem-solving (Fig. 6.2), according to the terminology employed by Bush (1987).

Finally, we may say that Veblen's theory of behavior in the interrelation between propensities (instincts) and habits of thought, challenges the type of economic development that a country should follow. A particular kind of economic development that ensures business prosperity may not imply industrial efficiency if the flow of knowledge is constrained. It may even conflict with public interest if less profitable but socially useful goods are not a priority of this type of development. At a more profound level, investment for profit which disregards social welfare indicates the predominance of self-regarding over group-regarding goals in the present model of economic development (McCormick 2006: 81–86, 91, 93–96, 130–131). This model might not be sustainable, either in terms of financial fragility and economic crises or in terms of socioecological sustainability (Hein et al. 2015: 36–42; Tymoigne 2011: 133). Hence, our encompassing institutional theory of development banks implies that the latter could become the vehicles of public intervention toward a more sustainable economic model by promoting institutional structures and habits of thought that would favor group-regarding propensities in agents' behavioral patterns. This means that the proposed theory is both an analytical tool for explaining the past performance of development banks in their historical institutional setting of particular financial regimes and, at the same time, a useful theoretical model that can guide government policy to cope with modern economic, financial, and environmental sustainability issues in development finance.

6.5 Historical Specificity, Pattern Modeling, and Storytelling: A Methodological Note

The way this book is structured reveals a methodological approach that appears to the author to be the most appropriate to the research question. The desideratum was to first form a comprehensive theory of development banking and then test it on the Greek case. The aim was to understand the nature of these banks and derive possible implications about their potential usefulness in current economic conditions in Greece. Hence, this research is more about understanding and interpreting rather than measuring, and about tracing possible paths of evolution rather than predicting in a rigorous mathematical manner (Whalen 2022: 257, 261; Cohen 1991). The foregoing analysis has followed this methodological path by setting at the forefront the history of development finance and development banking both as an idea and as a practical policy applied in different economies around the world, especially in the post-World War II period. Therefore, our claim that history matters in economic analysis leads this research close to both the theoretical approach and the methodology of Original Institutional Economics. Because "history matters" implies the primacy of understanding versus measuring and, at the same time, it highlights purposeful action that cannot be represented by any kind of mathematical optimization (Atkinson and Oleson 1996).

Moreover, the subject matter of this book, development banking, calls for a methodological and theoretical approach that will be dynamic, evolutionary, and open to alternative future paths. The discussion in Chaps. 2

and 3 showed the dynamic character of development banks in their interaction with the general institutional environment which takes the form of a particular financial regime in different historical periods. In addition, our discussion in this chapter demonstrated the inability of conventional banking theory to provide a comprehensive theory of development banks as macro-micro organizations. On the other hand, the current theories of development banking that we have surveyed approach different aspects of it that demand a consistent theoretical basis. If we believe in pluralism in economic methodology and if the subject matter of research decides its methodological approach rather than the other way round (Wilber and Harrison 1978) then, a research procedure that is based on historical specificity, pattern modeling, and storytelling is the appropriate for forming and testing a theory of development banking.

Our observation, which has been derived from the examination of the historical record of development banking, that it is not possible to understand development banking independently of its macro-institutional environment, calls for a holistic approach. In such a methodological approach the relationships between parts (development banks) and whole (financial regime) are described by a pattern model that grasps both the strategic or critical similarities that form a development bank as a going concern and its evolution over time (Atkinson and Oleson 1996; Wilber and Harrison 1978). Identifying similarities and differences, or "lumpers" and "splitters" (Kindleberger 2000: 88) is the natural way to proceed if the reality a researcher wants to explain is complex enough, evolving, and inadequately studied as is the case with development banking. On the other hand, looking for "lumpers" and "splitters" does not imply a decision between the two but rather the dialectical interrelationship between the evolving whole and its parts. Dialectics as a form of dynamic interaction implies evolution and institutional change (Stanfield 1999; Wilber and Harrison 1978) which is a defining characteristic of the history of development banking.

Eventually, understanding development banking in its historical evolution under different financial regimes amounts to recounting a story that will combine historical facts, economic theory, and social values. Pattern models are such coherent narratives of part-whole relationships that form alternative scenarios and working hypotheses that may guide economic policy-making (Whalen 2022: 251, 255, 261). Values are important because they condition economic actors' beliefs and guide their purposeful actions. Hence, understanding is incomplete if values are not taken into account (Cohen 1991). In addition, the social usefulness of a theory of development banking is indispensable for a research project that inspires to be useful for policymakers. Hence, "instrumental reasoning" in the sense of forming a theory that is able to inform government policy for economic development financing and institutional change (Stanfield 1999: 237) is another reason why values and visions for a better world should be part of our storytelling. Hence, our approach combines all three major elements of the analysis in the context of Original Institutional Economics namely, the focus on the cultural context, the emphasis on evolution, and the demand for both understanding and informing policy (Mayhew 2018).

The second part of this book is a case study of the Greek experience in development banking during the post-World War II period as an application of the aforementioned methodology of storytelling. We aim to test the institutional evolutionary model we expounded on in this chapter and to gain more insights into the nature of development banking from this case study (Figart 2017). We may consider our evolutionary theory of development banking as a pattern model derived from the examination of the historical experience we reviewed in this book so far and using the theoretical tools supplied by the Original Institutional Economics. It is a theory based on historical empirical data and already-developed theories (Cohen 1991). Then, this case study will attempt to apply this theory to understand the Greek economic reality (a "lumpers" effect) and possibly fill the gaps in terms of historical and country specificity (a "splitters" effect). Statistical analysis will only be used as a means to illustrate the points made in our historical recount (Atkinson and Oleson 1996) of development banking in Greece within the context of the evolution of the Greek economy during these years. Our storytelling will make use of a variety of historical sources including juridical sources, social documents, and narrative sources (Bracarense and Reeves Johnson 2016: 94) with an emphasis on development banks' annual reports and the relevant literature about the Greek financial system, the institutional context and the conditions of Greek post-World War II economic development. Hence, our units of analysis are development banks as going concerns in the context of alternating financial regimes as financial regulation/repression gives its place to financial liberalization and deregulation in the Greek post-World War II economy up to its present situation within the Eurozone.

References

Arestis, P. and Stein, H. (2005) "An Institutional Perspective to Finance and Development as an Alternative to Financial Liberalization." *International Review of Applied Economics* 19 (4): 381–398.

Arestis, P., Nissanke, M. and Stein, H. (2003) "Finance and Development: Institutional and Policy Alternatives to Financial Liberalization", The Levy Economics Institute of Bard College Working Paper No 377 available at https://www.levyinstitute.org/pubs/wp377.pdf Accessed 18 Nov. 2023

Atkinson, G. W. and Oleson, T. (1996) "Institutional Inquiry: The Search for Similarities and Differences", *Journal of Economic Issues*, 30(3) 701–718.

Bhattacharya, S. and Thakor, A. (1993) "Contemporary Banking Theory", *Journal of Financial Intermediation*, 3(1):2–50.

Bracarense, N. and Reeves Johnson, A. (2016) "Historical Method and Data", in Lee, F. S. and Cronin, B. (eds.) *Handbook of Research Methods and Applications in Heterodox Economics*, Cheltenham, UK & Northampton, MA, USA: Edward Elgar, pp. 92–109.

Bush, P. D. (1987) "The Theory of Institutional Change." *Journal of Economic Issues* 21(3): 1075–1116.

Cameron, R. E. (1953) "The Crédit Mobilier and the Economic Development of Europe." *The Journal of Political Economy*, 61(6): 461–488.

Castro, L. B. (2018) "Financial Regulation and Risk Management in Development Banks", in Griffith-Jones, S. and Ocampo, J. A. (eds.) *The Future of National Development Banks*, N.Y.: Oxford University Press, pp. 231–254.

Cohen, M. (1991) "Principles of Institutionalist Research Methodology", Staff Paper, No SP 91-11, Cornell University, Charles H. Dyson School of Applied Economics and Management, Ithaca, NY available at https://www.econstor.eu/bitstream/10419/276843/1/Cornell-Dyson-SP199111.pdf Accessed 14 Dec. 2023

Colombo, M. and Cuda, M. (2023) "The Role of Public Development Banks & Institutions in the Implementation of the United Nations' Agenda 2030: A Survey in Europe", Discussion Paper No. 179. Directorate General Economic and Financial Affairs (DG ECFIN), European Commission available at https://economy-finance.ec.europa.eu/document/download/2e0e5ab7-c684-40d7-9d03-e21432e99b62_en?filename=dp179_en.pdf Accessed 21 Oct. 2023

De Luna-Martínez, J., Vicente, C. L., bin Arshad, A., Tatucu, R., and Song, J. (2018) "2017 Survey of National Development Banks", World Bank Group Global Report, (May) available at https://documents1.worldbank.org/curated/en/977821525438071799/pdf/2017-Survey-of-National-development-banks.pdf Accessed 13 Oct. 2023

De la Torre, A., Gozzi, J. C. and Schmukler, S. L. (2017) *Innovative Experiences in Access to Finance. Market-Friendly Roles for the Visible Hand?*, Washington D.C.: World Bank Group.

Diamond, W. (1982a) "The Preoccupations and Working Style of Chief Executives of Development Banks" in Diamond, W. and Raghavan, V. S. (eds.) *Aspects of Development Bank Management*, EDI Series in Economic Development, Baltimore & London: The Johns Hopkins University Press, pp. 5–17.

Diamond, W. (1982b) "Notes on Purposes and Strategies" in Diamond, W. and Raghavan, V. S. (eds.) *Aspects of Development Bank Management*, EDI Series in Economic Development, Baltimore & London: The Johns Hopkins University Press, pp. 35–56.

Figart, D. M. (2017) "Three Short Stories of Progressive Institutional Change", *Journal of Economic Issues*, 51(2): 263–284.

Francisco, M., Mascaró, Y., Mendoza, J. C., and Yaron, J. (2008) "Measuring the Performance and Achievement of Social Objectives of Development Finance Institutions", World Bank Policy Research Working Paper WPS4506 available at https://documents1.worldbank.org/curated/en/949841468036879814/pdf/wps4506.pdf Accessed 21 Oct. 2023

Gerschenkron, A. (1962) *Economic Backwardness in Historical Perspective*, Cambridge MA.

Gordon, D. L. (1983) "Development Finance Companies. State and Privately Owned. A Review." World Bank Staff Working Papers, No 578, available at https://documents1.worldbank.org/curated/en/928181468741004629/text/multi-page.txt Accessed 25 Oct. 2023

Gottschalk, R., Castro, L. B., and Xu, J. (2022) "Should National Development Banks Be Subject to Basel III?", *Review of Political Economy*, 34(2): 249–267.

Griffith-Jones, S., Spiegel, S., Xu, J., Carreras, M. and Naqvi, N. (2022) "Matching Risks with Instruments in Development Banks", *Review of Political Economy*, 34(2): 197–223.

Griffith-Jones, S. (2022) "The Role Public National Development Banks Play in the Structural Transformation of Developing Countries", United Nations Conference on Trade and Development, April, available at https://unctad.org/system/files/information-document/BRI-Project_policy-brief-01_en.pdf Accessed 30 Oct. 2023

Griffith-Jones, S. and Naqvi, N. (2021) "Leveraging Policy Steer? Industrial Policy, Risk-Sharing, and the European Investment Bank", in Mertens, D. Thiemann, M., and Volberding. P. (eds.) *The Reinvention of Development Banking in the European Union. Industrial Policy in the Single Market and the Emergence of a Field*, New York: Oxford University Press, pp. 90–112.

Griffith-Jones, S., Ocampo, J. A., Rezende, F., Schclarek, A. and Brei, M. (2018) "The Future of National Development Banks." in Griffith-Jones, S. and Ocampo, J. A. (eds.) *The Future of National Development Banks*, New York: Oxford University Press, pp. 1–36.

Groenewegen, J., Kerstholt, F. and Nagelkerke, A. (1995) "On Integrating New and Old Institutionalism: Douglass North Building Bridges." *Journal of Economic Issues,* 29(2): 467–475.

Gutierrez, E., Rudolph, H. P., Homa, T., and Blanco Beneit, E. (2011) "Development Banks. Role and Mechanisms to Increase their Efficiency", World Bank Policy Research Working Paper WPS5729 available at https://documents1.worldbank.org/curated/en/912941468045550498/pdf/WPS5729.pdf Accessed 28 Oct 2023

Hein, E., Dodig, N., and Budyldina, N. (2015) "The Transition towards Finance-Dominated Capitalism: French Regulation School, Social Structures of Accumulation and Post-Keynesian Approaches Compared" in Hein, E., Detzer, D. and Dodig, N. (eds.) *The Demise of Finance-Dominated Capitalism*, Edward Elgar, pp. 7–53.

Kemp, T. (2009) *Progress and Reform. The Economic Thought of John R. Commons*, Saarbrücken, Deutschland: VDM Verlag Dr. Müller.

Keynes, J. M. (1936 [1973]) *The General Theory of Employment, Interest and Money*, reprinted in *The Collected Writings of J. M. Keynes*, Vol. VII, MacMillan.

Kindleberger, C. P. (2000) "Lumpers and Splitters in Economics, a Note", *The American Economist*, 44(1): 88–92.

Krahnen, J. P. and Schmidt, R. H. (1994) *Development Finance as Institution Building. A New Approach to Poverty-Oriented Banking*, London & New York: Routledge.

Lazzarini, S. G., Musacchio, A., Bandeira-de-Mello, R., and Marcon, R. (2015) "What Do State-Owned Development Banks Do? Evidence from BNDES, 2002-09", *World Development*, 66: 237–253.

Lewis, W. A. (1955) *The Theory of Economic Growth*, Homewood, Ill: Irwin.

Loizos, K. (2018) "The Financial Repression-Liberalization Debate: Taking Stock, Looking for a Synthesis." *Journal of Economic Surveys,* 32 (2): 440–468.

Loizos, K. (2023) "Prolegomena to an Evolutionary Theory of Development Banking for a Sustainable Future", *Journal of Economic Issues*, 57(2): 606–612.

Levy-Yeyati, E. L., Micco, A. and Panizza, U. (2004) "Should the Government Be in the Banking Business? The Role of State-Owned and Development Banks", Inter-American Development Bank Working Paper No 517, available at https://publications.iadb.org/en/publications/english/viewer/Should-the-Government-Be-in-the-Banking-Business-The-Role-of-State-Owned-and-Development-Banks.pdf Accessed 2 Nov. 2023

Marois, T. (2022) "A Dynamic Theory of Public Banks (and Why it Matters)", *Review of Political Economy*, 34(2): 356–371.

Mayhew, A. (2018) "An Introduction to Institutional Economics: Tools for Understanding Evolving Economies", *The American Economist*, 63(1): 3–17.

Mazzucato, M. and Penna, C. R. C. (2018) "National Development Banks and Mission-Oriented Finance for Innovation" in Griffith-Jones, S. and Ocampo, J. A. (eds.) *The Future of National Development Banks*, New York: Oxford University Press, pp. 255–277.

Mazzucato, M. and Penna, C. R. C. (2016) "Beyond Market Failures: The Market Creating and Shaping Roles of State Investment Banks", *Journal of Economic Policy Reform*, 19(4): 305–326.

McCormick, K. (2006) *Veblen in Plain English. A Complete Introduction to Thorstein Veblen's Economics*. New York: Cambria Press.

Minsky, H. P. (1996) "Uncertainty and the Institutional Structure of Capitalist Economies", *Journal of Economic Issues*, 30(2): 357–368.

Minsky, H. P., Papadimitriou, D. B., Phillips, R. J., and Randall Wray, L. (1993) "Community Development Banking. A Proposal to Establish a Nationwide System of Community Development Banks", The Jerome Levy Economics Institute of Bard College, Public Policy Brief No 3 available at https://www.researchgate.net/publication/5163193_Community_Development_Banking_A_Proposal_to_Establish_a_Nationwide_System_of_Community_Development_Banks Accessed 5 Nov. 2023

Musacchio, A., Lazzarini, S. Makhoul, P. and Simmons, E. (2017) "The role and impact of development banks. A review of their founding, focus, and influence", (Report to the World Bank). Washington, D.C.: World Bank. Available at https://people.brandeis.edu/~aldom/papers/The%20Role%20and%20Impact%20of%20Development%20Banks%20-%203-9-2017.pdf Accessed 5 Nov. 2023

Myrdal, G. (1960) *Beyond the Welfare State: Economic Planning and its International Implications*, New Haven, Connecticut: Yale University Press.

Polanyi, K. (1944 [2001]) *The Great Transformation: The Political and Economic Origins of Our Time*, Boston, MA: Beacon Press.

Ramstad, Y. (2001) "John R. Commons's Reasonable Value and the Problem of Just Price", *Journal of Economic Issues*, 35(2): 253–277.

Ramstad, Y. (1991) "From Desideratum to Historical Achievement: John R. Commons's Reasonable Value and the 'Negotiated Economy' of Denmark." *Journal of Economic Issues*, 25(2): 431–439.

Rezende, F. (2018) "Financial Sustainability and Infrastructure Finance" in Griffith-Jones, S. and Ocampo, J. A. (eds.) *The Future of National Development Banks*, New York: Oxford University Press, pp. 302–334.

Ricz, J. (2016) "Developmental States in the 21st Century: Analytical Structure of a New Approach", *Centre for Economic and Regional Studies of the Hungarian Academy of Sciences – Institute of World Economics*, Working Paper no 223 available at https://real.mtak.hu/39512/1/WP_223_Ricz.pdf Accessed 5 Jan. 2024

Rudolph, H. P. (2009) "State Financial Institutions. Mandates, Governance, and Beyond", World Bank Policy Research Working Paper WPS5141 available at https://papers.ssrn.com/sol3/papers.cfm?abstract_id=1517013 Accessed 12 Jan. 2024

Rutherford, M. (1995) "The Old and New Institutionalism: Can Bridges be Build?" *Journal of Economic Issues* 29(2): 443–451.

Santomero, A. M. (1984) "Modeling the Banking Firm: A Survey", *Journal of Money, Credit and Banking*, 16(4): 576–602.

Schumpeter, J. A. (1912 [1934]) *The Theory of Economic Development: An Inquiry into Profits, Capital, Credit, Interest and the Business Cycle*, Cambridge, MA: Harvard University Press.

Smallridge, D. and de Olloqui, F. (2011) "A Health Diagnostic Tool for Public Development Banks", Inter-American Development Bank (IDB) Technical Notes No. IDB-TN-225 available at https://publications.iadb.org/en/publications/english/viewer/A-Health-Diagnostic-Tool-for-Public-Development-Banks.pdf Accessed 3 Nov. 2023

Stanfield, J. R. (1999) "The Scope, Method, and Significance of Original Institutional Economics", *Journal of Economic Issues*, 33(2): 231–255.

Studart, R. (1995) *Investment Finance in Economic Development*, London and New York: Routledge.

Swank, J. (1996) "Theories of the Banking Firm: A Review of the Literature", *Bulletin of Economic Research*, 48(3): 173–207.

Torres, E. and Zeidan, R. (2016) "The Life-Cycle of National Development Banks: The Experience of Brazil's BNDES", *The Quarterly Review of Economics and Finance*, 62: 97–104.

Tymoigne, É. (2011) "Financial Stability, Regulatory Buffers, and Economic Growth after the Great Recession: Some Regulatory Implications" in Whalen, C. J. (ed.) *Financial Instability and Economic Security after the Great Recession*, Northampton: Edward Elgar, pp. 114–140.

Van Damme, E. (1994) "Banking A Survey of Recent Microeconomic Theory", *Oxford Review of Economic Policy*, 10(4): 14–33.

Whalen, C. J. (2022) "Storytelling and Institutional Change. The Power and Pitfalls of Economic Narratives" in Whalen, C. J. (ed.) *Institutional Economics. Perspectives and Methods in Pursuit of a Better World*, London & N.Y.: Routledge, pp. 247–270.

Wilber, C. K. and Harrison, R. S. (1978) "The Methodological Basis of Institutional Economics: Pattern Model, Storytelling, and Holism", *Journal of Economic Issues*, 12(1): 61–89.

PART II

A Case Study: The Post-World War II Experience of Development Banking in Greece and Its Prospects

CHAPTER 7

The Post-World War II Greek Economy: The Great Transformation

7.1 The Post-War Greek Economy in a Global Context: Periodization and Patterns of Development

Conducting a historical analysis of economic organizations implies the choice of a specific historical period and economy as the object of research. In our case, the post-war Greek economy and especially the period between the early 1960s and early 2020s constitutes the object of research for establishing our arguments. The choice for this period has manifold reasons: The first part of this bout between the early 1960s and early 2000s can be characterized as the main period of development banking in Greece during the post-World War II era. This epoch saw the operation and demise of the three Greek development banks, the National Investment Bank for Industrial Development (ETEBA), the Investment Bank (TE), and the Hellenic Industrial Development Bank (ETBA). The second part of this era from the early 2000s to the early 2020s has been the period of Greece's participation in the European Monetary Union (EMU) with major consequences for its institutional and economic development. In addition, during this time the idea of development banking found new momentum in both the European Union and Greece and the latter saw the establishment of a new development bank, the Hellenic Development Bank (HDB), and its subsidiary, the Hellenic Development Bank of Investments (HDBI). At the same time, the entire period 1960s to the

K. Loizos, *Between Markets and Governments*,
https://doi.org/10.1007/978-3-031-88527-3_7

2020s has been a historical period of major economic and institutional transformation for the economy as a whole.

However, making sense of the economic, social, and institutional developments during these sixty years implies a proper periodization that will identify possible patterns of change (Jordanova 2006: 107). Brenner (1998: 9), in his paper on the post-War World II economy, distinguishes three phases that the world's major economies passed through: The long boom (1950–1965), the interim period when the transition from boom to crisis takes place (1965–1973) and the long downturn (1973–late 1990s). The data for manufacturing in the G-7 economies indicate that the average net profit for the period 1950–1970 was 26.2% while it fell to 15.7% in the period 1970–1993. Brenner (1998: 7) points out that depressed profitability during the latter period brought about a decline in investment and output growth which both contributed to falling productivity rates and rising unemployment. Indeed, unemployment rates in the private sector of the economy were on average 3.1% in the period 1950–1973 but rose to the level of 6.2% on average in 1973–1993 (Brenner (1998: 5, Table 1).

Maddison (1983) also underlines the difference between the pre-1973 and the post-1973 period. In his research about six major economies (France, Germany, Japan, the Netherlands, the UK, and the USA), he observes an average annual growth rate of GDP in constant prices of 5.3% between 1950 and 1973 compared to 1.9% for the period 1973–1982. Besides, Maddison (2005: 12, Table 6) who covers a wider period estimates the per capita GDP annual average growth rates for Western Europe to be 4.05% for the period 1950–1973 and 1.88% for the period 1973–2001. The main causes for this trend reversal were for Maddison (1983): (1) The long-term fall in productivity rates as the gap between the US economy on the one hand and the European economies and Japan on the other narrowed in the post-war period. (2) "System shocks" in the sense of the change in the economic environment provoked by the breakdown of the Bretton Woods system and the ensuing oil crises. The widespread sense of uncertainty that followed affected both entrepreneurial expectations and the ability of governments to respond successfully to the new challenges for policy. (3) Changes in the "establishment view" of economic policy. By "establishment" Maddison (1983) means officials in central banks and ministries of finance along with politicians and academics who jointly constitute the elite of economic policy decision-making. The change of the point of view refers to the shift from the

Keynesian-inspired mix of policies in the 1950s–1960s to the new consensus founded on the ideas of Monetarists and New Classicals. The new consensus rejected the demand management fine-tuning approach and more generally the idea of big government along with a well-developed welfare state. In its place, it propagated the need for fiscal restraint and the ability of markets to self-correct themselves even with employment and output losses. In this sense, government policies aimed primarily at curbing inflation may be considered partly responsible for the fall in output and the rise in unemployment rates. This is how the Great Inflation of the period 1965–1982 was followed by the Great Moderation from 1982 to 2006 just before the Great Recession of 2007–2009 (Bordo 2015: 364; Bordo and Orphanides 2013: 1; Rich 2013; Whalen 2011: 1–2). The aftermath of the Global Financial Crisis and the Great Recession gave rise to the debate about sustainability in its various forms and about sustainable development in particular. The seventeen Sustainable Development Goals of the United Nations which were adopted in 2015 refer to both social, environmental, and economic objectives to be accomplished by 2030 that bring to the forefront the multiple dimensions of economic development (Katila et al. 2020: 1–2; Giovannoni and Fabietti 2013: 21). Maddison (2007: 335–372) just before the onset of the Global Financial Crisis and the Great Recession, speculated about the conditions in the world economy that might have been realized in 2030. His projections for the period 2003–2030 yielded an average annual rate of change in per capita GDP of 1.73% for the rich countries as opposed to 1.69% during the period 1990–2003. The respective rates of change were 3.01% (2003–2030) as opposed to 2.64% (1990–2003) for the rest of the world and 2.23% (2003–2030) in contrast to 1.81% (1990–2003) for the World. Although he had not predicted the effects of the financial crisis or the pandemic crisis, he warned about possible disruptive factors such as energy shortfalls, political upheavals, and climate change.

How did the Greek economy fit into this international context with the multiplicity of dimensions and alternating phases? The Greek economy shows two clear patterns of growth during the post-war period. According to Alogoskoufis (1996), the period from 1954 to 1973 is characterized by high growth rates of about 7% on average, along with low inflation rates not exceeding 4% on average. This pattern changes in the ensuing period 1974–1993 with a percentage growth rate as low as 2% on average and an inflation rate of about 18% on average. The author describes these two periods of development in the Greek economy as "the two phases of

Ianus". On the other hand, Dimelis et al. (1996) spot the point of inflection in the path of Greek economic development around the early 1980s. Hence, they argue that the Greek economy was growing "relatively too fast" till 1980 and "relatively too slow" afterward. In terms of the growth rate of GDP per capita, average annual growth rates as high as 4.58% (1950–1959), 6.80% (1960–1969), and 3.68% (1970–1979) were followed by much lower average growth rates of 1.10% (1980–1989) and 0.60% (1990–1994) (Dimelis et al. 1996: 74, Table 1). Despite the differences in opinion concerning the exact turning point in Greek economic growth, there is agreement concerning the deterioration of economic performance during the 1980s and early 1990s. However, Bosworth and Kollintzas (2001: 177) provide evidence for the recovery of the Greek economy after 1995 with the growth rate of GDP being 3.3% on average for the period 1995–2000. It is therefore fair to describe the post-war evolution of the Greek economy as being characterized by a great cycle (Drakatos 1997).

According to Drakatos (1997),[1] the great cycle of the Greek economy is analyzed in the following phases: (1) A phase of "reconstruction" after the Second World War and the devastation of the country by the ensuing Civil War. The period 1945–1952 was characterized by a popular demand for economic stabilization along with a reorganization of the production base of the economy. A major development of that period was the establishment of the Monetary Committee in 1946 to control money issuing although it soon became the governmental agency for financial affairs. A successful outcome that could be attributed to the efforts spent by the government in that period was the combatting of inflation which reversed the environment of monetary instability in 1952. (2) A "preparation" phase during 1953–1956 which was marked by the devaluation of 1953 that aimed at supporting the competitiveness of the economy. In the same period, there was an increase in domestic savings in the form of bank deposits as a consequence of rising confidence in the currency. In addition, government policy provided incentives for foreign direct investment such as those referred to the Law 2687/1953 "On investment and protection of foreign capital". Besides, a new income tax law was introduced in 1955 in an attempt to modernize the domestic fiscal system. (3) The

[1] This paragraph is based on the article Loizos (2017) published in the journal *Economic Alternatives*, 2017, available on line https://www.unwe.bg/eajournal/en/journalissues/article/10987

period of economic development 1957–1972 which was characterized by the establishment of large industrial units in sectors such as aluminum, metal industry, shipyards, petrochemicals, cement, etc., the acquisition of foreign know-how especially in management techniques, and the rise of the share of secondary production to total output at the expense of primary production. This period was also marked by the consolidation of macroeconomic stability due to the containment of inflationary pressures, the rapid growth of domestic output supply to meet growing demand, and the reduction of workers' demands for wage increases along with international monetary stability. In the highlights of this period, we should include the association agreement between Greece and the European Economic Community which was signed in 1961. However, the most important development in the financing of Greek economic development during this period was the establishment of the three development banks: the Hellenic Industrial Development Bank (ETBA), the National Investment Bank for Industrial Development (ETEBA) and the Investment Bank (TE). (4) The turning point observed in the period 1973–1980 was characterized by the two oil crises of 1973 and 1979 and the ensuing fluctuation in exchange rates after the abolition of the Bretton Woods regime. The typical feature of this period was the resurgence of inflation that reached levels ranging from 15.5% in 1973 to 24.9% in 1980 and the entrenchment of conditions of uncertainty and instability that hurt entrepreneurial activity and the inducement to invest and therefore, GDP growth. Despite these adverse developments, Greece became the 10th member of the European Economic Community in 1981. Finally, (5) the phase of a weak economy between 1981 and 1995 which was characterized by great macroeconomic imbalances and deindustrialization, especially during the stagflation period of 1981–1985. The government attempted to deal with rising inflation by proposing a stabilization program in 1986–1987. However, according to Garganas and Tavlas (2001: 58–59), the latter was short-lived for reasons relating to the political business cycle. During the early 1990s and specifically in 1991–1993 and 1994–1995, further stabilization programs were implemented in the context of the national goal for nominal convergence with the European average according to the criteria of the Maastricht Treaty. These criteria suggested significant adjustments concerning the inflation rates, budget deficits as a percentage of GDP, public debt as a percentage of GDP, and nominal long-term interest rates.

The Greek economy during the period 1994–2007 demonstrated high GDP growth rates. In particular, from 1996 onward, the reported growth rates were higher than the European Union average while the annual rate of change in investment expenditure, both public and private, was similar to that of the high growth years in 1961–1973 (Fragiadis 2007: 220). During this period the country benefited from falling interest rates which, however, generated a vicious circle of external borrowing, rising imports, and increasing consumption expenditure. It seems that macroeconomic imbalances were present at least from 2004 but were widely recognized due to the Global Financial Crisis of 2008. Thereafter, Greece entered a prolonged period of economic contraction with adverse social and economic consequences (Psalidopoulos 2014: 57–58).

Kazakos (2001: 35, 542) also characterizes the evolution of the Greek economy during the post-war period as a great cycle but he uses a slightly different periodization influenced by both economic and political events. The period 1944–1952 is marked by the Civil War together with reconstruction efforts. The period of development began in 1953 and ended in 1967 when the Greek junta came to power. The seven-year dictatorship (1967–1974) is then characterized by both crisis and development. In the next period 1974–1981, democracy was restored and stabilized while the following decade of 1981–1990 was the decade of economic populism. Finally, in the next decade 1990–2000, the country enters the era of the Maastricht criteria.

According to the previous discussion, one may choose to set the starting point of our review of the Greek economy in 1945 as the beginning of the reconstruction period (Drakatos 1997) or in 1954, just after the devaluation of 1953 (Alogoskoufis 1996) or even in 1950 which was marked by the end of the civil war and the stabilization program introduced by G. A. Kartalis (Zouboulakis 2023–2024). On the other hand, the main period of development banking in Greece begins in the early 1960s. In fact, there are too many different dates that are related to significant events in Greek economic history and could be chosen as the starting point of our recount. However, our interest is in the main and subsequent periods of development banking in Greece and how development banks were embedded in the Greek economy of that particular era. Hence, since the decade of the 1960s is the decade in which all three institutions of the main period of development banking in Greece were established, we will focus on the period 1960–2022 for the purpose of our analysis without disregarding the effects of the 1940s and 1950s.

The different subperiods of economic development in Greece during the period 1960–2022 are reflected in the evolution of three major macroeconomic variables, constant GDP per capita, GDP growth rates, and inflation which are presented in Figs. 7.1, 7.2, and 7.3.

The evolution of real GDP per capita from the 1960s to the early 2020s (Fig. 7.1) indicates the long process of economic development and transformation in the Greek economy. Despite significant bouts of fluctuation and stagnation of GDP per capita levels during the 1980s and early 1990s, the upward trend reached its peak in 2007 and entered a phase of a phenomenal contraction of the economy until 2013 and stagnation thereafter combined with the effects of the pandemic during the early 2020s.

Figure 7.2, which shows the path of the GDP growth rate during the same period tells a similar story. GDP growth rates were positive until 1973 but fluctuated between positive and negative values from 1974 to 1993. Between 1994 and 2007 GDP growth rates returned to positive values as opposed to the extreme fluctuation thereafter and the extreme

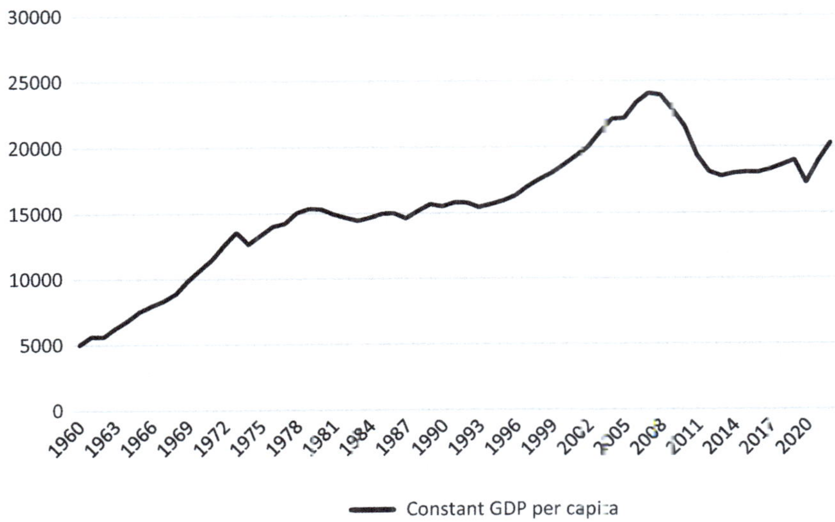

Fig. 7.1 Constant GDP per capita for Greece, 2010 U.S. dollars, annual, not seasonally adjusted, 1960–2022. Source: World Bank. World Development Indicators, retrieved from FRED, Federal Reserve Bank of St. Louis, and author's elaboration

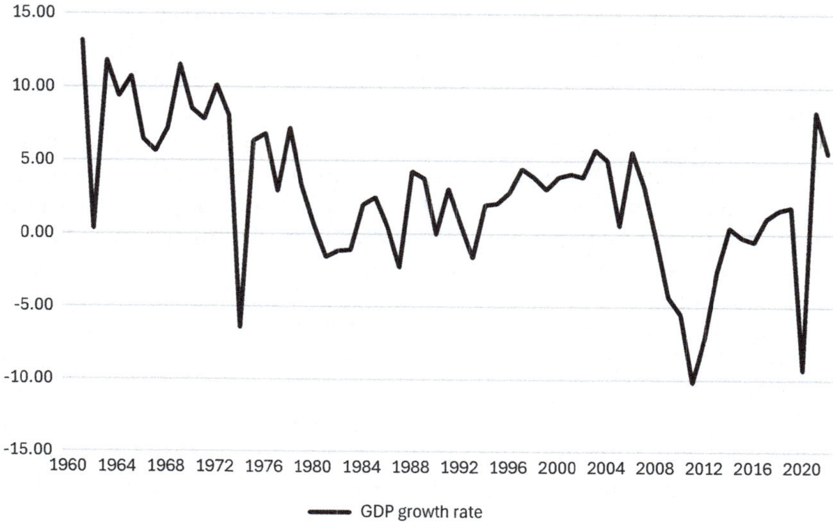

Fig. 7.2 GDP growth for Greece, percent, annual, at market prices based on constant local currency, 1960–2022. Source: World Bank national accounts data, and OECD National Accounts data files and author's elaboration

negative outliers in 2011 and 2020, offspring of the multiple crises that hit the Greek economy. Finally, inspecting the evolution of the inflation rate in Fig. 7.3 at least two observations stand out: A period of low inflation, below 5% until 1972 is followed by a highly inflationary period between 1973 and 1993. Moreover, while inflation fell sharply between 1994 and 1999, it entered a period of volatility that intensified from 2008.

These distinct trends are summarized in Tables 7.1 and 7.2. In terms of mean and median values of GDP growth rates, there is a clear cyclical pattern of peaks and troughs which confirms Drakatos (1997). The high growth period of the 1960s and early 1970s is followed by a period of both low average growth rates and high inflation rates. Then, both the preparation years before entering the European Monetary Union (1994–2001) and the first "short" decade within the EMU are marked by rising average growth rates and falling inflation rates while the period of multiple crises and restructuring 2008–2022 is characterized on average by economic contraction and low inflation.

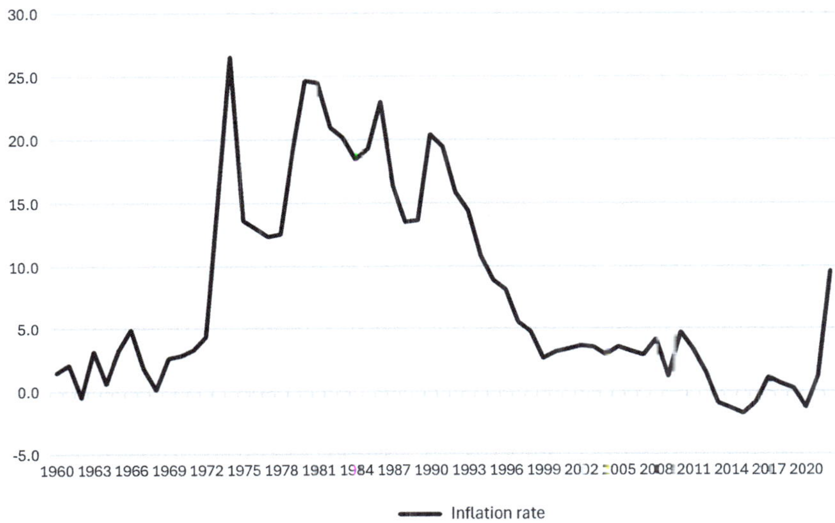

Fig. 7.3 Inflation, consumer prices for Greece, percent, annual, not seasonally adjusted, 1960–2022. Source: World Bank, World Development Indicators, retrieved from FRED, Federal Reserve Bank of St. Louis, and author's elaboration

Table 7.1 GDP growth rate, Greece, summary statistics, 1960–2022

	1960–1973	*1974–1993*	*1994–2001*	*2002–2007*	*2008–2022*
Mean	8.55	1.51	3.31	4.05	−1.39
Median	8.56	1.36	3.48	4.49	−0.34
St. Dev.	3.32	3.42	0.94	1.96	5.18
Min	0.36	−6.44	2.00	0.60	−10.15
Max	13.20	7.25	4.48	5.79	8.38

Source: Author's elaboration based on World Bank national accounts data, and OECD National Accounts data files

The above discussion points to a periodization of Greek economic development which is divided into five subperiods: The first period roughly extends from 1960 to 1973 and it is characterized by high growth rates and macroeconomic stability. The second period 1974–1993 is marked by macroeconomic imbalances and stagflation. The third period 1994–2001 is a prolonged period of macroeconomic adjustment with intervals of

Table 7.2 Inflation rate, Greece, summary statistics, 1960–2022

	1960–1973	*1974–1993*	*1994–2001*	*2002–2007*	*2008–2022*
Mean	3.2	18.1	5.9	3.3	1.4
Median	2.7	18.8	5.2	3.4	1.1
St. Dev.	3.81	4.44	3.05	0.33	3.01
Min	−0.5	12.4	2.6	2.9	−1.7
Max	15.4	26.6	10.9	3.6	9.6

Source: Author's elaboration based on World Bank, World Development Indicators

regression and progress toward the goal of Greece's participation in the European Monetary Union. The fourth period 2002–2007 is the period of illusions and hopes characterized by both rising GDP growth and unsustainable levels of consumption expenditure as will be shown below. Finally, the fifth period 2008–2022 is a period of both economic and social hardship as the economy contracted under the pressure of adverse international developments and domestic imbalances. It is also the period of reflection and deliberation about the necessary change in Greece's model of economic development which allows alternative value systems and policy proposals to compete with each other. This is the present state of affairs to which this book hopes to contribute. In the rest of this chapter, we review basic economic indicators of the Greek economy in order to identify the major characteristics of the aforementioned subperiods in economic development and outline the macroeconomic context for both institutional development and development banking in Greece. However, our brief description of the main features of each subperiod is neither complete nor thorough since such a venture would neither be possible nor be desirable from the point of view of this book. We argue that the process that characterizes the entire period from the early 1960s to the early 2020s is a process of continued and profound transformation which, however, is open to interpretation concerning its sustainability and future direction.

7.2 High Growth and Economic Development 1960–1973

The "golden age" of Greek economic development which is roughly represented by the period covering the 1960s and early 1970s (Maniatis and Passas 2013) was founded on a series of economic and social developments that took place during the 1950s when the devastating wars of the

1940s had come to an end. The devaluation of 1953 and the ensuing monetary stabilization shaped a macroeconomic framework that would be able to support economic development during the 1960s and early 1970s. The low levels of inflation have been accommodated by a stable exchange rate between the drachma and the dollar, the minimization of public deficits as a permanent policy concern, and the ability of the post-civil war state to curb labor demands for a rising share in national income as productivity rose. In addition, a strict system of regulation and administrative controls, of which more will be said in the next chapter, directed banking financing toward sectors of key importance for Greek economic development such as manufacturing, agriculture, and export trade (Kostis 2018a: 757–759; Psalidopoulos 2014: 40–41). Kostis (2018b: 357) characterizes the whole period from 1953 up to 1973 as the era of "great transformation" in the Greek economy in which capital accumulation played a central role. According to a prominent politician of the era, the question was that of high investment rates and rapid capital accumulation within a liberal and democratic political environment (Psalidopoulos 1996: 143–144 cited by Kostis 2018b: 357–358). Figures 7.4 and 7.5 illustrate this process of transformation at the economic level. A simple inspection of these

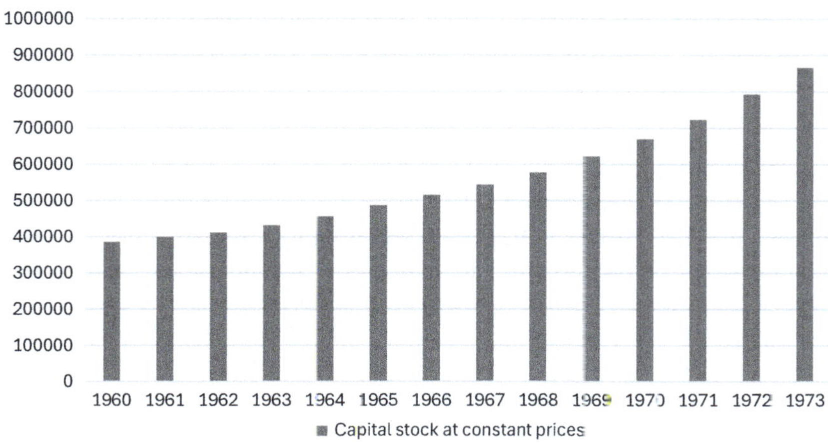

Fig. 7.4 Capital Stock at constant national prices for Greece, millions of 2017 U.S. dollars, annual, not seasonally adjusted, 1960–1973. Source: University of Groningen and University of California, Davis, Penn World Table 10.01, retrieved from FRED, Federal Reserve Bank of St. Louis and author's elaboration

Fig. 7.5 Total Factor Productivity at constant national prices for Greece, index 2017 = 1, annual, not seasonally adjusted, 1960–1973. Source: University of Groningen and University of California, Davis, Penn World Table 10.01, retrieved from FRED, Federal Reserve Bank of St. Louis and author's elaboration

diagrams indicates a similar pattern of continuous and consistent rise in both capital stock in real terms and in Total Factor Productivity which defines how efficiently labor and capital factors contribute to economic growth.[2]

However, the great transformation of Greece during the post-World War II period was both economic and social. The share of the primary sector of the economy in terms of the active employed labor force contracted by less than 13% between 1928 and 1961 but by more than 14% in just ten years between 1961 and 1971 in favor of the secondary and tertiary sectors of the economy. Notably, the ratio of people living in the cities to the total population rose steadily from 37.7% in 1951 to 43.3% in 1961 and to 53.2% in 1971. Hence, there was a clear trend of growing urbanization during the post-war period. On the other hand, the ratio of the active

[2] TFP (Total Factor Productivity) or MFP (Multi Factor Productivity) refers to the part of economic growth that cannot be explained by the increase in labor and capital inputs, the so-called residual, which usually reflects improvements in technology, the organization of production processes, etc. and is attributed to the effect of all factors of production together (Shackleton 2013).

labor force that was employed in the secondary sector remained close to 19.5% in 1951 and 1961 but rose sharply to 27% in 1971 (Kostis 2018b: 360–364). The period 1961–1973 was a period of rapid industrialization and structural transformation of the Greek economy, a decisive step from a developing to a developed economy. The role of the state was critical since more than half of the value of investment expenditure during this period can be attributed to government support in the form of various tax exemptions, interest rate subsidies, or direct capital disbursement. Manufacturing more than tripled its gross product and increased its share in GDP from 25% in 1961 to 33% in 1973. Rising productivity was accompanied by the establishment of new industrial units in heavy industry such as steel mills, shipyards, and refineries (Fragiadis 2007: 185–186).

Economic growth and structural change went hand in hand with social transformation. Life expectancy improved impressively through the years as shown in Fig. 7.6. In 1951 life expectancy at birth was 63.44 years for men and 66.5 years for women. In 1961 life expectancy at birth for men was 67.30 years and 70.42 years for women while in 1971 the respective figures were 70.13 and 73.64 years (Kostis 2018b: 368). Although the

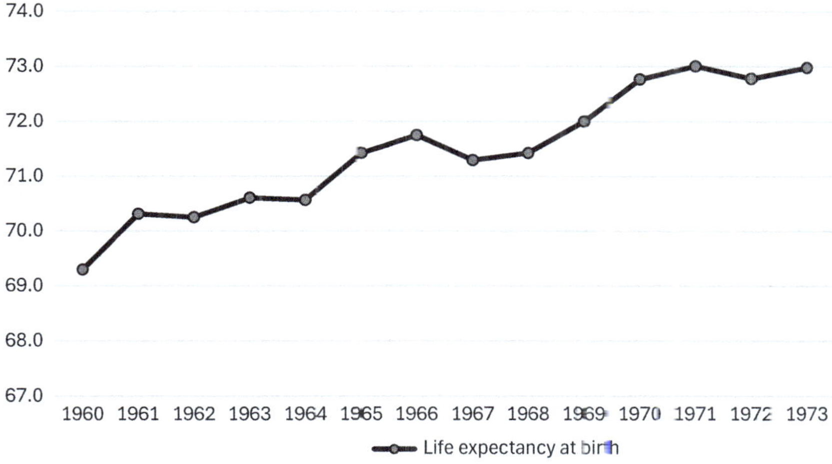

Fig. 7.6 Life expectancy at birth, total for Greece, number of years, annual, not seasonally adjusted, 1960–1973. Source: World Bank, World Development Indicators, retrieved from FRED, Federal Reserve Bank of St. Louis, and author's elaboration

increase in the standard of living of Greek workers lagged behind the increase in productivity, especially during the period of dictatorship (1967–1974), there was a significant improvement in human capital accumulation for the Greek economy. First of all, there was a significant reduction in child labor and at the same time, a rise in schooling as access to secondary education became universal. Illiteracy decreased substantially from 40.9% of the population over the age of 8 in 1928 to 13.9% of the population over the age of 10 in 1971. Furthermore, higher and technical education entered an era of continuous expansion with a rising student population and the establishment of new universities in the cities of Patras and Ioannina. Between 1959 and 1974 the number of students in Greek universities more than tripled from 24.896 to about 80.000 students (Kostis 2018a: 788–789; Fragiadis 2007: 188). Figure 7.7 depicts the evolution of a human capital index which is based on years of schooling and returns to education. As can be seen from this diagram, the index of human capital per person in Greece is consistently rising during the whole period indicating the importance of education in Greek economic and social transformation in the 1960s.

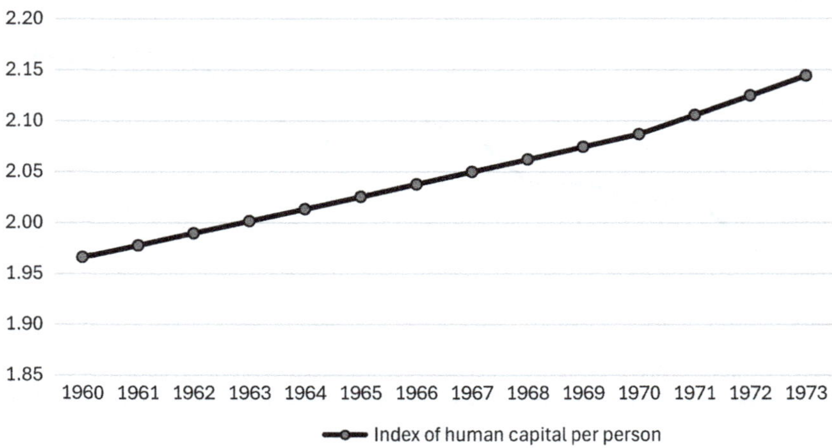

Fig. 7.7 Index of human capital per person for Greece, index, annual, not seasonally adjusted, 1960–1973. Source: University of Groningen and University of California, Davis, Penn World Table 10.01, retrieved from FRED, Federal Reserve Bank of St. Louis and author's elaboration

A major milestone of this period was the Association Agreement with the European Economic Community (EEC) which was signed in 1961. Besides the economic benefits that this agreement implied in terms of capital inflows to support public investment, there were also significant strategic and structural implications for the country. Through this Agreement, Greece was establishing a close and continuous connection with Western Europe and at the same time was becoming less dependent on US influence while following a necessary and much-needed path of modernization even though this process was interrupted during the dictatorship period (Kostis 2018a: 761–763).

7.3 Stagflation, Social Justice, and European Community Membership 1974–1993

The period 1974–1993 was marked by the oil shocks of the 1970s which challenged the sustainability of the model of economic growth that was followed by the Greek economy during the 1960s. Despite achievements in terms of "quantities" there were serious weaknesses concerning the "quality" of the process of economic development which hinged on domestic demand, state support, and a favorable international environment. State subsidies and financial support to private businesses were mainly directed to large industrial units thus, shaping monopolies in specific sectors. On the other hand, in the absence of effective long-term planning and sectoral policies, investment was driven by current demand, usually related to the construction sector of the economy. There was not any consistent policy for developing other key sectors for economic development such as machine manufacturing. Furthermore, the industrial policy of the era was not favorable to craftsmanship which, however, employed a significant share of the labor force and did not have the chance to modernize. Finally, the model of economic development that was followed during the 1960s did not improve the international competitiveness of the country and had adverse consequences for the natural environment in industrial areas (Fragiadis 2007: 189–192).

After 1973 the favorable international conjuncture that supported the "Greek miracle" of the 1960s ceased to exist. The impressive performance of the Greek economy during the preceding decade was accommodated by the significant emigration from Greece to Germany, Belgium, Australia, Canada, and the US. Emigration was instrumental as an outlet for a

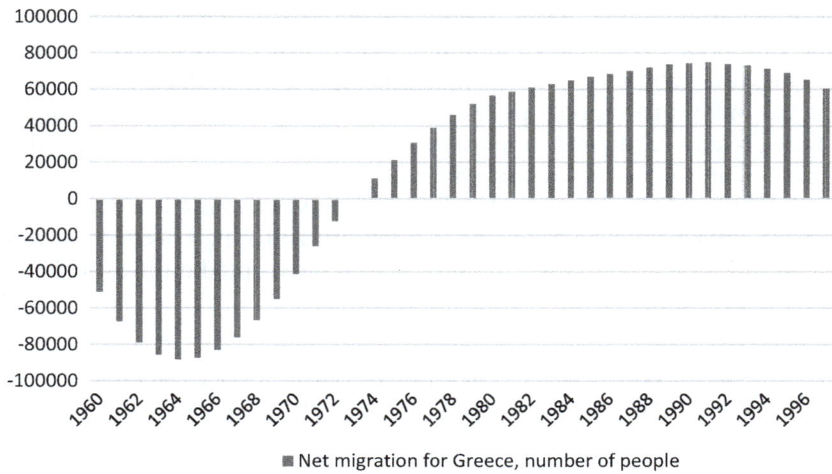

Fig. 7.8 Net migration for Greece (total number of immigrants less the number of emigrants) 1960–1997. Source: World Bank, World Development Indicators, and author's elaboration

surplus labor force which in addition, provided a significant source of capital inflow in the form of migrant remittances. However, after 1973, due to the adverse economic conditions that world economies experienced, the migration flow was reversed as it is shown in Fig. 7.8. Furthermore, the Greek industry faced fierce competition in manufacturing goods from low-cost developing countries and at the same time, was not able to diversify toward new industrial activities with high components of advanced technology (Kostis 2018b: 369–370; Fragiadis 2007: 187, 191–192).

The year 1974 is a turning point for Greece for many reasons. It was not only the pressure from developments in the international economy that manifested in that year but also a major political change in the country which marked the end of the seven-year dictatorship and the inauguration of a new democratic era. It has been argued that the Greek state of the post-war period until 1974 has been predominantly a state of the Cold War. Its Western orientation was an outcome of its choice to take sides in the Cold War divide but, at the same time, its Association Agreement with the EEC gave its people a European liberal perspective. This vision, despite the political setback during the dictatorship era, was reinvigorated with the restoration of democracy in 1974. The Karamanlis government officially applied for Greece's accession to the EEC in June 1975 and signed the Accession Agreement in May 1979 which rendered Greece the 10th member of the EEC as of 1981 (Kostis 2018a: 784–785, 792, 803).

The restoration of democracy was followed by a rise in popular demand for "social justice" since the oppressive regime of the colonels had kept wages at very low levels. Hence, a series of political, economic, and social demands became the object of social struggle that led to significant rises in wages above productivity levels (Fragiadis 2007: 197). It is notable that between 1974 and 1981 took place the most significant income redistribution in decades which witnessed the rate of absolute poverty fall from 23.5% in 1974 to 8.8% in 1981/82 (Kostis 2018a: 807–808). In terms of relative poverty, this decrease is less impressive but still significant from 23.5% in 1974 to 16% in 1981/82. In any case, there was certainly a shift toward a more equitable income distribution since the relevant Gini coefficient fell from 0.382 in 1974 to 0.309 in 1981/82 (Iordanoglou 2008: 76, 82).

However, as Figs. 7.1, 7.2, and 7.3 above showed the economy entered a period of slowdown and stagnation, especially after 1981 thus, diverting from the European developed economies (Kostis 2018b: 436–437). Figure 7.9 depicts the evolution of indices of private consumption and private gross investment in constant prices. The contrast between the two is striking. Private consumption manifests a consistent upward trend with minor fluctuations during the whole period. On the contrary, private investment passes through three phases: the initial upward trend until 1973 turns into a wide fluctuation until 1984. Afterward, there seems to be a tepid recovery until 1991. Indeed, the model of economic development in Greece during the period 1960–1973 was based on investment while the one from 1974 onward is founded on consumption expenditure. The share of investment expenditure as a percentage of GDP in constant 1995 prices was 30% for the period 1960–1973, 26% during the period 1974–1980 and just 20% in the following period 1981–1995 (Kostis 2018b: 438).

The characterization "stagflation" for this period is illustrated by the average GDP growth rate of 1.51% and the average inflation rate of 18.1% as shown in Tables 7.1 and 7.2 above. However, another variable with both economic and social significance is the unemployment rate which doubled from an average rate of 3.7% during the period 1960–1980 to 7.4% in the following period 1981–1993 (Fig. 7.10). Finally, this was also a period of rising imbalances in both the external and the public sector. As

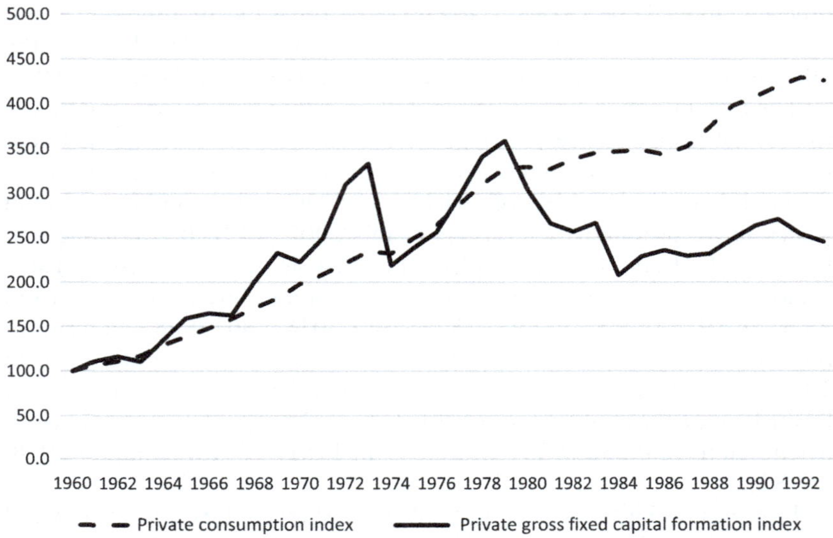

Fig. 7.9 Private consumption and private gross fixed capital formation index, 1960 = 100, based on constant 1995 prices, Greece, 1960–1993. Source: Iordanoglou (2008: 85–86, 96–97) and author's elaboration

Fig. 7.10 Unemployment rate, percentage, Greece, 1960–1993. Source: Ministry of National Economy (1998) and author's elaboration

shown in Fig. 7.11, Greece suffered from chronic current account deficits which, however, did not exceed −4% of GDP during the period 1960–1979. Although the trade deficit was large and exceeded −10% of GDP in most cases after 1965, receipts from tourism and remittances were able to significantly reduce this deficit. The situation deteriorated in the 1980s when the international competitiveness of Greek products declined, and the flow of remittances decreased (Kostis 2018b: 441). Moreover, as shown in Fig. 7.12, after 1975, and especially after 1979, Greece entered an era of exchange rate depreciation intending to boost output growth within an adverse international economic environment however disregarding the effect of such depreciation on inflation. Even so, this economic policy did not bear fruit since output growth during the period 1973–1980 was just 3.6% on average, compared to 8.5% in the long decade of 1960–1973, while in the period 1981–1989, the average growth rate did not exceed 0.8% (Iordanoglou 2008: 387–388).

The developments in public finances during the second half of the 1970s and in the 1980s reflected both the Greece-Turkey conflict in Cyprus in 1974 and the transition from the post-civil war state to an

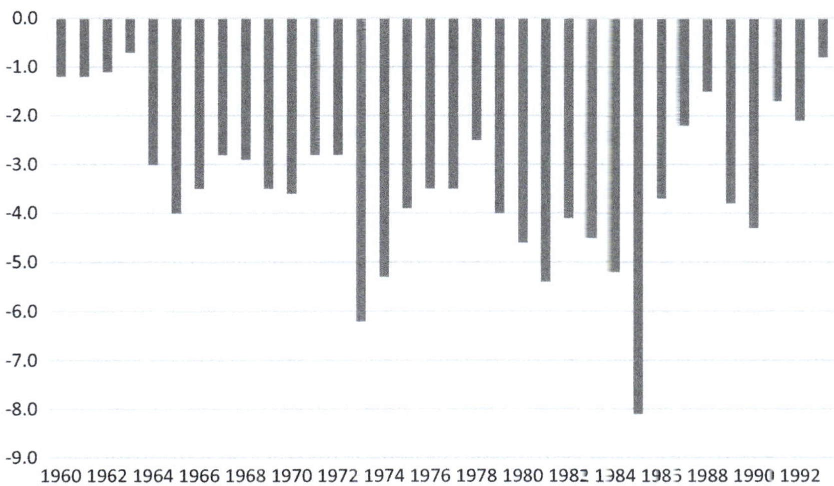

Fig. 7.11 Current account balance, percentage of GDP, Greece, 1960–1993. Source: Ministry of National Economy (1998) and author's elaboration

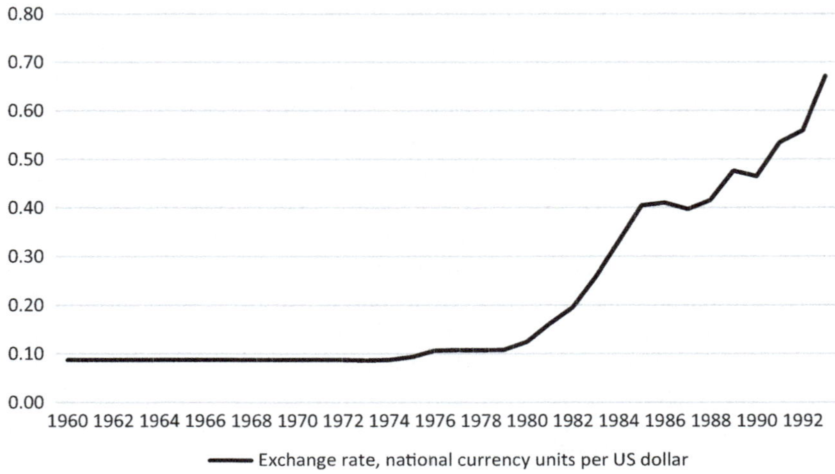

Fig. 7.12 Exchange Rate for Greece, national currency units per US Dollar, annual, not seasonally adjusted, 1960–1993. Source: University of Groningen and University of California, Davis, Penn World Table 10.01, retrieved from FRED, Federal Reserve Bank of St. Louis and author's elaboration

inclusive democratic polity. Hence, military spending was crucial for raising public spending initially, but public consumption and transfer payments have been the dominant factors of a continuous rise, especially after 1980. Notably, Central Government spending rose from 22.7% of GDP in 1973 to 26.2% in 1974, 29.2% in 1980, 35% in 1981, 44.4% in 1989 and 49.6% in 1993. Public consumption included wages payable to rising personnel employed in the public sector. The latter was expanding with the nationalizations of big banks and enterprises, the establishment of new firms under public control, the receivership of failed firms in the private sector, and the setup of the National Health System (Kostis 2018b: 448–449, 452–455; Pantazidis 2002: 45, 62, 102). However, the transition to a more inclusive state was not founded on sustainable economic policies since public deficit and inflation rose significantly between 1981 and 1985 and unemployment remained high (Fragiadis 2007: 205). Figure 7.13 depicts the evolution of the primary balance of the central government as a percentage of GDP indicating a clear deterioration in 1981. As a consequence, public debt rose with an average rate of 13.17% between 1981 and 1993 as opposed to an average rate of 5.38% between

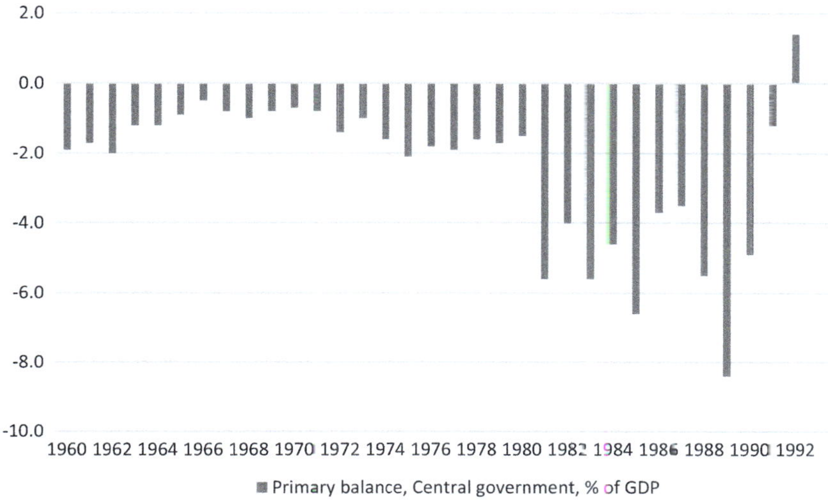

Fig. 7.13 Primary balance, Central government, percentage of GDP, Greece, 1960–1993. Source: Ministry of National Economy (1998) and author's elaboration

1961 and 1980, as can be derived from the data presented in Fig. 7.14. Through time, and as interest rates were liberalized, the service of public debt was the main cause of rising public deficits. Interest payable on public debt was 1.4% of GDP in 1980, 10% of GDP in 1990, and 13.9% of GDP in 1994. Moreover, financing these public deficits implied a diversion of resources that would otherwise support private investment expenditure (Kostis 2018b: 451–452).

7.4 Prolonged Macroeconomic Adjustment 1994–2001

On February 7, 1992, the Maastricht Treaty was signed which concerned the establishment of the European Monetary Union. Participation of Greece in this Union would entail a profound change of public policies with an emphasis on containing large fiscal deficits (Psalidopoulos 2014: 52–53). More analytically, the Maastricht criteria stipulated that until the year 2000 public deficit should have been below 3% of GDP, public debt should have been below 60% of GDP or approaching this level, inflation,

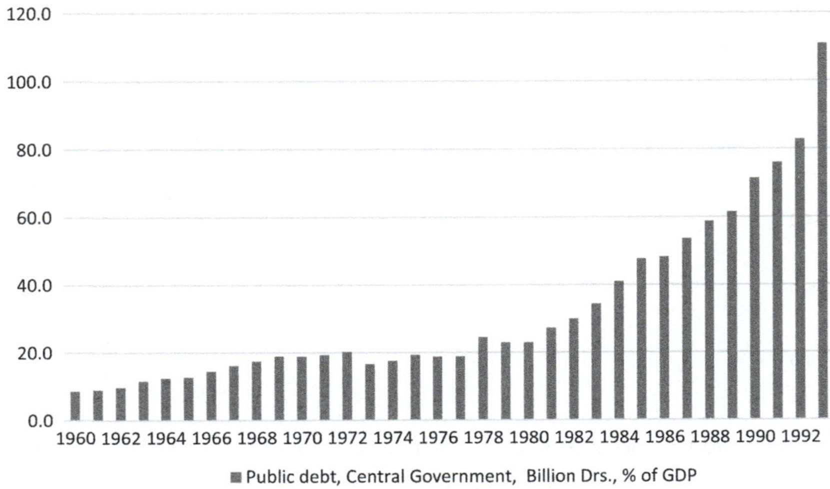

Fig. 7.14 Public debt, Central Government, Billion Drs., percentage of GDP, Greece, 1960–1993. Source: Ministry of National Economy (1998) and author's elaboration

in the case of Greece, should have been close to 2%–2.5% and long-term interest rates should have converged to the average of the three European Union countries with the lowest inflation rate with a margin of deviation of 2%. Finally, until that date, the national currency should have participated in the Exchange Rate Mechanism of the European Monetary System without being devalued for at least two years before locking into the Euro (Iordanoglou 2008: 525). The Maastricht criteria revealed the divide between two different directions of economic policy in Greece: The first one was followed during the period 1974–1990 and it was characterized by: (1) The "largesse" of economic policy that set the tone during this period, in the sense that there was a significant easing of monetary, fiscal, credit, and income policies. (2) Increased presence of the state in the economy with its interventionist policies. (3) Priority on re-distributional economic policies. (4) The foreign exchange policy ceased to be an anti-inflationary instrument, but it rather became an imperfect tool to restore the lost competitiveness of Greek exports. The negative effects of these policies were multiple: Expansionary policies stoked up inflation instead of production and employment, and the fact that productivity growth was short of wage rate growth contributed to a rise in unit production costs. The above had an adverse effect on investment expenditure while the deficit in trade balance rose. In a sense, all these implied a vicious circle that had its source in high fiscal deficits. Hence, the second direction in economic policy which was followed from 1990 until the accession of the country to the European Monetary Union in early 2000 was characterized by a major attempt at macroeconomic stabilization. This effort was effectively described by the Maastricht criteria mentioned above (Kostis 2018b: 463–469).

As shown in Figs. 7.15 and 7.16, the country moved from primary deficits until 1993 to primary surpluses from 1994 to 2001 while the General Government's deficit was reduced at a consistent pace after 1995 and until 2000. On the other hand, the General Government's gross debt (Fig. 7.17) fluctuated and finally rose after 1999. However, it should be noted that the data published at that time was more favorable indicating a continuous falling trend in public debt as a percentage of GDP from a value of around 110% in the period 1993–1997 and a peak of 111.3% of GDP in 1996 to 103.9% in 2000. In addition, the General Government deficit was

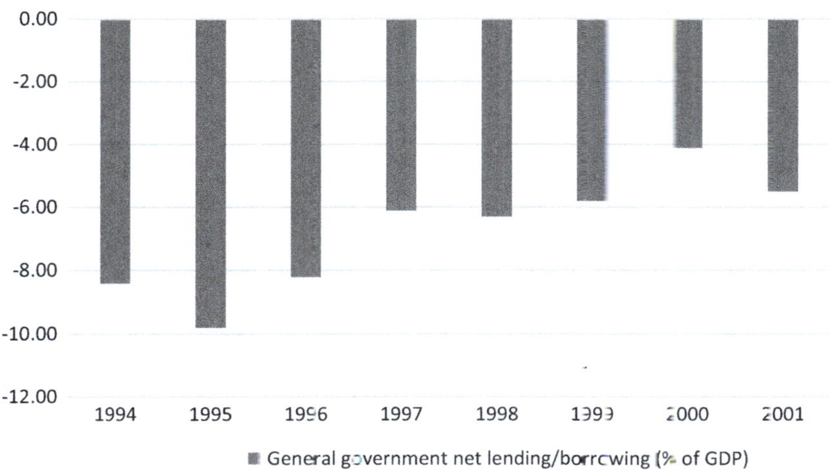

Fig. 7.15 General government net lending/borrowing (overall balance), Greece, percentage of GDP, 1994–2001. Source: IMF Fiscal Monitor, October 2023 and author's elaboration

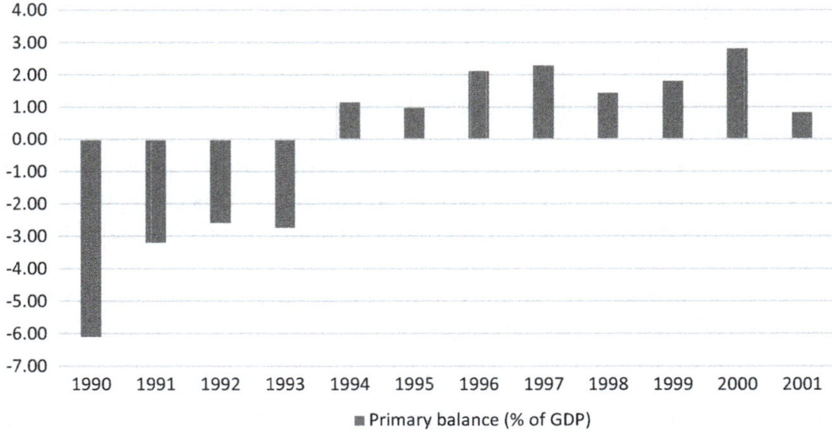

Fig. 7.16 Primary net lending/borrowing (primary balance), Greece, percentage of GDP, 1990–2001. Source: IMF Fiscal Monitor, October 2023 and author's elaboration

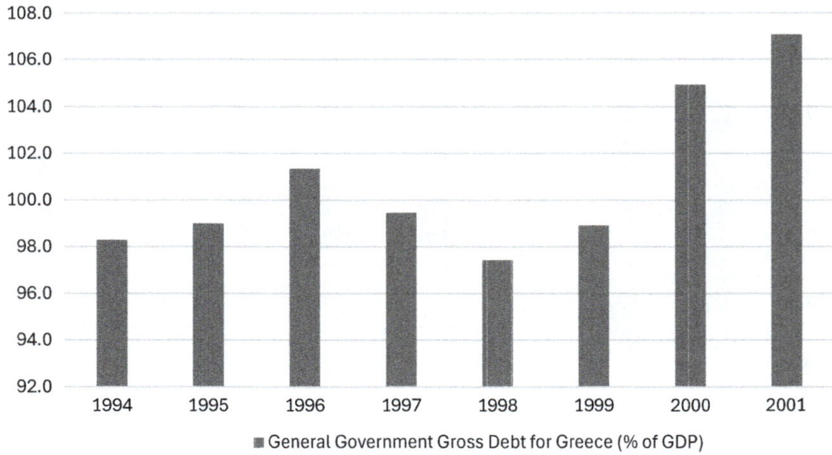

Fig. 7.17 General government gross debt for Greece, percent of GDP, annual, not seasonally adjusted, 1994–2001. Source: IMF, World Economic Outlook, retrieved from FRED, Federal Reserve Bank of St. Louis and author's elaboration

supposed to have been reduced from 13.8% of GDP in 1993 to 0.8% of GDP in 2000 (Manessiotis and Reischauer 2001: 133).

On the other hand, from 1995 onward Greece followed a consistent disinflation path that has been characterized by the literature as a new monetary regime for the country. This new monetary regime was established after a transition period between 1991 and 1994 when inflation fell from a figure close to 20% to a level as low as 11% (Garganas and Tavlas 2001: 45). Finally, as shown in Fig. 7.18, the long-term rate on government bonds for Greece fell sharply from a high of 23.9% in 1992 to a low of 5.3% in 2001. This impressive fall in long-term interest rates was the outcome of the increased credibility of anti-inflationary policies followed by Greek policymakers (Pantazidis 2002: 142). Eventually, from 1994 onward the country witnessed significant GDP growth rates between 2%, the lowest, and 4.5%, the highest. The growth rates achieved after 1996 were higher than the European average (Fragiadis 2007: 220), preparing the Greek economy and the Greek public opinion for accession to the European Monetary Union.

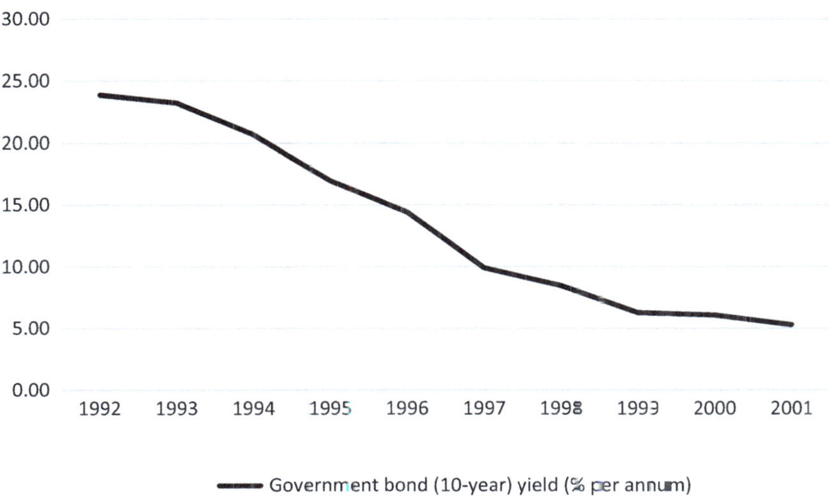

Fig. 7.18 Government bond (10-year) yield, Greece, percent per annum, 1992–2001. Source: IMF Data, International Financial Statistics and author's elaboration

7.5 European Monetary Union Membership and Illusions 2002–2007

The period of the first seven years of Eurozone membership for Greece was a bout of high expectations which were reflected in major macroeconomic variables. Tables 7.1 and 7.2 above summarize the favorable conditions of an average growth rate of 4% and an average inflation rate of 3.3%. Hence, the economy continued to grow at relatively high rates during this period with positive effects on both consumption and investment expenditure. Figure 7.19 shows the upward trend for both private consumption and gross capital formation. It is notable that consumption manifests an almost linear evolution through time as opposed to the fluctuations in investment expenditure. Rising consumption was also accompanied by increasing imports (Psalidopoulos 2014: 57) thus deteriorating the current account balance as shown in Fig. 7.20. The current account deficit rose from −6.3% of GDP in 2002 to the level of −13.9% of GDP in 2007.

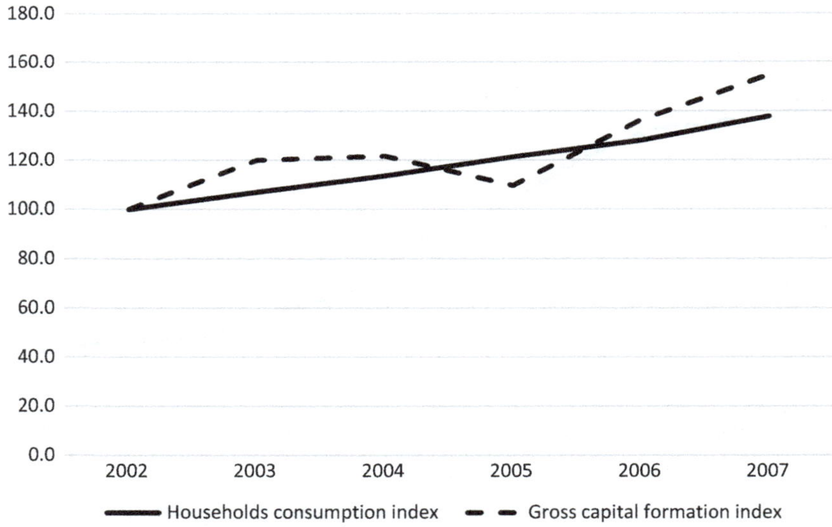

Fig. 7.19 Households consumption index and gross capital formation index, based on constant prices of the previous year, Greece, 2002 = 100, 2002–2007. Source: Hellenic Statistical Authority (ELSTAT) and author's elaboration

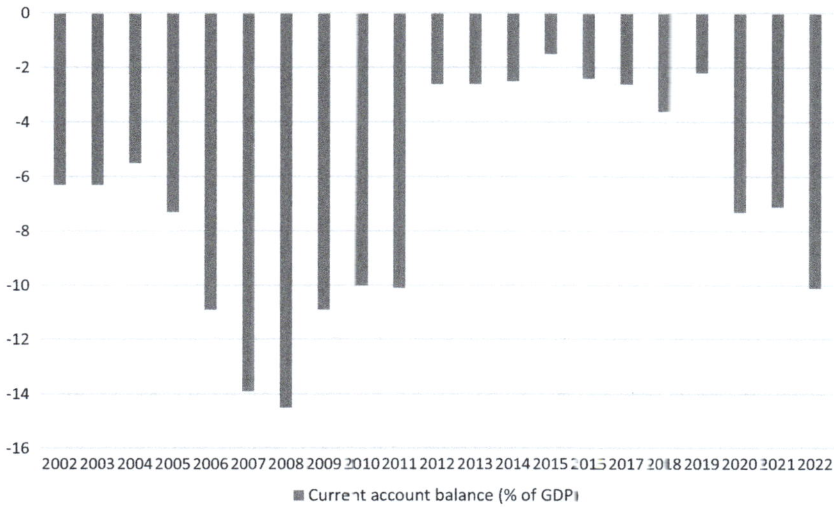

Fig. 7.20 Current account balance, percent of GDP, Greece, 2002–2022. Source: IMF country data and author's elaboration

Hence, despite reservations about the ability of the Greek economy of the first decade of the twenty-first century to smoothly integrate into an (imperfect) monetary union, because of the structural weaknesses it inherited from the previous decades, its initial performance in terms of growth was promising. The GDP of Greece in 2001 was just 76.1% of the European average (EU-15) while in 2009 reached the level of 85.7%. However, this was a short-lived period of increasing hope for convergence since during the crisis in 2016 Greece's GDP fell to 62.3% of the European average (Kostis 2018b: 501–505).

However, at the core of the subsequent crisis in the 2010s were the condition of public finances and the level of public debt. Therefore, it is plausible to assume that these imbalances have had their roots in the behavior of fiscal variables during the first years of Eurozone membership. Despite fluctuating deficits in overall and primary balances of the General government finances, public debt as a percentage of GDP was kept fairly stable until 2007 with an average value of 103.9%. Kostis (2018a: 857) spots a turning point in 2004 when national elections brought a new government into office and public debt rose from 94.1% of GDP at the end of

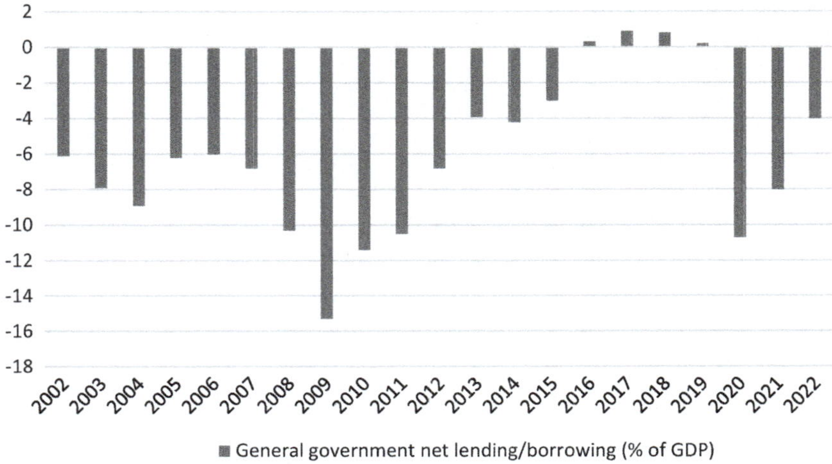

Fig. 7.21 General government net lending/borrowing (overall balance), Greece, percentage of GDP, 2002–2022. Source: IMF Fiscal Monitor, October 2023 and author's elaboration

2003 to 126.7% of GDP at the end of 2009. On the other hand, Argitis and Nikolaidi (2014) classify Greek government finances as either in the Ponzi or in the ultra-Ponzi category examining the period 1988–2012 which means that the Greek government either ran a primary surplus which was insufficient to cover its interest payments or ran a primary deficit during this period which called for new borrowing. The Greek government entered a Ponzi regime only in the interval of macroeconomic adjustment 1994–2002 and remained in an ultra-Ponzi regime in all other cases. Chronic inefficiencies of the Greek authorities in collecting taxes along with persistent structural problems of reduced competitiveness of the Greek economy contributed to the dismal situation of the public finances (Figs. 7.21, 7.22 and 7.23).

An assessment of this pre-crisis period by the Bank of Greece focuses on the same macroeconomic indicators. The Bank points out that the high growth of GDP between 2001 and 2007 was dependent on domestic demand and especially on private consumption which grew at an average rate of 4.2%. On the other hand, fixed capital formation grew at an average rate of 7.9% but most of it was related to buildings and dwellings. In addition, the international competitiveness of domestic businesses fell by 14%

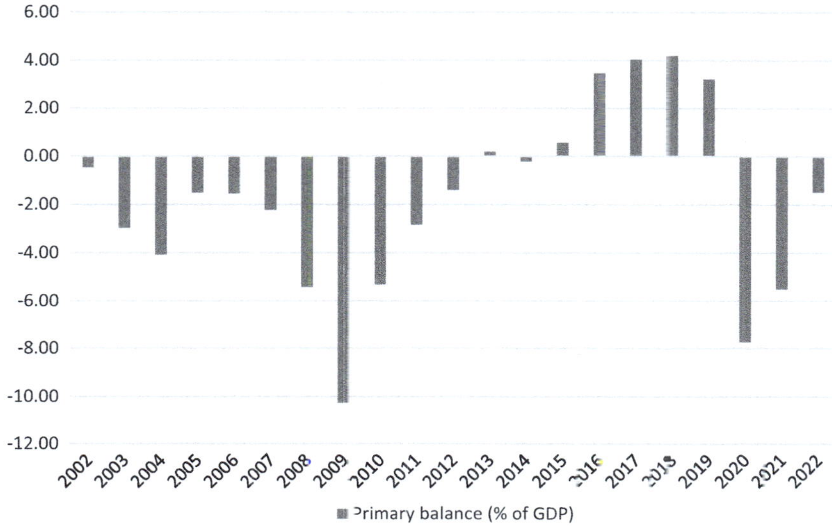

Fig. 7.22 Primary net lending/borrowing (primary balance), Greece, percentage of GDP, 2002–2022. Source: IMF Fiscal Monitor, October 2023 and author's elaboration

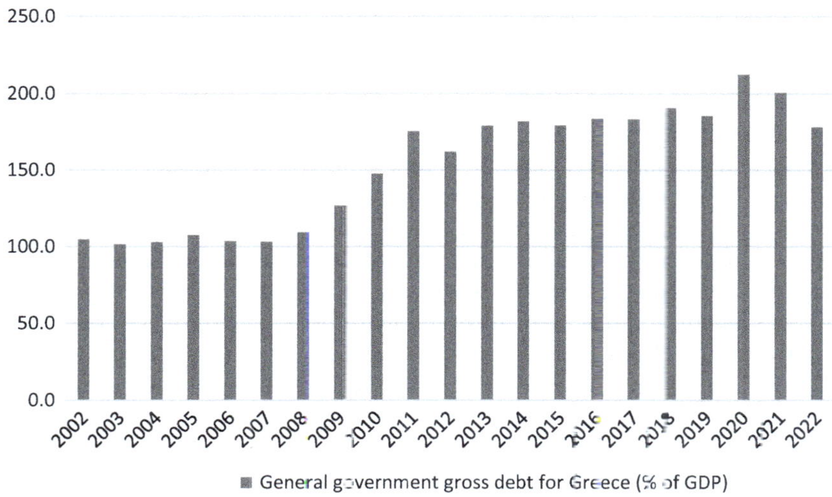

Fig. 7.23 General government gross debt for Greece, percent of GDP, annual, not seasonally adjusted, 2002–2022. Source: IMF, World Economic Outlook, retrieved from FRED, Federal Reserve Bank of St. Louis and author's elaboration

based on relative consumer prices and by 19.3% with respect to the relative cost of labor. Therefore domestic growth hinged on private consumption and dwellings' construction aided by rising incomes and increased borrowing. Imports in constant prices rose by an average annual rate of 4.5% to meet rising demand and the current account deficit increased from an average annual value of 3% of GDP during the period 1994–1999 to 8.5% in the ensuing period 2000–2007. Concerning the public finances, the Bank of Greece notes that fiscal policy, instead of being restrictive in order to support the country's membership in the Eurozone by contributing to a falling public debt, was rather expansionary until 2004 when the country was subjected to an Excessive Deficit Procedure by the European Commission. Lifting the constraints imposed due to the Excessive Deficit Procedure in June 2007 resulted in a period of expansionary fiscal policy and a deterioration of public finances. The above constituted a model of distorted and non-sustainable economic growth, as the subsequent decade would reveal (Bank of Greece 2014: 15–19, 26).

7.6 Protracted Crisis and Disillusionment 2008–2022

The Financial Crisis of 2007–2008 in the USA and its global repercussions were the initial cause of the Greek sovereign debt crisis and signaled the inauguration of an era of disillusionment and unprecedented economic contraction (Psalidopoulos 2014: 58). Hence, the Greek economic crisis in the second decade of the twenty-first century has had an international dimension both because it came as a consequence of the Global Financial Crisis and because of Greece's membership of the European Monetary Union. Besides, the efficiency of the latter has been questioned in the literature for ignoring crucial prerequisites of an optimum currency area such as a common fiscal policy. Structural imbalances within the EMU among the countries of the North and the South contributed to the weaker position of the latter in coping with the impact of the Global crisis. However, the Greek crisis depends mainly on a factor that is specific to this country and it is related to the model of economic development and growth that Greece followed at least from the 1970s and subsequently. The major issue for the Greek economy has been the one of reduced international competitiveness which relates to the model of production followed during this period (Kostis 2018a: 867–870). On the other hand, the international crisis adversely affected the public finances of nations worldwide due to government initiatives for shoring up the real and financial sectors of the economy and the role of automatic fiscal stabilizers. Greece was not an exception to that and both the General government deficit and public debt rose further in 2008. In 2009, the country entered a period when major macroeconomic variables deteriorated further, a development that revealed the long-lasting structural weaknesses of the Greek economy (Bank of Greece 2014: 28, 36–37). Figure 7.24 shows the steep rise of the long-term government bond yield from 2009 until 2012 as the country was downgraded by the international credit rating institutions due to doubts about the credibility of official statistics and the ability of Greek governments to implement a reliable program of fiscal consolidation (Bank of Greece 2014: 41–42). Hence, even if competitiveness is the major long-term problem of the Greek economy, public finances have been the trigger of the crisis and the issue that attracted the attention of policymakers and international organizations (Kostis 2018b: 523).

Fiscal consolidation has been the outcome of three Economic Adjustment Programs (EAPs) put into effect between 2010 and 2015 along with financial assistance provided by European and international

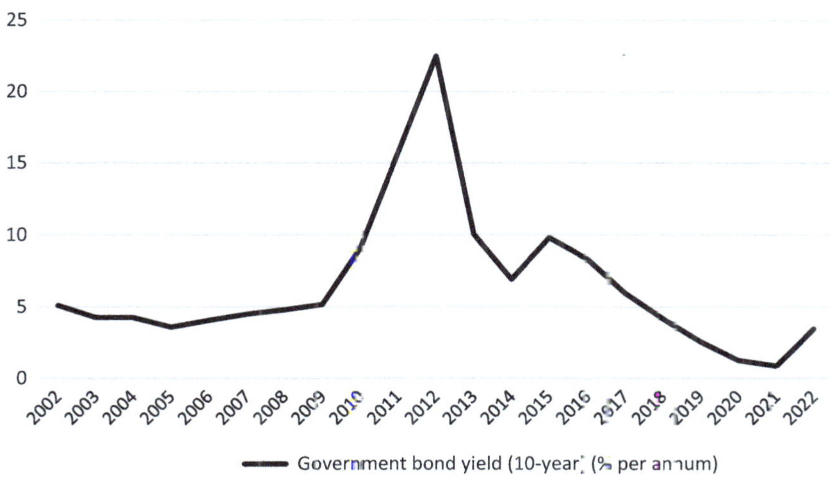

Fig. 7.24 Government bond (10-year) yield, Greece, percent per annum, 2002–2022. Source: IMF Data, International Financial Statistics and author's elaboration

sources under the monitoring of the European Commission, the European Central Bank, and the IMF. The short-term objectives of these programs were financial stability and fiscal consolidation and the medium-term ones were to increase competitiveness and promote an export-led model of economic development (Revuelta 2021).

Did these EAPs achieve their objectives? Is Greece able to change its economic development model toward a more sustainable, innovative, and equitable direction? The debate is still open and colored by different economic, political, and social views in the domain of public dialogue. It is predominantly an attempt to describe the past and understand it within particular theoretical frameworks. Should the researcher focus on the "institutional particularities of the Greek model of capitalism" which promotes a model of entrepreneurship that favors non-productive activities and a Veblenian "leisure class" culture instead of innovation and rising productivity (Argitis 2012: 51–54)? Or should they emphasize the continuous struggle between different social groups, political forces, and foreign influence that led to a new level of political and economic stability through reforms that were accepted by domestic "historical blocs" or "alliances" among social groups (Lapavitsas 2019; Kostis 2018b: 626–627)? Has the Greek economic crisis been a problem that goes beyond mere economic explanations to include issues such as government effectiveness, corruption, political stability, rule of law, and voice and accountability (Maris et al. 2021)? Or is there a more complex issue to address that takes into account crisis management and strategic planning in the intersection between the state, social interests, and effective democratic institutions in the simultaneous pursuit of innovation and reduced inequality (Thomadakis 2015)?

Figures 7.25 and 7.26 above describe the profound macroeconomic adjustment that the Greek economy passed through in the "long decade" of crisis in terms of consumption and investment expenditure and the unemployment rate. On the other hand, Figs. 7.27 and 7.28 indicate how these adverse macroeconomic developments impacted two crucial social variables such as the index of human capital per person and the net migration. It turns out that the crisis did not impair the accumulation of human capital, but it rather led to a continuous "brain drain", a new flow of migration abroad which peaked in 2013.[3] Furthermore, if there is an

[3] In World Bank data net migration for Greece turns negative as early as 2004 while in United Nations data (not presented here) it becomes negative in 2011 and peaks in 2012–2013. In any case, the conclusion about the impact of the crisis does not change.

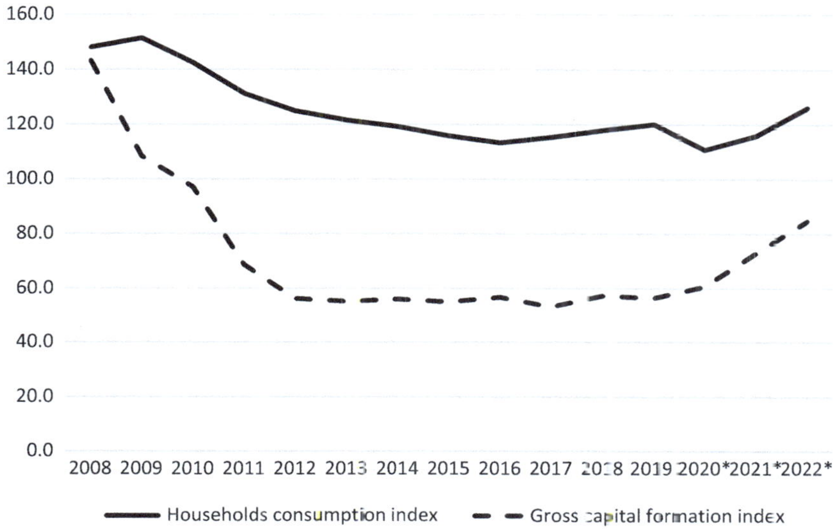

Fig. 7.25 Households consumption index and gross capital formation index, based on constant prices of the previous year, Greece, 2002 = 100, 2008–2022. Source: Hellenic Statistical Authority (ELSTAT) and author's elaboration (* indicate provisional data)

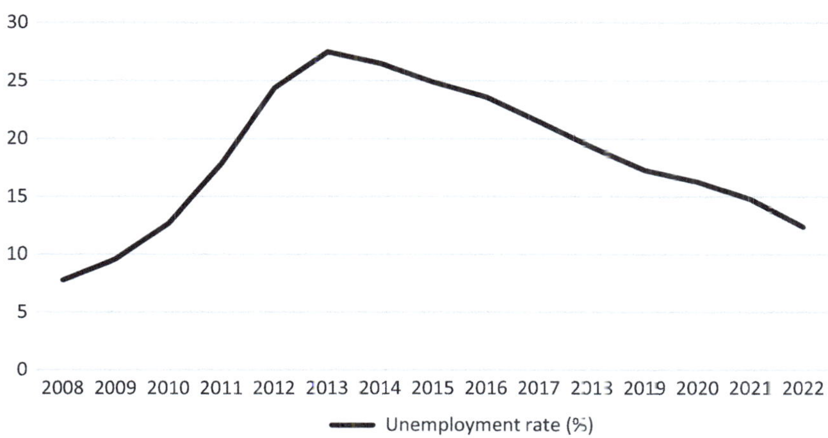

Fig. 7.26 Unemployment rate, percent, annual, Greece, 2008–2022. Source: IMF country data and author's elaboration

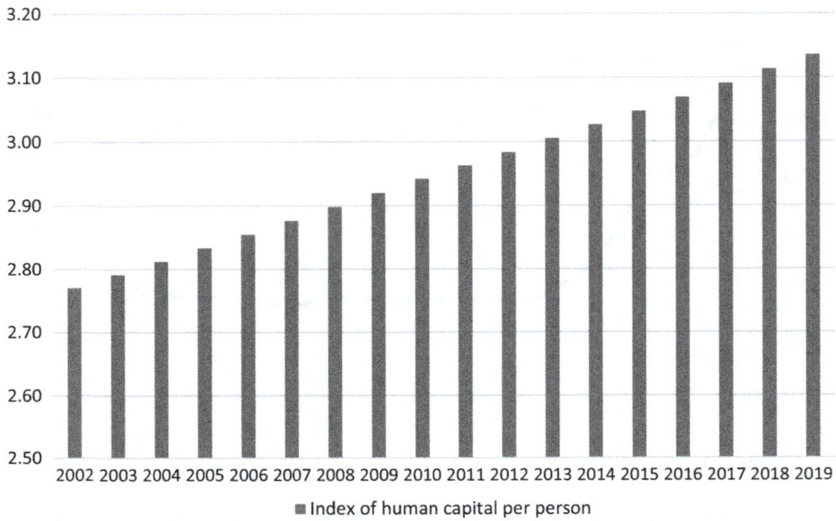

Fig. 7.27 Index of human capital per person for Greece, annual, not seasonally adjusted, 2002–2019. Source: University of Groningen and University of California, Davis, Penn World Table 10.01, retrieved from FRED, Federal Reserve Bank of St. Louis and author's elaboration

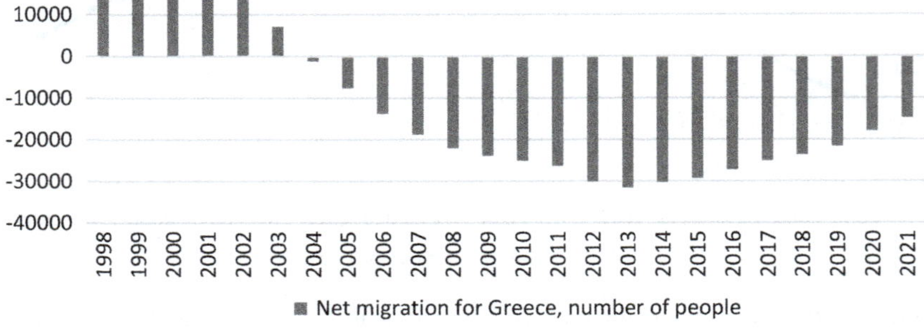

Fig. 7.28 Net migration for Greece (total number of immigrants less the number of emigrants) 1998–2021. Source: World Bank, World Development Indicators, and author's elaboration

agreement among different theoretical strands in the literature that competitiveness is the crucial problem that bedevils the Greek economy (Lapavitsas 2019; Kostis 2018b; Argitis 2012; Economakis et al. 2011; Mariolis and Papoulis 2011; Vlachou and Lambrinidis 2011) then it is worth considering the place of the Greek economy in various indicators of competitiveness as these are compiled in the Global Competitiveness Reports. In the Report of 2015–2016 when the Greek economy and society were still suffering the effects of the protracted crisis, Greece was in 36th place among 140 countries for its technological readiness, which is above the average, in the 34th place for its infrastructure, in the 43rd place concerning higher education and in the 41st place for primary education and health care. Of course, it ranked much lower with respect to other criteria such as business sophistication (74th place), innovation (77th place), institutions (81st place), the efficiency of the labor market (116th), financial development (131st), or the macroeconomic environment (132nd) (Kostis 2018a: 870–871). Despite possible reservations about the definition and interpretation of these criteria, the above indicates that the Greek economy and society managed to preserve in fair condition the most important factor for its future, its human capital. If this is the case, then the context in which this human capital is employed, developed, and interacts with the other factors of economic development and especially the institutional surroundings of human action is of primary importance.

The above analysis highlighted the main landmarks of Greek economic development during the last six decades. Summarizing this discussion we would emphasize the positive trend of socioeconomic transformation along with the internal weaknesses of the followed model of economic development. However, these achievements and deficiencies were supported and characterized by an underlying institutional evolution that was inscribed in the alternative financial regimes. Development banks assumed a significant role on both fronts, contributing to the pace of economic development described above and to institutional development and modernization of the Greek economy. The recount of the institutional evolution in the Greek economy which passed through alternative financial regimes is the subject of the next chapter while the main and the subsequent periods of development banking in Greece are examined in the following chapters.

References

Alogoskoufis, G. (1996) "The Two Phases of Ianus: Institutions, Economic Development and Balance of Payments in Greece", *Economic Policy Studies*, 1, 25–63 (in Greek).

Argitis, G. (2012) *Bankruptcy and Economic Crisis. Failure and Collapse of the Greek Model of Capitalism*, Athens: Alexandria Publications (in Greek).

Argitis, G. and Nikolaidi, M. (2014) "The Financial Fragility and the Crisis of the Greek Government Sector", *International Review of Applied Economics*, 28(3): 274–292.

Bank of Greece (2014) *The Chronicle of the Great Crisis. The Bank of Greece 2008–2013*, Athens: Bank of Greece (in Greek).

Bordo, M. D. (2015) "Reflections on the History and Future of Central Banking", in Humpage, O. F. (ed.) *Current Federal Reserve Policy Under the Lens of Economic History. Essay to Commemorate the Federal Reserve System's Centennial*, N.Y.: Cambridge University Press, pp. 364–368.

Bordo, M. D. and Orphanides, A. (2013) "Introduction" in Bordo, M. D. and Orphanides, A. (eds.) *The Great Inflation: The Rebirth of Modern Central Banking*, University of Chicago Press, pp. 1–22.

Bosworth, B. and Kollintzas, T. (2001) "Economic Growth in Greece: Past Performance and Future Prospects" in Bryant, R. C., Garganas, N. C. and Tavlas, G. S. (eds.) *Greece's Economic Performance and Prospects*, Athens and Washington, DC: Bank of Greece and The Brookings Institution, pp. 153–192.

Brenner, R. (1998) "The Economics of Global Turbulence", *New Left Review*, No 229, (May–June).

Dimelis, S., Kollintzas, T, and Christodoulakis, N. (1996) "Main Features of Economic Development in Post-War Greece", *Economic Policy Studies*, 1, 71–103 (in Greek).

Drakatos, K. G. (1997) *The Great Cycle of the Greek Economy (1945–1995)*, Athens: Papazisis (in Greek).

Economakis, G., Markaki, M., Anastasiadis, A., and Papalexiou, G. (2011) "Competitiveness of the Greek Economy: A Sectoral Approach", in Vlachou, A., Theocharakis, N., and Mylonakis, D. (eds.) *Economic Crisis and Greece*, Athens: Gutenberg Publications (in Greek), pp. 256–274.

Fragiadis, A. (2007) *The Greek Economy 19th – 20th Century. From the War of Independence to the Economic and Monetary Union of Europe*, Athens: Nefeli Publications (in Greek).

Garganas, N. C. and Tavlas, G. S. (2001) "Monetary Regimes and Inflation Performance: The Case of Greece" in Bryant, R. C., Garganas, N. C., and Tavlas, G. S. (eds.) *Greece's Economic Performance and Prospects*, Athens and Washington, DC: Bank of Greece and The Brookings Institution.

Giovannoni, E. and Fabietti, G. (2013) "What is Sustainability? A Review of the Concept and Its Applications" in Busco, C., Frigo, M. L., Riccaboni, A. and Quattrone, P. (eds.) *Integrated Reporting. Concepts and Cases that Redefine Corporate Accountability*, Springer International Publishing Switzerland, pp. 21–40.

Iordanoglou, C. I. (2008) *The Greek Economy in the "Long Term" 1954–2005*, Athens: Polis Publications (in Greek).

Jordanova, L. (2006) *History in Practice* 2nd Ed., London & N.Y.: Bloomsbury Academic.

Katila, P., Pierce Colfer, C. J., de Jong, W., Galloway, G., Pacheco P. and Winkel, G. (eds.) (2020) *Sustainable Development Goals: Their Impacts on Forests and People*, Cambridge University Press.

Kazakos, P. (2001) *Between the State and the Market. Economy and Economic Policy in post-war Greece 1944–2000*, Athens: Patakis Publications. (in Greek)

Kostis, K. (2018a) *'The Spoiled Children of History'. The Formation of the New Greek State 18th – 21st Century*, 2nd Ed. Athens: Patakis Publications. (in Greek)

Kostis, K. (2018b) *The Wealth of Greece. The Greek Economy from the Balkan Wars to the Present Day*, Athens: Patakis Publications (in Greek)

Lapavitsas, C. (2019) "Political Economy of the Greek Crisis", *Review of Radical Political Economics*, 51(1): 31–51.

Loizos, K. (2017) "Alternative Financial Regimes and Development Banks in Greece 1963–2002: What Have We Learned?", *Economic Alternatives*, 1: 34–50.

Maddison, A. (1983) "Economic Stagnation since 1973, its Nature and Causes: A Six Country Survey", *De Economist*, 131(4): 585–608.

Maddison, A. (2007) *Contours of the World Economy, 1-2030 AD. Essays in Macro-Economic History*, N.Y.: Oxford University Press.

Maddison, A. (2005) "Measuring and Interpreting World Economic Performance 1500–2001", *Review of Income and Wealth*, 51(1): 1–35.

Manessiotis, V. G. and Reischauer, R. D. (2001) "Greek Fiscal and Budget Policy and EMU" in Bryant, R. C., Garganas, N. C., and Tavlas, G. S. (eds.) *Greece's Economic Performance and Prospects*, Athens and Washington D.C.: Bank of Greece and The Brookings Institution, pp. 103–152.

Maniatis, T. and Passas, C. (2013) "Profitability, Capital Accumulation, and Crisis in the Greek Economy 1958 – 2009: A Marxist Analysis", *Review of Political Economy*, 25(4): 624–649.

Maris, G. Sklias, P. and Maravegias, N. (2021) "The Political Economy of the Greek Economic Crisis in 2020", *European Politics and Society*, 23(4): 447–467.

Mariolis, T. and Papoulis, K. (2011) "'Twin Deficits' and International Competitiveness of the Greek Economy" in Vlachou, A., Theocharakis, N., and Mylonakis, D. (eds.) *Economic Crisis and Greece*, Athens: Gutenberg Publications (in Greek), pp. 275–289.

Ministry of National Economy (1998) *The Greek Economy 1960 – 1997. Long Term Macroeconomic Statistical Series*, Athens

Pantazidis, S. N. (2002) *Macroeconomic Developments and Economic Policy in Greece from the Restoration of Democracy until EMU Accession (1975 – 2000)*, Athens: Kritiki Publications (in Greek).

Psalidopoulos, M. (2014) *History of the Bank of Greece 1928 – 2008. From Bank of the State, Guarantor of Financial Stability*, Athens: Bank of Greece (in Greek).

Psalidopoulos, M. (ed.) (1996) *Panagis Papaligouras, Speeches, Articles*, Athens: Aiolos Publications (in Greek).

Revuelta, J. (2021) "The Effects of the Economic Adjustment Programmes for Greece: A Quasi-Experimental Approach", *Sustainability*, 13(9), 4970.

Rich, R. (2013) The Great Recession. Federal Reserve History, available at https://www.federalreservehistory.org/essays/great-recession-of-200709 Accessed 20 Feb. 2024

Shackleton, R. (2013) "Total Factor Productivity Growth in Historical Perspective", Congressional Budget Office Working Paper 2013-01, Washington, D.C. available at https://www.cbo.gov/sites/default/files/113th-congress-2013-2014/workingpaper/44002_TFP_Growth_03-18-2013_1.pdf Accessed 23 Feb. 2024

Thomadakis, S. B. (2015) "Growth, Debt and Sovereignty. Prolegomena to the Greek Crisis", LSE Hellenic Observatory, European Institute, GreeSE Paper No.91, available at https://eprints.lse.ac.uk/62081/1/Thomadakis_Growth%20%20Debt%20and%20Sovereignty%20Prolegomena%20to%20the%20Greek%20Crisis_Author.pdf Accessed 14 Jan. 2024

Vlachou, A. and Lambrinidis, G. (2011) "Crisis and Unequal Development in the Context of EMU: The External Balance of Trade and International Competitiveness of the Greek Economy", in Vlachou, A., Theocharakis, N., and Mylonakis, D. (eds.) *Economic Crisis and Greece*, Athens: Gutenberg Publications (in Greek), pp. 229–255.

Whalen, C. J. (2011) "Introduction: Instability, Prosperity and Economics after the Great Recession", in Whalen, C. J. (ed.) *Financial Instability and Economic Security after the Great Recession*, Cheltenham, UK & Northampton, MA USA: Edward Elgar. pp. 1–12.

Zouboulakis, M. (2023–2024) "The Economic Thought of George A. Kartalis (1908–1957)", *Tetradia*, 83–84: 141–153. (in Greek).

CHAPTER 8

Institutional Evolution and Alternative Financial Regimes in Post-World War II Greece

8.1 The Greek Financial System in the International Post-War Context

The path of Greek economic development that was presented in the previous chapter was influenced by the evolution of the institutional structure of the Greek economy in the context of the changing international financial environment. The new international monetary order was decided near the end of the Second World War at Bretton Woods, New Hampshire in 1944 with the participation of 44 countries. The aim was the establishment of an international system that would prevent episodes such as the collapse that occurred in international financial transactions in the 1930s. The new international system should abandon any thought of returning to the gold exchange standard, and it should avoid protectionism, competitive devaluations, and deflation. Floating exchange rates may become a source of uncertainty in economic relations between nations that would hinder the development of international trade and would encourage destabilizing speculation. Therefore, in Bretton Woods, a fixed exchange rate system was established based on a fixed dollar-gold parity of 35 dollars per ounce. In addition, the International Monetary Fund (IMF) was set up to monitor and promote international monetary cooperation and guarantee the proper functioning of the fixed exchange rate system, thus promoting the growth of international trade. To ensure current account convertibility, controls on speculative capital flows were put in place together with

K. Loizos, *Between Markets and Governments*,
https://doi.org/10.1007/978-3-031-88527-3_8

heavy regulation of financial markets. This tight control over both domestic and international capital markets, which was also expressed in negative real interest rates, associated the Bretton Woods system with the financial repression regime. The Bretton Woods system operated successfully from March 1947 until August 1971 when it collapsed due to the massive increase in US balance of payments deficits and the inability of the dollar to support its convertibility into gold. The result was the abandonment of fixed exchange rate regimes and return to free capital flows between countries in the 1970s and 1980s in the context of financial liberalization policies which, however, added to the general economic turmoil that accompanied the two oil crises of the 1970s. The response of the European economies (those that were part of the European Economic Community in the early 1970s) was the creation of the Snake on April 24, 1972, as a system that allowed currencies to float between member countries and the dollar within predetermined limits. The Snake was replaced by the European Monetary System (EMS) on March 13, 1979, which entailed the establishment of the Exchange Rate Mechanism (ERM) and the European Currency Unit (ECU). The rationale behind all these initiatives was the formulation of a zone of monetary stability among European countries. However, these developments were also the first necessary step toward the European Monetary Union, an idea that preoccupied European policymakers throughout the 1990s (Mullin 2021; Hoffmann 2019; Reinhart et al. 2011; Pilbeam 1992: 282–289, 298, 358, 368–371).

In the above international context of institutional developments, the Greek economy has also been characterized by a parallel shift in policy objectives from actively planning and organizing economic development to passively accommodating market forces, with the active role now focused on monetary variables such as inflation. This shift of attention in economic policy and the developments in the financial sector are reflected in the description of monetary regimes during this period by Garganas and Tavlas (2001). They distinguish two monetary regimes and an interim transition period: (1) The monetary regime of 1975–1990 is characterized by high and persistent inflation. The authors point to the inability of monetary policy to reduce inflation, as it was constrained by the financially repressed system that prevailed in Greece, with a highly concentrated and regulated banking sector, thin capital markets, and the decisive role of the government in setting the objectives of monetary policy. Financial repression reduced the efficiency of monetary policy instruments such as interest rates. Direct control of prices or quantities that were vulnerable to evasion by agents undermined the effectiveness of monetary policy. In short, the monetary regime of 1975–1990 was one of inflationary finance in the face of large fiscal deficits. (2) The ensuing transition period from high to moderate inflation rates during 1991–94 and the gradual process of financial liberalization/deregulation, that began in 1982, enhanced the effectiveness of monetary policy. Interest rates became the main instrument of monetary policy, together with the use of indirect instruments such as open market operations, a refinancing facility, and reserve requirements, all of which reflected a market-oriented policy. Financial deregulation was effectively completed by 1995. (3) The period between 1995 and 2000 was characterized by a new disinflation regime facilitated by the prohibition of monetary financing of the government's budget deficit along with the tightening of monetary policy. The conclusion of the Maastricht Treaty in 1992 and the announced goal of the Greek government to join the EMU became the framework for the convergence program for the period 1994–1999. The main objective of this program was to significantly reduce the large budget deficit. An important instrument in this context was the "hard-drachma" policy according to which the drachma would depreciate against the ECU by only 3% per year without fully offsetting the differences in inflation between Greece and the rest of the Union. In this sense, pegging a country's currency to that of a low-inflation area would discourage increased government spending and wage policies that could add to inflationary pressures and thus undermine the country's competitiveness. It was in fact, a self-discipline measure that succeeded in lowering inflation and enhancing the credibility of the government to pursue anti-inflationary policies. To the same end, an important institutional measure was the declaration of the independence of the Bank of Greece in December 1997, with a specific mandate to pursue price stability. On the 16th of March 1998 the drachma joined the Exchange Rate Mechanism of the European Monetary System while in January 1999, when eleven members of the EMS adopted the Euro, Greece participated in ERM II. In short, the whole period 1995–2000 was characterized by the pursuit of the Maastricht convergence criteria, which led to Greece's entry into the euro area on January 1, 2001. The subsequent institutional developments in the Greek financial sector have been an integral part of those in the European Monetary Union of which Greece has been a member (Psalidopoulos 2014: 53–57; Garganas and Tavlas 2001: 43–82).

8.2 The Political Economy of Development Finance in Post-War Greece

It seems that the Greek economy during the second half of the twentieth century and the first two decades of the twenty-first century has followed the developments in the international institutional evolution from financial repression/regulation to financial liberalization along with the related changing attitudes toward development finance. However, historical specificity demands an explanatory framework that would take into account the salient features of this evolution that appear in the Greek case. Such a framework should focus on the role of the state and the major socioeconomic groups, the conditions of entrepreneurial activity and its practices, and the role of the financial system and especially of the banking system. This section analyzes the political economy conditions that supported the model of development finance in post-war Greece in the above context. The term "political economy" is used to highlight the importance of political and social factors in economic development and development finance from the point of view of Original Institutional Economics. The next section elaborates on the change in policy emphasis from development finance toward financial development with the change in the financial regime during the 1980s.

Katseli (1990) uses the term "state corporatism" to characterize the model of economic development in Greece in the post-war period. According to her view, a nexus of, mainly political, relationships between the state, banks, and traditional industrial families running major private enterprises—sometimes supported by trade unions—set the form and nature of development but also eventually undermined its future. The main feature of state corporatism was the regulation of conflicts between social and economic groups as a specific model toward industrialization. However, what is of interest here is the influential role of the state concerning the financial sector to the degree that the latter acted in support of the corporatist model. There was a close relationship between political and economic interests, the latter being represented by the family-controlled subsidized large firms. Hence, according to this view, the financial repression/regulation regime that prevailed in post-war Greece was the necessary complement of "state corporatism" that determined the relations between financial institutions, the government, and incumbent firms.

The effects of this model of post-war development, according to Katseli (1990) were manifold. Financial repression in the service of corporatist relations between large firms and the state contributed to capital market underdevelopment and weak entrepreneurship to the degree that financing decisions and project approval hinged on the close ties between political agents and the family-controlled firms. A second effect with relevance to the financial sector was the existence of a "dual" structure of the economy and its institutional apparatus which was divided into an official and an unofficial sector. The first was identified with the large, subsidized firms which were benefited from state regulation in the form of concessional credit and protection from competition. The unofficial sector, on the other hand, consisted of firms with a smaller size, less access to bank financing, and less bargaining power in the corporatist framework and hence, more competitive in their practices. A distinctive characteristic of these two sectors and the corporatist model that underpinned them was the "soft-budgeting" practice of "official" industrial firms. "Softness" of the budget constraint they faced, took the form of price-setting in consultation with the government, particular tax exemptions or concessions along with explicit subsidies and preferential credit offered to them without considering the ability of these firms to repay their debts. Important institutional implications of the corporatist model were the higher transaction costs for the more competitive unofficial sector and the reduced amount and low quality of information concerning the riskiness and return of firms' projects. The flow of information was additionally impeded by the family control of enterprises and by the absence of modern management and accounting practices. The corporatist model was supplemented by the oligopolistic structure of the banking system and the thin capital market. Both contributed to the smooth operation of the system since underdeveloped capital markets were favored by industrialists who wanted to keep the enterprise in family hands to preserve their negotiation power versus the government and the bank oligopolies.

To our understanding, what Katseli (1990) describes is in fact an attempt in post-war Greece to run some kind of a "negotiated economy" where "an essential part of the allocation of resources is conducted through institutionalized negotiations between independent decision-making centers in the state, organizations, and corporations" (Nielsen and Pedersen 1988, referred in Ramstad 1991: 431). Ramstad (1991) relates such an economy to Commons's ideas of "reasonable value" and "regulated capitalism". We have seen in our previous analysis how Commons associated these concepts with public purpose and democratic processes. Assessing the Greek "corporatist" post-war model in these terms reveals its shortcomings and fundamental flaws. Our historical account in Chap. 7 makes us skeptical about the quality and depth of democracy in Cold War Greece until the fall of the 1967–1974 dictatorship. At least the working classes and small businesses had significantly reduced bargaining power during the golden age of Greek economic development. The situation changed during the 1980s with increasing participation of labor in national income but at the expense of productivity gains as we have noted. However, Commons's ideas are heavily dependent on the effective operation of a regulatory framework where reasonable rules emerge as a compromise among social groups in the context of fair bargaining that avoids unfair "economic coercion". Hence for Commons, regulation is necessary to bring about a more fair outcome in the context of a market economy (Ramstad 1991). On the contrary, regulation or government intervention to favor political cronies and big incumbent firms, as Katseli (1990) implied that happened in the Greek case, does not serve the public purpose of inclusiveness and it is in complete contrast to the "negotiated economy" that Commons would have in mind.

Alogoskoufis (1996), on the other hand, attributes the disappointing performance of the Greek economy during the period 1974–1993 to the inability of the political system to replace the institutional framework of the post-war period that was conducive to economic development with another one equally successful in this respect. The post-war institutional framework was characterized by a tax system that favored private investment and protected property rights. Industrial relations guaranteed the return on investment projects as labor wage demands could not exceed productivity rates. However, this was the outcome of an authoritarian political regime that prevailed in Greece after the Civil War. In addition, the Bretton Woods system of fixed exchange rates in which the drachma participated contributed to a stable monetary environment, while fiscal rules that prevailed during that period assigned priority to public investment instead of public consumption and favored balanced government budgets. Furthermore, Alogoskoufis (1996) considers the combination of free product markets after the 1950s and the maintenance of a regulated financial market under the guidance of the Monetary Committee as positive for economic development. He thinks that the financial repression regime was efficient in allocating savings to selective sectors with high returns during the post-war period. In short, the post-war institutional framework assisted by a stable international monetary environment and despite its authoritarian structures was the ultimate cause of high growth rates during this period. The situation changed dramatically after the demise of the Bretton Woods system and the fall of the seven-year dictatorship in 1974. Nationalizations and extra taxes on profits rendered property rights at risk. Wage demands exceeded productivity rates while political business cycles affected public expenses and public debt soared. In such conditions, financial repression acted as a mechanism for keeping alive inefficient and problematic enterprises instead of being the developmental factor of the previous period. In short, the political system failed in substituting the authoritarian framework of the post-war period with a new consensual one that would be equally conducive to economic development by guaranteeing long-term investment returns and macroeconomic stability. In the terminology of Old Institutional Economics, the new political situation failed at building a true negotiated economy exactly because it failed to substitute the previous authoritarian regime with an efficient consensus among different social groups that would be conducive to inclusive economic growth. Such an efficient compromise would not sacrifice inclusiveness for the sake of growth or vice versa.

Pagoulatos (2003) examines in more detail the close relationship between the post-war political economy model for Greece's economic development and the prevailing financial structure. According to his argument, Greek economic development was triggered by unilateral initiatives from the government and the Bank of Greece in the absence of civil society, although the relationships between the political personnel and the economic oligarchy cannot be denied (Pagoulatos 2003: 41). This approach does not contradict Katseli's (1990) argument to the degree that it acknowledges the role of three major players in this game: the state, the banks, and the entrepreneurial families. However, even if the civil society in Greece in the post-war period was very weak in expressing demands and formulating economic policy (Pagoulatos 2003: 40), the relationships between the political and economic elite confirmed also by Pagoulatos (2003: 41) justify Thomadakis (1995: 105) assertion that government policies should be conceived as responses to social pressures. This means that government policies both reflect the predominance of the interests of a particular social group or groups over others and they also produce the legitimation to act in this way. However, Thomadakis's (1995: 105) claim may be subject to modification concerning the external constraints to domestic policy. In this respect, we agree with Pagoulatos (2003: 39) that the Greek state's developmental initiative in the 1950s and 1960s was strongly influenced by its role in the Cold War environment to defend the Western political and economic structures thus highlighting an urgent need for economic development. In this respect, issues of power and claims voiced by collectives and social groups in the context of civil society are in fact manifestations of Commons's rationing transaction (Kemp 2009: 70–71). According to Commons, the rationing transaction is correlated with the distribution of power among constituents and is the basis for carrying out the bargaining and managerial transactions (Guedes and Jeronimo 2023; Pessali and Fernández 1999; Ramstad 1996). In this context, the initiative of the Greek government and the Central Bank to support the post-war financial repression regime as a rationing transaction that allocates power was a strategic decision (strategic transaction in Commons's terminology) that improved the allocation of resources in the particular era and transcended the problems of the inter-war arrangements. In the specific case of Greece, this decision also depended on the need for local elites to take sides in the international Cold War scene.

Be that as it may, the model proposed by the Governor of the Bank of Greece in that period 1955–1967 Xenophon Zolotas, was founded on a policy mix that compounded price stability with bank credit to finance industrialization with the help of the state. This was a rather eclectic view not completely identified either with the Keynesian or with the neoclassical tradition. For example, the developmental state of the post-war period in Greece employed banks as instruments of development along with a policy of administered low interest rates. However, neither of these policies can be uniquely identified with the Keynesian or neoclassical theoretical tradition (Pagoulatos 2003: 29–30) although, according to Zolotas, the problem that developing countries faced was that of structural weaknesses rather than insufficient effective demand. In this sense, monetary stability was important for the additional reason that Greek economic development ought to be driven by export-oriented growth rather than by increases in domestic demand such as consumption expenditure (Psalidopoulos 1990: 52–53). On the other hand, this financial regime was characterized by a credit policy that contributed to both economic development and macroeconomic stability. The policy tools used included quantitative controls on the supply of credit and special reserve requirements for banks with the Central Bank. Credit rationing was used to limit credit expansion when price stability was threatened by high liquidity in the banking system. In the context of this policy, there was no need to raise interest rates to restrain monetary expansion (Pagoulatos 2003: 32–33).

In this context, of particular importance was the Currency Committee established in January 1946 with the authority to decide on monetary, credit, and foreign exchange policies (Pagoulatos 2003: 48). Although the initial intention was one of a short-lived institution to control credit expansion and channel financial aid to productive uses (Kostis 1997: 90), eventually the Committee evolved into a powerful mechanism of detailed control of the credit system until its abolishment in 1982 (Garganas and Tavlas 2001: 48). The Currency Committee consisted of the economic ministers, the Governor of the Bank of Greece and two foreigners, an American, and a British citizen. However, from 1951 onward its composition changed and only Greek nationals participated in the committee. These included the ministers of coordination, finance, agriculture, commerce, industry, and the Governor of the Bank of Greece. The Committee decided on the purposes for which bank loans could be granted, the sectors to which preferential loans should be granted according to mandatory percentages, the interest rates to be charged, the terms of the loans, the procedures to be followed by the banks and the security required depending on the type of loan (Halikias 1978: 27–29). Qualitative and quantitative controls along with administered interest rates played the double role described above: (1) The achievement of monetary stability for fear of early post-war hyperinflation. (2) The direction of credit to preferred sectors together with credit rationing for firms in less-priority sectors. However, the latter resulted in a double paradox. At first, a few large oligopolies co-existed with many small firms (Ellis et al. 1964: 173–175), the first comprising the "official" subsidized sector and the latter the so-called "unofficial" sector which depended on retained earnings for its financing or on the curb markets. Hence, economic policy and institutional conditions favored the oligopolistic profits of large firms which were subsidized by the government through preferential credit and by various measures of protection against external competition without considering their efficiency. Secondly, there was significant over-indebtedness of favored firms that borrowed funds from banks at preferential rates and in turn provided loans to credit-rationed firms at higher interest rates thus becoming "unofficial" financial intermediaries (Katseli 1990).

Therefore, a critical feature of the financial system was the oligopolistic structure of the Greek banking sector which was characterized by the dominance of two big commercial banks, the National Bank of Greece and the Commercial Bank of Greece (Kostis 1997: 91; Psilos 1964: 186) and the thin capital market. After the stabilization of 1953–1955 that restored public confidence in the currency, there was a period of both monetary stability and increasing accumulation of savings in the form of bank deposits (Pagoulatos 2003: 48–49; Ellis et al. 1964: 50). This was the "era of emancipation" of commercial banks which saw also the increase of their bargaining power in the Greek economy (Kostis 1997: 93). It is noteworthy that as early as the mid-1960s, Psilos (1964: 17) pointed out that the main problem of the Greek financial system was not insufficient savings, but rather an inefficient mechanism for channeling excess liquidity into productive investment. Such inefficiencies were related to the reluctance of large family-owned firms to go public, the inability of small firms to access the capital market, the inadequacy of Greek corporate law to protect shareholders' interests, and the lack of competition in the banking industry that resulted in the paradox of excess supply of savings combined with a high cost of capital (Psilos 1964: 246–251). Capital market underdevelopment described in this way gave rise to state intervention intending to funnel these funds to preferential outlets to boost development by using a rather complex system of rules and controls. According to Courakis (1981), there were two major instruments of government intervention between surplus and deficit units: (1) Controls on commercial banks concerning the required reserve ratios with the Central Bank, reserve/rebate ratios on bank credits, credit ratios on bank liabilities for specific sectors' financing, lending limits for unflavored sectors, interest rate ceilings on lending and deposit rates, and prescribed terms on loans supplied and deposits accepted. (2) Controls on special credit institutions—such as the Postal Savings Bank, the Agricultural Bank, the development banks, the mortgage banks, and the Consignations and Loans Fund—concerning the permitted range of their business and the structure of their balance sheets. Besides, as Pagoulatos (2003: 11) indicates, in developing economies with oligopolistic banking systems, market-determined credit allocation would have favored import trade at the expense of more productive and developmental activities because of the higher profit rates of the former. The above justifies the interventionist role of the Greek state during the period of financial repression that gave rise to the Greek economic development "miracle" as serving that public purpose amidst competing social groups with unequal bargaining power. In a sense, the government attempted to establish more "reasonable" terms for the financing of economic development having in mind the prevailing post-War development finance model.

However, as we mentioned above, "reasonableness" for Commons does not reflect only the public purpose of economic development but also the fair procedure to achieve it in an inclusive manner. In this respect, the distortions of the Greek version of financial repression made financial reform necessary in the coming years.

Therefore, the need for financial development remained a task resulting from the weaknesses of the Greek financial system during the period under consideration. An urgent task, in this direction, was to break up the oligopolistic structure of banking persisting during the post-war period (Katseli 1990; Psilos 1964: 186). Banking oligopolies were initially favored by the Bank of Greece to maintain the stability of the Greek banking system (Pagoulatos 2003: 76). On the other hand, banking oligopolies and industrial family-ran oligopolies reinforced each other (Pagoulatos 2003: 73) and contributed to financial underdevelopment given the eagerness of banks to finance these firms and the reluctance of the latter to resort to the capital market (Pagoulatos 2003: 70). In a sense, there has been a special relationship between the commercial banks and the large industrial firms (Halikias 1978: 166). On top of that, the system of administered low interest rates provided a disincentive for firms and the government to raise funds in the capital market. Restricting the supply of financial assets as an alternative (to bank deposits) placement of savings resulted in excessive liquidity for banks and an underdeveloped capital market (Karatzas Committee 1987: 22, 66; Harissopoulos Committee 1979: 6). In this sense, financial repression also reinforced the oligopolistic structure of the banking system. In addition, Psilos (1964: 191–194) argues that the major commercial banks hindered the development of the capital market either by opposing the establishment of specialized institutions for long-term credit (such as the OXOA in the 1950s) or by demanding that those competing institutions should limit their operations to sectors unprofitable for commercial banks. Besides, they made use of their affiliated insurance companies to stifle competition in the insurance market. The issues of competition and capital market development remained major problems in the Greek financial system even in the late 1980s as is evident in the Karatzas Committee (1987: 34) report where such issues were related to the need for modernization of the Greek banking system in the context of economic stabilization and fiscal consolidation (Karatzas Committee 1987: 11). Indeed, as Katseli (1990) states, public deficits increased enormously during the crisis years. More importantly, however, the bulk of these expenditures covered public consumption rather than public investment and mostly acted as a cushion to absorb social reactions within a political cycle framework. This was especially the case after 1973 when trade unions also emerged as interest groups (Pagoulatos 2003: 88). This is probably the reason why Bosworth and Kollintzas (2001: 168–169) identify labor market rigidities that permitted the rise in real wages above labor productivity as a major factor for the productivity slowdown during the late 1970s and 1980s together with macroeconomic instability and financial regulation. However, this argument disregards the distorted nature of the model of economic development in Greece in the sense of lack of inclusiveness in the context of reasonableness as explained above. Labor market rigidities and productivity slowdown in the 1980s make sense when perceived in the context of the crippled "negotiated economy" of the 1960s and 1970s. However, they do not justify the intertemporal myopia of Greek governments concerning the false dilemma between growth and social fairness.

On the other hand, Thomadakis and Seremetis (1992) seem to support the view of Katseli (1990) regarding the direction of public expenditures as they examined the fiscal management during the decade of the 1980s in Greece under the theoretical notion of "fiscal regime". The interesting point in this notion is that it embodies both the economic and political parameters of fiscal management by relating the effectiveness of institutional arrangements concerning tax collection and public expenditure to the ability of the state to intervene in a developmental direction without endangering financial stability. In this respect, a fiscal regime might become unsustainable either because of mere financial reasons or because of a lack of "social legitimation", or both (Thomadakis and Seremetis 1992: 206). The demands of vested interests or even the existence of pessimistic expectations might put at risk the state's credibility as a manager of public funds. For example, the chronic disparity in the tax burden between salaries and pensioners, on the one hand, and corporate profits and property income, on the other, revealed the political/electoral weight of the latter interest groups. Such differential tax treatment accommodated tax laxity and, in a sense, institutionalized tax evasion from income categories other than wages or pensions such as rents, profits, or self-employment incomes. This led to a fall in "tax morality" for all income categories as some groups found that tax evasion was indeed possible for them while others, being the permanent victims of the prevailing tax regime, sought every possible way to escape their fate (Thomadakis and Seremetis 1992: 231–235). On the other hand, on the expenditure side of the budget, the Greek state undermined its credibility as a developmental state by attributing to its income policy—and thus to the transfer component of its budget—a developmental role that it could never have had in the first place (Thomadakis 1995: 105), and by using government expenditure for political-electoral reasons (Thomadakis 1995: 110). Despite that, Thomadakis (1993: 367, 370–371; 1995: 119–121) makes the point that the state still has a role to play even in the new conditions of economic integration and increased capital mobility. This role should emphasize the importance of public investment for economic development, mainly through its effect on infrastructure and the subsequent favorable impact on private investment returns and volumes. In addition, a declared commitment of the state to long-term economic stability and growth would create an attractive environment for foreign capital investments. However, this was not the case of the Greek experience during the 1980s and especially after 1984. In an environment of growing debt-service expenditures, public investment expenditure fell in favor of increased transfer payments in the government budget. Hence, there was a substitution of capital formation, that would have contributed to the structural change of the economy, by income formation. Such income formation targeted specific social groups in the form of pensions and social security contributions, or it provided investment incentives in the form of grants that were, however, transformed into rent-seeking income formation by particular groups. The policy commitment toward developmental change degenerated into a policy of social subsidization (Thomadakis 1995: 106, 119; Thomadakis and Seremetis 1992: 243, 247, 251–252). However, this "social subsidization" was not able to restore "reasonableness" in the Greek case by a rationing transaction that redistributes power between social groups. The reason is that this redistribution was not a long-term policy conducive to growth but a short-sighted policy of remedying injustices by favoring particular social groups. Fair bargaining, as Commons would have wished, was still lacking because inequalities in bargaining power still persisted despite the fact that democracy was making progress in Greece. To put it differently, fairness is not just about righting wrongs but it is mainly the way you do that. This is why Commons put such emphasis on democratic procedures and the negotiation process. In any case, the public purpose of inclusive economic development seemed not to be so well served by the old financial repression regime.

8.3 The Policy Emphasis from Development Finance to Financial Development: Changing Financial Regimes

Every institutional arrangement is historically specific to the degree that it serves the economic and social conditions of its era. If these conditions change, then the relevant institutional arrangement, that serves the public purpose of economic development, enters a period of transformation and mutation that culminates in a new institutional framework. In this context, the shortcomings of the credit policy pursued and its underpinning financial regime became apparent during the 1970s and 1980s when the international environment altered. Two major issues stated by Halikias (1978) stand out. First, the negative impact of official interest rate policy on bank profitability, which rendered qualitative and quantitative controls on both investment and monetary policy ineffective. The structure of interest rates—at least until 1966, when a system of equalizing bank profits on different types of loans was introduced—made long-term lending unprofitable for banks. On the other hand, banks were allowed to charge various fees on short-term loans thus increasing the effective return on these loans (Halikias 1978: 52, 168, 185, 187). Furthermore, lending to small firms was effectively discouraged because of the high administrative costs of such small amounts of loans, the lower official lending rates for handicrafts as opposed to the manufacturing industry, and the lower creditworthiness of these small-sized firms (Halikias 1978: 191–192). Thus, the incompatibility of the official interest rate policy with the profit maximization of the commercial banks created a disincentive for the banks to cooperate with the monetary authorities in the successful implementation of the preferential credit system. Qualitative credit controls on the allocation of credit to priority sectors failed because of the unofficial indirect financing of imports and trade as industrial enterprises became financiers of commercial enterprises (Halikias 1978: 232, 212). In addition, qualitative and quantitative controls proved ineffective due to banks' excess liquidity, their reluctance to cooperate with the authorities given their own preference for short-term lending, and insufficient demand for long-term loans from industrial firms. Acceptance by commercial banks of credit regulations would be tantamount to maintaining excess idle funds and thus accepting loss of profits (Halikias 1978: 220–221). Finally, the success of a system of comprehensive controls required the operation of an effective mechanism to inspect and monitor both the activities of banks and the use of borrowed funds by their clients. However, such a detailed monitoring mechanism was unlikely to be effective in identifying "socially desirable" versus "undesirable" lending (Halikias 1978: 221–222).

The second issue relates to the ultimate failure of easy finance policies, which led to corporate over-indebtedness, increased risk, and the diversion of corporate funds into unproductive activities such as real estate rather than reinvesting retained earnings in more competitive productive uses. The easy access of large industrial enterprises to bank financing, together with their unofficial indirect financing of trade, increased the indebtedness of these enterprises and the risks assumed by both these enterprises and their lending institutions. In addition, the Greek entrepreneurs were characterized by a low propensity to save as they reinvested only a small proportion of their profits in their business. The most favored outlet for industrial profits was real estate, which, unlike the more risky industrial ventures, had the lure of security and also guaranteed high capital gains due to rising prices and increasing trading volumes in the real estate market. For these reasons, industrial enterprises in Greece operated below their optimal size despite the intention of official financial policies to encourage industrial investment (Halikias 1978: 195–204).

Courakis (1981) adds another adverse consequence of the system of administered interest rates and credit controls. This system was based on the calculation of apparent yields of various categories of loans and disregarded the actual returns and the cost-benefit structure of banks' financing decisions. However, the expected return on loans could fall at a given official interest rate, as the risk of default increases for each type of loan. In addition, lending rate ceilings increased the emphasis banks placed on collateral requirements to limit their risk exposure, which discouraged small and new firms with limited collateral from taking on investment initiatives. More importantly, it discouraged those firms that wanted to pursue projects that were more risky but socially desirable to the degree that high collateral requirements made such firms ineligible as potential borrowers. As a result, government policy did not favor the very activities its regulatory apparatus was designed to promote.

The situation changed gradually from 1982 and especially from 1987 onward when financial liberalization proper commenced in view of the 1992 milestone for European market integration (Karatzas Committee 1987: 15). The two major reports on the Greek banking system, the Harissopoulos Committee (1979) and the Karatzas Committee (1987) illustrate the policy change that took place under the pressure of external factors relating to Greece's accession to the European Community in 1981 (Harissopoulos Committee 1979: 1). The Harissopoulos Committee (1979: 29–30) pointed out that the Greek economic development in the 1960s and early 1970s was not accompanied by a corresponding financial development, so that the anachronistic structure of the financial system became an obstacle to further growth. This structure came under further pressure following Greece's accession to the European Community, the associated liberalization of the capital account, and the harmonization of the Greek financial system with the European one.

The above observations indicate that Robinson's (1952: 86) dictum, "where enterprise leads finance follows", did not materialize effectively in the Greek case. We saw in the previous sections of this chapter how the rationing of power among social groups within the financial regulation/ repression regime was not able to achieve inclusiveness and fairness in a way conducive to economic growth. The above-mentioned distortions in the Greek financial system, which prevented financial development from keeping pace with economic development, illustrate a different aspect of the same issue. The Greek political and economic elite was not able to fully understand the dialectical interrelationship between economic development and financial development and its social impact. It seems that they were trapped into a cheap-lending perception of the financial regulation/ repression regime without paying the necessary attention to financial development as a support to the process of economic development. They did not understand that "reasonableness" did not mean concessional finance irrespective of the historically specific domestic and international economic context. Moreover, in the above description of the developments in the Greek banking sector, no special reference was made to the role of the Greek development banks and their distinct role with respect to the commercial banks. The argument of this book is that development banks are, by their very nature, privileged instruments of both economic and financial development. Whether they assumed such a role in the Greek case is the object of the next Chapter. However, as we shall demonstrate in that Chapter these banks were also victims of the inconsistencies of government policy concerning the relationship between economic and financial development.

The two major reports on the reform of the Greek banking system that appeared in the late 1970s and mid-1980s provide a sense of the institutional changes that took place in the process of financial liberalization. The proposals of the Harissopoulos Committee included: (1) The abolition of the administrative setting of lending rates according to different loan types and the gradual increase of both the lending and the deposit rates to market levels. This implied that indirect subsidization of manufacturing, exports, and agriculture through the interest rate policy would no longer be possible. Subsidies should appear explicitly as entries in the government budget. (2) The abolition of the complex reserve-rebate system imposed on commercial banks. (3) The financing of budget deficits through recourse to the money and capital markets. (4) Measures for the development of the money market, the foreign exchange market, and the capital market. (5) Measures to reduce oligopolistic conditions in the banking sector. (6) Liberalization of the sources of financing of special credit institutions, including the issuance of their own securities. (7) Restructuring of the Postal Savings Bank, the Agricultural Bank, and the National Mortgage Bank to face the new competitive environment. (8) Measures for the modernization of the three development banks. These included reducing administrative costs, a healthier portfolio, and a greater role for ETBA in the capital markets. With respect to private banks, the Committee suggested that they diversify their sources of funding and expand their lending to other sectors of the economy, as well as play a more active role in the development of the capital market (Harissopoulos Committee 1979: 38–46).

On the other hand, the Karatzas Committee's (1987) suggestions for the reform of the Greek financial system included issues such as interest rates and credit rules, competition and bank portfolio management, bank accounts disclosure and supervision along with particular suggestions concerning agricultural credit, development banks, and the capital market. More specifically: (1) Concerning the required changes to interest rates and credit rules, the Committee identified three stages. The first stage should ensure the return to positive real deposit and lending rates, as well as the disengagement of the credit system from the obligation to support social and developmental tasks, the latter being transferred to the government budget. The second stage should activate the market forces in the determination of deposit and lending rates except for long-term lending rates for handicraft and agricultural enterprises. The third stage should make market forces the main determinant of interest rates and the allocation of resources, with the abolition of various credit controls and compulsory reserves for industrial financing. In addition, the government should resort to the market to finance its deficit. In the context of these stages, both the Harissopoulos Committee (1979: 38) and the Karatzas

Committee (1987: 11, 25) emphasized the need for gradual liberalization in tandem with the stabilization of the economy. Lower inflation rates and balance of payments deficits were necessary conditions for the convergence of interest rates to lower levels, and for lower budget deficits which would contribute to the smooth functioning of money and capital markets (Karatzas Committee 1987: 25). (2) Competition in the Greek banking system should be promoted by gradually increasing the importance of smaller banks, rather than by reducing the power of the big banks. This is because a financial system that consists of sizable institutions is in a better position to cope with international competition. In addition, new innovative products such as leasing, credit factoring, forfeiting, venture capital services, loan securitization, and syndicated loan techniques should be included in those offered by the banking system. Furthermore, portfolio management for commercial banks should distinguish between investments in financial services companies, which should be further expanded, and those in industrial and tourism companies. The latter should not exceed a certain limit and should be handled by independent holding companies, while investments that lead to more permanent relationships between banks and specific companies should be avoided (Karatzas Committee 1987: 34–35, 38–39). (3) Adoption of uniform accounting principles and standards that would improve economic information disclosure for banks. In addition, a new supervisory system of banks by the Bank of Greece was proposed that included the close monitoring of banks in terms of capital adequacy, liquidity, and quality of assets (Karatzas Committee 1987: 48–50). (4) Suggestions for special credit institutions such as the Agricultural Bank of Greece and the three development banks. Concerning the latter, it was proposed that they should continue to offer financing for long-term investment projects but they should also expand their activities to include modern investment banking practices such as participation in syndicated loans, underwriting of share and bond issues, and participation in the restructuring of enterprises through mergers and acquisitions. Concerning the sources of their funds, the Committee suggested that development banks should have the right to accept time deposits and borrow directly from insurance companies and pension funds. They should have access to the interbank, money, and capital markets. They should also be allowed to offer loans for working capital on a more permanent basis and long-term financing for a wide range of activities including trade, real estate, and services. Finally, the gradual adaptation of development banks to a more liberalized environment required the phasing out of government subsidies for bank bond issues (Karatzas Committee 1987: 61–62). (5) The development of the capital market should be based on measures concerning both the supply and demand of securities and the modernization of the Athens Stock Exchange. Financial instruments such as long-term government bonds, commercial paper, certificates of deposit, private bond issues underwritten by banks, and long-term bond issues by banking institutions could increase the supply of alternative securities offered to savers. Measures on the tax treatment of interest income and emphasizing the role of institutional investors such as insurance companies and pension funds, together with foreign investors, could boost demand (Karatzas Committee 1987: 67–69). Both reports indicate the crucial role of the Bank of Greece which should lead this operation freed from its obligation to monetize government deficits or to support the balance sheets of commercial banks (Karatzas Committee 1987: 30; Harissopoulos Committee 1979: 20–21, 39).

The financial liberalization process in the banking sector was followed by initiatives for the modernization of the capital market and especially the Athens Stock Exchange. The reforms in the capital market took place during the second half of the 1990s and the early 2000s and they included: (1) The establishment of the Capital Market Committee in 1995 by Law 2324 in the context of the European Directive 93/22/EEC. (2) The modernization of transactions in the Athens Stock Exchange with the adoption of new technological improvements such as the integrated automated system of electronic transactions and the process of digitalization. (3) The setup of markets for derivative products as of the summer of 1999. (4) A series of measures for the security of market transactions such as the setup of an insurance capital, regulations concerning capital requirements for brokerage firms, or the adoption of a code of conduct for market participants. (5) The publication of the “white paper for corporate governance” in 1999 and (6) measures against market abuse as early as 1999 although the European legal framework did not take its final form before 2004. The country indeed experienced a major stock exchange crash in 1999 but the consequences of this exuberance would probably have been worse than they actually had been for the economy if these institutional developments concerning the regulation of the capital market had not been in place (Thomadakis and Loizos 2025).

The decision for financial liberalization was taken in response to both external and domestic factors. The main external constraints were related to the European single market program and the liberalization of capital flows while the domestic determinant was the need for disinflation and the determination of the Bank of Greece to achieve it (Pagoulatos 2003: 112–114) as called for in the reports of the Harissopoulos and Karatzas Committees. Pagoulatos (2003: 114, 159–160) highlights the "policy strength" of the central bank which is a feature distinct from its formal dependence on the government. Even if a central bank is institutionally dependent, it may have control in policy areas where the government does not have the technical expertise to exert its influence (Pagoulatos 2003: 120). Hence, according to Pagoulatos (2003: 160) the state-driven directed-finance developmental process of the post-war period was followed by an equally government-initiated financial liberalization process in which, on the one hand, social group pressures played a minor role and on the other hand, the contribution of the Bank of Greece was essential. In particular, the central bank had a technically competent staff and its own agenda of policy objectives that considered financial liberalization necessary for the effectiveness of monetary policy in curbing inflation. It also had the determination and the ability to insulate policy from the demands of various group pressures. In this context, the organizational weaknesses of different interest groups to express uniform demands along with the government's escape route of avoiding pressure by invoking the external European factor or the Bank of Greece authority were crucial in the ultimate success of the financial liberalization policy (Pagoulatos 2003: 159). Furthermore, the outcome of financial liberalization was also a transformation of the state itself from a "developmental state" to a "stabilization state" in the sense of prioritizing macroeconomic stability over development. To the degree that the former was considered to be a precondition for the latter and not vice versa, the balance of power had turned against government intervention and in favor of globalized financial markets and institutional investors (Pagoulatos 2003: 203–205). However, the problem is that the financial liberalization process in Greece did not strike a balance between policies that would be both conducive to growth and socially inclusive. The lack of effective participation of various social groups in this process, especially those with the least bargaining power, was of critical importance. In this respect, the result was less "reasonable" than expected by the less privileged social groups because it did not come as the outcome of effective negotiation among them but, as Pagoulatos (2003) indicated it was the offspring of top-down initiatives of experts for whom Commons had his reservations (Ramstad 1991). Moreover, the government's and the Bank of Greece's actions that determined the content of the public purpose of the era emanated from their "ethical beliefs" which reflected the "sovereign's class position" or the "private purpose endorsed by the sovereign as a public purpose" as Commons would have stated (Ramstad 2001: 258). We hesitate to declare the unconditional success of a financial liberalization process that was not the outcome of negotiation among social groups because the latter, as Pagoulatos (2003) argues, were not well organized to express their demands. On the other hand, we claim that, even in such conditions, the role of development banks as agents of institutional change was important and usually disregarded. Development banks, as will be explained in the next Chapter, played an important role in changing beliefs and habits of thought in the business and investors' community during the financial regulation/repression era which subsequently supported the top-down process of financial liberalization. If we identify the modernization of the financial system through financial development, which responds to economic development, as a process ultimately founded in technological change then, in Veblenian terms development banks contributed to a change in the index of ceremonial dominance in Greek society. However, the democratic process is more apt to guarantee the progressive direction of this institutional change. Depending on the degree of democratic participation, the social groups with more bargaining power are able to impose their own ideas, beliefs, and mental models in a society thus, framing the perception of alternative policies (Altman 2023; Bush 1987). For Commons, informed decision-making through bargaining in the context of democratic participation is essential for a "reasonable" reform (Kemp 2009: 89–90). On the contrary, it seems that in Greece the new policy convention has been that fairness is not a constituent part of the reform process but it is somehow derived from liberalized markets. In other words, if markets are left to operate freely they will deliver fair results. The minimum condition for this is prudential regulation as opposed to the strict financial repression of the past. However, the fact that this new liberalized regime was imposed by the government did not guarantee that the latter fully grasped the economic development-financial development dialectics. On the contrary, it seems to us that the political and economic elite substituted the cheap-lending fallacy with another one. The latter is the assumption that free, from government intervention, markets are able to achieve the public purpose of fair economic and financial development at a minimum cost. However, is it not also a fallacy to believe that the dogma of "free markets" does not imply some sort of government intervention in shaping these markets, in the sense of Polanyi (1944 [2001]) (Mazzucato and Penna 2016), and in this respect the support of the state for specific social groups with more bargaining power than others? Hence, it is an open question whether the content of prudential financial regulation was adequate to restore the bargaining power of the weaker social groups such as small businesses or small investors and retail savers. After all, the content, direction, and depth of financial regulation are themselves affected by the unequal bargaining power of the same social groups.

8.4 Financial Development and Financial Instability

Despite the above reservations about its shortcomings, institutional evolution in Greece has progressed in tandem with economic development passing through the alternative financial regimes during the post-World War II era. In a sense, Greece's membership to the European Monetary Union as of 2001 has been a milestone in terms of institutional development as well since it testifies to its integration into the core of the Western developed world. In other words, despite less progress in terms of income and productivity convergence of Greece with other Euro area countries and regardless of its financial cycles being more intense than others (Franks et al. 2018), the country has been on an institutional convergence path for at least the last two decades. Of course, institutional convergence as an indicator of institutional development does not necessarily imply beneficial results for economic development. The first part of this book was an attempt to show that institutional evolution is correlated with changes in habits of thought and beliefs in the context of conflicting interests of different social groups rather than with uniformity of formal rules and regulations. But let us put that caveat aside for the moment to think in terms of the fruits yielded by the country's path from financial repression/regulation to financial liberalization. Recalling the discussion in Chap. 3 of this book, the main feat of financial liberalization has been a wave of financial development which allegedly is positively correlated with economic growth. On the other hand, financial liberalization has been accused of being responsible for financial instability and crises worldwide. Hence, there seems to be a connection between the level of financial development or financial deepening and the degree of financial stability in an economy. Interestingly, this is also the theme of an IMF paper published in May

2015. According to this paper, the relationship between financial development and growth is neither linear nor monotonically increasing. On the contrary, there is a "bell-shaped" association between these variables since initially, financial development has a positive effect on growth but too much financial deepening turns the relationship into a negative one. A similar result is obtained in terms of financial stability. Rising financial deepening, especially in terms of the "depth" of financial institutions, increases financial instability since financial institutions are assuming more debt and risk. Hence, despite initial beneficial effects, high levels of financial development are correlated with lower economic growth and higher financial instability (Sahay et al. 2015).

The International Monetary Fund has introduced a new, more comprehensive, measure of financial development which is an aggregate of separate indices for financial institutions and financial markets. Instead of the traditional simple measures of private credit to GDP and stock market capitalization to GDP, the above indices take into account a wide variety of financial institutions' and markets' depth, access, and efficiency features. For example, the overall measure for Financial Institutions includes profitability and cost ratios such as Net Interest Margin, Return on Assets, Return on Equity, or Overhead costs to total assets along with depth and access measures like Private sector credit to GDP or Bank branches per 100,000 adults. Similarly, the Financial Markets index combines among other measures Stock market capitalization to GDP with the percent of market capitalization outside of the top 10 largest firms and Stock market turnover ratio (Svirydzenka 2016). In short, the financial development index of the IMF can be considered a summary measure of both financial deepening and efficiency of the financial sector.

Figure 8.1 shows that there was an upward trend in the aggregate measure of the Financial Development index until 2008 and a downward trend afterward, during the Global Financial crisis and the subsequent Greek crisis. The value of this index in 2021 (0.47) returned close to its value in 2001 (0.48) indicating the adverse effect of the crisis on the financial sector. However, as Table 8.1 depicts, both on average and in median values, the aggregate index of financial development rises persistently through time, including the last period 2008–2021 despite the negative average output growth portrayed in Table 7.1. Therefore, it seems that the ability of the financial sector to develop by passing through institutional transformations that were characterized by alternative financial regimes was not fully impaired by the Greek economic crisis, but the latter

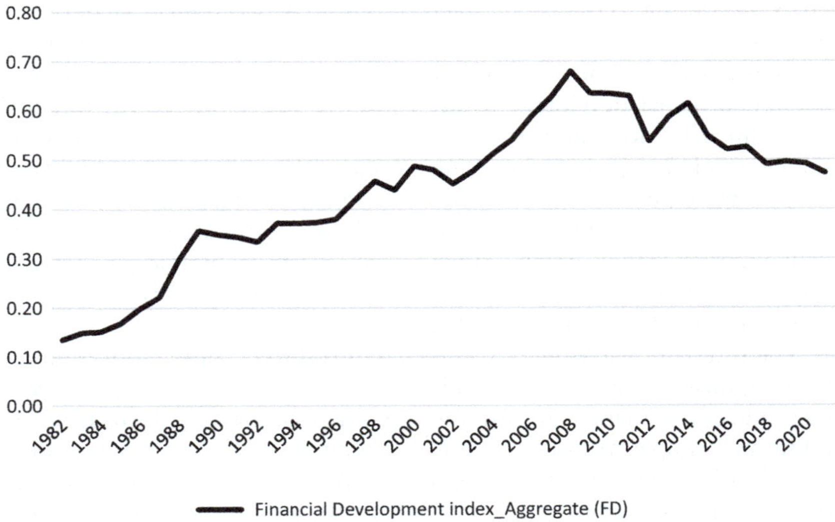

Fig. 8.1 Financial Development index for Greece (FD) (aggregate of Financial Institutions index and Financial Markets index), 1982–2021. Source: IMF Data, Financial Development Index Database, and author's elaboration

Table 8.1 Financial Development Index, Greece, summary statistics, 1982–2021

	1982–1993	*1994–2001*	*2002–2007*	*2008–2021*
Mean	0.26	0.43	0.53	0.56
Median	0.26	0.43	0.53	0.54
St. Dev.	0.09	0.05	0.07	0.07
Min	0.14	0.37	0.45	0.47
Max	0.37	0.49	0.63	0.68

Source: Author's elaboration based on IMF Data, Financial Development Index Database

surely left its scar. On the contrary, Greece confirms the interrelationship between financial development and financial instability, especially the point made by Sahay et al. (2015) that advanced economies with high levels of financial development face decelerating or lower growth and increased output volatility.

It is interesting to disentangle the puzzle of financial development-financial instability by looking at the financial institutions and financial markets indices separately and by focusing on specific individual measures of performance for each one of them. Figure 8.2 shows that financial intermediation in Greece increased sharply until 1989 and then fell until 1995. The index rose again from 1996 until 2008 only to follow a downward trend thereafter thus, falling to a value of 0.43 in 2021. This is not the case for the financial development index concerning financial markets depicted in Fig. 8.3 which rises consistently until 2008 and then fluctuates widely before it stabilizes to a value equal to 0.50. It seems that financial institutions and the capital market followed different paths during the period of institutional evolution in the financial system. The period of financial liberalization during the late 1980s and early 1990s adversely affected financial institutions while it benefited the development of the capital market. In Greece, the presence of commercial banks in the financial sector is overwhelming. Indeed, in 2020 commercial banks possessed an astonishing 90% of total financial sector assets while insurance companies, mutual funds, investment companies, and other financial institutions all together accounted for the rest 10% (Black Sea Trade and Development Bank 2020). Therefore, Fig. 8.2 portrays the unfavorable impact of

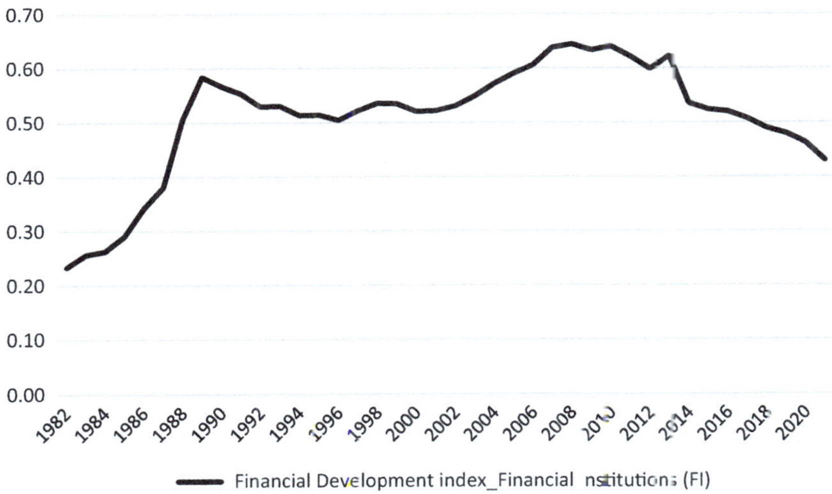

Fig. 8.2 Financial Development, Financial Institutions Index for Greece (FI), 1982–2021. Source: IMF Data, Financial Development Index Database, and author's elaboration

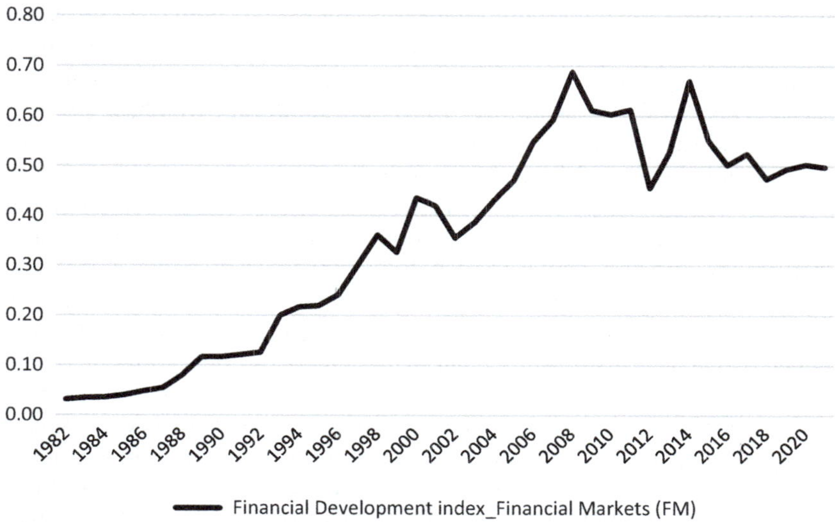

Fig. 8.3 Financial Development, Financial Markets index for Greece (FM), 1982–2021. Source: IMF Data, Financial Development Index Database, and author's elaboration

financial liberalization on the efficiency and financial intermediation offered by the Greek banking sector with an emphasis on the profound downward trend after 2008. Indeed, as Fig. 8.4 shows, Greek banks faced an extreme rise in non-performing loans between December 2008 and September 2017 when bad loans reached the level of 49.1% of total loans. Only as late as September 2022 did non-performing loans fall to one-digit levels. On the other hand, the stock market too went through two major booms and busts between February 1997 and March 2003 the first, and between March 2003 and March 2009 the second with peaks in September 1999 and October 2007 respectively as shown in Fig. 8.5. However, financial instability in this case did not reverse the upward trend of financial development in the capital market at least until 2008 confirming the Thomadakis and Loizos (2025) assertion that modernization and institutional development in the Greek capital market during the late 1990s and early 2000s have had a long-term impact irrespective of market exaggerations. Even the situation after 2008, despite fluctuations, shows rather a stabilization than a clear downward trend in financial development.

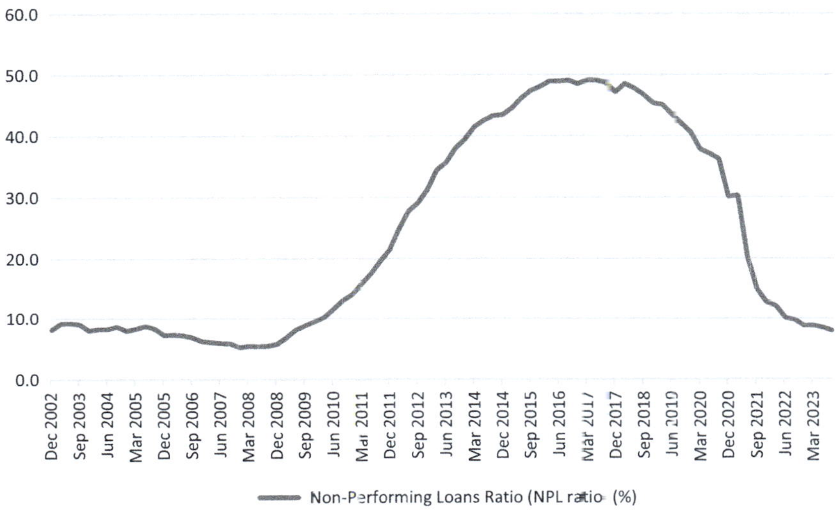

Fig. 8.4 Non-Performing Loans ratio (NPL ratio), percentage, total Greek banks (commercial and cooperatives), solo basis, on balance, Dec. 2002–Sep. 2023. Source: Bank of Greece statistics and author's elaboration

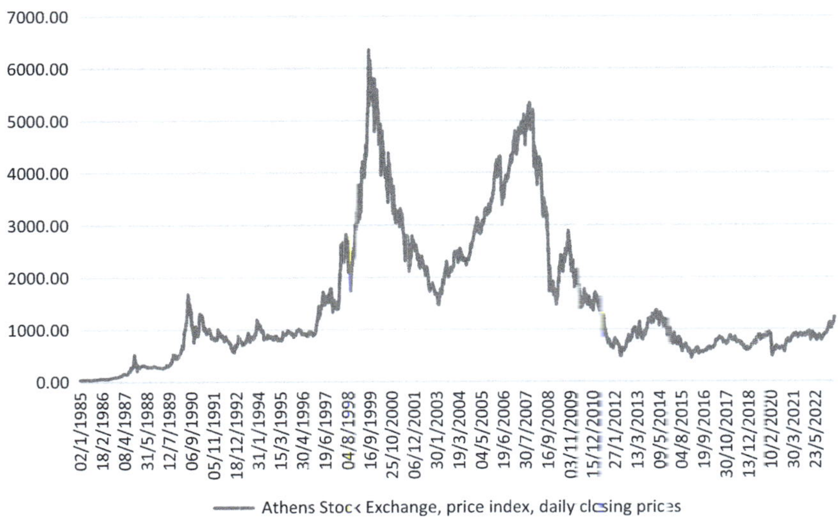

Fig. 8.5 Athens Stock Exchange, price index, daily closing prices, 2/1/1985–2/6/2023. Source: https://www.capital.gr/finance/historycloses/%ce%93%ce%94/ and author's elaboration

According to the IMF paper mentioned above, there is a possibility to combine higher financial development with lower risks for growth and financial stability. The solution lies in the quality of institutions that secure property rights, information diffusion, and effective regulation in the context of the rule of law although there is no "one-size-fits-all" recipe (Sahay et al. 2015). At this point, the initial argument of this book reasserts itself in the sense that institutions matter in a historically specific context. More than that, an institutional analysis proper is not possible without taking into account changing habits of thought and beliefs in the context of conflicting interests among social groups and their influence on the political process. The last section of this chapter attempts a recapitulation of institutional evolution in Greece along these lines.

8.5 Development Banking and Institutional Change in Greece

The above analysis reveals the central role of alternative financial regimes in our understanding of Greek economic development in the post-war years. This role hinges on how these different financial regimes provided different sets of incentives to social groups that conditioned their behavior. Commercial banks and big industrial firms composed the main "official" nexus of development finance with the help of the state. The latter pursued its developmental goals in conditions of post-war reconstruction and urgent industrialization within a favorable international environment. Therefore, the state took the initiative for institutional development to serve its goals of industrialization and economic development. After all, this was the conventional wisdom of the era that endorsed government intervention in favor of macroeconomic management and economic growth. In this context, government involvement in the Greek economy took the form of a financial repression/regulation regime during the 1950s and 1960s which was, however, succeeded by a financial liberalization regime during the mid-1980s. During the 1980s the international conditions had changed and so did the dominant ideas in academia and international organizations. The shift toward market liberalization left its mark in Greece's attempt to deregulate and develop the financial sector including the capital market. Both periods, of financial repression/regulation and financial liberalization were marked by the degree of consistency and the determination of the government to carry out the task of economic and institutional development. More so, they were characterized by the balance of power among social groups and the bargaining process that underpinned government initiatives both during the financial repression and in the financial liberalization regime. However, unequal bargaining power favored initially policies that were conducive to growth but less inclusive. This was the case at least until the fall of the dictatorship regime in the mid-1970s. On the contrary, policies that favored inclusiveness, sometimes at the expense of economic growth, prevailed in the 1980s. Hence, the era of financial regulation/repression in Greece was not able to serve the public purpose of socioeconomic development in the context of "reasonableness" that would embrace economic growth as the outcome of fair bargaining. The ensuing financial liberalization inherited the model of unequal bargaining power and gave priority to restoring free markets relegating fairness to the background as a byproduct. The content of prudential financial regulation which may increase the bargaining power of weaker social groups is itself a field of power antagonisms between these groups. In addition, the political and economic elite of Greece in both financial regimes did not fully understand the interplay between economic and financial development but rather juxtaposed the one with the other. Beyond issues of inclusiveness and participation of all social groups in the fruits of economic and institutional development, there were also effects on financial stability. The performance of the Greek financial sector, measured by the degree of accomplished financial development, showed a path of disintermediation in favor of markets during the financial liberalization era. It was also characterized by the presence of financial instability on at least three occasions: during the early 1990s, early 2000s, and after the Global Financial Crisis. Hence, financial instability seems to have gone hand in hand with financial development in the Greek case as well as in other developed countries.

Development banking has been historically a crucial link between development finance and financial development as the analysis in the first part of this book revealed. The Greek financial sector saw the establishment and operation of three development banks for four decades from the 1960s to the early 2000s. These institutions, which were meant both to bridge the gap between affluent savings and investment demand as substitutes of the capital market and to prepare the development of the latter, might have made the difference in the above-mentioned political-economic nexus or, equally possible, might not have been able to overcome it. In addition, during the twenty-first century, there were also different forms of development finance in Greece along with the establishment of a new development bank in the late 2010s in the context of the European architecture of promotional banking to cope with the modern challenges. If development banks are indeed dynamic institutions with a double role to play in promoting both economic and institutional development, did they assume such a role in the Greek case? What was their contribution to industrialization and structural transformation in terms of both their financing activities and their initiatives for institutional change? Was the Greek state supportive of their engagement with these tasks? How did the change in financial regimes affect their performance and their financial viability? Did they manage to carry out successfully their internal transformation so as to be able to adjust to the new liberalized financial regime? What are the lessons to be learned from the main period of development banking in Greece and how these can inform the current revival of development banking in this country? In the current reality of financial disintermediation, the rising role of the capital market, and the episodes of financial instability what is the role that development banking should play to support both financial development and financial stability?

The chapters of this book that follow attempt to provide some answers to these questions bearing in mind that development banks should be conceived as dynamic organizations that balance between markets and governments. This means that development banks as hubs of both development financing and institutional change should play a multilevel role characterized by "reasonable" loan pricing, negotiation between social groups and the government, and a commitment to promote goals serving the public purpose. The public purpose may have been described by the need for industrialization during the financial repression era or by the need to control inflation and adjust the growth model of the Greek economy in a globalized international environment during the financial liberalization era. The public purpose may also dictate in the post-crisis present era a new model of economic growth with multiple sustainability characteristics such as economic, environmental, and financial sustainability. The above describes a way to read the history of development banking and to ascribe a role to the current model of development banking in Greece in accordance with the institutional theory that was developed in Chap. 6 of this book.

References

Alogoskoufis, G. (1996) "The Two Phases of Ianus: Institutions, Economic Development and Balance of Payments in Greece", *Economic Policy Studies*, 1, 25–63 (in Greek).

Altman, M. (2023) "Mental Models, Decision-Making, Bargaining Power, and Institutional Change", *Journal of Economic Issues*, 57(4): 1241–1259.

Black Sea Trade and Development Bank (2020) "Overview of the Financial Sector in Greece", available at https://www.bstdb.org/BSTDB_Overview%20of%20the%20financial%20sector_GREECE.pdf Accessed 24 Apr. 2024.

Bosworth, B. and Kollintzas, T. (2001) "Economic Growth in Greece: Past Performance and Future Prospects" in Bryant, R. C., Garganas, N. C., and Tavlas, G. S. (eds.) *Greece's Economic Performance and Prospects*, Athens and Washington D.C.: Bank of Greece and The Brookings Institution, pp. 153–192.

Bush, P. D. (1987) "The Theory of Institutional Change", *Journal of Economic Issues*, 21(3): 1075–1116.

Courakis, A. S. (1981) "Financial Structure and Policy in Greece: Retrospect and Prospect", *Greek Economic Review*, 3(3): 205–244.

Ellis, H. S., Psilos, D. D., Westebbe, R. M., and Nicolaou, C. (1964) *Industrial Capital in Greek Development*, Center of Economic Research, Research Monograph Series, No 8, Athens.

Franks, J., Barkbu, B., Blavy, R., Oman, W., and Schoelermann, H. (2018) "Economic Convergence in the Euro Area: Coming Together or Drifting Apart?" IMF Working Paper WP/18/10 available at file:///E:/Work%20in%20Progress/Book%20Proposal/data/Macro%20data/Financial%20Development%20and%20Instability/wp1810.pdf Accessed 23 Apr. 2024.

Garganas, N. C. and Tavlas, G. S. (2001) "Monetary Regimes and Inflation Performance: The Case of Greece" in Bryant, R. C., Garganas, N. C. and Tavlas, G. S. (eds.) *Greece's Economic Performance and Prospects*, Athens and Washington D.C.: Bank of Greece and The Brookings Institution, pp. 43–102.

Guedes, S. N. R. and Jeronimo, R. C. (2023) "A Concept of Two Authors: Commons and Williamson on Transactions", *Journal of Interdisciplinary Economics*, 35(1): 61–82.

Halikias, D. J. (1978) *Money and Credit in a Developing Economy The Greek Case*, N.Y.: New York University Press.

Harissopoulos Committee (1979) *Banking System Study Committee. Recommendation*, Athens: Bank of Greece (in Greek).

Hoffmann, A. (2019) "Beware of Financial Repression: Lessons from History", *Intereconomics*, 54(4): 259–266.

Karatzas Committee (1987) *The Committee's Report for the Reform and Modernization of the Greek Banking System*, Athens: HEA (in Greek).

Katseli, L. (1990) "Structural Adjustment of the Greek Economy", CEPR Discussion Paper, No 374.

Kemp, T. (2009) *Progress and Reform. The Economic Thought of John R. Commons*, Saarbrücken, Deutschland: VDM Verlag Dr. Müller.

Kostis, K. (1997) *Cooperation and Competition: The 70 Years of the Union of Greek Banks*, Athens: Alexandria Publications (in Greek).

Mazzucato, M. and Penna, C. R. C. (2016) "Beyond Market Failures: The Market Creating and Shaping Roles of State Investment Banks", *Journal of Economic Policy Reform*, 19(4): 305–326.

Mullin, J. (2021) "A Look back at Financial Repression" *Econ Focus*, 22–25.

Nielsen, K. and Pedersen, O. K. (1988) "The Negotiated Economy: Ideal and History", *Scandinavian Political Studies*, 11(2): 79–101.

Pagoulatos, G. (2003) *Greece's New Political Economy. State, Finance and Growth from Postwar to EMU*, Houndmills, Basingstoke and New York: Palgrave Macmillan.

Pessali H. F. and Fernández, R. G. (1999) "Institutional Economics at the Micro Level? What Transaction Costs Theory Could Learn from Original Institutionalism (In the Spirit of Building Bridges)", *Journal of Economic Issues*, 33(2): 265–275.

Pilbeam, K. (1992) *International Finance*, Houndmills Basingstoke Hampshire and London: The Macmillan Press.

Polanyi, K. (1944 [2001]) *The Great Transformation: The Political and Economic Origins of Our Time*, Boston, MA: Beacon Press.

Psalidopoulos, M. (2014) *History of the Bank of Greece 1928 – 2008. From Bank of the State, Guarantor of Financial Stability*, Athens: Bank of Greece. (in Greek).

Psalidopoulos, M. (1990) *Keynesian Theory and Greek Economic Policy: Myth and Reality*, Athens: Kritiki (in Greek).

Psilos, D. D. (1964) *Capital Market in Greece*, Center of Economic Research, Research Monograph Series, No 9, Athens.

Ramstad, Y. (2001) "John R. Commons's Reasonable Value and the Problem of Just Price", *Journal of Economic Issues*, 35(2): 253–277.

Ramstad, Y. (1996) "Is a Transaction a Transaction?", *Journal of Economic Issues*, 30(2): 413–425.

Ramstad, Y. (1991) "From Desideratum to Historical Achievement: John R. Commons's Reasonable Value and the 'Negotiated Economy' of Denmark." *Journal of Economic Issues*, 25(2): 431–439.

Reinhart, C., Kirkegaard, J. F., and Sbrancia, M. B. (2011) "Financial Repression Redux", *Finance and Development*, 22–26.

Robinson, J. (1952) "The Generalization of the General Theory" in Robinson, J. *The Rate of Interest and Other Essays*, London: Macmillan, pp. 67–142.

Sahay, R., Čihák, M., N'Diaye, P., Barajas, A., Bi, R., Ayala, D., Gao, Y., Kyobe, A., Nguyen, L., Saborowski, C., Svirydzenka, K., and Yousefi, S. R. (2015)

"Rethinking Financial Deepening: Stability and Growth in Emerging Markets", IMF Staff Discussion Note SDN/15/08 available at https://www.imf.org/external/pubs/ft/sdn/2015/sdn1508.pdf Accessed 23 Apr. 2024.

Svirydzenka, K. (2016) "Introducing a New Broad-based Index of Financial Development", IMF Working Paper WP/16/5 available at https://www.imf.org/external/pubs/ft/wp/2016/wp1605.pdf Accessed 23 Apr. 2024.

Thomadakis, S. (1995) "The Greek Economy and European Integration: Prospects for Development and Threats of Underdevelopment" in Constas, D. and Stavrou, T. (eds.) *Greece Prepares for the Twenty-first Century*, Washington, D.C. and Baltimore: Woodrow Wilson Center & John Hopkins University Press.

Thomadakis, S. (1993) "European Economic Integration, the Greek State, and the Challenges of the 1990s" in Psomiades, H. and Thomadakis, S. (eds.) *Greece, the New Europe, and the Changing International Order*, New York: Pella Publishing Company.

Thomadakis, S. and Loizos, K. (2025) "Modernization and Instability in the Capital Market. The Decade of the 1990" in Kostis, K. and Rizas, S. (eds.) *Histories of Metapolitefsi*, Athens: Patakis Publications (in Greek).

Thomadakis, S. and Seremetis, D. (1992) "Fiscal Management, Social Agenda, and Structural Deficits", in Kariotis, T. (ed.) *The Greek Socialist Experiment. Papandreou's Greece 1981–1989*, Pella Publishing Company.

CHAPTER 9

The Main Period of Development Banking in Greece (1963–2002)

9.1 Development Banking in Post-War Greece: An Introduction

The early attempts to introduce development banking in post-war Greece included the establishment of the Economic Development Financing Organization (OXOA) in 1954 and the Industrial Development Corporation (OBA) in 1960. The OXOA participated in the reconstruction of the Greek economy after the war by acting as a development finance institution and by attracting foreign capital for domestic firms. However, OXOA's operation was marked by the interconnection between the state, commercial banks, and industrial families which has not always been beneficial either for economic growth or for capital market development. Loans provided at low cost were directed to projects with high risk and low efficiency which were guaranteed by commercial banks oligopolies in exchange for high commission fees (Loizos 2012: 229; Psilos 1964: 221–222, 226–230; Psilos and Westebbe 1964). On the other hand, the semi-public Industrial Development Corporation's (OBA) contribution to economic development was rather meager as it provided funds to only 13 small enterprises during the period 1960–1964. However, it is notable that OBA contributed to the modernization of existing companies by providing technical and financial assistance and by training technical personnel. In addition, OBA prepared feasibility studies and facilitated the flow

K. Loizos, *Between Markets and Governments*,
https://doi.org/10.1007/978-3-031-88527-3_9

of information to foreign and domestic investors (Loizos 2012: 230; Halikias 1978: 246; Psilos 1964: 231–232).

In the early 1960s, the main part of the post-war history of development banking in Greece begins with the establishment of ETBA (Hellenic Industrial Development Bank), ETEBA (National Investment Bank for Industrial Development), and TE (Investment Bank). However, this milestone for development finance in Greece was characterized by a competition between the commercial banks, i.e. the National Bank of Greece and the Commercial Bank of Greece, and the government. ETBA was the offspring of government initiative while the ETEBA and the TE came as an attempt of the commercial banking duopoly to gain a share in development financing. Hence, development banking in Greece was founded from the beginning on competition rather than cooperation between the government and banking incumbents (Loizos 2012: 230; Kostis 1997: 99, note 152: 193).

The mandate of the three development banks was trivial for development finance during the post-war era namely, to promote industrial development and to develop the capital market. Both were parts of the public purpose of the era to promote economic and institutional development as explained in Chap. 8. However, four specific points concerning all three development banks are in order before looking at the evolution of each particular institution separately. First, there was a gradual weaning off the government financial support over time since after 1975 development banks were able to float their own bonds to the public thus, increasing the share of this form of funding from a range between 42% to 69% in the mid-1980s to 90% in the early 1990s, including foreign borrowing. This change in the source of funds that backed their lending activity was, in Commons's terms, the transformation of a managerial transaction into a bargaining transaction and highlighted the dynamic nature of these banks and their ability to adapt to changing economic conditions.

The second point concerns a difference in lending priorities between the state-owned ETBA on the one hand and the ETEBA and the TE on the other hand, which were established with the initiative of commercial banks. ETBA as a public institution emphasized socioeconomic returns and disregarded financial returns as opposed to the other two banks, and in particular ETEBA. In addition, ETBA had the dominant share in long-term lending among development banks (Xanthakis 1995: 177–180, 207; Karatzas Committee 1987: 59–60). Figures 9.1 and 9.2 illustrate the credit activity of Greek development banks. All three development banks

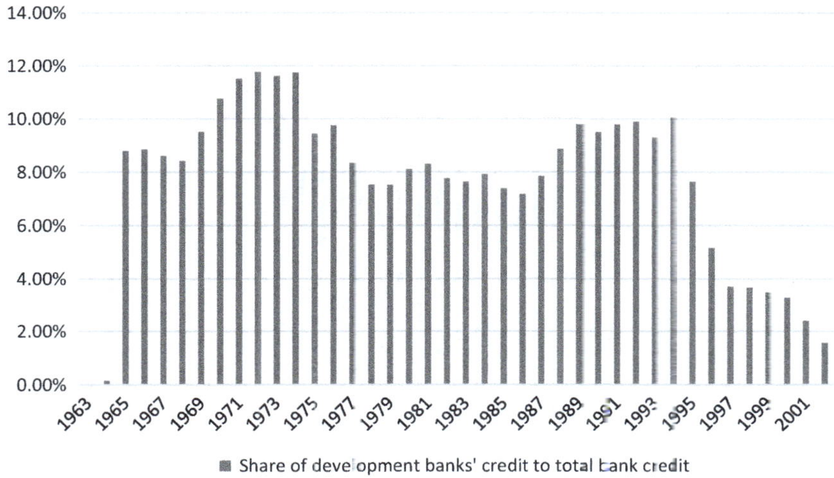

Fig. 9.1 Share of development banks' credit to total Greek banking sector credit, percentage, 1963–2002. Source: TE, ETEBA and ETBA Annual Reports and Bank for International Settlements, Credit to Private Non-Financial Sector by Domestic Banks, Adjusted for Breaks, for Greece, retrieved from FRED, Federal Reserve Bank of St. Louis, and author's elaboration

together did not exceed 12% of the total credit provided by the banking sector. On average, the share of development banking credit to the economy was 8.5% of total banking credit in 1963–1974, 8.1% in 1975–1986 and 6.6% in 1987–2002. Although the amounts of loans provided may seem insignificant compared to commercial bank lending, the importance of the development of the industries financed, the socioeconomic benefits derived despite the risks taken, and the institutional initiatives taken by the development banks multiplied the impact of the loan disbursements. On the other hand, ETBA was dominant among development banks with an average share in total development banking credit of 83% in 1965–1974, 69% in 1975–1986, and 84% in 1987–2002 indicating its major role in development finance in the post-war Greek economy. In short, development banks, and especially the public ETBA, ranked their mandate to serve the public purpose above their profitability. In this sense, as explained in Chap. 6, their bargaining and managerial transactions were governed by a rationing transaction to the degree that development banks contributed to resource allocation in favor of economic development.

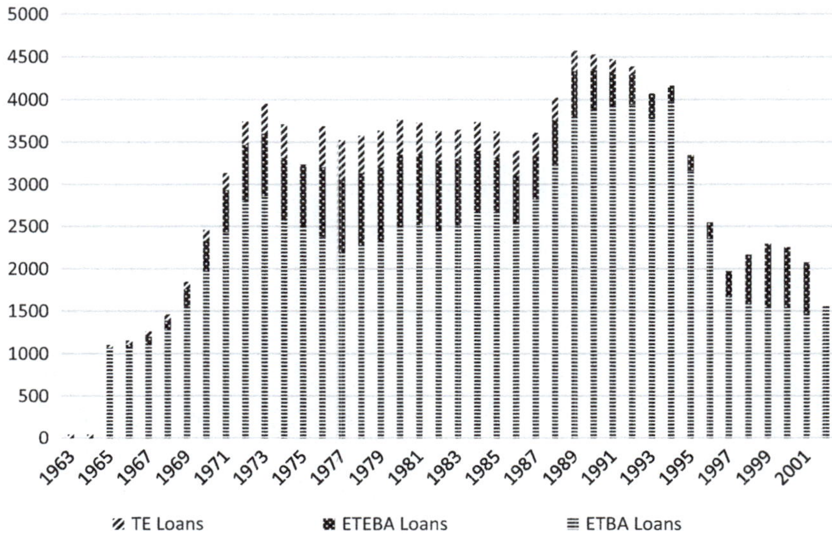

Fig. 9.2 TE, ETEBA, and ETBA, loans, million Euros, constant 2015 prices, 1963–2002. Loans are classified as long and medium-term loans (1963–1993) and claims against customers (1994–2002). Source: TE, ETEBA, and ETBA Annual Reports, various years, and author's elaboration

The third point is that all three banks contributed to the capital market and institutional development through activities such as securities underwriting, trading on their own portfolio of securities, providing services of fund management, advising companies in mergers and takeovers, and offering technical and management support to businesses. In this sense, development banks were instrumental in institutional development and reform by identifying limiting factors and providing solutions based on the best available practices. In Commons's terminology, a limiting factor is a problem that causes a systemic failure and calls for remedial action (Kemp 2009: 56). In Chap. 8 we discussed several such limiting factors that inhibited the development of the capital market in Greece during the 1960s, 1970s, and 1980s. The above activity of development banks that contributed to capital market and institutional development was in fact a strategic transaction in Commons's terminology that corrected the prevailing limiting factors (Kemp 2009: 62) and supported the wave of financial liberalization that followed during the 1990s. In Veblenian terms, development banks underpinned the gradual process of institutional development by contributing to changing habits of thought and social conventions about business practices. It would be naïve for someone to believe that financial liberalization would have been possible without a minimum level of internalization of the new practices and behavior by market participants. In turn, this process of "institutionalization" (Arestis and Stein 2005; Arestis et al. 2003) would not have been possible without the institutional activity of development banks. To the degree that development banks provided financial and technical solutions to problems faced by businesses, they promoted instrumental values at the expense of ceremonial ones. In this sense, they reduced the index of ceremonial dominance in the Greek economy which was transformed from a less developed to a developed one. However, the degree of progressiveness of this institutional change depended on the quality of the democratic process and the participation of different social groups in the bargaining process as explained in previous Chapters (Altman 2023; McCormick 2006: 24–25; Bush 1987).

The final point highlights the difficulties posed in their financial viability as the macroeconomic conditions deteriorated and the financial regime changed gradually during the 1980s. Financial liberalization implied higher financing costs and increased competition with commercial banks while their balance sheets suffered losses from non-performing loans (Xanthakis 1995: 177–180, 207; Karatzas Committee 1987: 59–60). Given that the main period of development banking in Greece ended officially in 2002 when ETEBA and ETBA were absorbed by the National Bank of Greece and Piraeus Bank respectively (Loizos 2012: 232) opinions on the performance of these banking organizations were mixed. The positive account stresses their contribution to economic, financial, and business development with their multiple activities. The negative evaluation highlights the shortcomings of public institutions such as ETBA and focuses on their role as competitors to commercial banks, their support of industrial oligopolies, and their inability to stave off government pressures (Karatzas Committee 1987: 60; Halikias 1978: 246–247).

The above points about profitability and mixed opinions highlight the changing meaning of "reasonableness" as the financial regime changes. A "reasonable" outcome reflects the public purpose inscribed in the public opinion and custom of a particular historical period (Kemp 2009: 75–77), and reasonable pricing is associated with bargaining power and fairness as perceived in that period (Ramstad 1991, 2001). Moreover, the deteriorating financial condition of development banks reflects the impact of a changing financial regime along with the institutional-political risk that characterizes them. An issue that emerges at this point is whether and how development banks managed to cope with these problems. It seems that the solution they gave was an internal organizational mutation from traditional development banks of the financial repression era to investment banks of the financial liberalization period by substituting long-term lending with short-term activities that provided fee-income (Loizos 2017; Loizos 2012: 231). In this respect, the evolution of development banking in Greece during the period 1963–2002 shows that development banks can be understood comprehensively as a dynamic combination of bargaining, managerial, and rationing transactions with a view to problem-solving institutional reform, serving the public purpose and adapting to changing economic and institutional conditions. The success or failure of their transformation as economic and institutional conditions change depends on the prevailing government policies that govern their operation in the context of a rationing transaction and the stated public purpose.

The following sections of this chapter outline the evolution of each of the three development banks in Greece during the period beginning in the early 1960s and ending in the early 2000s when Greece joined the European Monetary Union. The periodization that is followed depends on both the subperiods of economic development expounded in Chap. 7 and the particularities that characterize the history of each bank. In addition, the discussion below takes into account the great transition from financial repression to financial liberalization in the Greek economy that took place in the 1980s as reflected in the evolution of the Financial Development Index of Fig. 8.1. However, the analysis sets the year 1987 as the turning point in the financial regime. Although the abolition of the Currency Committee in 1982 was a crucial step toward financial liberalization, the year 1987 coincides with the publication of the Karatzas Committee report for the reform in the Greek banking system and saw the beginning of a series of reforms that gradually liberalized the financial sector in Greece (Eichengreen and Gibson 2001: 581; Garganas and Tavlas 2001: 61, 85–91). Therefore, in an attempt to combine institutional-political events with the historical evolution of these banks, financial performance ratios are calculated setting as turning points the year 1974 when the Greek dictatorship fell and the country entered a period where the European vision prevailed and the year 1987 as the milestone of financial liberalization.

9.2 The National Investment Bank for Industrial Development (ETEBA)

9.2.1 The Economic Growth Period: 1964–1973

ETEBA was established on 13th November 1963 by the National Bank of Greece and several foreign shareholders but the statutes of ETEBA and the approval of the Monetary Committee were published in the Official Gazette on December 10, 1963. The foreign shareholders included Chase International Investment Corporation, Manufacturers Hanover International Banking Co., Hambros Bank Ltd, Deutsche Bank AG, Banca di Credito Finanziario (Mediobanca) S.p.A., Crédit Lyonnais, Banque Nationale pour le Commerce et l'Industrie, Crédit Commerial de France, Banque Lambert, and Compagnie Financière et Industrielle Confinindus SA. In 1965, ETEBA's capital increased and four new foreign shareholders were added to the old ones: Crédit Suisse, International Finance Corporation, Nordfinantz-Bank Zurich, and Svenska Handelsbanken (Vousvounis 2010: 42, 44; ETEBA Annual Report 1964, 1965).

The scope of the activities of ETEBA included both the long-term financing of the Greek industry—in a complementary role to the existing commercial banks—and the development of the capital market in the Greek economy. In addition, the bank intended to play a significant role in the modernization of Greek industry by financing joint ventures between Greek and foreign firms which would imply the transfer of know-how and modern management techniques. In terms of its sources of financing, the bank's ability to accept time deposits was included in its charter, as was its ability to expand its operations to include fee-based banking activities. However, in its 1964 Annual Report, the bank emphasized the lack of a framework for the operation of investment banks in Greece at the time when the latter had to respond to the pressing needs of the Greek economy (Vousvounis 2010: 42; ETEBA Annual Report 1964: 9, 21–22, 34).

According to the same report, the situation of the economy and especially of manufacturing in 1964 was characterized by the significant structural and quantitative developments that occurred during the post-war period. There was a widespread transition from large handicraft enterprises to small and medium-sized industrial units in the context of increased production growth. However, these industrial units were mainly labor-intensive and focused on the production of consumer goods. The inadequacy of their own capital resources for investment in capital equipment reflected their low productivity. On the other hand, the small size of the market and the existence of protective tariffs contributed to both the low competitiveness of the industry and the small size of its units. Finally, these industrial units were less specialized and more concentrated around Athens and Piraeus because of the proximity of the labor market in this area and the inadequate infrastructure and transportation facilities away from Attica. On the other hand, there was a tendency to overcome these problems, as evidenced by the increasing demand for mechanization of production and the rising capital-labor ratio. However, the lack of skilled labor and the ownership structure of Greek enterprises (sole proprietorships and family-owned firms) were additional institutional impediments to both the optimal size of the industry and the need to increase productivity through the use of new technologies. Furthermore, the introduction of modern management techniques and the employment of professional technical and administrative staff were considered crucial to the development of the Greek industry. Another issue of concern was the underdevelopment of the capital market which could not play a significant role in funding investment. At the same time, attracting foreign capital in the form of direct investment was of vital importance. A possible rise in equity investments would have the additional institutional effect of reviving the capital market in the Greek economy. The peculiarity of the Greek case was that domestic firms were not generating sufficient profits to finance new ventures but they were using short-term bank borrowing to meet long-term funding needs (ETEBA Annual Report 1964: 10–19).

It is noteworthy that ETEBA identified these problems in its first year of operation and proposed measures to alleviate them. According to the bank, the establishment of development banks created a healthier environment in the Greek banking system by distinguishing the role of traditional commercial banks from that of institutions that have as their special purpose to finance long-term investment. More importantly, it emphasized its active role in institutional development as a private Development Finance Corporation alongside the public Hellenic Industrial Development Bank (ETBA). Hence, it highlighted the need for the development of the capital market in Greece, the consolidation of new forms of financing of industry such as equity participation, and the establishment of a rational relationship between short-term and long-term interest rates. Especially, concerning the capital market, ETEBA has sought to develop it by underwriting issues of shares and bonds and by placing its investments in securities on the market when the respective firms have reached a level of maturity (ETEBA Annual Report 1964: 19–20, 22). This means, that ETEBA's financing decisions were market-oriented at least as far as equity participations were concerned. In this respect, we can see the interrelation between the issue of industrial development and that of financial development in the way the bank's owners and managers thought about its mission.

During the first period of its operation, ETEBA took an active role in the development process, both by providing loan financing and by participating in the share capital of companies. In this way, entrepreneurs received finance at lower interest rates in exchange for the participation of the bank in potential profits. ETEBA also offered government-guaranteed foreign exchange loans with the support of the International Bank for Reconstruction and Development and the European Investment Bank, while transferring the foreign exchange risk to its clients. In general, the forms of financing in which the bank was active were the following: (1) loans involving payment of interest and participation in profits; (2) participation in share capital without voting rights for a specified period, converted into ordinary shares or repurchased by the existing shareholders; (3) loans convertible into share capital; (4) accelerated repayment of the loan if the borrower's cash generation exceeds a specified level; (5) long-term loans with foreign exchange clauses. In order to finance its lending activity ETEBA drew funds from the Bank of Greece (the central bank of the country) and the National Bank of Greece (its parent institution). Furthermore, the bank proposed to the government some measures to facilitate capital market development. These included: tax exemption on dividend income under certain conditions, extension of tax exemption on capital gains to banks and insurance companies, tax exemption on capitalization of corporate income, reduction of fees and transaction costs of capital market operations, and the establishment of investment companies and a Capital Market Committee along with a unified accounting system (ETEBA Annual Report 1965: 21–22, 25–26, 27).

The bank played also an active role in facilitating mergers, especially in the metal industry, to increase the size and competitiveness of industrial units, while at the same time supporting the decentralization of industrial activity by financing the setup of factories in the new industrial zones outside of the Attica region. It is noteworthy that, as early as 1966, the bank sought to diversify its lending by financing a variety of sectors such as chemicals, paper, building materials, metals, textiles, food, and even tourism (ETEBA Annual Report 1965: 24; 1966: 8). In addition, it has not abandoned its goal of playing an active role in the development of the capital market. In this regard, it held a growing portfolio of bonds and equities intending to channel them to the stock market in the future. This eventually happened in 1971 (ETEBA Annual Report 1966: 12; 1971: 8). In addition, in the field of legislation, it has prepared drafts for the establishment of closed and open-end investment companies in order to give small investors, pension funds, and Greeks in the Diaspora the opportunity to place their savings in outlets with minimal risk, contributing to the development of the capital market. The idea, as expressed by the bank (ETEBA Annual Report 1968: 10) was that the acquisition of shares in firms by investment companies would increase public confidence and would stabilize price fluctuations on the stock exchange. Besides, these companies would be a new source of funds directed to the industry in the form of equity capital. In this context, it established the Diethniki management company and the Delos Mutual Fund in 1972 which entered the market early in 1973. In the same year, it also floated its own preferred non-voting shares (one-third of its total share capital) on the stock market in an attempt to raise additional share capital by attracting savings from the general public. ETEBA pointed out that for its attempt to attract local savings to be successful, the bank should maintain a reasonable profitability ratio along with a balanced debt/equity ratio (ETEBA Annual Report 1972: 2, 12, 14). In addition, in 1967, ETEBA recognized the need for special technical and management support for Greek companies and, in cooperation with the international consulting firm Arthur D. Little, established Arthur D. Little Hellas Consultants SA (ETEBA Annual Report 1967: 10). In 1969, this company contributed to the reorganization and introduction of Electronic Data Processing systems in the National Bank of Greece, the Agricultural Bank of Greece and the Postal Savings Institution (ETEBA Annual Report 1969: 6).

This first period of the operation of ETEBA highlighted its ability to identify the limiting factors in Greek economic development and propose solutions for their overcoming. In this context, ETEBA served the public purpose of the era putting a special emphasis on institutional development which was accompanied by specific proposals to the government. These initiatives introduced new ideas and institutions in the Greek financial system and the business community that affected their habits of thought and everyday practices. On the other hand, it attempted to specify the "reasonable" conditions for development finance in such a way that the latter would associate industrial financing with financial development without jeopardizing the financial viability of the bank. We think that the key to such an exercise was what the bank identified as "reasonable" profitability and "balanced" leverage position which directly echoes Commons's idea of "reasonableness" as a defining principle of fair pricing in specific historical conditions.

9.2.2 *The Stagnation Period: 1974–1986*

Despite the quantitatively astonishing results achieved by the Greek industry in the previous period, its development was based on a rather short-sighted model with weaknesses, especially in its technological and organizational structure. These shortcomings became more apparent when the economy was hit by the oil shocks of 1973 and 1978–1979 and the subsequent period of stagflation. The industry also had to contend with workers' demands for a higher share of GDP, especially after the fall of the dictatorship in 1974, and with increased international instability, both in terms of demand and exchange rate fluctuations. In addition, the need to control rising prices due to rising inflation limited their profitability and ability to self-finance their operations. The immediate result of all these adverse developments was the proliferation of firms with problems of economic viability, the so-called "*provlimatikes*" [1] Investment rates fell especially due to the inability of Greek firms to respond to the changing international environment, while prices and unemployment increased. In the case of ETEBA, arrears represented 10.2% of the loan portfolio at the end of 1980, compared with only 1.7% at the end of 1974. Therefore, much of the financing during this period was directed toward the modernization of existing capital assets rather than the construction of new facilities. However, an important part of funds was directed, especially from 1984 onward, to the restructuring of "*provlimatikes*" through the relevant

[1] The term "*provlimatikes*" in Greek literature, or firms in distress refers to firms experiencing difficulties as a result of excessive borrowing. This phenomenon emerged in the late 1970s, shortly after the second oil crisis, and reached its peak in the mid-1980s. A number of factors contributed to this issue, including unfavorable international monetary developments, an increase in industrial production costs, the leniency of the criteria for credit provided to industrial firms, the poor management of these industrial units and the gradual removal of tariff protection and government subsidies to industry due to the country's accession to the European Economic Community. (Vousvounis 2010: 139–140).

organization established by the state, the "OAE" (Organization for Business Restructuring). Therefore, a common practice at that time was to reschedule companies' debts to the bank along with their reorganization to become viable. Such measures included the conversion of a part of the outstanding non-serviced debt into equity participation by ETEBA in the relevant firms and the provision of new loans along with support in management and structural reorganization (Vousvounis 2010: 162; ETEBA Annual Report 1983: 5–6; 1984: 7).

Generally, the bank participated in three kinds of firms: (1) companies in the financial sector that were complementary to its own activities. Such firms were the Bank of Macedonia and Thrace, the insurance company "Insurance ETEBA", the FrancoGreek Bank of International Trade and Navigation, and the EΔEX—a firm for international portfolio investments. (2) Firms included in the development mandate of the bank such as the EΛEBME—a firm with the aim of carrying out big development projects in the chemicals and metal sector—the exporting firm HEDCO, and the MEBIOP SA. (3) Companies in distress ("*provlimatikes*") to help them restructure (ETEBA Annual Report 1975: 7; 1979: 9; 1984: 8–11).

Despite the adverse conditions in the real economy, the bank did not abandon its developmental role. In this context, ETEBA emphasized the importance, not only of the financial viability of the projects it financed but also of their economic rate of return concerning the development of the Greek economy. As a result, from 1974 onward, it began evaluating these projects in terms of their contribution to certain indicators, such as technological improvements, additional exports, import substitution, creation of new jobs, development of provincial industry, and impact on agricultural incomes (ETEBA Annual Report 1974: 8). In addition, the bank conducted several case development studies such as: (1) The possibility of establishing a petrochemical industry in Greece. (2) The study of the development of tourism in the Mediterranean countries. (3) The consequences of Greece's accession to the EEC (in collaboration with ETBA and the Foundation for Economic and Industrial Research, IOBE). (4) The possibility of exports to the Middle East and for Greece to become the commercial link between Europe and that part of the world. (5) A study for the exploitation of quartz mineral deposits in Northern Greece and the production of petroleum coke. (6) A case study for the introduction of leasing and the establishment of mutual funds related to real estate in the Greek market (Amoivaia Ktimatika Meridia). (7) Studies on the use of lignite as a substitute for oil and the recycling of by-products from the aluminum and tire industries. In addition, ETEBA took the initiative to support companies in distress (*"provlimatikes"*) by approving loans for the modernization of their capital equipment and by rescheduling outstanding debts of companies that were deemed financially viable. In addition, the bank proposed measures such as the conversion of part of the outstanding loans into equity participation and the provision of new loans subject to organizational restructuring of the borrowers (ETEBA Annual Report 1978: 7; 1979: 10; 1980: 15; 1981: 5; 1983: 9; 1984: 7).

During this period, the Bank expanded its sources of funding by adding the German Kreditanstalt für Wiederaufbau and the US Bank of Exports-Imports to its lenders. It also added the Greek Postal Savings Bank to its domestic lenders. ETEBA also issued its first bond to the public in 1976, which became an important source of financing for the bank's activities in the following years (ETEBA Annual Report 1976: 8–9) However, in 1985 the foreign shareholders withdrew from the bank's capital (Vousvounis 2010: 47).

During this period, ETEBA's profits from its portfolio management began to play an increasing role in maintaining its profitability as opposed to profits from its long-term loans. It is not surprising, then, that in 1978 the bank complained about the policy of offering below-market rates on long-term loans that could not keep pace with the increased cost of borrowed funds. It was felt that government subsidies on interest rates were not sufficient to alleviate the problem, which was exacerbated by depressed economic activity (ETEBA Annual Report 1978: 6, 15). Hence, as early as 1979, in the relevant Annual Report the bank advocated a more liberalized financial system in view of the accession of the country as a full member of the EEC. The bank's demands echoed the international discussion on the financial repression model and its effects on the viability of the financial system and the efficiency of investments. On the same basis, and because of the depressed activity in the industry, the bank sought to expand its lending to a wider range of activities such as shipping, trade, and construction (ETEBA Annual Report 1979: 4).

In this second period of its existence which coincides with the stagnation of the Greek economy, ETEBA sought for a balance between the traditional development bank model and the new one that seemed to emerge in the context of a more liberalized financial regime. The bank carried out its role in the context of the rationing transaction by allocating funds in accordance with government priorities but at the same time developed its managerial and bargaining transactions. In a sense, ETEBA did not lose its conduct with the capital market either as a borrower or as an investor without disregarding its contribution to economic development. Hence, the indicators it developed to evaluate the contribution of different projects in economic growth were a manifestation of its rationing function in serving the public purpose. They were also important in affecting the habits of thought in the business community since they prioritized specific aspects of entrepreneurship that were associated with technological change, contribution to regional development, and the social impact of business activity. In addition, the bank had an early understanding of how the definition of "reasonableness" was changing as the financial regime was about to change and voiced its concern about the evolution of its profitability.

9.2.3 The Transformation into a Merchant Bank 1987–2001

The financial system in Greece entered a period of liberalization after 1987 with the publication of the relevant resolutions of the Bank of Greece that referred to: (1) the liberalization of interest rates for loans offered to industry to finance the acquisition of fixed assets, (2) the ability of development banks to determine freely the interest rate and the terms under which they would issue their bonds. Although banks were still facing some restrictions on the kinds of loans they were able to provide and this was not consistent with a full liberalization of interest rates, the above resolutions signaled a new era which would be reflected in the changing nature of ETEBA during the last 13 years of its life (ETEBA Annual Report 1987: 5).

In this new environment, ETEBA sought to accomplish its new role in the context of an internationally integrated financial system with falling barriers to capital flows between countries and market-determined interest rates. Hence, in 1989 the bank announced its intention to transform itself from a traditional development bank into an investment bank. In this context, its operations would include activities such as underwriting new stock and bond issues on the stock exchange, advising on mergers, acquisitions, and international corporate cooperation, advising institutional investors on portfolio management, creating special mutual funds, and establishing venture capital. During this period, ETEBA played a leading role as an advisor on equity issues and as an underwriter (Vousvounis 2010: 198–199; ETEBA Annual Report 1989: 6–7). On the same basis, the bank gradually reduced the proportion of long-term loans in favor of equity participation in the companies it financed. It is noteworthy that long-term loans accounted for only 47% of total approvals in 1990, compared with about 90%–95% in the previous period. On the other hand, equity participation increased from a low of 5–10% to a substantial 53% of total approvals (ETEBA Annual Report 1990: 10). Hence, the bank changed the form in which it provided long-term finance to firms.

An even more important development was the ability of the bank to offer short-term loans starting in 1991. Short-term loans were provided to finance working capital instead of investment in capital equipment. Perhaps this was the key feature that changed the whole character of the bank, moving it away from the traditional DFC model. This was reflected in the evolution of ETEBA's lending activity, where approvals for long-term loans declined sharply, reaching 37% of total loans in 1992, compared with 65% in 1991. On the other hand, short-term loans reached a high level of 63% as opposed to 35% of total loans in 1991. Overdraft facilities increased only within one year from 1.6 billion Drs (4.7 million euros) in December 1991 to 6.2 billion Drs (18.2 million euros) in December 1992 in current prices (ETEBA Annual Report 1992: 15–16). In this context, the bank reconsidered its policy concerning equity participation in enterprises. The earlier concern with maintaining the viability of "*provlimatikes*" was now abandoned. ETEBA liquidated shares of companies when there was an opportunity to make a profit from this operation, and did not participate in any company that was not listed on the stock exchange after 1992 (Fig. 9.3) (ETEBA Annual Report 1993: 24–25). This was a prudent financial decision, not only because it enhanced the credibility of its portfolio, but also because it allowed the bank to easily assess the value of a company according to the price fluctuations of its shares on the stock exchange.

As far as ETEBA was a private development bank, it had an interest in its profitability along with its social role concerning the financing of industrial investment. The bank maintained positive and rising profits on average during the entire period of its operation as is apparent in Fig. 9.4. Return on assets rose on average from 1% in 1964–1974 to 2% in 1975–1986 and 3% in 1987–2001. Similarly, return on equity increased on average from 6% in 1964–1974 to 13% in 1975–1986 and to 18% in 1987–2001. However, its average cost of debt, measured as the ratio of financial expenses to total debt, rose steadily from 5% in 1965–1974 to 10% in 1975–1986 and 15% in 1987–2001. Furthermore, ETEBA's loss ratio, measured as provisions for losses over total earning assets, rose on

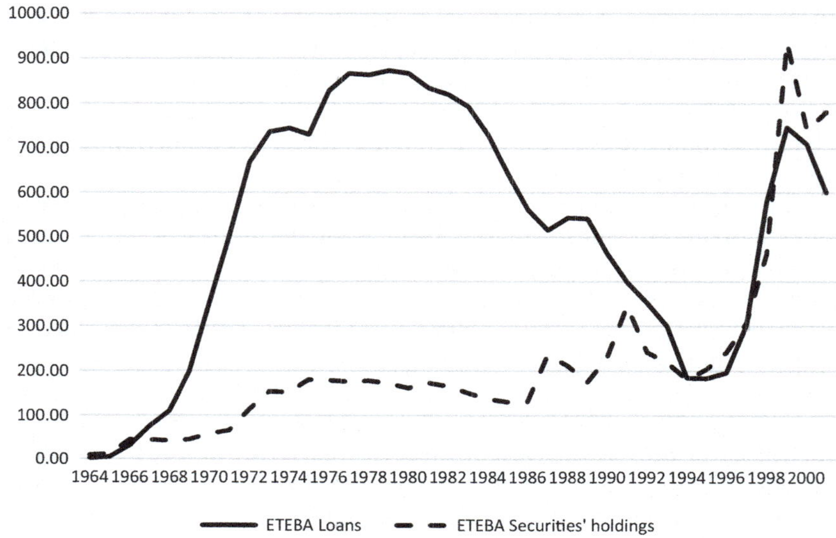

Fig. 9.3 ETEBA, loans, and securities' holdings, million Euros, constant 2015 prices, 1964–2001. Loans are classified as long and medium-term loans (1964–1991), loans (1992–1993), and claims against customers (1994–2001). Securities holdings include financial investments in shares, bonds, treasury bonds, and mutual funds. Source: ETEBA Annual Reports, various years, and author's elaboration

average from 3% in 1964–1974 to 7% in both periods 1975–1986 and 1987–2001 (Loizos 2012: 236–245).

However, the bank could not play its social role in the first place without the help of the state. Since, in the new financial environment interest rates were liberalized and since the state stopped subsidizing bank bonds and even taxed them after 1991, the bank could no longer uphold its long-term financing. It is worth noticing that ETEBA tried to maintain a balance between domestic borrowing and foreign borrowing, mainly from the European Investment Bank. It also sought to be self-financed by the regular floating of its own bonds. However, these sources of finance became extremely difficult to maintain after 1993 because of the competition from government bonds and Treasury Bills that remained untaxed. Hence, ETEBA limited its long-term loans only to those that were directly financed by the European Investment Bank. The result was a very low

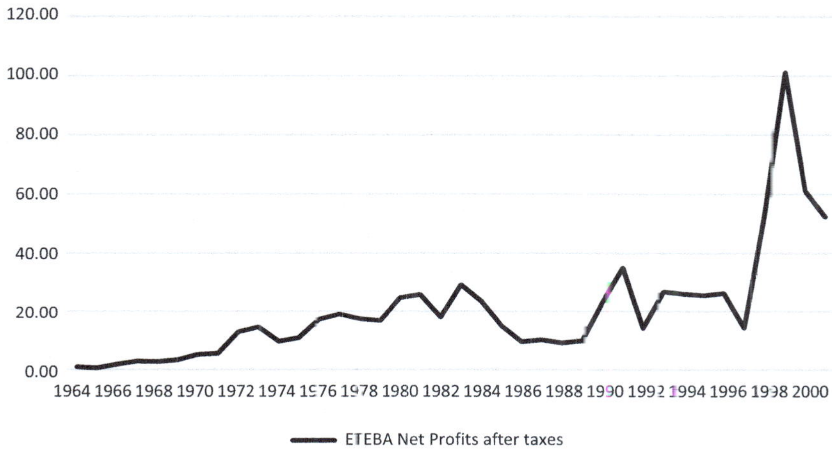

Fig. 9.4 ETEBA net profits after taxes, million Euros, constant 2015 prices, 1964–2001. Source: ETEBA Annual Reports, various years, and author's elaboration, reproduced with permission from Loizos (2017)

proportion of long-term loans relative to the total—about 18%—compared to 82% of short-term ones (ETEBA Annual Report 1993: 7–9, 18, 33).

In January 1994, ETEBA submitted a study on its future prospects to the National Bank of Greece. The proposal was that ETEBA should become a universal bank with activities complementary to those of the National Bank (Vousvounis 2010: 192–193). The transformation of ETEBA into a bank with both commercial and special investment activities was further facilitated by the 554/3/1995 Resolution of the Committee for Monetary and Credit Issues of the Bank of Greece that allowed ETEBA to (1) accept all kinds of deposits, (2) offer credit for working capital to all kinds of enterprises, (3) raise capital from the interbank market. This resolution allowed the bank to reduce its dependence on bond financing which had become quite expensive and increase its liabilities in the form of deposits (ETEBA Annual Report 1994: 3, 24).

Concerning the activities of the bank, the new era was characterized by an increasing involvement in consulting, mergers/acquisitions, and portfolio management. In this context, two major highlights were its investment banking activity in countries of Southeastern Europe and its participation in the privatization program for Public Enterprises and Organizations (DEKO). The bank expanded its operation in countries such as Bulgaria, Romania, Cyprus, Egypt, Albania, and Yugoslavia. In Bulgaria and Romania, it established two investment companies the ETEBA Bulgaria AD and the ETEBA Romania SA respectively. Concerning its consulting activities to the Greek government, it participated as an underwriter in the share issue of OTE, EYDAP, DEH, ΕΥΑΘ, ΟΠΑΠ, etc. In addition, it established two offshore venture capital companies the ETEBA Greek Fund and ETEBA Balkan Fund later renamed as NBG Greek Fund and NBG Balkan Fund. The bank offered its consulting services in project financing concerning the major projects of the Greek government such as the new Airport, the Rio-Antirio bridge, the Ymitos Avenue, etc. It also became an investment advisor to pension funds such as ΤΕΑΔΥ and ΤΑΑΣ (ETEBA Annual Report 1995: 14–15; 1997: 12–13, 20; 1998: 20–21; 1999: 19, 25–27, 33, 35).

The general characteristic of the last period of ETEBA's history was the change of the bank's focus from loan financing to various investment banking activities, including the active management of its portfolio during the stock market boom in 1999. The cost paid for the bank's reorientation was the reduction of its net profits before tax (in current prices) by 26% in 2000 and 3% in 2001 with respect to the previous year (ETEBA Annual Report 2000: 32; 2001: 32). ETEBA's high exposure to the stock market, which was reflected in its income from both dividends and capital gains/ losses on trading securities, made its financial performance dependent on the negative evolution of the stock market index during the last two years of the bank's operation, in 2000 and 2001. ETEBA was finally taken over by the National Bank of Greece at the end of 2002, following a decision announced in June of that year (Vousvounis 2010: 217; Hellenic Republic, Official Gazette 2002: 3).

However, a simple inspection of Figs. 9.3 and 9.4 above shows that ETEBA was successful in changing its business model and adapting to the changing financial regime. Its last period of operation is a testament to the dynamic character of development banks as a combination of all three categories of transactions identified by Commons with the ability to shift between them in different financial environments. In Veblenian terms, ETEBA contributed to changing habits of thought in Greek financial markets through its extensive investment banking activity which was just a follow-up of its institutional development activity in the previous years that included technical and managerial support of the Greek industry.

More so, it was successful in changing its own habits of thought and practices by moving from the traditional development banking model to the investment banking model in a liberalized financial environment. It was not an abandonment of the developmental public purpose but its realization in different conditions that demanded more market-friendly approaches to development finance. Irrespective of how significant was the share of ETEBA in Greek economic and institutional development it was certainly a model that showcased the dynamic character and adaptability of development banking.

9.3 The Investment Bank (TE)

9.3.1 The Period of High Expectations: 1963–1975

The Investment Bank (TE) was established in December 1962 with the Commercial Bank of Greece and the Ionian and Popular Bank of Greece as its main shareholders but its actual operation commenced in April 1963. However, during the period under examination, a host of other institutions also participated in the capital of the Bank. These included the Bank of America and Barclays Bank International Ltd. Minor shareholdings with participation ranging from 1.57% to 0.07% were possessed by the Commercial Bank of the Near East Ltd., Banque Nationale de Paris, Algemene Bank Nederland N.V., Banca Nazionale del Lavoro, Dresdner Bank AG, Société Générale pour Favoriser le Développement du Commerce et de l'Industrie en France SA, G. & C. Kreglinger SA, Banque de l'Union Européenne, Samuel Montagu & Co Ltd, the "Phoenix" Greek General Insurance Co SA, the "Ionian" Insurance Co SA, and General Insurance of Greece Co Ltd (TE 1975: 6; n.d.: 9; TE Annual Report 1963).

The purpose of the establishment of the bank was to provide long-term loans to firms engaged in industry, tourism, and shipping and to support these enterprises in managerial and technical aspects. In addition, the possibility of joint ventures between Greek and foreign firms was also considered in the mandate of the institution. The bank provided loans both for the modernization and expansion of existing enterprises and for the establishment of new enterprises of particular importance for the development of the Greek economy. The main form of financing was the provision of long-term loans. However, in addition to them, short-term loans to meet specific working capital needs could accompany long-term development loans. In some cases, as an alternative form of financing, the bank participated in the equity of the companies financed. Furthermore, it engaged in activities that would promote capital market development such as the promotion and underwriting of new issues of shares and bonds for both public and private firms (TE 1975: 8–12; n.d.: 11).

The main sources of financing for the first period of TE's operation were, in addition to its own capital, funds provided by the Commercial Bank of Greece, the Ionian and Popular Bank of Greece, and the Bank of Greece. However, the Bank was considering the possibility of issuing a domestic debenture loan of the order of 100 million Drs. as early as 1968 to diversify its sources of funds. It was finally issued in July 1969 as a ten-year debenture loan. It was considered by the TE both as an additional form of financing and as an activity that would help the development of the capital market (TE Annual Report 1969: 15). In addition, the TE received three loans from foreign sources. The first two were loans of 5 million Dollars each, granted in 1968 and 1971 respectively by the foreign institutions that participated in the capital of the Bank, namely the Bank of America, the Commercial Bank of the Near East Ltd., Banque Nationale de Paris, Algemene Bank Nederland N.V., Banca Nazionale del Lavoro, Dresdner Bank AG, Société Générale SA, Banque de l'Union Européenne, and Banque de Bruxelles. The third loan, also of 5 million Dollars was provided to the bank in 1971 by the National Bank of North America (TE 1975: 16). However, the downside of the above foreign borrowing was that it exposed the bank to exchange rate fluctuations after 1971.

On the other hand, the management of TE, as early as 1963, expressed in the relevant Annual Report its reservations about the efficiency of the prevailing financial structure of the economy and the dominance of the Monetary Committee with its restrictions on the operation of banks in general and investment banks in particular. The bank disagreed with "economic planning in the financing field of the economy" and believed that the reasons for the restrictive monetary policy that prevailed in the 1950s were no longer valid and hence, quantitative and qualitative credit controls hindered rather than helped the economic development of the country. In addition, such policies suppressed the profitability prospects of banking institutions and their ability to use their funds more efficiently (TE Annual Report 1963: 14). These observations reflected the continued interest of the bank in policies that would revitalize the capital market to form an environment conducive to operations such as equity participation in funded enterprises and the issuing of shares and bonds by both firms and the bank itself. The poor performance of the capital market in Greece was attributed by TE (TE Annual Report 1967: 39) to the small size of the productive units, the inadequacy of the corporate law, the absence of effective tax incentives, and the lack of available institutional means to attract savings to productive investments. In this context the bank offered its recommendations to the government to facilitate foreign purchases of securities in the Greek capital market and to adopt the appropriate legislative measures for the operation of financial corporations (for example unit trusts) (TE Annual Report 1964: 15). Besides, an important initiative of the bank concerning the institutional development of the Greek financial system was the establishment on April 2, 1972, of the first Mutual Fund Management Company in Greece, named Hellenic Mutual Fund Management Company. This was done in cooperation with Barclays Bank International and Merrill Lynch and should be credited to TE as an important institutional step in the development of the financial system. The idea was to increase the number and range of listings on the Athens Stock Exchange by investing a portion of the Fund's portfolio in unlisted shares, which the mutual fund would then list on the Stock Exchange. The second aim of the establishment of the Fund was to attract savings from small investors throughout the country (TE 1975: 34; TE Annual Report 1972: 31). Another innovation attributed to TE was the opening of a special office for dealings in unquoted shares in 1973. The goal was to create a parallel market that would serve as a clearinghouse for those holding such shares (TE Annual Report 1973: 11). Finally in 1974 TE entered the equity underwriting business by underwriting the first public share issue of Radio-Athinai SA in association with the Hellenic Mutual Fund Management Company (TE Annual Report 1974: 13).

The bank's lending activity grew steadily during this first period of operation, as shown in Fig. 9.5. Sectors that received financing included the engineering industry, electrical appliances, construction materials, automobile components, paper and printing products, fertilizers, pharmaceuticals, plastics and canning, cotton textiles and silk industries, tobacco industries, and oil. Furthermore, sectors such as shipping and tourism—especially hotel enterprises—were also offered loans. The bank preferred to provide loans of small and medium size to minimize the related risks of repayment and default by the borrowers. In addition, it followed some stringent criteria for selecting prospective clients such as the ability of the borrower to service the loan, the ability and experience of management, and the financial and technical planning of the project. Regarding the

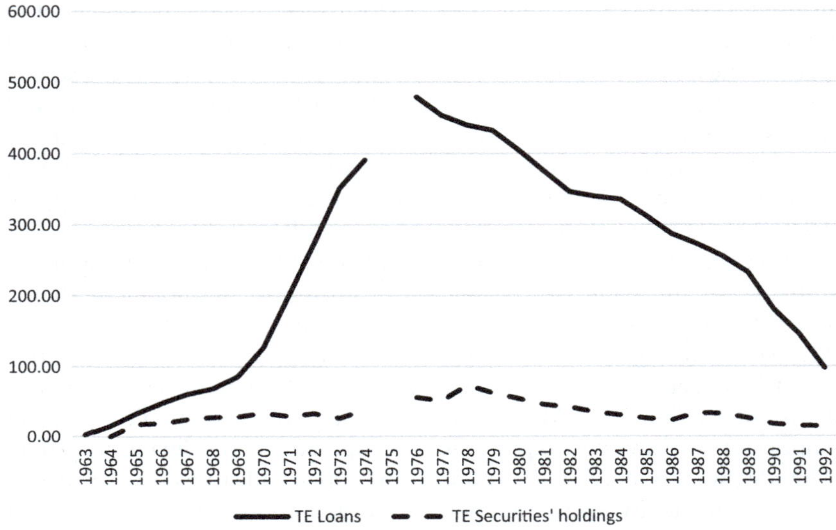

Fig. 9.5 TE loans and securities' holdings, million Euros, constant 2015 prices, 1963–1992. Loans are classified as long and medium-term loans. Securities holdings include financial investments in shares, bonds, treasury bonds, and mutual funds. Source: TE Annual Reports, various years, and author's elaboration

economic return of the proposed projects, an additional criterion was their contribution to the Greek economy in terms of increased employment and exports. An additional requirement that the Bank imposed on its clients for a project to be financed was that the borrower's financial participation in the project should be at least 30% of the total cost. In addition, loans were secured by appropriate real estate collateral or third-party guarantees. Hence, the bank did not suffer losses from defaulting borrowers during this period as reported in the Follow-up Report of 1975. In short, TE granted 659 loans during the period 1963–1975 amounting to 4350 million Drs. (12.8 million Euros). Of this amount, 691 million Drs (2 million Euros) were repaid while 678 million Drs (1.9 million Euros) were not yet drawn and 2,981 million Drs (8.7 million Euros) were outstanding by mid-1975 (TE 1975: 5, 21–22). Loans offered increased by 482.89 % during the first two years of operation and by 541.73% between 1965 and 1970. The corresponding figure for the period 1970–1973 was 183.36%.

In addition to extending long-term loans, the bank participated in the equity capital of various industries as an alternative form of financing. Its portfolio, by the end of 1974, included firms such as Eleusis Shipyards SA, Greek Industry for Sacks & Plastic Products Ltd, Hellenic General Enterprises Co SA, Phosphoric Fertilizers Industry Ltd, and others. Besides, in 1974, the bank sponsored a joint venture with Del Monte Corporation and the International Finance Corporation (IFC) to establish a canned food industry in Greece called Hellenic Food Industries SA. This was the first successful activity of the bank in the field of international joint ventures in an attempt to attract foreign investment capital to Greece. In addition, it participated in a joint venture with Crown Paints (Hellas) SA, a subsidiary of Reed International Ltd to build a paint factory in Greece (TE 1975: 11–12). Its holdings of shares and bonds rose until 1978 when they reached the level of 73.93 million euros in constant 2015 prices (Fig. 9.5).

The first period of operation of TE demonstrated its willingness to take initiatives in favor of institutional development and modernization of the Greek economy and the capital market. The establishment of the first mutual fund in Greece with international cooperation contributed to financial development and affected habits of thought concerning savings outlets, especially among small savers and investors. The same is true concerning the clearinghouse for unlisted shares which should have an impact on how market participants thought about the risks of unlisted firms. Furthermore, the bank, being a private institution as was also the case with ETEBA, experienced quite early the contradiction between socioeconomic and financial efficiency when it criticized the Monetary Committee and its restrictive practices. It was a contradiction between different meanings of "reasonableness" and "reasonable pricing" that would better serve the public purpose of the era. Of course, TE as a private bank emphasized its profitability. However, it did so in conjunction with its interest in the development of the capital market and its international cooperation. TE contributed to the rationing function of the prevailing financial regime by highlighting both the managerial and bargaining aspects of its operation seeking a balance between its developmental role and its financial viability.

9.3.2 *Crisis and Reorganization: 1976–1985*

The second period of the operation of TE was marked by the two oil shocks of the 1970s which had a negative impact on the Greek economy by increasing the proportion of enterprises in distress during the 1980s.

Notably, loan repayments in arrears concerning industrial loans as a percentage of total repayments in arrears amounted to 36.7% in 1976, 38.3% in 1977, and 51.8% in 1978 (TE Annual Report 1978: 25) thus, showing a persistence increase. This rate dropped from 47.8% to 38.6% between 1979 and 1981 (TE Annual Report 1981: 17) but remained substantial. Total loan repayments in arrears increased subsequently until the mid-1980s indicating the enduring problem of financial viability that the borrowers of the bank faced (TE Annual Reports 1982: 20; 1983: 18; 1984: 18; 1985: 20). In general, the financing activity of TE was adversely affected by the conditions of stagflation in the economy which particularly affected major companies that were associated with the bank such as the Eleusis Shipyards and AGET Herakles (TE Annual Report 1986: 14). Furthermore, the bank pointed out in the late 1970s the distorted development of Greek industry during the previous years in terms of its low rate of return and high entrepreneurial risk compared to other economic activities such as real estate, construction, and import trade. According to the bank, these shortcomings, together with increased international competition and the depressed expectations of Greek entrepreneurs, called for a reorganization of industrial policy. Otherwise, the effects would be negative both for the Greek economy and the bank's clients on the one hand and for the bank's performance on the other (TE Annual Report 1978: 19–20). These developments led the bank to recognize in 1981 the significant decline in its business along with an increase in non-performing loans that affected negatively the quality of its portfolio. In these conditions, the bank regarded its transformation into a merchant bank or Banque d' Affaires (TE Annual Report 1981: 9–11) as necessary to overcome the double problem of unprofitable long-term financing and the increased cost of borrowed funds.

Regarding the financial cost of TE's operations, the bank noted a decline in its profit margin from 2.65% in 1979 to 2.01% in 1980 (TE Annual Report 1979: 8). The problem was attributed by the bank to the existing financial system of quantitative and qualitative credit controls, together with the policy of administratively set interest rates. In this respect, the difficulty of drawing funds on the domestic market at reasonable rates was considered crucial for the financial viability of TE. On the other hand, the bank managed to obtain two loans from the European Investment Bank in October 1981 and April 1982 amounting to 620 million Drs. (1.8 million Euros) each. Its borrowing from the European Investment Bank continued during this period with additional loans in

1983 and 1984. In addition, in an attempt to diversify its domestic sources of funding, in 1981 the bank issued its own bonds (500 million Drs or 1.47 million euros) while obtaining a long-term loan from the Postal Savings Bank (TE Annual Report 1980: 8; 1981: 11; 1982: 7; 1983: 5).

Despite the relative stagnation of its lending activities, TE took initiatives in other banking activities of particular institutional importance for financial development. Hence, in 1979, the bank organized the first syndicated loan in Drs. at the amount of 700 million Drs. (2 million Euros) offered to Halkis Cement company (TE Annual Report 1979: 9). Two further loans of this kind were provided to Aspropyrgos Refineries and Achaia Paper Company in 1982. Furthermore, the bank, in association with US Leasing International, Barclays Bank, and Banque Nationale de Paris promoted the establishment a leasing company to meet the demand for capital equipment through this new form of financing (TE Annual Report 1979: 9). As early as 1980 the bank engaged in merchant banking operations such as brokerage in the domestic interbank market (TE Annual Report 1980: 9), while in 1981 it considered the possibility of expanding its activities to include medium-term financing of exports through factoring, mergers, and acquisitions, and consulting services to firms and public organizations (TE Annual Report 1981: 11). In general, the bank entered a reorganization phase during the 1980s concerning both the type of its activities and its internal structure such as the modernization of its management and the recruitment of specialized personnel. It also sought to differentiate its revenue and funding sources by introducing innovative merchant banking products and attracting low-interest deposits to improve profit margins (TE Annual Report 1985: 6–7).

The second period of the operation of TE was characterized by its attempt to survive in the crisis years of the Greek economy during the late 1970s and early 1980s. The conditions of reasonable pricing had now changed as the bank was burdened by rising non-performing loans in an environment of stagflation and faced administratively set interest rates. These developments affected the bank's ability to allocate funds effectively in the context of a rationing transaction within the financial repression/regulation regime. Nevertheless, TE sustained its institutional development function with its initiatives in organizing syndicated loans, promoting leasing solutions, and engaging in merchant banking activities. All these would prove useful in familiarizing the business community with financial instruments that would flourish in the forthcoming financial liberalization regime.

9.3.3 *The Merchant Banking Transformation That Never Realized: 1986–1992*

In the early years of this period, TE was still struggling with the problems that had accumulated during the crisis years. The assets side of its balance sheet suffered from the remaining non-performing loans from the previous period, while its income statements, even at current prices, showed losses rather than profits for most of the period 1986–1992 (Fig. 9.6). On average, the bank faced a falling return on assets from 1% in 1963–1974 to 0% in 1976–1986 and to −3% in the last period of operation 1987–1992. Its return on equity also followed on average a decreasing trend from 6% in 1963–1974 to 0% in 1976–1986 while it became deeply negative and equal to −47% in 1987–1992 with average net profits −5.06 million euros in constant 2015 prices during this last period. The bank's average cost of debt followed a rising trend on average with values of 4% in 1963–1974, 12% in 1976–1986, and 28% in 1987–1992. Moreover, the loss ratio which takes into account the provisions for losses rose from 1% in 1963–1974 to remain constant at 7% on average in 1976–1986 and 1987–1992 (Loizos 2012: 237–245).

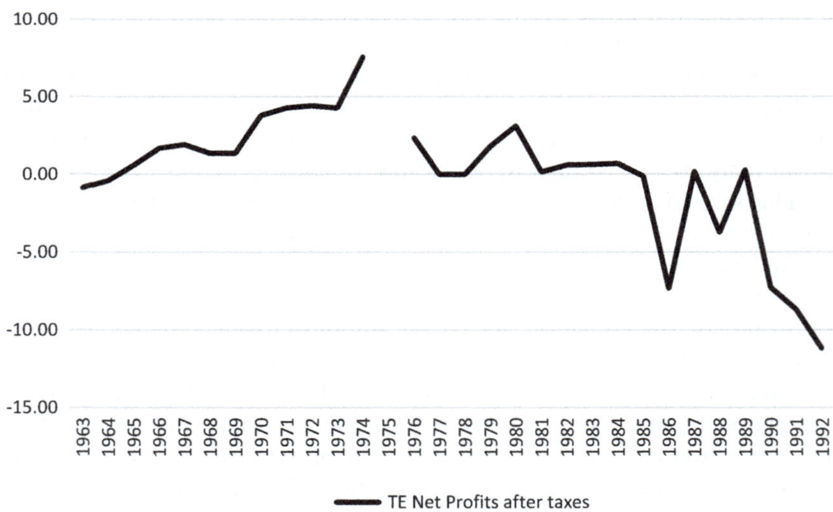

Fig. 9.6 TE net profits after taxes, million Euros, constant 2015 prices, 1963–1992. Source: TE Annual Reports, various years, and author's elaboration

The bank attributed these results to two main reasons: (1) the administratively low interest rate on loans that could not be rescheduled upward in accordance with the decisions of the Bank of Greece, and (2) the suspension of interest payments due of loans that became unprofitable during the crisis in the real economy. These loans were made during the period 1970–1980 and represented 11.9% of the total outstanding loans in 1986 (TE Annual Report 1986: 13–14). However, it is interesting to see how the percentage of these non-interest-bearing loans with respect to total outstanding loans evolved during the following years. According to the relevant Annual Reports of the Bank, this percentage reached the level of 15.5% in 1987 and increased further to 18.2% in 1989, 33.6% in 1990, and 36.1 % in 1991 but decreased to the level of 28.4% in 1992 (TE Annual Report 1987: 8; 1989: 8; 1990: 8; 1991: 1_; 1992: 7). Another reason was the forced securitization of outstanding non-performing loans through the acquisition by the bank of shares of the borrowed enterprises in lieu of the loan capital due. This was the case with distressed companies such as AGET Herakles SA, Kavala Plastics SA, Pournaras SA, and others which had the unfavorable effect of burdening the bank with assets having diminishing returns. Finally, the bank's low-yield participation in companies within the Emporiki Bank Group and the loans offered to Emporiki Bank's clients also hurt its profitability (TE Annual Report 1986: 14; 1987: 11; 1991: 12).

On the other hand, TE's bonds offered to the public represented 49.2% of total long-term borrowed funds in 1986 but increased to 55.1% in 1987 and followed a rising trend until 1989 (TE Annual Report 1987: 13; 1988: 35; 1989: 33). However, the change in the financial regime toward its liberalization during the late 1980s created new problems for TE, this time affecting its liabilities. The policy of long-term financing of development banks through the issuance of their own bonds was supported by the state through the subsidization of these bond issues. Starting in 1988, this subsidy was reduced from 4.5% to 3.25%, with the prospect of its complete elimination in the future (TE Annual Report 1988: 11). The bank underscored the dangers of this development by describing the disharmony between the government's attempt to fully liberalize the financial system and the preservation of the old status quo for development banks, which made them less competitive than their commercial counterparts. Commercial banks faced a lower cost of funds and a greater variety of opportunities to invest them while development banks were still constrained by low-return long-term loans and were dependent on the government for their sources of funds through the subsidization of their bonds. As far as TE was concerned, it seemed that by 1992 it had never been able to overcome the problem of the rising cost of its funds, as the bond subsidy diminished and the old low-interest loans from commercial banks and the European Investment Bank were reduced.

Despite these problems, the bank never abandoned the attempt to modernize and expand its operation to more profitable activities to the degree that this was permitted by the existing framework for development banks. It continued its fee-income activity as a manager in the field of syndicated loans concerning the financing of enterprises such as Athinaiki Brewery, EBO SA, and others. It also participated as an advisor and/or underwriter in the share issues of Petzetakis SA, Alouminion Attikis SA, Geniki Commercial and Industry SA, Rokas SA, BIOSOL SA, Radio-Athinai SA, 3Epsilon, Medical Center of Athens and others on the Athens Stock Exchange. It offered its services as an advisor for the issuance of Greek government bonds or their syndicated offering. Economic consultant services were offered also for important developmental public works such as the Rio-Antiorio bridge, and the Acheloos project (in association with Morgan Grenfell & Co Ltd). It also participated in the mergers/acquisitions of Delta SA, Chipita International SA, Biolex SA, Petzetakis SA, Keranis SA, and Bianca SA (TE Annual Report 1986: 19; 1987: 11, 15; 1988: 14; 1990: 13). However, all this activity came to an end in 1992 when the bank admitted that its operation in investment banking was anemic. Eventually, the accumulated losses of the bank during the 1990s resulted in the decision to stop its operation and to be absorbed by the Commercial Bank of Greece in 1992 (Eichengreen and Gibson 2001: 552; Xanthakis 1995: 195).

The last period of TE operation highlights a significant issue that characterized development banking in Greece and has to do with the role of government policy in the survival of these banks. As explained in Chap. 8, the government has pursued a top-down policy of financial liberalization that has put development banks at a competitive disadvantage. This was the outcome of a rationing transaction that changed the distribution of power and resources among market participants, redefined the meaning of "reasonable" pricing from above, and disregarded the possible role that development banks were able to play in the new financial regime. The new policy consensus did not recognize either the role in institutional development, changing habits of thought, and practices that development banks had played in the previous period or their attempt to adapt to the new conditions. The institutional-political risk that all development banks faced with the change in the financial regime is more evident in the case of TE and it was reflected in its depressed profitability over the years. This institutional-political risk also demonstrates the critical bond between development banks and the prevailing financial regime which is however mediated by a supportive or non-supportive government policy. The example of TE clearly shows that the Greek governments of that period did not maintain a long-term perspective of institutional policy design nor did they understand the dynamic nature and adaptability of development banks as a combination of managerial, bargaining, and rationing transactions in the service of the public purpose for economic and institutional sustainable development.

9.4 The Hellenic Industrial Development Bank (ETBA)

9.4.1 *The High Growth Period: 1964–1975*

The Hellenic Industrial Development Bank (ETBA) was established on September 16, 1964, by L.D. 4366, through the merger of three institutions: the Economic Development Financing Organization (OXOA), the Industrial Development Corporation (OBA), and the Tourist Credit Organization. Until 1973, ETBA was a Public Enterprise. However, by L.D. 1369 of 1973, the bank was transformed into a joint-stock company with only one shareholder, the Greek government. The Acts of 1964 and 1973 described the purpose of the establishment of ETBA, which was to promote large and medium-sized industries, mining, metallurgy, shipping, and tourism by providing loan and equity financing. To achieve its developmental objective, ETBA was expected to provide technical and financial assistance to existing enterprises, modernize their operations, and encourage the inflow of foreign capital. Finally, it had an institutional mission to fulfill by contributing to the development of the capital market. However, the legal framework of the bank's operation also indicated that, although the bank would operate as a private enterprise, its financing activity would take place within the framework defined by the development program of the government (ETBA Annual Report 1967: 7–8; 1972: 3). In this context, the Annual Report of 1975 stated that ETBA should undertake activities that, although unprofitable from a financial point of view, were, nevertheless, essential for the development of the country (ETBA Annual Report 1975: 13). The above shows how closely ETBA was tied to the Greek state, a fact that resulted, on the one hand, in a much larger scale of operations than the other two development banks and on the other hand, its much greater dependence on the decisions and the policy of the government.

ETBA assumed, from the beginning of its operation, a leading role in the long-term financing of both private and public enterprises. As the Annual Report of 1967 indicates, the bank handled 42% of total long-term financing in the Greek economy in manufacturing and mining and about 40% of total financing of enterprises operating in tourism (ETBA Annual Report 1967: 12). Furthermore, starting in 1968, ETBA offered preferential interest rates to export industries given the opportunities arising from the proximity of the country to the Middle East and Africa. On the other hand, it maintained a particular concern for the decentralization of industry by increasing the approval of loans to provincial firms. Such loans increased by 360% between 1966 and 1968 (ETBA Annual Report 1968: 3–4). It is characteristic that in 1972, loans provided to the greater Athens area were 32.7% of total loans offered, while the relevant proportion for the Macedonia and Thrace districts was 42.7% (ETBA Annual Report 1972: 18). It also approved loans for shipbuilding which increased from 80 million Drs (0.23 million Euros) in 1966 to 2,137 million Drs. (6.3 million Euros) in 1969 (ETBA Annual Report 1969: 10).

On the other hand, its activity in equity investments in industrial enterprises was also substantial as it accounted for 1/3 of the bank's total funds in 1967. Some of these enterprises were wholly-owned by the bank such as the Nitrogenous Fertilizers Industry SA, Metal Constructions of Greece SA, Hellenic Marble SA, and Hellenic Tanneries SA. In addition, ETBA participated in the equity capital of the Aluminium de Grèce SA, LYWANA Hellas SA, Gypsum-Hellas SA, Lavreotiki SA, ETANAL SA, Viohalco-Aluminium SA, Piraiki-Patraiki Cotton Mfg. Co. SA, Greek Exports SA, Hellenic Automobile Manufacturing Co SA, Steyr-Daimpler-Puch Hellas, and Greek Company of Industrial and Metallurgy Investments. In particular, the bank stated in its 1967 Annual Report that it intended to transfer ownership of its shares in these companies to the public in due course in order to contribute to the development of the capital market. Hence, for example, in 1972, ETBA sold its share participation in Lywana Hellas and Textile Mills "Ilios Ten Cate" SA (ETBA Annual Report 1967: 14–16; 1968: 7–9; 1970: 16; 1971: 12; 1972: 34–36)

The bank sought to promote foreign investments in Greece by opening an office in New York in 1963 and also an office in Cologne, Germany in 1967 and by publishing guides and pamphlets for investment legislation, taxation, and fiscal and other incentives for foreign investors (ETBA Annual Report 1967: 17–18). This policy bore fruit in 1968 with the agreement between ETBA and Kredittanstalt für Wiederaubau for a loan of 6,25 million dollars directed to shipbuilding (ETBA Annual Report 1968: 14). In addition, several contacts were made with German firms which were interested in investing in Greece in sectors such as chemicals, machinery, electrical appliances, rubber products and others (ETBA Annual Report 1970: 18; 1971: 14). Furthermore, four loans were obtained from the European Investment Bank in 1975 (ETBA Annual Report 1975: 19).

An important part of its operations was the derivation of techno-economic studies concerning surveys of certain industrial sectors or referring to general economic issues that were related to industrial policy. Such studies included: (1) feasibility studies for meat packing plants in Northern Greece, (2) a study for a new town gas plant in Athens-Piraeus, (3) studies for industrial complexes in Macedonia and Thrace for the exploitation of their forests, (4) study for the establishment of water desalination plants in the Greek islands, (5) the establishment of the General Company of Studies, Research, and Exploitation SA in order to prepare feasibility studies for the exploitation of the underground mineral wealth of the country. In the field of general economic surveys, the bank published in 1975 a study called "Anatomy of the Market Conditions of Greek Industry" that included a detailed survey of 110 industrial subsectors and the possibilities for their development (ETBA Annual Report 1968: 11–12; 1974: 15; 1975: 17).

A unique function of ETBA, which distinguished it from other development banks, was the Industrial Areas Program. The purpose of this plan was to select and acquire plots of land throughout the country and carry out the necessary infrastructure work to make them suitable for industrial estates. This program included areas in Thessaloniki, Volos, Patras, Herakion in Crete, Chania, Kavalas, and elsewhere (ETBA Annual Report 1967: 17; 1975: 21–22).

Another important initiative in the development of the capital market was the establishment by ETBA in 1972 of the Hellenic Investment Company SA, whose shares were listed on the Athens Stock Exchange the following year. The purpose of the new company was to facilitate the listing of shares of companies financed by ETBA. It also began to cooperate with foreign financial firms such as Bankers Trust Co N.Y. and Merrill Lynch, Pierce, Fenner, and Smith N.Y. In the same year, ETBA, together with other banks, underwrote two bond loans issued by Aluminium de Grèce (ETBA Annual Report 1972: 45; 1974: 14).

ETBA was a public institution and in this way, it was the primary instrument for the implementation of government's industrial and institutional development policy. Profit considerations were not a priority for ETBA and in this sense, it solved the contradiction between socioeconomic returns and financial returns in favor of the former. The public purpose, as this was defined by the government, fully characterized ETBA's lending activity and what it considered to be "reasonable" in terms of pricing and quantities allocation within the rationing function of the financial repression/regulation regime. The scale of its activity justified its close ties to the Greek government. This, in turn, seems to have enhanced its managerial transactions at the expense of its bargaining transactions as this was reflected in its loan activity and its financing by official funds. However, institutional development was also a priority for ETBA with an emphasis on the Industrial Areas Program, the techno-economic studies, and its initiatives for the development of the capital market. Therefore, although ETBA was a public enterprise until 1973 and under the complete control of the state thereafter, did not behave just as a cheap-lending vehicle. It had full knowledge of the importance of institutional development from below in the sense of spotting limiting factors that hindered industrial development through its techno-economic studies and providing solutions that would change conventional habits of thought and action. In this light only we can fully grasp the important institutional role of ETBA which supported its lending activity.

9.4.2 *The Years of Crisis: 1976–1986*

In the mid-1970s the bank expressed the need to reconsider its role in the Greek economy after its internal reorganization during the years that followed the fall of the dictatorship in 1974, and the pressure imposed on the economy by international events such as the recession of 1974–1975 and the prospective accession of Greece to the European Community. The bank described in detail the evolution of Greek industrialization during the 1960s and focused on three major shortcomings in this process: (1) the prevalence of small-scale industries that employed labor-intensive production methods which made them less competitive in the new international conditions. (2) The low degree of specialization and standardization of Greek industry which increased the cost of production. (3) The insufficient degree of vertical integration and the dependence of industrial units on imported semi-finished products and raw materials. The common cause of all these handicaps seemed to be the protective policy measures that directed the industry to inefficient and non-competitive production methods and put their export activity at risk in the new competitive international environment. In this context, the bank reconsidered its role in the Greek economy given that its imprudent lending policy during the dictatorship years had rendered it a promoter of the short-run political goals of the military regime rather than a developmental institution (ETBA Annual Report 1974: 11–12; 1975: 13–14; 1976: 13, 20).

The bank recognized that the sense of uncertainty among business owners was a key factor in holding back investment so it set as one of its primary goals to create favorable conditions for entrepreneurship by contributing to economic infrastructure works—the Industrial Areas Program included—and by providing technical assistance to firms. In these conditions, ETBA considered the role of development banks which are the banking institutions that specialize in long-term financing to be crucial. For each project considered, ETBA paid special attention to the criterion of competitiveness of the investment. Other criteria included the high ratio of value added, the utilization of domestic raw materials, the comparative advantage of the project, the degree of industrial decentralization and export orientation, the employment criterion, the prospective improvement of managerial skills, and the protection of the environment. In addition, the bank's evaluation process placed more emphasis on the importance of the proposed project for economic development than on the collateral provided by the company (ETBA Annual Report 1976: 29–31).

It is notable that ETBA accepted its responsibility for the delays observed concerning the development of the capital market. The bank was keen to undertake initiatives concerning the underwriting of securities issues of both newly established and incumbent firms that sought to improve their capital structure. ETBA had already underwritten the loan to Piraiki-Patraiki and placed several issues of bank bonds on the market. Furthermore, it would continue its activity of equity participation which could take three forms: (1) participation to improve the capital structure of borrowed firms, (2) equity participation in the context of debt restructuring of distressed companies, and (3) equity participation to support the Greek part of joint ventures with foreign firms. Moreover, a policy of recycling its equity portfolio through the capital market would revive the latter (ETBA Annual Report 1976: 32).

ETBA's main source of capital from its establishment in 1964 was the Central Bank. However, the bank acknowledged the need to gain more independence in terms of its financing sources and hence, sought to increase the proportion of its own bank bonds in its total funds. Moreover, ETBA emphasized the higher risks that it took compared to other development banks and therefore, it considered its preferential treatment, concerning the cost of its capital, as necessary (ETBA Annual Report 1976: 33). The funds acquired by the Bank of Greece as a proportion of total capital sources fell from 53% to 48.9% between 1976 and 1977 while the corresponding percentages for bank bonds were 6.9% and 12% respectively. Bank bonds continued to rise in subsequent years reaching the level of 14.31% in 1979 (ETBA Annual Report 1979: 42) and 17.9% in 1980 accompanied by a fall of Bank of Greece financing to 39.4% (ETBA Annual Report 1980: 45). The respective figures for 1982 were 32.2% for bond financing and 24.4% for Bank of Greece funds, while for 1984 bond financing rose to 48.1% and Bank of Greece funds fell to 9.9% (ETBA Annual Report 1982: 32; 1984: 21). On the other hand, foreign borrowing increased from 2.6% in 1975 to 16.4% in 1980 and 26.1% in 1984 including loans obtained from the European Investment Bank (ETBA Annual Report 1980: 45; 1984: 21). In addition, ETBA placed successfully its first bond issue on the Tokyo capital market in 1982 on favorable terms (ETBA Annual Report 1982: 6).

As shown in Fig. 9.7, in the context of the above developments, ETBA continued its long-term financing activity through loans or equity participation, in many cases in cooperation with foreign organizations. Examples of this activity were: (1) the industry of asbestos fibers in Kozani with MABE SA (financed through a bond-loan convertible into shares), (2) the industry of Ammonia Production with Greek Ammonia Industry SA, (3) Greek Electronics Industry SA with equity participation by ETBA (55%), (4) the Greek Arms Industry SA with equity participation 30% by ETBA and 70% by the Greek government, (5) the Hellenic Steel SA (participation of 14%), (6) the spinning mills Aegeon SA (12% participation), (7) Neorion-Shipyards Syros SA (both equity participation and loan extended), and (8) Spinning mills Aegeon SA. However, part of the investments of the bank in the form of equity participation and/or long-term loans

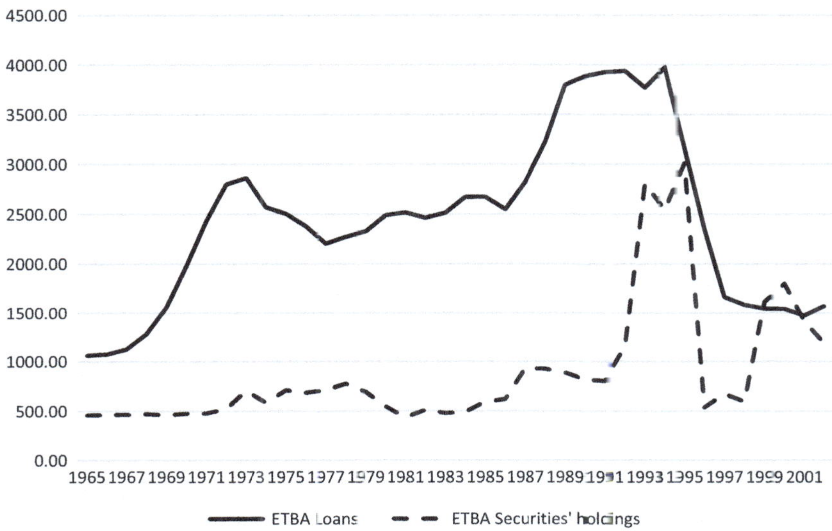

Fig. 9.7 ETBA, loans, and securities holdings, million Euros, constant 2015 prices, 1965–2002. Loans are classified as long and medium-term loans (1965–1993) and claims against customers (1994–2002). Securities holdings include financial investments in shares, bonds, treasury bonds, and mutual funds. Source: ETBA Annual Reports, various years, and author's elaboration

proved to be unprofitable or the respective enterprises were categorized as "*provlimatikes*" (being in distress). Hence, the bank introduced a program of assistance and reorganization of these firms. These included Hellenic Exports SA, GEMEE SA, the Nitrate Fertilizer Plant, Steyer Hellas, Thermis SA, Chandris –Cables SA, Deras Leather Industry, Piraiki-Patraiki SA, Skalistiris Group, Pyrkal SA, Hellenic Steel SA, Hellenic Shipyards SA and others. In 1982, the bank estimated the number of employees in firms in distress to have reached the level of 3,722 persons while in 1984 the respective number was 11,000. This finding made it necessary for the bank to support these firms with new loans, conversion of maturing debt, or rescheduling their debt along with the reorganization of these companies. Starting in 1983 the Bank cooperated with the Organization for Business Restructuring (OAE) established by Law 1386/1983 (ETBA Annual Report 1977: 24–26; 1978: 23; 1979: 40–41; 1982: 35–36; 1984: 20; 1985: 35).

As for the approved loans, it is notable that these increased at current prices by 210% between 1975 and 1977 of which those directed to industry and mining increased by 275% (ETBA Annual Report 1977: 29). The same figure at current prices between 1978 and 1980 was only 13.7% in industry but 208% in shipping (ETBA Annual Report 1980: 40–41). However, starting in 1982, the bank provided not only long-term capital for fixed assets but also the necessary start-up working capital for the first months of the operation of a project (ETBA Annual Report 1982: 6). Total loans continued to rise in the following years showing a percentage change of 25.4% between 1983 and 1984, and 19% in 1985. The majority of loans went to industrial and workshop units. For example, by the end of 1985, the portfolio of the bank was comprised of four kinds of loans: those to industry and workshops (70.5%), to shipping (6.4%), to tourism (18.7%), and miscellaneous loans (4.4%) (ETBA Annual Report 1983: 23; 1984: 17; 1985: 18–19).

The Industrial Areas and Workshop-Industry Centers program became a continuing concern for the bank. Hence, as reported in 1978, the number of industries installed in these areas rose to 148 from 42 that were in place in 1977 (ETBA Annual Report 1978: 19). These firms increased to 192 in 1981 while 4,800 enterprises were yet expected to locate there. The impact on employment was substantial with the creation of 11,500 jobs and the expectation of providing an additional 250,000 jobs in the future (ETBA Annual Report 1981: 3). Furthermore, in 1979, the bank established a subsidiary company named Industrial Areas-ETBA SA which in 1980 took over all the functions that were related to the design and construction of projects in the industrial areas. The amounts of funds disposed by the bank to the development of industrial areas rose at current prices from 160 million Drs. (0.5 million Euros) in 1975 to 1,280 million Drs. (3.75 million Euros) in 1980 (ETBA Annual Report 1979: 19–20) and to 10,807 million Drs (31.7 million Euros) in 1984 (ETBA Annual Report 1984). These projects were financed from the bank's own funds, proceeds from the sale of industrial land, the Public Investment Program, and loans from the European Investment Bank and the European Regional Development Fund.

A significant dimension of ETBA's activity was the conduct of various studies and research concerning the possibilities of the Greek industry. These included: (1) a study on the marble industry, on the construction of buses and telecommunication material, (2) a feasibility study on semisynthetic penicillin, on the use of solar energy, and the development of silk industry, (3) market research on fish processing industries, meat canning, and fruits and vegetables industry, (4) a study on the use of emery from the island of Naxos, (5) estimates of operating costs of new oil storage facilities, (6) a study in cooperation with ETEBA and the soviet firm TSVETMETPROMEXPORT for the construction of an Alumina plant, and (7) a study for Maritime Industrial Areas (NA.VI.PE.). In addition, ETBA conducted a study in cooperation with IOBE on the conditions of industry in Greece as compared to the corresponding sectors in the European Community. Finally, the bank established in 1980 a special Technical Assistance Company staffed with financial and technical experts so as to consult small and medium-sized businesses on matters such as internal organization, production, and market conditions (ETBA Annual Report 1977: 23–24; 1978: 21, 24; 1980: 34, 47; 1982: 6).

Concerning the development of the capital market, the bank floated the shares of Greek Portfolio Investment SA on the Stock Exchange in 1978 (ETBA Annual Report 1978: 26). However, ETBA attributed its poor performance in this area to unfavorable economic conditions, which also affected the capital market and made it difficult for it to recycle its portfolio on the market without losses. This meant that many of its equity investments were tied up in its portfolio and yielding low returns, further reduced its funding capacity but also hampered its efforts to support the capital market (ETBA Annual Report 1979: 16). However, the main contribution of ETBA to capital market development was the operation of its affiliated company, the Hellenic Portfolio Investment Company which attracted new shareholders, and 14 insurance funds, thus enabling ETBA to reduce its equity participation in it (ETBA Annual Report 1980: 46).

During the crisis years, ETBA combined its role as an instrument of government policy and a factor of its rationing function in the financial repression/regulation regime with its ability to promote institutional development. It was the only development bank that sustained its lending policy despite losses and the shortcomings of the Greek industry. It even recognized in a rather Keynesian fashion the role of uncertainty in business expectations and its responsibility to uphold investment demand. All the above show that ETBA fully embraced its role as a supporter and promoter of the public purpose of the era which was to overcome the crisis and reorganize industry in the new competitive environment. It is noteworthy that the bank not only continued its diverse institutional activities but it also took responsibility for the less-than-expected progress in capital market development. This is an indication of how serious it considered its mission for institutional development to be. In the crisis years, ETBA showed that a public development bank is able to conduct both an anti-cyclical lending policy and to promote financial development and institutional activity. Its extensive research and studies program proved that overcoming a crisis demands long-term planning and institutional and structural reform together with the necessary funds. This is where the Veblenian notion of changing habits of thought and Commons's strategic transactions for reform, meet Keynes's emphasis on fundamental uncertainty and long-term expectations for investment. In other words, a public development bank that serves the public purpose and acts as an instrument of rationing funds and specifying "reasonable" prices is well placed to promote both short-term anti-cyclical policies and long-term institutional and economic development.

9.4.3 From a Public Developmental Agency to a Private Universal Bank: 1987–2002

The late 1980s, especially from 1987, were important years for ETBA, as for the other two development banks, in terms of the nature of their operations. It is noteworthy that in the Annual Report of 1987, the bank noted a slowdown in the process of raising funds from the domestic bond market because of the competition faced by the government's Treasury Bills. The latter offered higher interest rates than those permitted for the bank's bonds and hence, ETBA's funds through bonds' issue fell to 22,549 million Drs (66.2 million Euros) compared to 49,328 million Drs. (144.8 million Euros) in 1986. This was certainly a turning point in the character of the bank as far as it indicated a gradual withdrawal of the support of the state to the development banking model prevailing in the previous decades. ETBA acknowledged this change and requested that the government separate its role as a competitive investment banking institution from its role as a manager of the government's programs within the Public Investment Program. The bank stated that the original need for long-term financing in the Greek Economy which motivated its establishment in 1964 was now satisfied by a variety of institutions. Hence, there was no reason for ETBA to be locked into this business which, in many cases, was unprofitable. In the new environment of financial liberalization and integration of money and capital markets within the European Community in 1992, the bank sought a new role as a modern investment bank by incorporating in its operation activities such as counseling, underwriting, promotion of mergers and acquisitions, factoring, leasing, and venture capital (ETBA Annual Report 1987: 7–9). The aim of the bank was not to abandon its previous role but to integrate it into the new competitive environment. What ETBA wanted was a new compromise between the traditional development banking model and the modern merchant banking model both operating at the same time and within the same entity. However, this would prove to be difficult in the following years. Indeed, in its Annual Report for 1989, the bank raised again the problem of the government's interest in firms such as the Greek Coastal Shipping Company, Porcel, and others that were financially unviable and deteriorated the quality of the portfolio of ETBA. It also proposed to sell or liquidate its manufacturing subsidiaries to the private sector in order to build a healthier investment portfolio (ETBA Annual Report 1989: 7). In 1990, nineteen such firms went into liquidation and seven of them went bankrupt (ETBA Annual Report 1990: 9). In 1994, the bank published a business plan in which it indicated its determination to follow a conservative financial policy that would minimize the risks assumed by ETBA in the future along with the full liquidation of its portfolio of firms in distress. Based on this plan and Law 2359/1995, the bank underwent a restructuring process to adapt to its new role in the context of the modernization of the Greek banking system (ETBA Annual Report 1994: 11; 1995: 5). Finally, in 1998, ETBA in cooperation with ABN-AMRO—the latter acting as a consultant—defined its strategy toward the three branches of its operation: commercial banking, investment banking, and development banking (ETBA Annual Report 1998: 10). In 1999, ETBA Bank was listed on the Athens Stock Exchange after a public offering that took place on 17th December 1999. Hence, the government was no longer the only shareholder of the Bank as its share contracted to 65.56%. The process of privatization of the bank continued in the following years until its absorption by the Piraeus Bank in 2002 (ETBA Annual Report 1999: 11; 2001: 7; 2002: 2).

Nevertheless, the bank continued its industrial areas program along with its long-term financing activity. A novelty, however, was the new proposal of ETBA to establish "technopolises" which are special industrial estates for manufacturing plants that will use technologically advanced production processes with the least environmental impact (ETBA Annual Report 1989: 7). Furthermore, it launched a program within the government's Regional Development Plan by raising funds from the EEC Structural Funds. In the context of this program ETBA conducted the relevant feasibility studies concerning the exploitation of lignite deposits, the exploitation of the geothermal field at Nea Kessani in Xanthi, a study for the identification of investment opportunities in the area of water supply and drainage, and a pre-feasibility study into the Area Heating of Megalopolis. The bank also participated in other European Community programs such as INTERREG (inter-regional development), VALOREN (conservation of energy), ENVIREG (protection of the environment) (ETBA Annual Report 1989: 48; 1991: 14, 27–28), and JEV (Joint European Venture) for encouraging joint European ventures in SMEs (ETBA Annual Report 1998: 24). In ETBA's development projects, we should include its financing for the modernization of existing industries such as Nitrogenous Fertilizers Industry SA (AEBAL), Hellenic Alumina SA, and NA.VI.PE, and an investment project concerning spa tourism in N. Apollonia and Icaria. As far as the technical aid to domestic enterprises was concerned, the bank participated in the PRISMA program aimed at the improvement of the quality and standardization of produced products and the RETEX program for the modernization of enterprises (ETBA Annual Report 1990: 32–35).

Loans provided by ETBA increased, at current prices, by 28% between 1986 and 1987, while for industrial estates total expenditure in 1987 reached the level of 16,131 million Drs (47.3 million Euros) at current prices (ETBA Annual Report 1987: 15, 18). However, the financing of this activity became more difficult in the early 1990s, when the interest subsidy on bank bonds was reduced by 25% in 1990 and eliminated in 1991. In addition, ETBA's bonds were taxed, unlike government securities, and the bank was unable to adjust the interest rates on its loans, which accounted for 1/3 of its portfolio (ETBA Annual Report 1990: 9; 1991: 12). Loans continued to rise at current prices but at lower rates. Hence, the rate of change of loans approved between 1991 and 1992 was 20.7% while between 1992 and 1993 was only 9.5%. This figure for 1994 was 3.3% while in 1995 there was for the first time a decrease of −6.2% in loans offered which continued in the next years to become −20.3% between 1996 and 1995 and −24.4% between 1996 and 1997. However, starting in 1998 loans increased again by 10% compared to 1997 and showed a positive percentage change of 55% between 1998 and 1999. This trend lasted until 2000 while in 2001 newly approved loans fell again. However, the criteria on which these loans were granted were completely different from those of the past, as the profitability of the proposed projects was now the determining factor (ETBA Annual Report 1993: 19; 1994: 15; 1995: 15; 1996: 15; 1997: 15; 1998: 12; 1999: 21; 2000: 9; 2001: 7).

Despite the adverse conditions in the bond market, ETBA's bonds remained the main source of funds being 60.4% of the total in 1987 and 64.8% in 1988. However, this percentage fell to 59.9% of the total in 1989 with a rise of funds raised from abroad from 20.6% in 1988 to 27.6% in 1989. Foreign funds consisted of loans provided by the European Investment Bank and funds drawn on the international capital markets—especially the German and Japanese markets. Part of the foreign exchange risk was assumed by the Bank of Greece (ETBA Annual Report 1989: 24). In addition, ETBA was looking for new sources of funding and, in this context, proposed to the Bank of Greece in 1990 that investment banks be allowed to accept time deposits in Drachmas and foreign exchange and that the maximum limit for raising capital on the interbank market be raised to up to 50% of the bank's capital. These amendments were accepted and enacted in 1991 along with the issuance of new one-year "6,9,12" bank bonds that were able to compete with Treasury Bills on the grounds of their early redemption attractive terms. Furthermore, in the same year, the establishment of a secondary market for bank bonds and the renewal of old non-taxable bonds with an interest payment option strengthened the liquidity position of ETBA (ETBA Annual Report 1990: 10; 1991: 13). However, bank bonds dropped continuously as a percentage of total sources of funds reaching the level of 51.5% in 1992 and 38.5% in 1993 with the parallel increase of own funds (share capital, reserves, and provisions) from 12.5% in 1992 to 27.5% in 1993. In 1996, bonds accounted for only 7.8% of total funding sources (ETBA Annual Report 1993: 24; 1996: 25).

Since ETBA, during most of its active presence in development financing, had been a public agent, its financial performance had not been its primary concern. However, ETBA showed on average a falling return on assets from 1% in 1967–1974 to 0% in 1975–1986 and −4% in 1987–2002. In addition, its return on equity which was on average 2% in 1967–1974 and 1% in 1975–1986 became negative −47% in 1987–2002 when the bank also reported negative average profits −212.88 million euros in constant 2015 prices (see Fig. 9.8). Besides, its average cost of debt rose on average from 4% in 1967–1974 to 9% in 1975–1986 and 13% in 1987–2002. Finally, ETBA's loss ratio fell on average from 6% in 1965–1974 to 5% in 1975–1986 to 2% in 1987–2002 It seems as if ETBA considered the period of financial liberalization less risky in terms of accumulated provisions for losses, especially after 1994 when its lending activity declined sharply as is evident from Fig. 9.7 (Loizos 2012: 237–245).

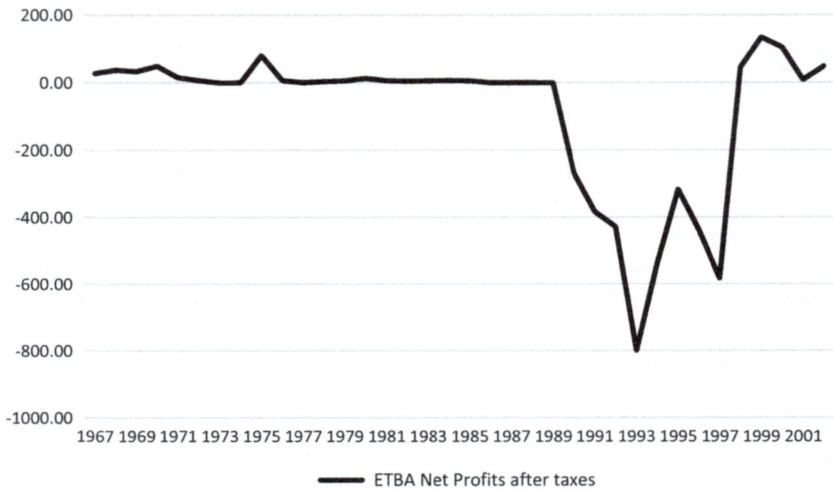

Fig. 9.8 ETBA net profits after taxes, million Euros, constant 2015 prices, 1967–2002. Source: ETBA Annual Reports, various years, and author's elaboration

In an attempt to promote its new role in the financially liberalized environment as a merchant or a universal bank, ETBA established ETBA Leasing SA in 1988 while upgrading the role of its old company Hellenic Investment Company SA. These firms along with ETBA Bank and the Hellenic Import-Export Bank SA, founded in 1989, were parts of the ETBA Group (ETBA Annual Report 1989: 47). ETBA Insurance Brokers SA was added to the Group in 1991 so as to act as brokers for the Bank's insurance-related portfolio (ETBA Annual Report 1991: 14). In addition, the bank launched a new Capital Market Service in order to provide consultancy services to public and private firms concerning the offering and underwriting of new share and bond issues on the Athens Stock Exchange and to help the restructuring of enterprises through mergers and acquisitions. Such services were provided to firms such as Natural Gas (DEPA SA) (a public corporation), EKO-Chemicals SA, Hellenic Shipyards SA, HELEXPO, Petzetakis SA, Macedonia Plastics SA, Kavala Plastics SA, E.D. Mouzakis SA, OP. Darig & Co SA, the Bank of Central Greece, SANYO HELLAS SA, Public Petroleum Corporation (DEP), Hellenic Sugar Industry, OTE, and others (ETBA Annual Report 1989: 47; 1993: 37; 1994: 32). Furthermore, the bank established a Privatization

Committee in 1990 to help the privatization program of its subsidiaries (ETBA Annual Report 1990: 11). These included Hellenic Marble SA, Porcel SA, Nafsi Sa, Elvior SA, Helenic Shipyards SA, Shipyards of Greece SA, Thraki SA, Filiates Textiles SA, Akti Mirinis SA, GEMEE SA, Hellenic Asbestos SA and others (ETBA Annual Report 1991: 13; 1992: 7–8). Furthermore, ETBA together with the Agricultural Bank of Greece were appointed in 1990 as intermediaries and financial advisors on behalf of Greece for the provision of economic assistance to 6 countries of Central and Eastern Europe within the PHARE Programme. The services that the bank would provide included the assessment of investment programs and the prospective companies, the determination of the preliminary steps toward the establishment of joint ventures, and the provision of related technical assistance (ETBA Annual Report 1990: 61; 1991: 14). In the context of its international operations, we should mention its participation in the MENTOR Programme for the establishment of an international business center in Romania (ETBA Annual Report 1991: 14; 1992: 6–7). Besides, in 1992 ETBA established its own Dealing Room that became a valuable link between the bank, the interbank market, and the REPOS and Swaps market (ETBA Annual Report 1992: 9). In 1993, the bank played a significant role in the development of the fixed-income bond market by being appointed as a lead manager together with Midland Bank for the issuance of bonds of the European Investment Bank and by offering similar services and products in cooperation with international organizations such as the EBRD, the International Finance Corporation, and the International Monetary Fund (ETBA Annual Report 1993: 36–37). In 1994 ETBA participated in two new firms in the context of its transformation within the new financial environment: ETBA-Natwest Mutual Fund Management (in cooperation with National Westminster Bank) and DANUBE Fund (Venture Capital) (ETBA Annual Report 1994: 32; 1995: 31). In short, by the end of 2001, the bank was completely privatized and transformed into a modern universal bank with activities in corporate banking, retail banking, investment banking, and treasury services. The history of the bank as a separate entity ended in October 2002 with the decision of the Board of Directors of ETBA and Piraeus Bank for its absorption by the Piraeus Bank (ETBA Annual Report 2001: 7–9; 2002: 2).

The last period of the operation of ETBA illustrates a story of the successful transformation of a public traditional development bank into a modern universal bank with a wide range of activities. It was successful because ETBA managed to maintain its lending and trading activity at satisfactory levels as shown in Fig. 9.7 despite the fierce competition it faced. It also turned its losses into profits during the last years of its operation as shown in Fig. 9.8. Most importantly, ETBA maintained its extensive institutional role by providing a great variety of products, some of them quite innovative such as the "technopolises" initiative. However, all these were not enough for the government to continue its support of the bank. The complete privatization of the bank signals a different aspect of the institutional-political risk faced by all development banks. ETBA was an emblematic public development bank of the main period of development banking in Greece which came to an end the moment a fully liberalized financial market came into effect. At least this was the perception of the Greek government in that era. The public purpose may have been modified, and the meaning of "reasonableness" may have changed but the dynamic nature of development banks as a combination of the three transactions that Commons identified to serve Veblenian institutional development and reform have not changed even in liberalized markets.

9.5 The Main Period of Development Banking in Greece: An Assessment

The above analysis indicates the possibly positive role that development banks assumed concerning financial development in Greece both indirectly through their lending activity and promotion of economic development and directly through specific initiatives. This happened because, as it was explained in Chap. 3, financial development emerges both as a need of a growing economy and as a catalyst of the latter. In this close relationship between economic and financial development Greece is not an exception (Eichengreen and Gibson 2001: 548). Hence, the contribution of development banks in this economic growth-financial development nexus might be pivotal in the context of the economic development policies followed in post-war Greece which were inspired and guided by the internationally dominant academic and policy doctrines of the era.

As explained in previous chapters, the idea of pro-development government intervention was at the core of the policy prescriptions, and development banking was one of its means to carry out development finance in key sectors of the economy. Did the three development banks succeed in this role? In a complex multifactor real world is difficult to isolate the contribution of development banks. The share of development banking credit in total banking credit might be a criterion but it is an imperfect one as far as it does not take into account the impact of individual investment projects in economic development. As described in this chapter, development banks and especially the public ETBA had a crucial contribution in the financing of a wide range of major industrial projects that transformed the Greek economy from a developing to a developed one. In addition, there was an equally important "intangible" beneficial impact of all three banks on institutional development, especially in the development of the capital market and modern entrepreneurship in the Greek economy. The historical evolution of these banks as described in this chapter provides some examples of this major contribution of development banks in institutional development.

However, equally crucial was the role of the state in development banks' contribution to economic and institutional development. In the Greek case, as has been shown above, this role passed through two phases: a first one which was supportive of the traditional development banking model during the financial repression period, and a second one during the deregulation period which could be characterized as indifferent. If this is the case then the operation of Greek development banks should be assessed not just in terms of management quality and pure economic efficiency but also in terms of the constraints imposed on them by the government policy in place. In this context, a further question about the motives of government policy may complicate things further. Following Thomadakis (1995: 105–106, 110, 119–121), Thomadakis and Seremetis (1992: 243, 247, 252) and Psalidopoulos's (1990: 20,75) remarks about the consistency of the implemented economic policy in Greece compared to the dominant economic doctrines and the developmental role of the state as opposed to the electoral cycle a question is raised about the identification of each phase of government policy with a consistent program of financial repression or liberalization to promote economic development or with an expedient means to obtain short-term political goals. The latter may take the form of a degeneration of financial repression policies to policies aiming at financing short-sighted government consumption—instead of long-term government investment. In the same manner, financial liberalization may become a means to defending ideological prejudices in praise of free markets, when the international environment favors them, at the expense of long-term planning about structural reform toward a more sustainable economic growth model. The point here is that development banking failure or success may disproportionately reflect the failure or success of government policies rather than their internal competencies as organizations.

Related to this issue is the dynamic character and internal transformation of these banks. As shown in the previous analysis, the change in financial regimes from financial repression to financial liberalization signaled the need for an internal transformation of these banks from the classic development banking model of the post-war era to a modern investment banking model. All three banks entered this process of transformation but not all of them succeeded in carrying it out. The indifferent role of the state against these banks and the lack of a long-term plan for their new role in the globalized and liberalized financial environment marked their fate. The Greek case of development banking is an illustration of how institutional-political risk, in the sense of a poorly designed and implemented government policy and the possible dominance of the ideas that were inimical to an interventionist policy in the financial sector, determined the evolution and demise of development banking in Greece. The point here is not that the classic development banking model of the 1960s should have survived in the new globalized environment. The argument is that in favor of a pro-free markets prejudice the particular role of development banking as a means to advance the public purpose in parallel with private banking was dismissed in the Greek case. Furthermore, the ability of development banks to transform themselves in association with the prevailing financial regime and to contribute to institutional development was also disregarded.

Development banks do have a role to play in the new liberalized environment as is evidenced by the experience of other European countries and will be explained in the next chapter. The rise of the capital market as an alternative source of funding does not preclude the role of modern development banks which have a wide mandate as explained in previous chapters. The new challenges of financial stability, climate change, and the multiple dimensions of sustainability in an ever more uncertain world call for a new role in development banking. However, neither the Greek experience nor the revival of development banking both globally and in Europe is intelligible without the institutional foundations of development banking theory that were expounded in Chap. 6. The role of the three Greek development banks under different financial regimes was dependent on the collective bargaining between social groups in post-war Greece in the context of Commons's "rationing transaction". This is an illustrative way to characterize the policy of preferential credit to key economic sectors and the respective social groups in favor of economic development. Greek development banks themselves as a combination of bargaining, managerial, and rationing transactions showcased their dynamic character, their contribution to the development of the capital market, and their determination to serve the public purpose of the era. In their operation, development banks in Greece were guided by what Commons characterizes as "reasonableness" to the degree that their pricing policies and their lender-borrower relationships served the public purpose and transcended conventional private banking practices. Such a "reasonable" attitude which was conducive to economic and social development may have also become a burden to them when these banks attempted to support firms in distress during the crisis years of the 1970s and 1980s. In any case, "reasonableness" depends on the public prevailing opinion and hence, is a dynamic notion as development banks themselves. Furthermore, the Greek development banks, as explained above, were also agents of institutional change and reform in the everyday practices of firms by providing solutions to practical problems, introducing new working rules and methods, and contributing to institutional and financial development. The latter, according to Veblen, is a rather painstaking and long-lasting process because it entails a change in habits of thought and social conventions along with technological change. The Greek development banks were present in this process since it is difficult to argue that the new legal framework that was introduced in support of the liberalization of the banking sector and the development of the capital market did not find a foothold on the preceding initiatives of development banks. After all, for an institutional reform to be successful people should believe in it and adjust their behavior accordingly. This implies a process of changing habits of thought conducive to financial development among entrepreneurs who "internalize" the new practices in their behavior. Ignoring this role, which development banks have played since the 1960s leaves the question of institutional development in the Greek financial sector without a satisfactory and well-founded answer. Moreover, this question assumes critical importance in the current challenges of development banking in Greece as these will be examined in the next chapter.

References

Altman, M. (2023) "Mental Models, Decision-Making, Bargaining Power, and Institutional Change", *Journal of Economic Issues*, 57(4): 1241–1259.

Arestis, P. and Stein, H. (2005) "An Institutional Perspective to Finance and Development as an Alternative to Financial Liberalization", *International Review of Applied Economics*, 19(4): 381–398.

Arestis, P., Nissanke, M. and Stein, H. (2003) "Finance and Development: Institutional and Policy Alternatives to Financial Liberalization", The Levy Economics Institute of Bard College Working Paper No 377 available at https://www.levyinstitute.org/pubs/wp377.pdf Accessed 18 Nov. 2023

Bush, P. D. (1987) "The Theory of Institutional Change", *Journal of Economic Issues*, 21(3): 1075–1116.

Eichengreen, B. and Gibson, H. D. (2001) "Greek Banking at the Dawn of the New Millennium", in Bryant, R. C., Garganas N. C., and Tavlas, G. S. (eds.) *Greece's Economic Performance and Prospects*, Athens and Washington D.C.: Bank of Greece and The Brookings Institution, pp. 545–601.

ETBA Annual Reports 1967–2002, Athens.

ETEBA Annual Reports 1964–2001, Athens.

Garganas, N. C. and Tavlas, G. S. (2001) "Monetary Regimes and Inflation Performance: The Case of Greece" in Bryant, R. C. Garganas, N. C. and Tavlas, G. S. (eds.) *Greece's Economic Performance and Prospects*, Athens and Washington D.C.: Bank of Greece and The Brookings Institution, pp. 43–102.

Halikias, D. J. (1978) *Money and Credit in a Developing Economy: The Greek Case*, N.Y.: New York University Press.

Hellenic Republic, Official Gazette (2002) Issue of Joint Stock Companies and Limited Liability Companies, No. 12826.

Karatzas Committee (1987) *The Committee's Report for the Reform and Modernization of the Greek Banking System*, Athens: HBA (in Greek).

Kemp, T. (2009) *Progress and Reform. The Economic Thought of John R. Commons*, Saarbrücken, Deutschland: VDM Verlag Dr. Müller.

Kostis, K. (1997) *Cooperation and Competition: The 70 Years of the Union of Greek Banks*, Athens: Alexandria Publications (in Greek).

Loizos, K. (2017) "Alternative Financial Regimes and Development Banks in Greece 1963–2002: What Have We Learned?", *Economic Alternatives*, 1: 34–50.

Loizos, K. (2012) "Development Banking in Greece 1963–2002: Performance and Institutional Transformation" in Petmezas, S., Charlafti, T., Lymperatos, A. and Papakonstantinou, K. (eds.) *Theoretical Inquiries and Empirical Research*. Proceedings of the International Conference in Economic and Social History. Rethymno 10–13.12.2008, Athens: University of Crete, School of Philosophy and Alexandria, pp. 229–258.

McCormick, K. (2006) *Veblen in Plain English. A Complete Introduction to Thorstein Veblen's Economics*, New York: Cambria Press.

Psalidopoulos, M. (1990) *Keynesian Theory and Greek Economic Policy: Myth and Reality*, Athens: Kritiki (in Greek).

Psilos, D. D. and Westebbe, R. (1964) *Public International Development Financing in Greece*, Public International Development Financing Research Project of Columbia University, Report No 10, New York.

Psilos, D. D. (1964) *Capital Market in Greece*, Center of Economic Research, Research Monograph Series, No 9, Athens.

Ramstad, Y. (2001) "John R. Commons's Reasonable Value and the Problem of Just Price", *Journal of Economic Issues*, 35(2): 253–277.

Ramstad, Y. (1991) "From Desideratum to Historical Achievement: John R. Commons's Reasonable Value and the 'Negotiated Economy' of Denmark", *Journal of Economic Issues*, 25(2): 431–439.

TE Annual Reports 1963–1992, Athens.

TE (1975) *Past Performance and Prospects. A Follow-Up Report*, Athens.

TE (n.d.) *Investment Bank S.A. Catering to the Capital Requirements of Greek Industry*, (no place).

Thomadakis, S. (1995) "The Greek Economy and European Integration: Prospects for Development and Threats of Underdevelopment" in Constas, D. and Stavrou, T. (eds.) *Greece Prepares for the Twenty-first Century*, Washington, D.C. and Baltimore: Woodrow Wilson Center & John Hopkins University Press.

Thomadakis, S. and Seremetis, D. (1992) "Fiscal Management, Social Agenda, and Structural Deficits", in Kariotis, T. (ed.) *The Greek Socialist Experiment. Papandreou's Greece 1981–1989*, Pella Publishing Company.

Vousvounis, A. A. (2010) *ETEBA, National Investment Bank for Industrial Development 1963–2002*, Athens: National Bank of Greece (in Greek).

Xanthakis, M. (1995) "Investment Banks: European and Greek Experience" in Alexakis, P., Giannitsis, T., Thomadakis, S., Xanthakis, M., and Hatzigiannis, N. (eds.) *Markets' Liberalization and Transformations in the Greek Banking System*, Athens: ETBA, Papazisis (in Greek).

CHAPTER 10

The 2003–2018 Interval in Development Finance and the "revival" of Development Banking in Greece Within the European Context (2019–Today)

10.1 The Modern European Context for Development Finance

As indicated in previous chapters, the presence of development banking in Europe has a long history. Despite the changing economic conditions in many European countries and the different institutional environments, development banking has survived by adapting. The heyday of development finance was the post-war period and the financial support of industrial policies while its antipode was the period of financial deregulation (Mertens et al. 2021: 19; Moslener et al. 2018: 63) However, contrary to the Greek case, in which the last development bank of the main era of Greek development finance stopped its operation in 2002, in other European countries, development or investment banks adjusted their organization and activity to the new conditions. The German Kreditanstalt für Wiederaufbau (KfW) was established in 1948 with a mandate to finance the reconstruction of the German economy with funds provided by the Marshall Plan. However, its focus changed later on by adapting to the changing needs of the era, for example by targeting small and medium enterprises (SMEs) or by providing development aid. When the European Commission considered guarantees provided to KfW by the German government as state aid that violates the European rules for competition, KfW

K. Loizos, *Between Markets and Governments*,
https://doi.org/10.1007/978-3-031-88527-3_10

went through an internal reorganization in 2002. The Italian Cassa Depositi e Prestiti (CDP) was established in the nineteenth century with a focus on postal savings and the aim of collecting savings from the population in rural areas and financing public works. Following the European Union regulation for competition and state aid the CDP was privatized in 2003 while its activity, such as the financing of infrastructure projects, should now take into account also profitability criteria. In addition, after 2009, in response to the crisis, it expanded its activity to include the financing of the private sector and further transformed itself into a modern National Development Bank. Another example is the Agence Française de Développement (AFD) which was established in 1941 in London by Charles De Gaulle with the original name Caisse Centrale de la France Libre (CCFL). Changing names reflected its changing focus as the economic and political conditions changed. Hence, before it became AFD in 1998 it was the Caisse Centrale de la France d'Outre-mer (CCFOM) in 1944 and the Caisse Centrale de Coopération Économique (CCCE) in 1975. AFD is currently providing financial and technical support to developing countries with a focus on green transition and sustainable development (Bilal 2021; Bulfone and Di Carlo 2021: 147–160; Mertens 2021: 120).

The skeptical attitude toward development banking in Europe changes in the 1990s and especially after the crisis of 2008. The recession of 1992 triggered the gradual development of a European eco-system of development finance or a "field of European development banking" which included the European Investment Fund (EIF), the European Investment Bank (EIB), and National Development Banks. At the Amsterdam Summit in 1997, the European Community urged National Development Banks to provide countercyclical lending while these banks were gradually established as "legitimate" instruments of European structural and anti-cyclical policies in a liberalized institutional environment (Mertens et al. 2021: 19–20). Furthermore, the recent global financial crisis and the ensuing recession rendered development banking topical against the background of the anti-cyclical credit policy that was followed in many countries (The Economist 2019; De Luna-Martínez et al. 2018: 10). Finally, National Development Banks gained further support after the European Commission acknowledged their potentially significant contribution to addressing procyclicality, encouraging innovation, and assisting the green transition in the European economies (Moslener et al. 2018: 63). In this document, the European Commission recognized the indispensable role of National Promotional Banks (as it calls them) in advancing its "Investment Plan for Europe" that was put forward in 2014. The Commission justified the participation of development banks in the implementation of this plan in cooperation with the EIB on the grounds of their expertise and knowledge of local conditions and policies and for this reason, it encouraged member states to set up a National Development Bank in case they do not already have one in operation. In this sense, the document of the European Commission aimed to provide guidelines based on best practices that would help member states to establish a National Development Bank including the reasons for doing so, following the market failure argument. It also includes some principles that should guide policymakers in setting up such a bank, issues concerning state-aid regulations and the Stability and Growth Pact, and the cooperation between National Development Banks and the EIB (European Commission 2015).

The above-mentioned European Commission Communication expressed a decisive change of attitude toward development banking which now seems to find its proper place within the liberalized global economy facing new demanding challenges. Indeed, the special role of Public or National Development Banks in promoting sustainability in its various forms is highlighted in subsequent studies. For example, Griffith-Jones (2016) focuses on the contribution of the emblematic KfW in providing green lending and setting environmental standards for the projects that receive finance. Furthermore, Colombo and Cuda (2023) stress the importance of Public Development Banks around Europe in promoting the United Nations Agenda 2030 concerning 17 Sustainable Development Goals that include economic, environmental, and social issues such as innovation, responsible consumption, economic growth, zero hunger and good health, quality education, reduction of various inequalities, climate and environmental action and strong institutions for peace and justice.

This is the context in which development finance developed in Greece shortly after the country joined the Eurozone in 2001. The following section follows the different stages of this process and the different forms in which development finance was provided until the establishment of the modern development banking institution in the Greek economy, the Hellenic Development Bank (HDB) in 2019. Then the next section highlights the major issues concerning the operation of the HDB including its mandate, areas of activity, performance, and possible future prospects within the new European context of development finance. The analysis is carried out in the light of the institutional model developed in this book.

10.2 Development Finance in Greece 2003–2018

After the absorption of ETBA by the Piraeus Bank and the end of the main era of development banking in Greece, development finance assumed a different form which was characterized by smaller public outfits that made extensive use of European Union funds. Hence, if the Greek development banks of the previous era were dependent on the support and national economic and institutional policies of the Greek state, this new form of development finance was much more determined by the ideas and policies that were prevalent in the European Union institutions and dependent on EU funding (Bastian 2021: 288–289). This means that the epicenter of decision-making that characterizes the institutional structure of the Greek financial sector and the way the prevalent financial regime affects development finance was shifted from the national to the Union level. The new idea on which development finance was now founded was that of public-private partnerships (PPP). The European Investment Bank (EIB) and the European Investment Fund (EIF), in cooperation with some national public institutions such as the Hellenic Fund for Entrepreneurship and Development (ETEAN), provided loans or guarantees for loans made by private commercial banks to SMEs or households. Hence, private commercial banks were an indispensable part of this funding mechanism, and development banking was relegated to a complementary role (Bastian 2021: 288–289). In terms of our institutional model, these small public development finance outfits were deprived of both their independent lending policy and their distinct role in institutional development and change. This does not mean that they did not take the initiative to promote the public purpose defined by the government within the European framework of development finance. However, their ability to make a difference in terms of economic and institutional development was limited and dependent on the necessary cooperation of private commercial banks.

In 2003 the Greek government established the Guarantee Fund for Small and Very Small Businesses (TEMPME).[1] The establishment of TEMPME was co-funded by the Greek state (33%) and the European Regional Development Fund (67%). The rationale behind the setting up of this fund was a goal of financial inclusion rather than development finance. The idea was that this fund would facilitate access to financial resources for SMEs. TEMPME aimed to promote entrepreneurship

[1] The Greek initials for this organization are *ΤΕΜΠΜΕ*.

among all socioeconomic groups in Greek society and to mitigate the consequences of business failure. The permanent residence of a businessman who joined the guarantee program of TEMPME was exempt from mortgage lien while their financing at a lower cost would curb usury and other activities of the informal economy. Hence, the "Guarantee Fund" signaled the shift from direct lending of the traditional development banking variety to more indirect instruments such as grants and guarantees. Indeed, TEMPME was empowered to manage programs funded by the government's budget or by EU funds such as lending rate subsidies provided to small and very small enterprises with an annual number of employees up to twenty workers and annual turnover up to 10 million euros. Eventually, TEMPME pursued to promote a different way of thinking in the relations between banks and small enterprises that would focus on supporting financially viable and economically promising units in all areas of activity by covering long-term and medium-term risks. However, the emphasis was on enterprises that did not have access to financial resources because of a lack of sufficient collateral or because of the high risk of their projects such as start-ups, innovative firms, or "new economy" enterprises (Bastian 2021: 289; TEMPME Annual Report 2006: 5–7). In 2007 TEMPME managed six guarantee programs concerning small enterprises: (1) Guarantees for setting up or developing new small enterprises, (2) guarantees for very small enterprises, (3) guarantees for small enterprises, (4) guarantees for small loans to very small enterprises (5) guarantees for mergers and acquisitions of small enterprises and (6) leasing guarantees for small and very small enterprises. Most of these guarantee programs required that the firm was profitable in at least one of the last two years before its application to the program (TEMPME Annual Report 2007: 28–29).

However, it is worth noting that the guarantee programs provided by TEMPME faced, in many cases, the reluctance of commercial banks to participate in them and the lack of familiarity of small businesses with this financial instrument. The Fund attributed these phenomena to the inadequate experience of the Greek banks and businesses concerning the institution of guarantees and the centralized system of application assessment that operated in most banks. In the latter case, bank officers did not spend time probing the different applications they received but they simply relayed this responsibility to a centralized assessment system. The Fund attempted to solve these issues by conducting seminars for bank managers and officials, by formulating proposals for the development of new products that would address the needs of each bank and its clientele, and by participating in workshops and other initiatives that aimed at informing the enterprises about its guarantee programs (TEMPME Annual Report 2007: 50–59). In 2008, TEMPME introduced a new program concerning the provision of guarantees and interest rate subsidies for working capital loans offered to small and very small enterprises and secured the participation of 36 out of 37 banks in this program (TEMPME Annual Report 2008: 8).

The next year 2009 was significant for TEMPME for many reasons. At first, it was a year in which guarantees supplied skyrocketed as is evident in Fig. 10.1. According to the management of the Fund, this was proof of the ability of TEMPME to act anti-cyclically in adverse macroeconomic conditions and support small and very small firms which received more than 86% of guaranteed loans in 2009. In addition, for the first time, the Fund showed losses before taxes because of the unprecedented rise in guarantees supplied as Fig. 10.3 depicts (TEMPME Annual Report 2009: 7–8).

In February 2011, according to Law 3912/2011, TEMPME was renamed as the Hellenic Fund for Entrepreneurship and Development

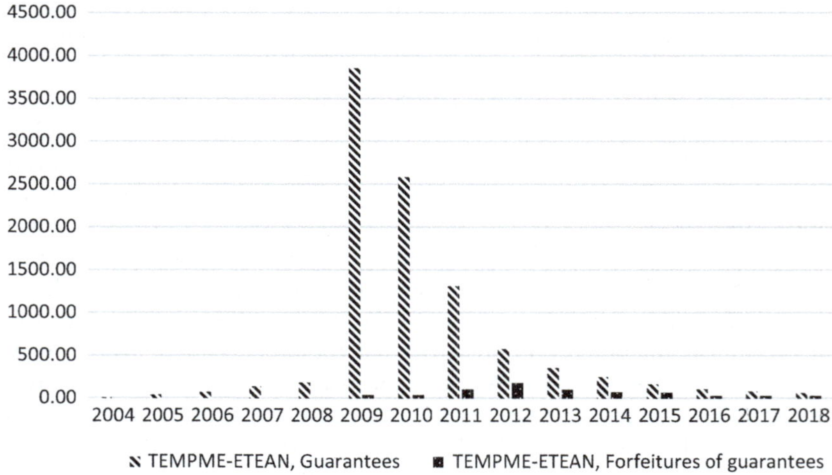

Fig. 10.1 TEMPME and ETEAN, Guarantees supplied and Forfeitures of guarantees, million euros, constant 2015 prices, 2004–2018. Source: TEMPME and ETEAN Annual Reports, various years, and author's elaboration

(ETEAN) and its mandate was extended to include medium-sized firms.[2] In addition, ETEAN would have the ability to co-invest funds provided by the Greek government in financial engineering instruments such as loan funds, guarantee funds, venture capital funds, seed funds, and others. In this context, until May 2011 four such funds had been established including a fund for agricultural entrepreneurship, a fund for investments in fisheries, and a fund for loans to households to render their houses more energy efficient. ETEAN remained a public institution that operated within the financial mechanism described above consisting of European Union financial institutions, the Greek government, and Greek private banks. The dependence on European Union structural funds becomes obvious if one considers the fact that the Greek participation was only a small part (10%–25%) of the total (Bastian 2021: 289–290; TEMPME Annual Report 2010: 7–8).

ETEAN continued TEMPME's activity concerning the provision of guarantees despite the restricted conditions on the guarantees which the Greek government was able to supply according to the adjustment programs agreed with the IMF, the European Commission, and the European Central Bank. Hence, ETEAN launched in July 2010 its new product "Guarantee of low interest rate loans to cover the purchase costs of raw materials, goods, and services". Firms that benefited from this program were able to cover their short-term needs with medium to long-term funding at a cost lower than the market. Loan disbursements reached 86% of total approved loans in 2011 which was, however, lower than 2010 as Fig. 10.2 shows. Both a lower demand for loans on behalf of firms because of reduced economic activity and high interest rates, and more strict lending criteria on the part of banks were responsible for this result. On the other hand, ETEAN faced in December 2011 forfeitures of guarantees that reached the level of 3% of initial guarantees supplied and 7.6% of its equity capital. However, this negative performance reflected the situation in the Greek banking sector in general during that period (ETEAN Annual Report 2011: 8, 14).

[2] According to the European Commission "SME Country Fact Sheet" for Greece for the period 2010–2022, the share of SMEs in the total number of enterprises did not fall below 99.9%. In addition, the share of SMEs in employment was on average 85.6% and their share in value added was on average 67.9% of the total. In comparison, the EU-27 averages for the same period were 66.4% for the share of total employment and 56.5% for the share of total value added while the share of EU-27 SMEs in the total number of enterprises was 99.8%.

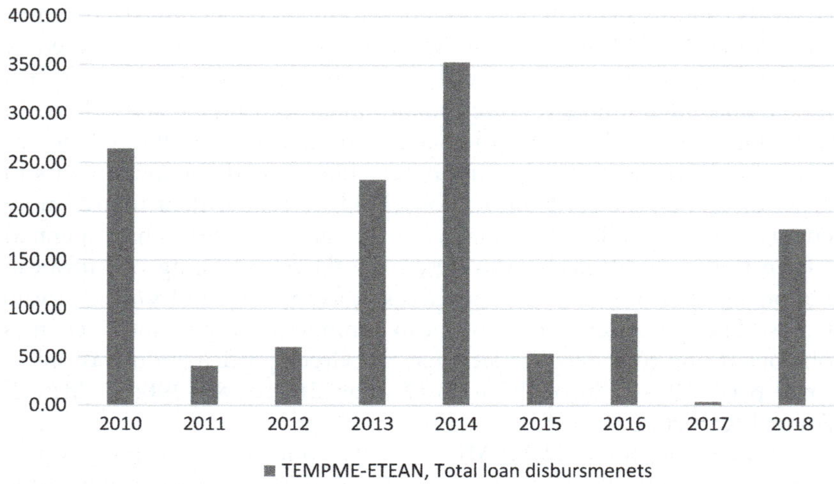

Fig. 10.2 TEMPME and ETEAN, Total loan disbursement, million euros, constant 2015 prices, 2010–2018. Source: TEMPME and ETEAN Annual Reports, various years, and author's elaboration

Under these conditions, the viability of ETEAN was called into question since its profits before and after taxes were consistently negative from 2009 up to 2011 because of the devaluation of Greek government bonds which were included in the equity capital of ETEAN and the provisions due to possible forfeitures of guarantees (see Fig. 10.3). As a result, both its return on equity (ROE) and its return on assets (ROA) were deeply negative during this period, especially in 2011 as Fig. 10.4 shows, reflecting losses of −1091.52 million euros in constant 2015 prices during that year (ETEAN, Annual Report 2012: 6–7). Eventually, ETEAN managed to return to positive profits in the next year because of the reversal of provisions against losses concerning the valuation of Greek government bonds. Moreover, the government bonds that supported ETEAN's equity capital did not participate in the private sector involvement (PSI) (ETEAN Annual Report 2013: 7). However, as shown in Figs. 10.3 and 10.4, ETEAN net profits remained close to zero from 2013 to 2018 with an average value of −10.05 million euros in constant 2015 prices while the average values for both ROA and ROE during the same period were equal to −1%. Despite this financial performance, ETEAN continued to support

Fig. 10.3 TEMPME and ETEAN, Net profits after taxes, million euros, constant 2015 prices, 2004–2018. Source: TEMPME and ETEAN Annual Reports, various years, and author's elaboration

Fig. 10.4 TEMPME and ETEAN, ROA and ROE, percentage, 2004–2018. Source: TEMPME and ETEAN Annual Reports, various years, and author's elaboration

its clients by restructuring loans in arrears, improving the conditions required by its guarantee programs, and managing its holding funds to support both households and businesses with an emphasis on energy efficiency, business restart, especially for small economic units, tourism, and agricultural entrepreneurship (ETEAN Annual Report 2013: 8–11). In the next year, ETEAN participated in the setup of the Institute for Growth (IfG) by representing the Greek government while KfW represented the German government (ETEAN, Annual Report 2014: 7). The change of government in 2015 signaled also a change in the strategic goals of ETEAN which was now considered to be a major instrument in support of the national development plan. However, ETEAN remained complementary to commercial banks despite its aim to address market failures in the credit market. In this context, ETEAN was called upon to focus on start-ups and innovative firms and to develop new financial instruments such as microcredit along with its provision of consulting services to small and very small businesses (ETEAN Annual Report 2015: 7). Until its transformation into the Hellenic Development Bank, ETEAN assumed important initiatives such as the memorandum of understanding which was signed between ETEAN and the European Investment Fund, the participation of ETEAN in the EIF-NPI Equity Platform together with 29 National Promotional Banks from 18 European Union member states, and the establishment of new holding funds including one with a regional focus. As Fig. 10.2 shows, total loan disbursements, including guarantees and financing from the holding funds of ETEAN to support entrepreneurship, fluctuated between 2011 and 2018 with an average value of 127.69 million euros in constant 2015 prices. It seems that ETEAN played indeed an anti-cyclical role in the Greek economy by supporting 16,844 small and medium-sized enterprises during the turbulent years (HDB Annual Report 2019: 3; ETEAN Annual Report 2017: 13–14; ETEAN Annual Report 2016: 7–11).

Two years before the establishment of TEMPME, the New Economy Development Fund (TANEO) was set up with the initiative of the Greek Ministry of Economy and Development. The goal of TANEO as a "fund of funds" was to address the needs of SMEs for venture capital financing by participating in such financing schemes. Participation in these instruments took the form of equity or quasi-equity in the context of the Greek state's Strategic Investment Plan. It is important to note that TANEO was able to attract capital also from non-European sources such as the Mubadala Investment Company based in Abu-Dhabi. This example indicated the ability of TANEO to capitalize on its good name and reputation in the market in turbulent times for the Greek economy as was the case in March 2018 when the relevant agreement was signed (Bastian 2021: 290–291). TANEO became a subsidiary company of ETEAN in December 2016 (ETEAN Annual Report 2016: 7).

TANEO's investments and other earning assets were on average 116.94 million euros in constant 2015 prices and showed a falling trend during the period 2009–2015 while they remained quite low in the following three years 2016–2018 with an average value of only 18.33 million euros in constant 2015 prices (Fig. 10.5). Moreover, net profits after taxes were consistently negative until 2016 as shown in Fig. 10.6 with an average value of −8.38 million euros in constant 2015 prices and an average ROA equal to −8%. Only in 2017 did net profits turn positive but they became negative but close to zero in 2018. The reasons for this poor financial performance were many and varied, including the mark-to-market valuation of TANEO's portfolio, which reflected the adverse macroeconomic environment in Greece, and the decline in operating income that followed the decline in Eurozone interest rates (TANEO Annual Report 2011: 9; 2012: 9).

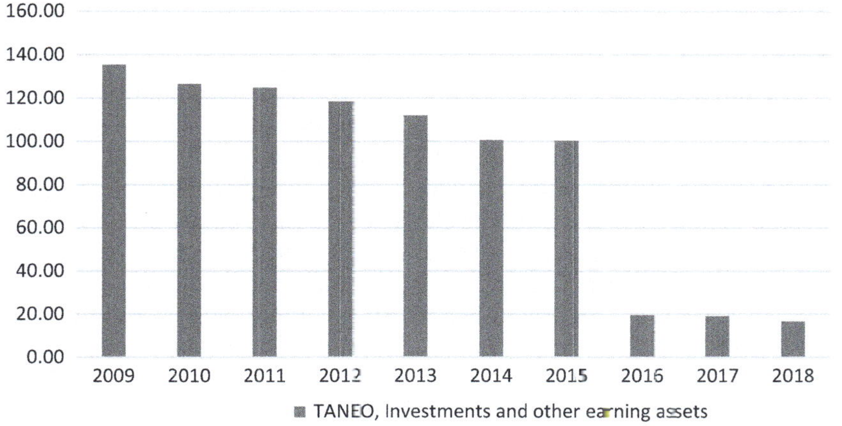

Fig. 10.5 TANEO, Investments, and other earning assets, million euros, constant 2015 prices, 2009–2018. Source: TANEO Annual Reports, various years, and author's elaboration

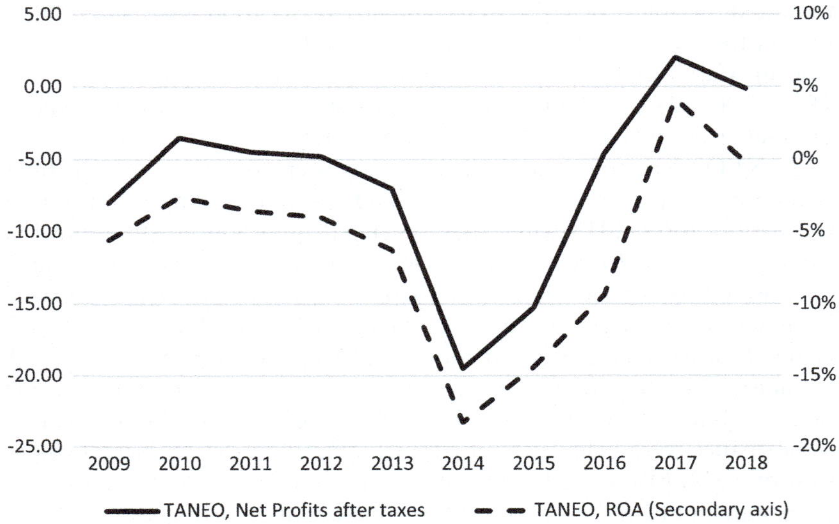

Fig. 10.6 TANEO, Net profits after taxes, million euros, constant 2015 prices and ROA, percentage, 2009–2018. Source: TANEO Annual Reports, various years, and author's elaboration

Two more examples of the dispersed landscape of development finance in Greece before the establishment of the Hellenic Development Bank in 2019 were the EquiFund Greece and the Institution for Growth (IfG). The EquiFund was set up in 2018 and attracted capital from the EIB, the EIF, the European Fund for Strategic Investments (EFSI), the Black Sea Trade and Development Bank (BSTDB), and domestic private sources. When the Greek government established this fund, the idea was to channel the capital collected from the above sources into equity investments in the form of private equity and venture capital to SMEs and start-ups in sectors such as tourism, new technologies, and others. On the other hand, the short-lived IfG was established in 2014 as a non-bank institution with three sub-funds dedicated to loan and equity financing of SMEs and financing of infrastructure works. Both the Greek government and the German development bank KfW participated in the share capital of IfG but the institution eventually died out because it did not find support by the new government that took office in 2015 (Bastian 2021: 291–295).

The period 2003–2018 was marked by a dispersed model of development finance with many small institutions with limited capabilities and complementary roles. It was a model faithful to the cheap-finance myopic mentality that characterized the Greek governments over time. It reflected a fragmented development finance model where the various functions of development banking that we have analyzed in previous chapters were performed in a fragmentary way and without coordination within a unified independent organization. TEMPME-ETEAN performed a limited form of managerial transaction in forced cooperation with private commercial banks while TANEO's activities and those of EquiFund and IfG were more akin to bargaining transactions. The rationing transaction that correlates with sovereignty and the prevailing financial regime seems to have faded out in the case of these institutions. The allocation of funds and prices was a matter to be solved by the market with a minimum participation of the government and European institutions which favored SMEs with their indirect financing instruments. In this case "reasonableness" was determined more by market forces than by the bargaining of social groups within a democratic process. The contribution of these institutions to institutional development and change was also limited or non-existent. TEMPME-ETEAN took some initiatives in this direction to encourage entrepreneurship among various social groups, promote inclusiveness, and familiarize market participants with its financial instruments. However, these actions were rather complementary to the main goal of this organization which was of the cheap-lending variety even if it involved co-financing with commercial banks.

10.3 HDB and HDBI: A New Era for Development Banking in Greece

As explained in Chap. 7, the Greek economy experienced a prolonged economic recession from the late 2000s, just after the Global Financial Crisis, which revealed the serious weaknesses of its production model and the urgent need to transform it toward a more viable alternative. According to the Greek legislative document concerning the establishment of the Hellenic Development Bank (HDB), the latter should be able to play a significant role in promoting "fair, sustainable, and holistic" economic development at both national and regional levels (Hellenic Parliament 2019). Furthermore, according to the Explanatory Statement of the relevant bill (Ministry of Economy and Development 2019), the point is the restructuring of the production system of the country within a holistic development process that satisfies the economic, social, and environmental dimensions of development altogether. Consequently, the idea was for HDB to fill a gap in development banking in Greece that had existed for a period of seventeen years after the absorption of ETBA from Piraeus Bank in 2002. The European experience of major development banks described in the first section of this chapter together with the importance attributed to national development banks by the European Commission (European Commission 2015) contributed to the realization of this idea. Despite the presence of public initiatives to promote development finance during these seventeen years in the form of the different Funds described above, a comprehensive approach to development banking in the footsteps of the new European context for development finance was only adopted with the creation of HDB. In this respect, the argument of this book is that the nascent development bank cannot succeed in fulfilling its purpose unless it operates as a major agent of the Greek government, an "institutional accelerator" in promoting a model of development characterized by both efficiency and sustainability. This cannot be done unless it is left to fully embrace the dynamic character of the development banking model we analyzed in Chap. 6 as a comprehensive combination of managerial, bargaining, and rationing transactions in the direction of development finance and institutional development.

10.3.1 Mandate and Organization

According to its founding legal framework (Hellenic Parliament 2019), HDB integrates its strategy in the context of national development policy by focusing its activities on meeting a series of intermediate objectives such as: supporting entrepreneurship, developing financing instruments with a special emphasis on new innovative and Small and Medium Enterprises (SMEs), promoting the innovation and competitiveness of enterprises, providing consulting services to the private and public sectors of the economy, and encouraging a Social Solidarity Economy. In general, the legislative document emphasizes the emergence of HDB's role as a significant attractor of capital as well as a promoter of investment projects.

The Hellenic Development Bank aims to provide multifaceted support to companies operating in leading sectors of the Greek economy, especially those that are new, innovative, developing, and exporting and their products are of high value added. The majority of these enterprises should be SMEs that have difficulty accessing external sources of financing. Furthermore, the scope of HDB's activity expands further to include the support of local authorities' development projects, projects with environmental and developmental dimensions in the context of circular economy policies as well as the promotion of Social and Solidarity Economy. HDB's composite role is not limited to assisting the aforementioned economic and social entities in obtaining financing for their projects. HDB should also be able to carry out studies by sector and industry. In addition, it will seek to disseminate its expertise in economic planning and its range of consultancy services to businesses and the state. Finally, it is within the duties of the new development bank to coordinate public developmental agencies and cooperate with financial institutions, public policy agents, and research institutes (Hellenic Parliament 2019; HDB Annual Report 2019: 23–24).

The above indicates the wide mandate of HDB which differs qualitatively from the previous model of development funds. Although HDB is in fact a mutation of ETEAN, the relevant legislative document emphasized the complementary role of ETEAN with respect to the domestic banking system. On the contrary, the intention of the legislator is for HDB to assume a more comprehensive developmental and consulting role even though it lacks the ability of direct lending to the economy (Ministry of Economy and Development 2019). Therefore, HDB is structured as an organization that aims at maximizing developmental and socioeconomic returns. On the other hand, it should be financially sound in order to be able to fulfill successfully its mandate. In this sense, HDB should aim to increase the value of its assets to achieve its twin goals of being financially viable and socioeconomically efficient. That is why there is a provision for the government to have a majority stake in HDB's capital while, at the same time, the bank will operate as a private firm, which will be self-financed and whose pricing policy will follow market practices. On top of this, HDB should follow the basic principles of corporate governance and the best practices that ensure transparency in its activity while, at the same time, it should function with private economic criteria (Hellenic Parliament 2019; Ministry of Economy and Development 2019).

Finally, the HDB will be a multifaceted developmental agency with three major dimensions: (1) the financing dimension which refers to the conclusion of loan contracts and the provision of grants and guarantees; (2) the administrative dimension which pertains to the use of financial engineering instruments, the management of holding funds and the implementation of financing programs funded by government and European funds; and (3) the consultative dimension which relates to counseling and dissemination of know-how to the private and public sector, conducting research or preparing studies on issues about various economic sectors. In any case, HDB is not expected to compete with incumbent financial institutions. Rather, HDB will take a leading executive role in designing credit market interventions to support SMEs and innovative enterprises, which will be implemented through private banks (Ministry of Economy and Development 2019).

The mandate and structure of HDB are reconstructing a comprehensive development finance model that conforms to our understanding of development banks in this book. The legislative documents describe an organization that seems capable of contributing to sustainable economic development and institutional change within the modern European context. It is certainly a major step forward concerning the previous dispersed model. It is also an advancement compared to the old traditional model since it accounts for an increasing role of market mechanisms, the balance between socioeconomic returns and profitability, and the role of the bank in a liberalized financial environment. It is certainly progress for the Greek government to recognize the role of a comprehensive development bank with a multiple developmental role in modern market conditions. HDB looks able to play an essential role in developing new, more efficient, and more sustainable practices and contribute to changing habits of thought and at the same time be itself viable. It seems that rationing, bargaining, and managerial transactions reconnect in a dynamic way although the co-financing requirement with private commercial banks restricts the efficiency of its managerial transactions. In any case, the public purpose for "fair, sustainable, and holistic" economic development is clear and sets "reasonableness" on a new modern level which combines sustainability with a holistic approach to development and a process of fair bargaining among social groups. Of course, all of the above are only expectations to be fulfilled by the future operation of the bank, of which we can only describe the first few years.

10.3.2 Activities

In the context of the mandate described above, HDB is allowed to develop a variety of activities such as the following: (1) Provision of credit to businesses through third parties such as financial sector entities, investment growth funds, and other funding bodies; (2) Provision of guarantees to firms against their liabilities to other financial institutions; (3) Designing and management of financial engineering instruments that serve the statutory purpose of the bank; (4) Targeted financing of businesses aiming at their restructuring toward improving their effectiveness, innovation, and competitiveness; (5) Participation in various financing mechanisms and bodies to serve its purpose along with developing cooperation with international investment organizations; (6) Support of new and innovative entrepreneurs and businesses that are export-oriented; (7) Financial support of scientific research and studies at the enterprise level to the degree that they promote firms' productive efficiency; (8) Financing of institutions that encourage social and economic cohesion and promotion of alternative ways of funding, such as microcredit; (9) Supply of services of consultancy and dissemination of know-how concerning a wide range of issues to firms (especially SMEs) and other bodies. These services may include consultancy and transmission of know-how about the design of financing instruments, business restructuring, capital structure, organization and corporate governance, human resource management, formulating investment projects, and others; (10) Preparation of macroeconomic and microeconomic studies in various sectors of the economy so that policymakers can spot financing needs and fill in the gaps in institutional development caused by market deficiencies (HDB, Annual Report 2019: 25–26).

In pursuit of the above objectives, HDB redesigned the existent Entrepreneurship Fund II and established the COVID-19 Guarantee Fund. It also signed cooperation agreements with the Black Sea Trade and Development Bank, the research center "Democritus", the EIB, the EIF, and others. The result was a surge in lending since in 2020 loans granted were seven times more than those provided in the period 2010–2014 and ten and a half times more than those offered in the period 2015–2019 (HBD Annual Report 2020: 4). Indeed, as shown in Fig. 10.7 loan disbursements in 2020 reached the level of 6,399.72 million euros in constant 2015 prices as opposed to only 273.58 million euros in 2019. The bank describes the economic and social impact of its activity in terms of an increase in employment by 15,600 more workers employed and its positive impact on GDP of 6.2 billion euros using a multiplier of 2. In addition, it refers to the 8th Assessment Report of the European Commission that acknowledges the contribution of HDB to the 8.3% rise in bank credit

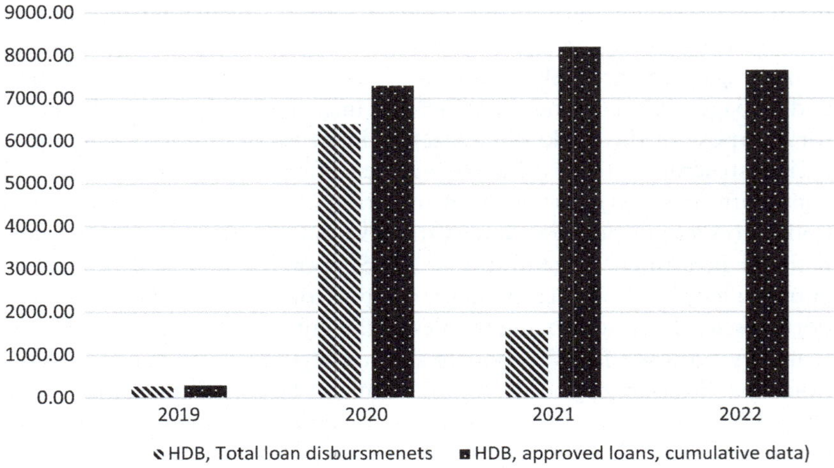

Fig. 10.7 HDB, total approved loans (cumulative data) and loan disbursements, million euros, constant 2015 prices, 2019–2022. Source: HDB Annual Reports, various years, and author's elaboration. Note: Data for loan disbursements in 2022 were not available

to non-financial firms in September 2020 (HBD Annual Report 2020: 4). The following year 2021, HDB expanded its cooperation with market participants and other institutions, both domestic and foreign ones, to include the Athens Stock Exchange, the Hellenic Federation of Enterprises (SEV), the Chamber of Commerce and Industry, the National Technical University of Athens, the French development bank BPI France and others. In addition, it was accepted as a full member of the D20-Long Term Investors Club, the European Long-Term Investors (ELTI), and the Network of European Financial Institutions for SMEs (NEFI). The participation of HDB in these clubs is a recognition of its role and potential in the Greek economy and an opportunity for exchanging good practices, and know-how and expanding international collaborations. The bank designed six new financing instruments with a focus on particular regions of the country and specific economic sectors. More importantly, HDB in collaboration with BPI France has started to provide also non-financial services to firms such as the inauguration of "InnoAgora", a business and investor interface platform, or the provision of counseling to very small enterprises on how to formulate a business plan (HDB Annual Report

2021: 5, 7–8, 18, 20). Finally, in 2022 HDB introduced two new financing instruments concerning the provision of guarantees to innovative SMEs and to audiovisual enterprises that were engaging in the preservation of cultural heritage in which Environmental, Social, and Governance (ESG) criteria were taken into consideration. It also prepared a new non-financial service called "KYC by HDB" which is a "know-your-customer" platform and helps firms to apply for financing to participating banks through the programs introduced by HDB. After all, the bank in 2022 focused on promoting entrepreneurship in SMEs and contributing to the green and digital transition of the economy according to the European and national priorities (HDB Annual Report 2022: 13–14, 18–20).

Cumulatively, in 2022 approved loans reached the level of 7,665.71 million euros in constant 2015 prices, lower than their size in the year 2021, which was 8,207.32 million euros in constant 2015 prices while loan disbursements in 2021 were just 1,581.86 million euros as opposed to the astonishing 6,399.72 million euros in constant 2015 prices in 2020. Differing macroeconomic, social, and geopolitical conditions should be taken into account when explaining this discrepancy between different years. For example, the year 2020 was the time when HDB responded to the effects of the COVID-19 pandemic (HDB Annual Report 2020: 3). Furthermore, it is worth noting that average loan disbursements of HDB in the period 2019–2021 were equal to 2,751.72 million euros in constant 2015 prices which were much higher than the average in the case of TEMPME-ETEAN which was just 142.94 million euros in constant 2015 prices during the period 2010–2018. On the other hand, it is interesting to describe the composition of HDB's approved loans during the period 2019–2022 as shown in Figs. 10.8, 10.9, 10.10, and 10.11.

As Fig. 10.8 shows, the great majority of loans approved in terms of value were directed to retail and wholesale trade (38.3%) with manufacturing in the second place (26.6%) and services provided to tourism in the third place (14%). These three sectors together amounted to about 80% of total approved loans in value. In addition, as Fig. 10.9 depicts, the majority of loans were approved to firms with an age of operation between 15 and 30 years (42%) while older firms came second in place (24%) followed by firms with a range of years of operation between 7 and 15 years (23%). The above indicates that enterprises in trade, tourism, or manufacturing with an age of more than 7 years are the most likely to receive financing through the programs of HDB. In addition, Figs. 10.10 and 10.11 show that these firms are most probably small since about 53% of them have less

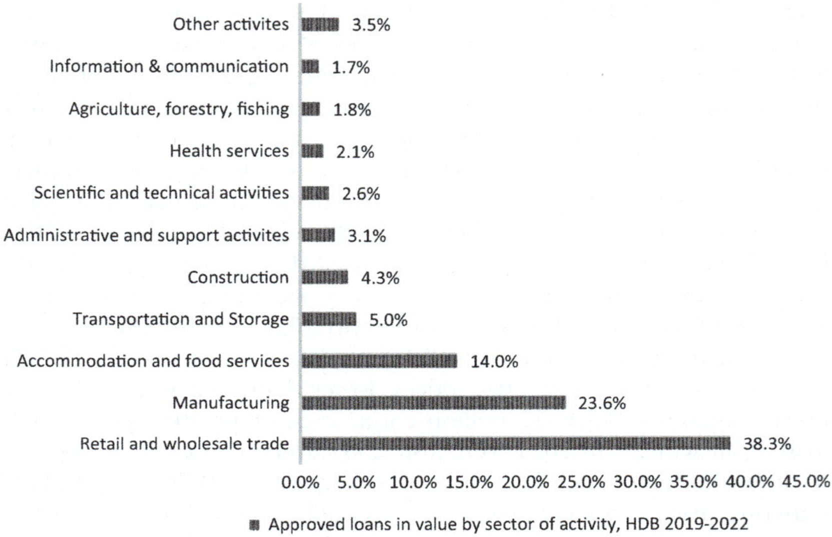

Fig. 10.8 HDB, Approved loans in value by sector of activity, percentage, 2019–2022. Source: HDB Annual Report, 2022, and author's elaboration

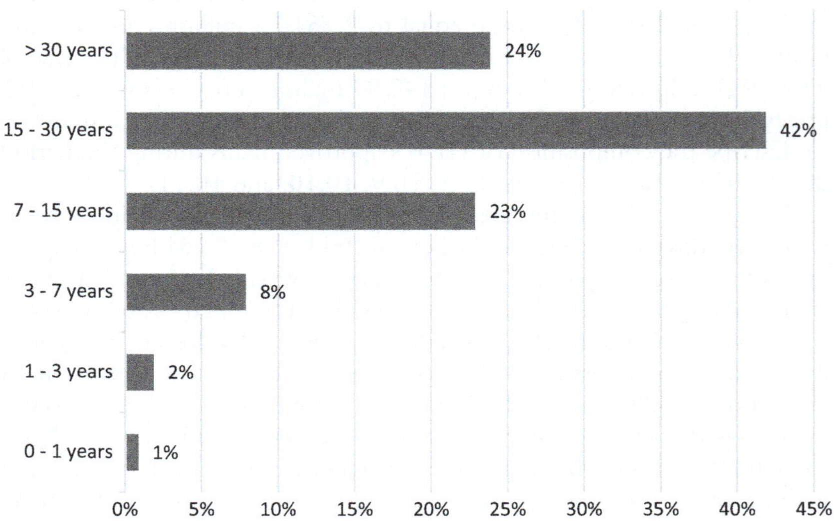

Fig. 10.9 HDB, Approved loans in value by borrowers' business age, percentage, 2019–2022. Source: HDB Annual Report, 2022, and author's elaboration

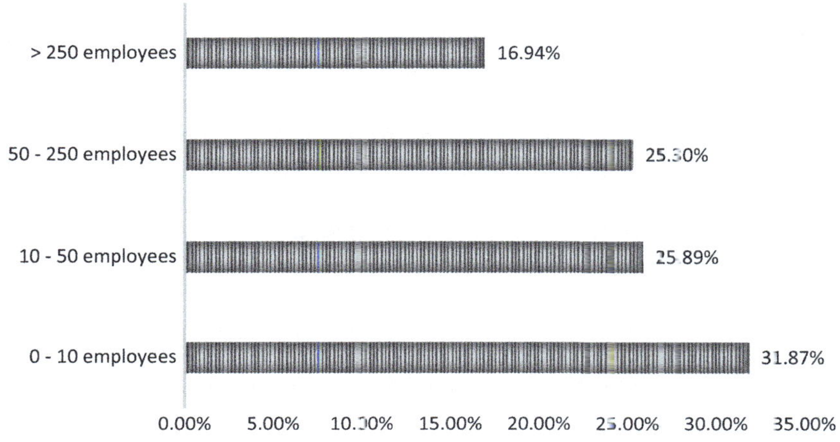

Fig. 10.10 HDB, Approved loans in value by number of borrowers' employees, percentage, 2019–2022. Source: HDB Annual Report, 2022, and author's elaboration

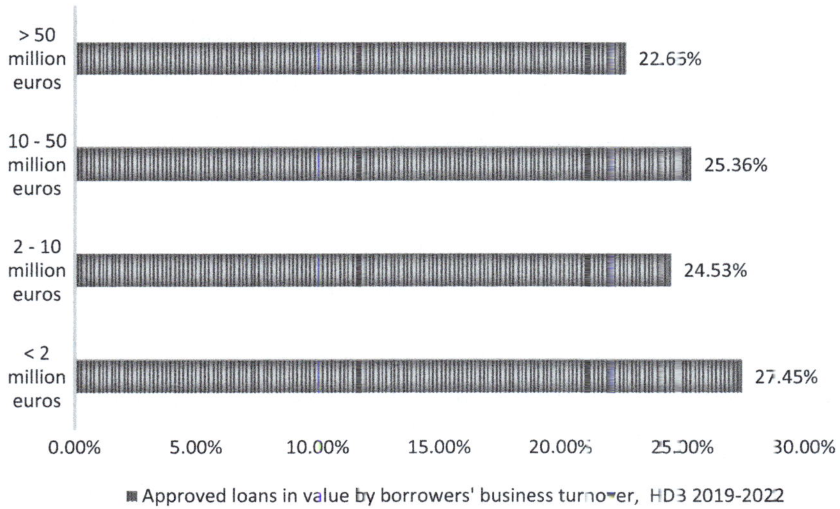

Fig. 10.11 HDB, Approved loans in value by borrowers' business turnover, percentage, 2019–2022. Source: HDB Annual Report, 2022, and author's elaboration

than 50 employees and about 52% of them have a turnover of less than 10 million euros according to the European Commission criteria (European Commission 2003).

Furthermore, the Hellenic Development Bank of Investments (HDBI), former TANEO, being member of the group of HDB continued the activity of TANEO in participating and managing venture capital funds with emphasis on business restructuring, innovation, research and development and start-ups (HDB Annual Report 2019: 36; 2022: 78–80; HDBI Annual Report 2018: 18; 2019: 20). As shown in Fig. 10.12 investments and other earning assets of HDBI rose from 10.49 million euros in constant 2015 prices in 2019 to 13.07 million euros in 2021 but fell at the level of 9.81 million euros in constant 2015 prices in 2022. In general, the average level of HDBI earning assets during the period 2019–2022 was equal to 11.60 million euros in constant 2015 prices which was lower than the corresponding average for TANEO during the period 2016–2018 which was 18.33 million euros.

The activity of both HDB and HDBI in the first few years of operation is an indication of their potential which has yet to be realized. For example, the data for HDB lending show a sustained activity. However, in terms of its composition is less encouraging for a development model that wants to target new and innovative firms with an ability to change the production model of the country. On the other hand, HDB has taken some institutional initiatives in the field of non-financial services and counseling but needs to do much more to support entrepreneurship in SMEs in the context of green and digital transition. Finally, the activity of HDBI in venture capital financing is rather modest and lower than that of its predecessor.

10.3.3 Financial Performance

Financial performance has been a point of criticism both for development banks in general and for Greek development banks in particular, as it is explained in previous chapters. In addition, the financial performance of the precursor of HDB and HDBI was rather disappointing as was shown above. This is not the case for the Hellenic Development Bank and its subsidiary as Figs. 10.13, 10.14, 10.15, and 10.16 depict. Net profits after taxes are consistently positive and rising for HDB until 2021 and remain positive in 2022 with an average level of 21.46 million euros in constant 2015 prices. In addition, HDB managed to attain a rising yield both in

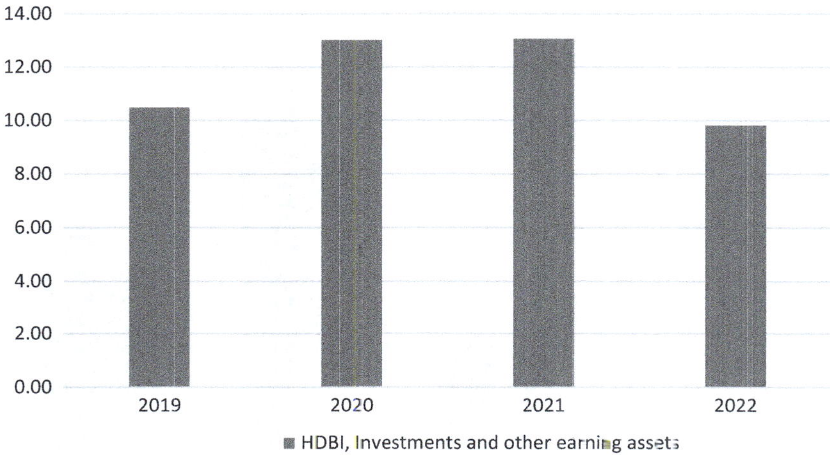

Fig. 10.12 HDBI, Investments, and other earning assets, million euros, constant 2015 prices, 2019–2022. Source: HDBI Annual Reports, various years, and author's elaboration

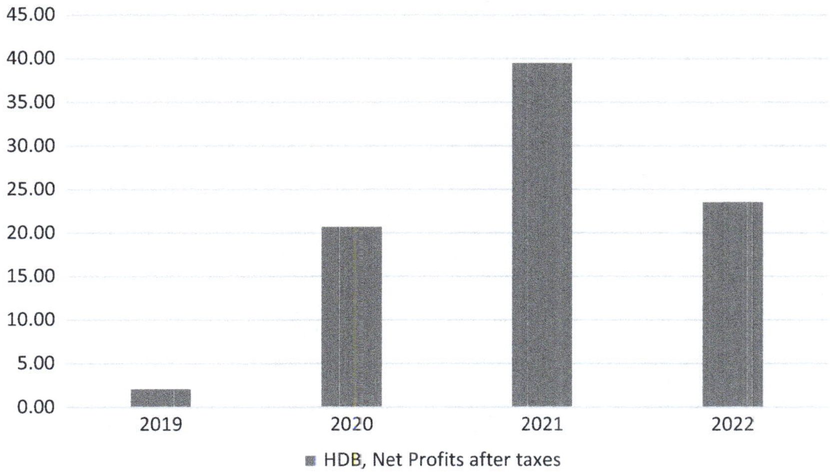

Fig. 10.13 HDB, Net profits after taxes, million euros, constant 2015 prices, 2019–2022. Source: HDB Annual Reports, various years, and author's elaboration

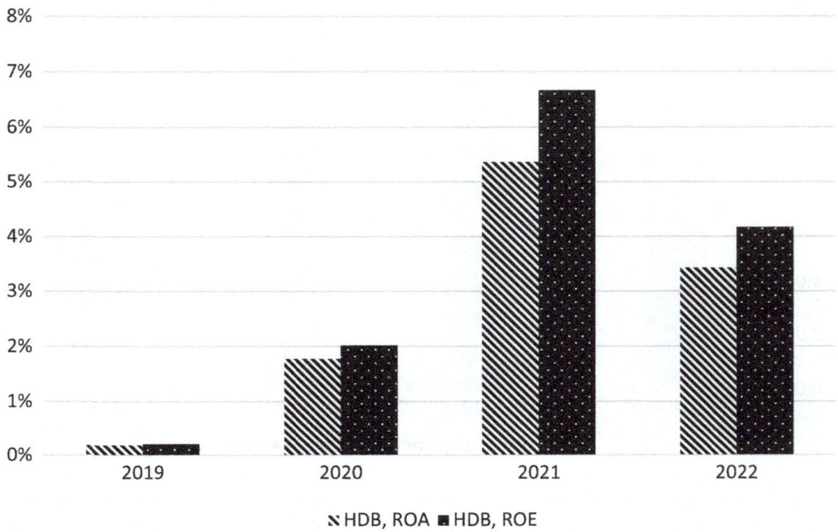

Fig. 10.14 HDB, ROA, and ROE, percentage, 2019–2022. Source: HDB Annual Reports, various years, and author's elaboration

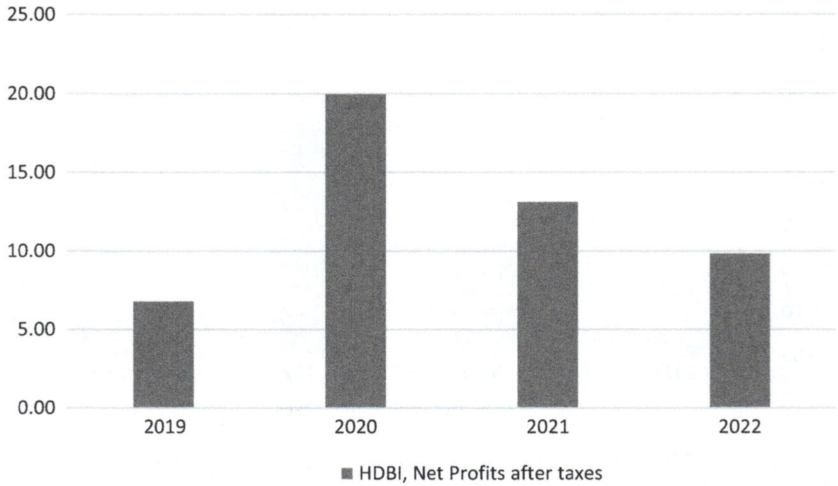

Fig. 10.15 HDBI, Net profits after taxes, million euros, constant 2015 prices, 2019–2022. Source: HDBI Annual Reports, various years, and author's elaboration

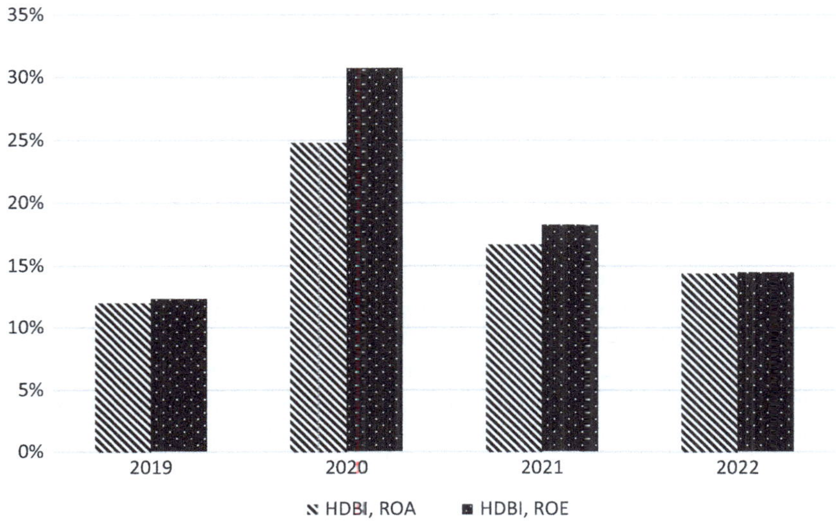

Fig. 10.16 HDBI, ROA, and ROE, percentage, 2019–2022. Source: HDBI Annual Reports, various years, and author's elaboration

terms of ROA and in terms of ROE during its first three years of operation while average values for the period 2019–2022 were 3% for both performance ratios although in their peak in 2021, ROA was 5% and ROE was 7%.

Similarly, HDBI, despite the smaller size of its investments, managed to achieve positive financial results every year from 2019 to 2022 with an average of 12.43 million euros in constant 2015 prices (Fig. 10.15). This is in sharp contrast to the consistent underperformance of its predecessor TANEO. In addition, as Fig. 10.16 shows, HDBI's investments yielded quite high returns on both assets and equity with an average value of 17% for ROA and 19% for ROE.

Thus, both HDB and HDBI have so far managed to strike a balance between their development finance role and their financial viability. This is encouraging for the new Greek model of development banking within the European framework, as it emphasizes the financial sustainability of these institutions without neglecting their development objective. Of course, profitability cannot be the main criterion for development banks, but it should not be neglected either, as explained in the previous chapters of this book.

10.3.4 HDB Prospects

The Hellenic Development Bank was founded during a critical era for the Greek economy, in agreement with the long international experience which indicates that development banks have played a pivotal role in crucial moments in economic history throughout the world. In this sense, it may be considered the appropriate mechanism to act as a developmental catalyst in the Greek economy, which needs a new production model. Moreover, development banks have always been engaged in a double role of financing by targeting investment projects and emphasizing and promoting the institutional preconditions of economic development.

The above analysis showed that HDB has the ability to act according to the expectations of Greek firms and the Greek government and has taken significant initiatives in this direction. There is a lot more to be done especially at the institutional level so that HDB to prove its role as a catalyst and financial planner for economic development rather than a mere cheap-lending mechanism. Four years of operation is too short a time for HDB to deploy its possibilities and it could be rather characterized as a transition period to building the new development banking model in Greece within the European development banking framework.

Certainly, the success of this venture depends on how clearly the objectives of the HDB have been defined, the quality of its staff, and its corporate governance. In various Annual Reports HDB has mentioned its constant attempt to modernize its organization and operation and improve the capabilities of its staff (HDB Annual Report 2020: 12; 2021: 4–5; 2022: 20). This is and should be a continuous process informed by the new challenges that the bank faces. However, the greatest challenge for the Hellenic Development Bank is the balanced satisfaction of the criteria of its efficiency in terms of financial viability and socioeconomic returns. The data presented above show a reassuring picture concerning financial performance and a positive impact in terms of social and economic criteria such as the rise in employment and GDP. It seems that the management of HDB acknowledges that it is important for the bank to be able to fulfill credibly, effectively, and transparently its task as a critical arm of the national strategy for inclusive and sustainable development.

The omens look favorable but the unknowns are multiple and include the future macroeconomic environment, the changing institutional environment the possible developments in the prevailing financial regime, and finally, the omnipresent institutional-political risk that haunts development banking. Is the Greek government sincerely committed to development banking as a long-term mechanism of institutional and socioeconomic transformation or is it a victim of short-term cheap-lending policies to serve the political clientele? As explained above, the HDB and its subsidiary possess the properties that are necessary to realize a comprehensive development banking model that combines J. R. Commons's managerial, bargaining, and rationing transactions in a dynamic way to serve institutional and economic development. However, the above is subject to the role of the government and the institutional-political risk that characterizes development banking as we have argued in this book. Development banks worldwide have proved their ability to survive and adapt to changing financial regimes if they have the support of their governments. This support implies the government's commitment to a long-term development and financial policy which set the framework for the operation of development banks under alternative financial regimes. This long-term plan is the antidote to the political short-termism and crony capitalism that breed corruption and have plagued so many development banks in the past. If the Greek government draws and follows such a long-term policy then HDB will be able to realize its potential for supporting sustainable socioeconomic development within a modern liberalized financial system. Such a long-term plan should mainly define what is "reasonable" in terms of prices and quantities in modern financial markets by defining the "rules of the game" after the deliberation and bargaining of the interested social groups. Then "reasonableness" informs the way the public purpose of sustainable development should be sought and set the basis for institutional reform in Veblenian terms as a bottom-up process where the emphasis is not on drafting laws and formal rules but the focus is on changing habits of thought and practices. In this context, HDB has a major role to play as an organization having the expertise to spot limiting factors and proposing solutions to everyday problems in the Greek business community with a view to inclusiveness, sustainability, and growth.

References

Bastian, J. (2021) "The Rise, Fall, and Return of Promotional Banking in Greece" in Mertens, D., Thiemann, M., and Volberding, P. (eds.) *The Reinvention of Development Banking in the European Union. Industrial Policy in the Single Market and the Emergence of a Field*, New York: Oxford University Press, pp. 283–305.

Bilal, S. (2021) "The Rise of Public Development Banks in the European Financial Architecture for Development", Elcano Royal Institute Working Paper 12/2021, Madrid: ETTG/Elcano Royal Institute. Available at https://media.realinstitutoelcano.org/wp-content/uploads/2021/12/wp12-2021-bilal-rise-of-public-development-banks-in-european-financial-architecture-for-development.pdf Accessed 23 May 2024.

Bulfone, F. and Di Carlo, D. (2021) "Privatization, Crisis, and the Transformation of Cassa Depositi e Prestiti", in Mertens, D., Thiemann, M., and Volberding, P. (eds.) *The Reinvention of Development Banking in the European Union. Industrial Policy in the Single Market and the Emergence of a Field*, New York: Oxford University Press, pp. 144–171.

Colombo, M. and Cuda, M. (2023) "The Role of Public Development Banks & Institutions in the Implementation of the United Nations' Agenda 2030: A Survey in Europe", Discussion Paper No. 179. Directorate General Economic and Financial Affairs (DG ECFIN), European Commission, available at https://economy-finance.ec.europa.eu/document/download/2e0e5ab7-c684-40d7-9d03-e21432e99b62_en?filename=dp179_en.pdf Accessed 21 Oct. 2023

De Luna-Martínez, J., Vicente, C. L., bin Arshad, A., Tatucu, R., and Song, J. (2018) "2017 Survey of National Development Banks", World Bank Group Global Report, (May) available at https://documents1.worldbank.org/curated/en/977821525438071799/pdf/2017-Survey-of-National-development-banks.pdf Accessed 13 Oct. 2023

ETEAN Annual Reports 2011 – 2017, Athens available at https://hdb.gr/oikonomika-stoixeia/ Accessed 23 Jan. 2023

European Commission (2015), COM/2015/361 "Working Together for Jobs and Growth: The Role of National Promotional Banks (NPBs) in Supporting the Investment Plan for Europe" Communication from the Commission to the European Parliament and the Council. Available at https://eur-lex.europa.eu/legal-content/en/TXT/?uri=CELEX%3A52015DC0361 Accessed 23 May 2024.

European Commission (2003) Commission Recommendation of 6 May 2003 Concerning the Definition of Micro, Small and Medium-Sized Enterprises. Available at https://eur-lex.europa.eu/legal-content/EN/TXT/PDF/?uri=CELEX:32003H0361 Accessed 30 May 2024.

Griffith-Jones, S. (2016) "National Development Banks and Sustainable Infrastructure; the Case of KfW", Boston University, Global Economic Governance Initiative Working Paper 006. Available at https://www.bu.edu/pardeeschool/files/2016/07/GriffithJones.Final_.pdf Accessed 23 May 2024.

HDB Annual Reports 2018 – 2022, Athens available at https://hdb.gr/oikonomika-stoixeia/ Accessed 23 Jan. 2023

HDBI Annual Reports 2018 – 2022, Athens available at https://hdbi.gr/el/h--eate/financial-reports Accessed 23 Jan. 2023

Hellenic Parliament (2019) "Hellenic Development Bank and Attracting of Strategic Investments and Other Provisions", passed Bill, Hellenic Parliament, Minutes of PIB', April 17th, 2019 (in Greek).

Mertens, D., Thiemann, M. and Volberding, P. (2021) "Introduction: The Making of the European Field of Development Banking" in Mertens, D., Thiemann, M., and Volberding, P. (eds.) *The Reinvention of Development Banking in the European Union. Industrial Policy in the Single Market and the Emergence of a Field*, New York: Oxford University Press, pp. 1–32.

Mertens, D. (2021) "A German Model? KfW, Field Dynamics, and the Europeanization of "Promotional" Banking", in Mertens, D., Thiemann, M., and Volberding, P. (eds.) *The Reinvention of Development Banking in the European Union. Industrial Policy in the Single Market and the Emergence of a Field*, New York: Oxford University Press, pp. 117–143

Ministry of Economy and Development (2019), Explanatory Statement on the Bill of the Ministry of Economy and Development, "Hellenic Development Bank and Attracting of Strategic Investments and Other Provisions", April 8th, 2019 (in Greek).

Moslener, U., Thiemann, M. and Volberding, P. (2018) "National Development Banks as Active Financiers. The Case of KfW", in Griffith-Jones, S. and Ocampo, J. A. (eds.) *The Future of National Development Banks*, New York: Oxford University Press, pp. 63–85.

TANEO Annual Reports 2010 – 2017, Athens available at https://hdbi.gr/el/h--eate/financial-reports Accessed 23 Jan. 2023.

The Economist (2019), "National Development banks are back in vogue", March 7

TEMPME Annual Reports 2006 – 2010, Athens available at https://hdb.gr/oikonomika-stoixeia/ Accessed 23 Jan. 2023.

CHAPTER 11

Three Questions About the Future of Development Banking

11.1 Taking Stock to Set Questions

This book was about development banking, an idea and a policy instrument that is closely related to economic development and development finance. As explained in the previous chapters, development banking emerged as a way to address both financial issues and institutional underdevelopment in developing economies trying to catch up with the more advanced ones. To the degree that economic development was related to the industrialization of less developed economies, development banking was associated with industrial financing as early as the nineteenth century and with the reconstruction of war-torn economies after the Second World War. In any case, development banks have been instruments in the hands of governments that wished to transform their economies and integrate them into the global economic system of the era. In this sense, development banks served the dominant public purpose in every historical period as organizations that assumed a position between financial markets and governments. They responded to the underdevelopment of capital markets, but they also took initiatives in favor of institutional and economic development that would result in more developed financial markets. They were endowed with mandates and funds by governments, and they followed public policy objectives in support of economic development in its various dimensions, but they also quite often put at risk their financial viability by doing so. This was the main reason why development banks

K. Loizos, *Between Markets and Governments*,
https://doi.org/10.1007/978-3-031-88527-3_11

fell out of fashion in the context of liberalized financial regimes when the mediocre profitability of many of them was read as a sign of mismanagement and short-term political influence. The same financial underperformance was conceived as the inescapable outcome of supporting risky projects which were nevertheless necessary from a developmental point of view in the context of the financial repression/regulation regime.

In this context, the chapters of the first part of this book were the result of a review of the literature about development finance and development banking in an attempt to clarify the idea within its historical and theoretical context. The purpose of this analysis was to formulate a comprehensive theory of development banking based on Original Institutional Economics since a major argument of this book is that development banks are development finance organizations that aim to support institutional development and change. Original Institutional Economics has been chosen as a more encompassing and realistic institutional approach to economic theory and policy. The second part of this book was a case study of development banking in the post-World War II Greek economy. Assessing the role of development banking in the Greek economy was a useful exercise for both theoretical and policy reasons. The Greek economy changed its status from a developing to a developed economy during the post-World War II period and development banks had a significant contribution to this economic and institutional transformation. Furthermore, this evolution was characterized by the prevalence of alternative financial regimes which affected the operation of development banks. Finally, Greece has been a member of the European Economic Community since the early 1980s, a member of the Euro-area since the early 2000s, and one of the most hardly stricken economies during the recent Global and European crisis. Hence, the last chapter of the empirical part of this book discussed the current situation of development banking in Greece as a peripheral economy within the Eurozone.

The book sought to contribute to the current literature on development banking on both theoretical and empirical grounds. Going beyond a mainstream discussion about market failures and government failures, it provided the institutional foundations for the heterodox view of development banking in the context of a state that is active in shaping markets. Development banks were defined as hybrid institutions with features pertaining to both capital markets and typical banks being a dynamic combination of bargaining, managerial, and rationing transactions. They were also characterized by their priority to serve the public purpose, in the context of "reasonableness", over private profitability. In this context, they may contribute to progressive institutional reform which nowadays takes the form of sustainable socioeconomic development. Describing development banks in this way, our theory located the major risk of development banking, the institutional-political risk, in government policies about the prevailing financial regime. Then, our dynamic theory of development banking was founded on both their critical role in promoting institutional change and their internal transformation and adaptation. The empirical part of this book attempted to shed light on the understudied Greek case of development banking over a period of six decades through the lens of our Original Institutional Economics model. According to our knowledge, this was a novel application of Original Institutional Economics theoretical and methodological tools in our understanding of development banking in general and the Greek case in particular. The analysis showed the role of development banking in supporting the economic and institutional transformation of the Greek economy. It also confirmed that the major risk for Greek development banks was the institutional-political risk that emerged from the dependence of Greek development banks on the policy followed by the Greek government with respect to the prevailing financial regime. In this respect, the ability of the government to follow, in a consistent way, a long-term institutional and economic development policy has been critical for the present and future of development banking in Greece, given conflicting socioeconomic interests.

However, in this final concluding chapter, three questions that summarize the arguments developed throughout this book are in order. The first question is a policy one: Do development banks, as policy instruments, have a future? The second question is a theoretical one: Should a theory for development banks be open-ended? And the final question is a country-specific one, derived from our case study: will, the new experimentation with development banking in Greece, be short-lived? In a sense, these questions summarize the argument of this book which has all these three dimensions: a theoretical, a policy, and a country-specific one. The following sections provide some preliminary answers to these questions.

11.2 Do Development Banks, as Policy Instruments, Have a Future?

For many decades, development banks were associated with financial repression/regulation regimes, especially those derived from the Bretton Woods international monetary arrangements that prevailed in the post-World War II era. Hence, the wave of financial liberalization that followed the demise of the Bretton Woods regime challenged the idea of development banking as a remnant of financial repression/regulation. The analysis provided in the chapters of this book questions this argument on various grounds.

First of all, we argue that development banking is mistakenly understood as a mechanism of cheap finance. The Greek experience in the period 2003–2018 is an illustration of this argument. During the above period various "funds" took the place of development banks in the provision of preferential credit with government support. Hence, cheap financing in support of government priorities is possible without development banks. Consequently, identifying development banks with cheap lending as their defining characteristic is misleading. On the contrary, development banks cannot be defined unless their distinctive institutional role is acknowledged. These banks emerge as an antidote to institutional underdevelopment in financial markets and, at the same time, development banks themselves take part in institutional and financial development. Furthermore, their characteristics as financial organizations are dependent on the prevailing financial regime while their dynamic nature makes possible their adaptation and internal transformation when the financial regime changes.

Focusing on the institutional aspect of development banking opens new horizons and poses new problems. It is now possible to transcend the sterile contradiction between pro-market and pro-government priorities in perceptions of development finance. According to the institutional analysis of Commons expounded above there is a continuum of transactions with differing characteristics that encompass all economic activity whether within a market, within an organization, or even within wider collectivities or groups of people. Moreover, development banks can be conceived as a dynamic combination of these various kinds of transactions. Hence, the problem is not whether development banks contrast market institutions in a static sense but whether these banks are able to cater to the needs of an economy with evolving institutional characteristics. The theory of development banking proposed in this book supports the idea that it is possible for development banks to do so. It is possible not only because development banks as internal structures are defined by their ability to combine managerial, bargaining, and rationing transactions but also because these banks serve by definition the public purpose with a view to institutional development and reform. Another misconception about development banking is to identify the public purpose with old-fashioned industrial policy. However, the public purpose itself is also a dynamic concept. For sure, it was in favor of the public purpose for economic development to focus on the industrialization of less developed countries which implied both preferential credit and institutional development. Why not conceive as a new public purpose the new challenges of economic development within a globalized and liberalized economy? Irrespective of the value judgments attached to each policy, this book asserts that development banks can serve the public purpose that prevails in every historical period. They can do so because, again in Commons's terms, the public purpose is the outcome of social negotiation that defines what is considered "reasonable" in every historical period and hence, how a "reasonable" value is defined. Development banks being between markets and governments are a locus of this "reasonably" priced financing. However, what was reasonable in the context of the post-World War II financial repression/regulation regime might not be reasonable in the financial liberalization regime of the 1990s. More importantly, what was reasonable in the financial liberalization regime of the 1990s and 2000s might not be reasonable in the same regime after the Global Crisis of 2008. Hence, Original Institutional Economics provides a platform for comprehending development banking in the evolution both between and within financial regimes.

Therefore, if development banks are perceived as organizations with the particular institutional characteristics described above then there is no reason to believe that they are not able to survive in the future as they did in various occasions in the past. Of course, the historical examples examined in this volume indicate that the contrary is also possible. The outcome will be the responsibility of governments in different countries and their ability to use development banks constructively and beneficially. It is their responsibility to prioritize long-term goals of institutional and economic development over short-term electoral objectives. Eventually, it is their responsibility to act in a way that would promote, rather than discredit, the idea of development banking. That is why we argue in this book that the major risk of development banking is institutional-political rather than economic or financial.

11.3 Should a Theory for Development Banks Be Open-Ended?

It is usual in economics as a social science to choose a theoretical framework as the most appropriate to conduct a particular analysis. The Original Institutional Economics is our choice for proposing a theory of development banking for the reasons explained above. In short, it is, in our opinion, a consistent choice in favor of interdisciplinarity and evolution which best characterizes the multiple dimensions of finance for economic development. In the early chapters of this book, it was evident that economic development is a much more rich concept than economic growth and this is why institutions are so important in this debate. After all, society is composed of institutions at various levels of activity that interact with each other. Economic, political, and social institutions act one upon the other in multiple ways and human economic behavior is in fact a combination derived from them.

Veblen's theory of institutional change supplements Commons's ideas expounded above concerning the contribution of development banks in institutional reform. This approach understands change in human society as the interaction between technological innovation and institutional structure where both progressive change and regressive outcomes are possible. Eventually, individual perception, habits of thought, and ideology are crucial in determining the path of change and deciding the weight of ceremonial and instrumental values. Hence, values are important because they are associated with how individuals understand the world around them and act upon their perception. Furthermore, the individual per se is a complex entity not possible to be described by preference orderings or rationality axioms. Veblen's theory is interdisciplinary itself looking at the individual as a member of both a biological and a social group. In this sense, one cannot speak of economic behavior irrespective of instincts being the proclivities of this behavior. Furthermore, one cannot understand economic behavior without taking into account how habitual behavior is formed within different social groups. Only on these grounds one can grasp the process through which ideology, a popular theme for North, is the outcome and, at the same time, the determinant of cognition. Veblen's theory of instincts and habit formation is both a well-founded and open-ended theory of ideology, cognition, and change because it does not contradict any assumption of "proper" rational behavior. It is all a matter of evolution at different paces and levels. Instincts as the biological substratum evolve more slowly than habits of thought which in turn evolve more slowly than beliefs. However, the outcome of change is neither predetermined nor guaranteed. There are no "correct" institutions that obey the axioms of rationality but probably antiquated institutions and ways of thinking that resist them. There are historically specific institutions that derive from the complex interaction between instincts, habits of thought, and technological innovations where value judgments are an integral part of institutional change. In this sense, adopting sustainable goals is not the outcome of rational calculations and selfish motives but rather the result of group-regarding instincts dominating over self-regarding ones.

If this is the case, then a theory of development banking should be open-ended as far as development banks are defined by an open-ended public purpose and intervene in open-ended human behavior. In this book, development banking theory has been constructed using the empirical and theoretical material of the past and present. The ideas of Commons and Veblen and the Original Institutional tradition in general drew the main lines of this theory but the theory per se is not a closed set of axioms or hypotheses. It is, or it aspires to be, a theory of evolution of these development finance organizations both because their purpose evolves and because their survival depends on their internal change as the external environment changes. More importantly, development banks are defined by institutional and economic change. Since these banks are not mere intermediaries between market participants but active in institutional change, their theory is bound to be open-ended given the uncertainty and innovation that characterizes human economic and social activity. Veblen's theory of institutional change described above provides a measure of these characteristics of economic behavior which development banks should take into account when they are engaging in institutional action. Finally, the choice of Original Institutional Economics instead of New Institutional Economics to formulate a theory for development banks is an additional argument for an open-ended, comprehensive, and more encompassing theory.

11.4 Will, the New Experimentation with Development Banking in Greece, Be Short-Lived?

Despite the size of the Greek economy and its small weight within the European economy, Greece has an interesting experience in development banking during the post-World War II era. The Greek financial system saw the operation of three development banks during the period 1963–2002 of which one public and two private ones. During the following period 2003–2018, the Greek government ran a variety of development finance funds before it embarked once more on the project of development banking proper with the establishment of the Hellenic Development Bank in 2019. The analysis in the second part of this book showed the interrelation between alternative financial regimes and the attempt of these banks to adapt to the new conditions. It also provided an account of both their contribution to economic and institutional development and their financial performance. The results could be read either as a financial failure, especially for ETBA and TE, or as the price paid in serving government priorities according to the public purpose of the era.

The account of the main period of development banking in Greece is an illustration of a theory of this kind of banking that puts the emphasis on how an economy is transformed with the contribution of development banks. It is a story of development finance that promoted structural change from a developing to a developed economy. In this sense, it is best read as a story of institutional transformation and change that goes beyond individual amounts of funds provided or investments made in firms' assets. Therefore, it is misleading to compare the size of funds provided by development banks as opposed to those provided by commercial banks when assessing their contribution to economic development. After all, development banks were meant to innovate and assume risks in the sense of opening up paths that commercial banks could follow afterward. In addition, the multiplicative effect of both their financing and institutional intervention in the economy cannot be directly measured but rather implied by the fact that it contributed to the transformation of the economy as a whole.

However, the history of development banking in Greece is also a testament to how the government conceives economic development financing. Development banks in Greece faced different government development policies which depended on how these governments understood the surrounding international policy environment and their position within it. In the context of the financial repression/regulation regime of the 1960s, 1970s, and early 1980s the government supported these banks to different degrees during different periods. The change of the financial regime into financial liberalization and deregulation during the late 1980s and early 1990s saw a gradual disengagement of the government from development banking institutions without considering their possible contribution to the new definition of the public purpose. This observation holds especially for the public ETBA which could become a public modern investment bank in the new liberalized conditions. The developments in major European countries described in the previous chapter during this period and the need to establish the Hellenic Development Bank seventeen years later prove that selling off ETBA should not have been the only course of action.

Hence, the historical account of the Greek experience in development banking is also an illustration of both the institutional theory of development banking and the key role of the state. If development banks are dynamic institutions defined by the Commons's categories of transactions and have the ability to transform themselves in a Veblenian fashion by changing their own habits of thought as the public purpose evolves, then their success to do so depends both on their management and government policy. Despite the different financial performances of the three development banks during the main period of development banking in Greece, which may have reflected the ability of their management, their common fate rather reveals the crucial role of government policy or the institutional-political risk they faced. Their story demonstrates that the ability of development banks to provide "reasonable" terms of financing and promote financial and institutional reform along with their ability to survive under different financial regimes ultimately depends on whether the government believes in them. It is not certain that the Greek governments of the 1990s and 2000s believed in development banking or understood the role of development banking in the new conditions of financial liberalization and globalization. We are inclined to believe that Greek governments intertemporally fall victim to simplistic approaches such as the one of "cheap financing" or "markets-versus-public development banks".

It is probably not a coincidence that the Greek government considered the establishment of a new development bank in 2019 only when it was urged to do so by the European institutions. Since economic relations between decision-makers both in the private and the public sector are characterized by their differing negotiation power, as the Original

Institutional Economics emphasizes, then it is probably the diminished negotiation power of vested interests within the Greek economy as opposed to European institutions that made this happen. However, despite the encouraging results of the HDB as explained above, its possibilities are far from been exploited to the full, especially in the field of institutional development toward a new production model for the Greek economy that would respect social, environmental, economic, and financial sustainability. The key for HDB to have a future is not to expand the range of its activities or even its ability to provide loans directly to its clients, although both would be desirable. The key is for the government to believe in HDB as an organization with long-term value for economic and institutional development in Greece. If it does, then a long-term development and financial policy plan is in order to substitute for short-sighted electoral objectives that generate political cronyism, corruption, and mismanagement. This long-term development and financial policy plan should define "reasonableness" in modern financial and economic conditions in the context of a democratic bargaining process among social groups with a view to socioeconomic, financial, and environmental sustainability.

Index[1]

[1] Note: Page numbers followed by 'n' refer to notes.

K. Loizos, *Between Markets and Governments*,
https://doi.org/10.1007/978-3-031-88527-3

The manufacturer's authorised representative in the EU is Springer Nature Customer Service Centre GmbH, Europaplatz 3, 69115 Heidelberg, Germany. If you have any concerns regarding our products, please contact ProductSafety@springernature.com

Printed and bound by CPI Group (UK) Ltd, Croydon, CR0 4YY
30/09/2026
02225565-0015